1/09

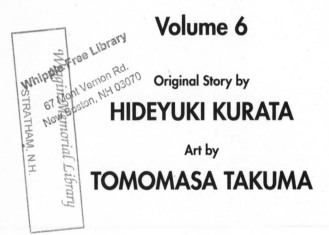

TRAIN ＋ TRAIN

Volume 6

Original Story by

HIDEYUKI KURATA

Art by

TOMOMASA TAKUMA

go!comi

Concerning Honorifics

At Go! Comi, we do our best to ensure that our translations read seamlessly in English while respecting the original Japanese language and culture. To this end, the original honorifics (the suffixes found at the end of characters' names) remain intact. In Japan, where politeness and formality are more integrated into every aspect of the language, honorifics give a better understanding of character relationships. They can be used to indicate both respect and affection. Whether a person addresses someone by first name or last name also indicates how close their relationship is.

Here are some of the honorifics you might encounter in reading this book:

-san: This is the most common and neutral of honorifics. The polite way to address someone you're not on close terms with is to use "-san." It's kind of like Mr. or Ms., except you can use "-san" with first names as easily as family names.

-chan: Used for friendly familiarity, mostly applied towards young girls. "-chan" also carries a connotation of cuteness with it, so it is frequently used with nicknames towards both boys and girls (such as "Na-chan" for "Natsu").

-kun: Like "-chan," it's an informal suffix for friends and classmates, only "-kun" is usually associated with boys. It can also be used in a professional environment by someone addressing a subordinate.

-sama: Indicates a great deal of respect or admiration.

Sempai: In school, "sempai" is used to refer to an upperclassman or club leader. It can also be used in the workplace by a new employee to address a mentor or staff member with seniority.

Sensei: Teachers, doctors, writers or any master of a trade are referred to as "sensei." When addressing a manga creator, the polite thing to do is attach "-sensei" to the manga-ka's name (as in Takuma-sensei).

Onii: This is the more casual term for an older brother. Usually you'll see it with an honorific attached, such as "onii-chan."

Onee: The casual term for older sister, it's used like "onii" with honorifics.

[blank]: Not using an honorific when addressing someone indicates that the speaker has permission to speak intimately with the other person. This relationship is usually reserved for close friends and family.

TRAIN + TRAIN
VOLUME 6

Episode. 32 ——————————— 7

Episode. 33 ——————————— 39

Episode. 34 ——————————— 71

Episode. 35 ——————————— 87

Episode. 36 ——————————— 103

Episode. 37 ——————————— 133

Episode. 38 ——————————— 165

TRAIN
+
TRAIN

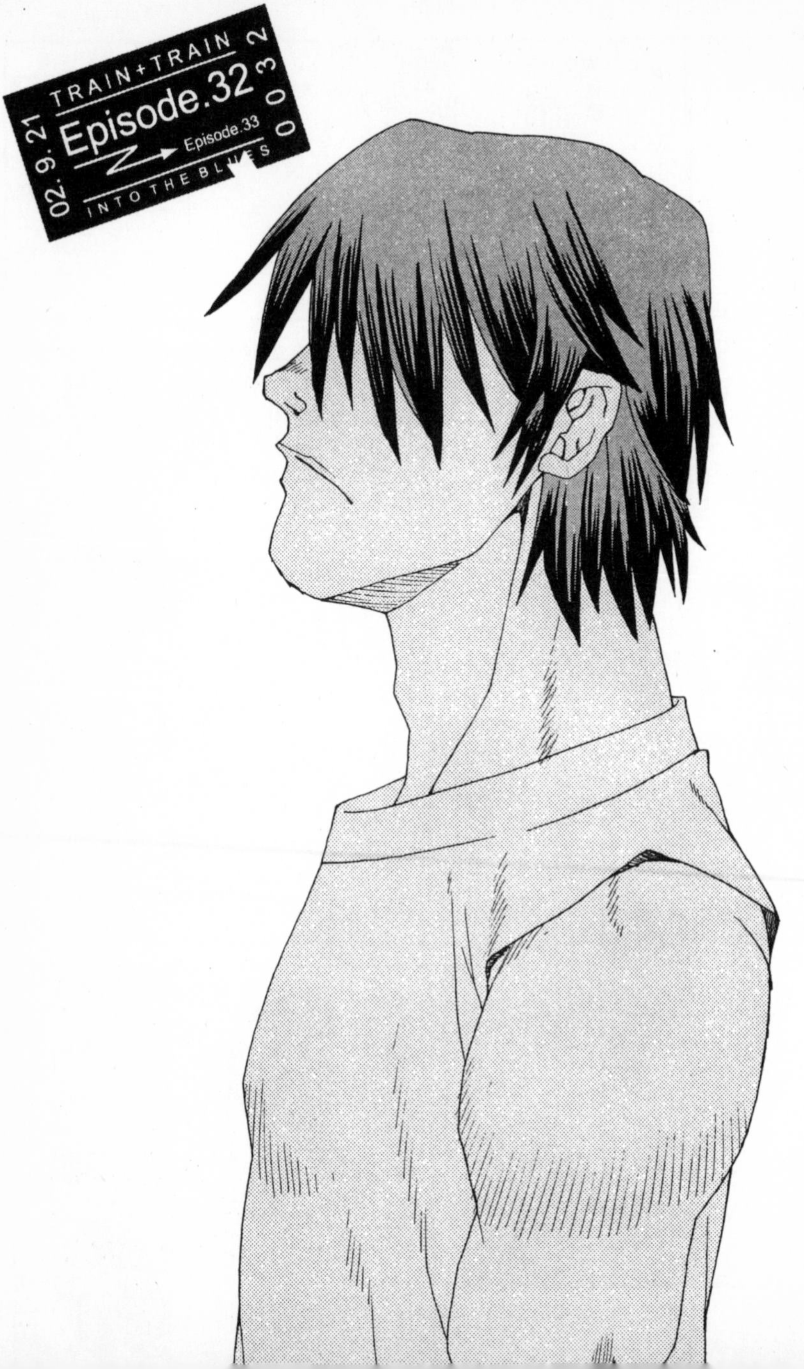
TRAIN+TRAIN
Episode.32
Episode.33
INTO THE BLUES
02. 9. 21
0032

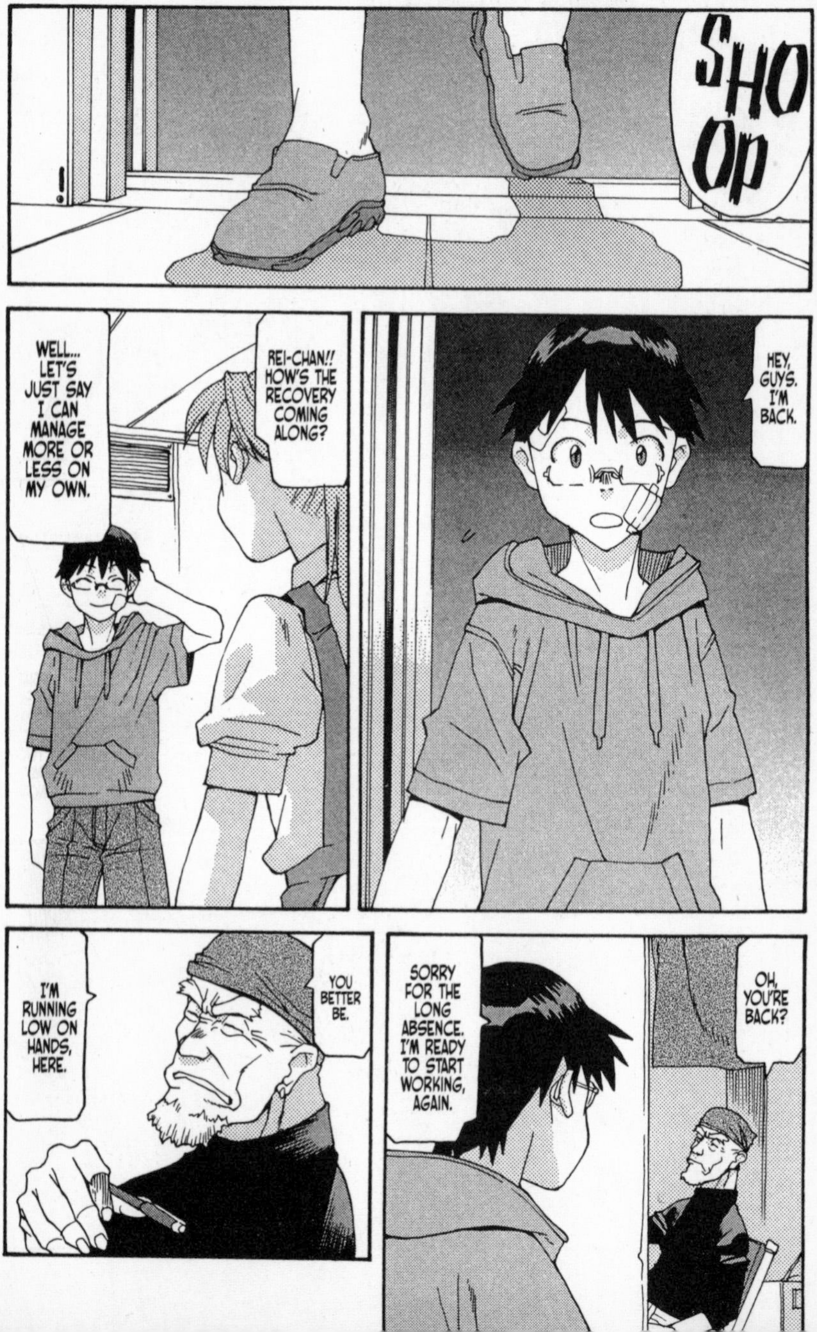
SHO OP
HEY, GUYS. I'M BACK.
REI-CHAN!! HOW'S THE RECOVERY COMING ALONG?
WELL... LET'S JUST SAY I CAN MANAGE MORE OR LESS ON MY OWN.
OH, YOU'RE BACK?
SORRY FOR THE LONG ABSENCE. I'M READY TO START WORKING, AGAIN.
YOU BETTER BE.
I'M RUNNING LOW ON HANDS, HERE.

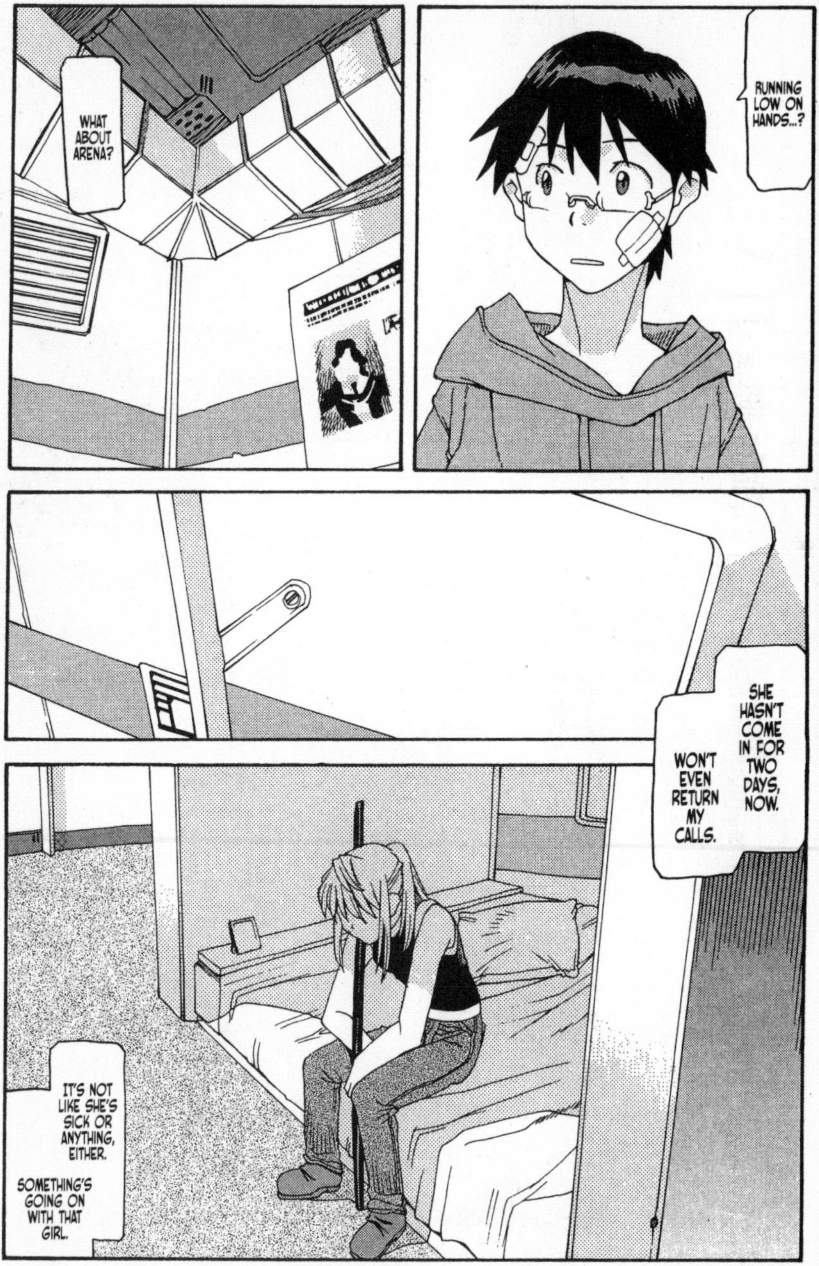
RUNNING LOW ON HANDS...?
WHAT ABOUT ARENA?
SHE HASN'T COME IN FOR TWO DAYS, NOW.
WON'T EVEN RETURN MY CALLS.
IT'S NOT LIKE SHE'S SICK OR ANYTHING, EITHER.
SOMETHING'S GOING ON WITH THAT GIRL.

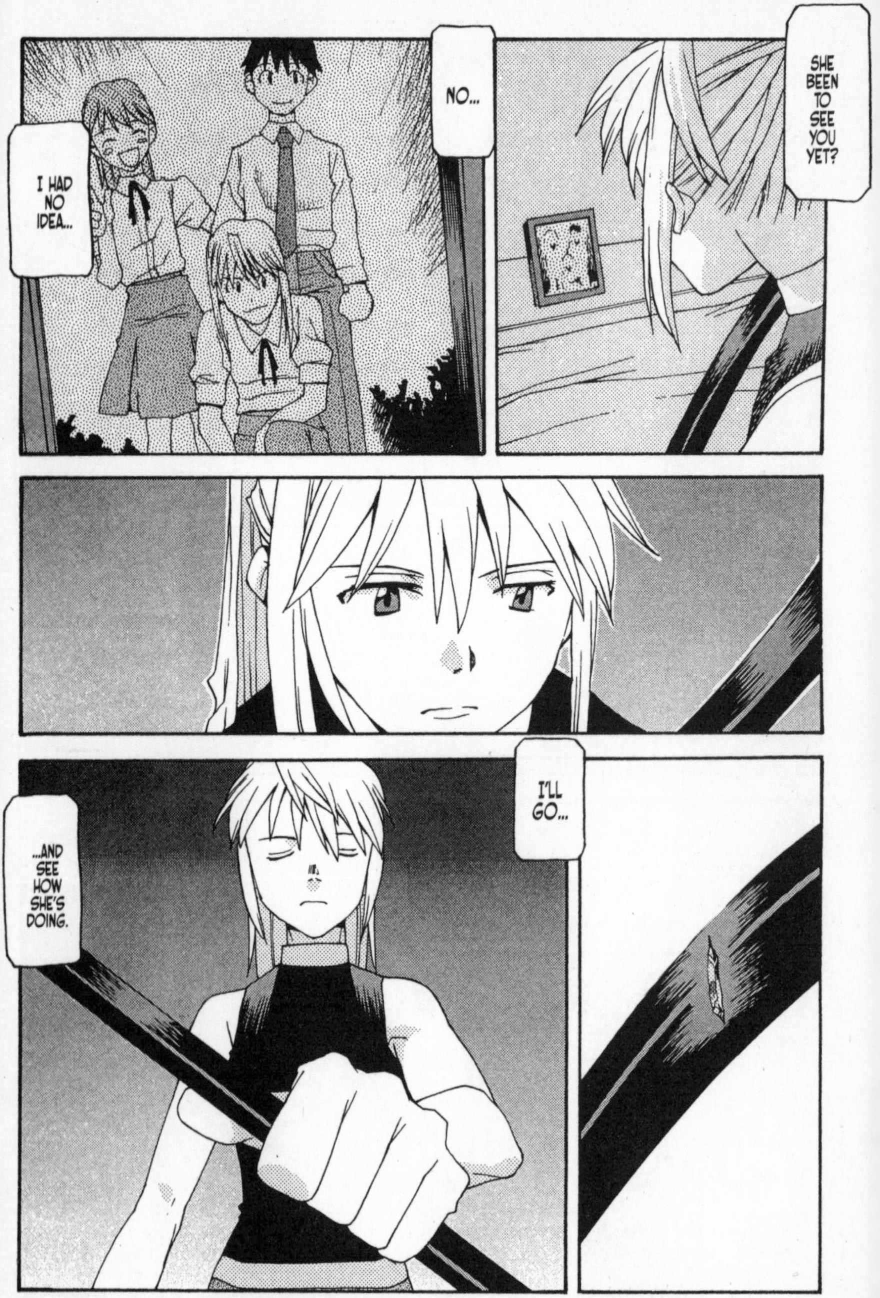
SHE BEEN TO SEE YOU YET?
NO...
I HAD NO IDEA...
I'LL GO...
...AND SEE HOW SHE'S DOING.

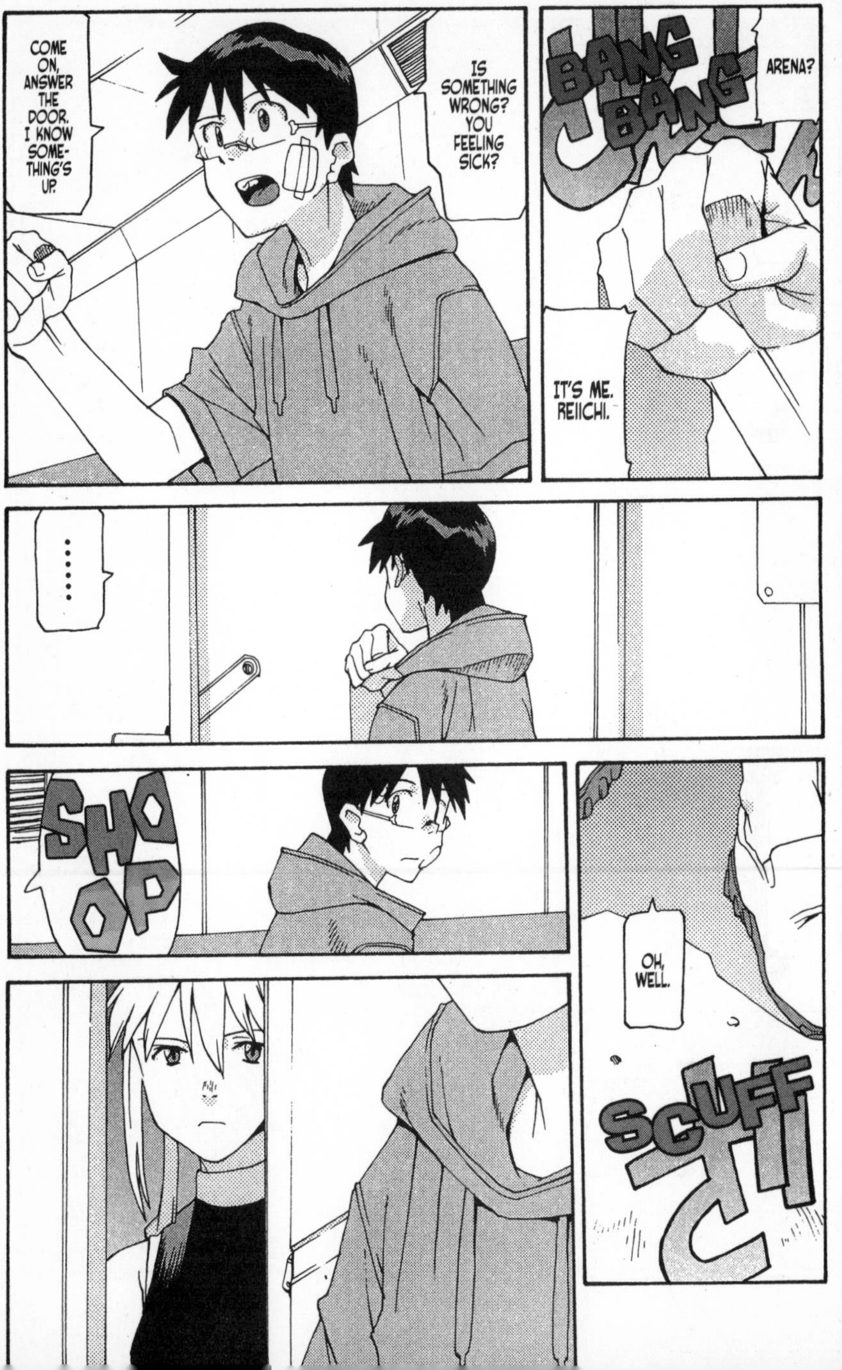
BANG BANG
ARENA?
IT'S ME. REIICHI.
IS SOMETHING WRONG? YOU FEELING SICK?
COME ON, ANSWER THE DOOR. I KNOW SOME-THING'S UP.
......
OH, WELL.
SCUFF
SHOOP

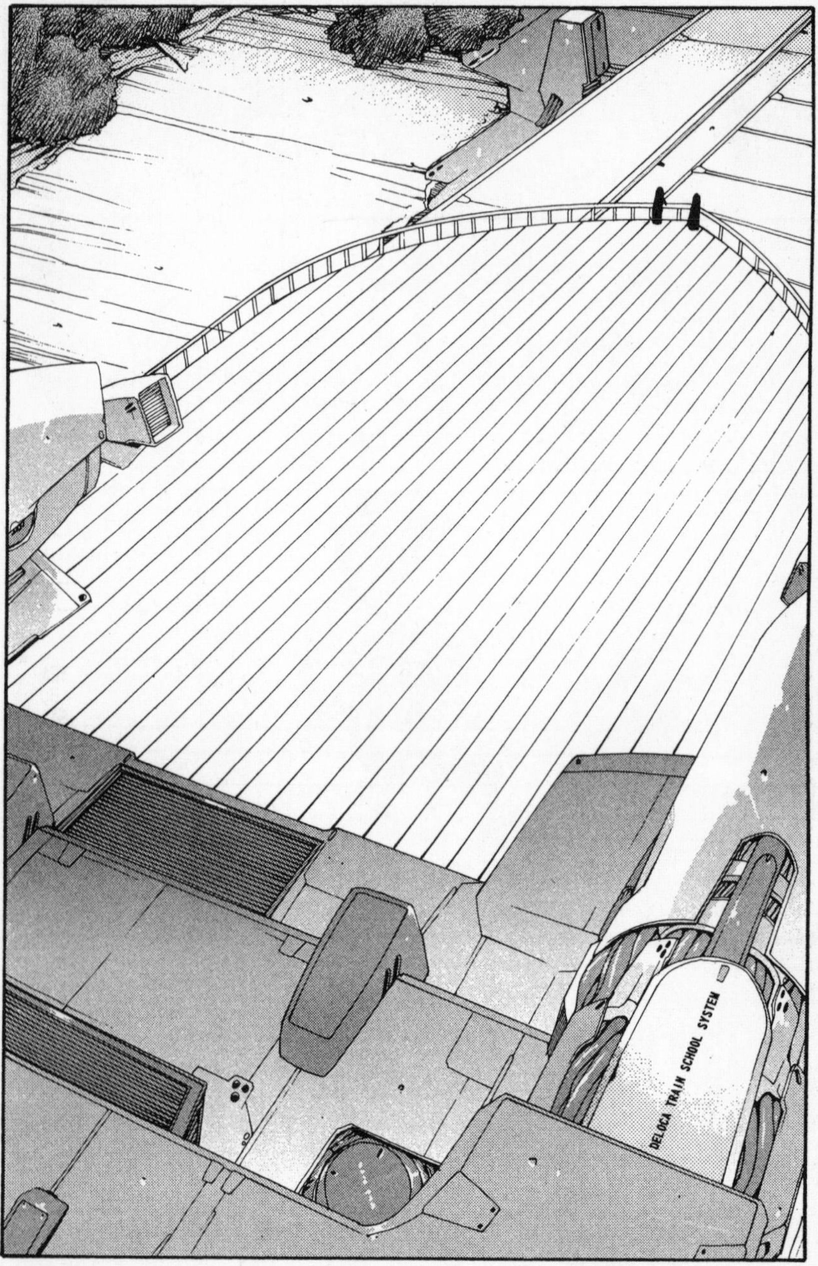
DELOCA TRAIN SCHOOL SYSTEM

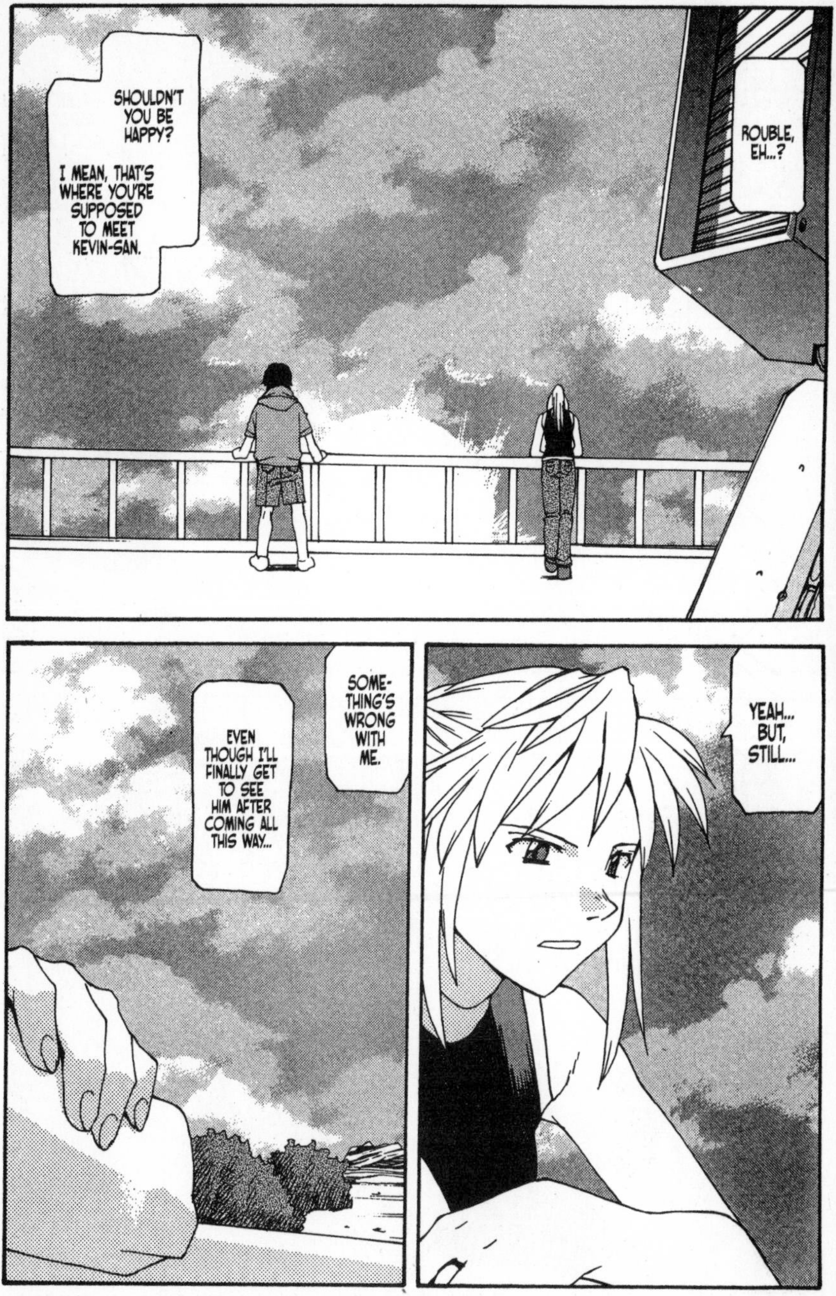
ROUBLE, EH...?
SHOULDN'T YOU BE HAPPY?
I MEAN, THAT'S WHERE YOU'RE SUPPOSED TO MEET KEVIN-SAN.
YEAH... BUT, STILL...
SOME-THING'S WRONG WITH ME.
EVEN THOUGH I'LL FINALLY GET TO SEE HIM AFTER COMING ALL THIS WAY...

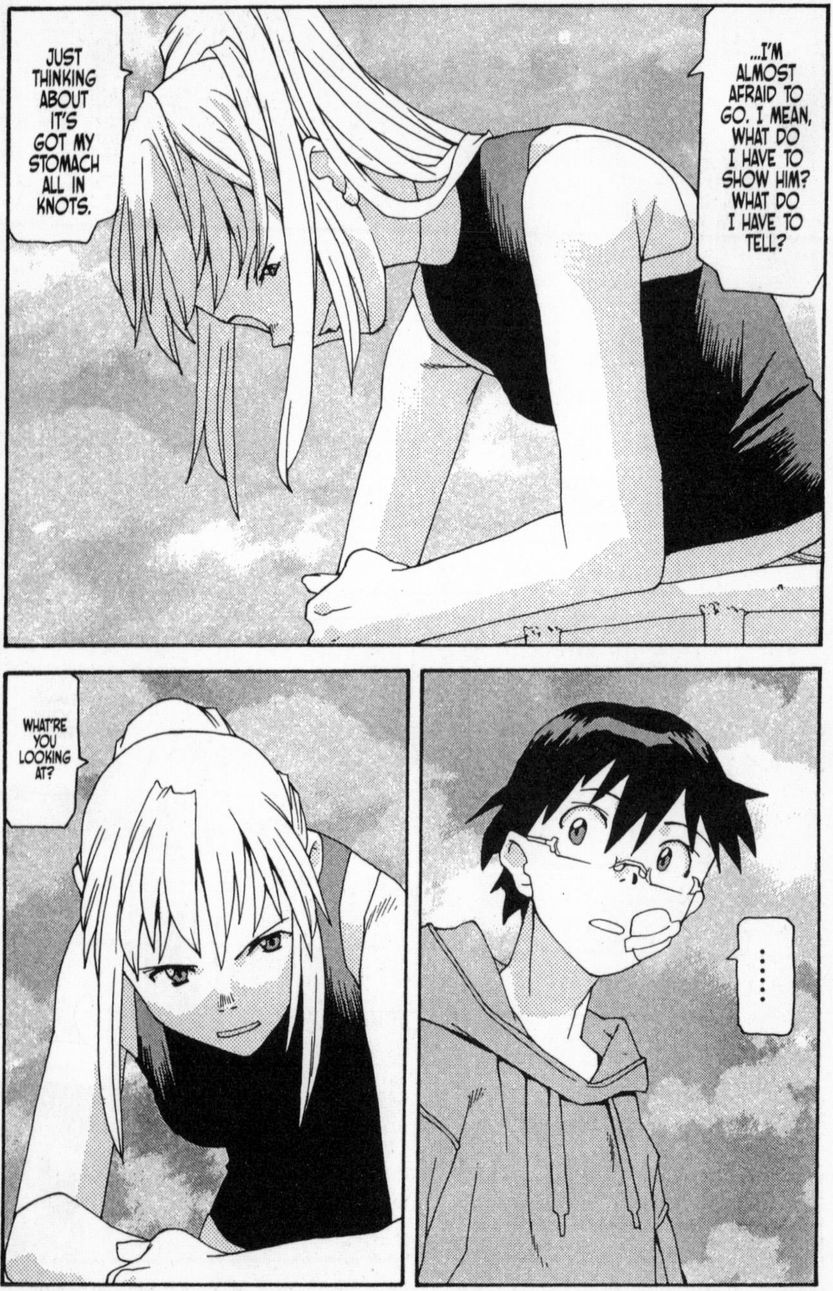
...I'M ALMOST AFRAID TO GO. I MEAN, WHAT DO I HAVE TO SHOW HIM? WHAT DO I HAVE TO TELL?
JUST THINKING ABOUT IT'S GOT MY STOMACH ALL IN KNOTS.
......
WHAT'RE YOU LOOKING AT?

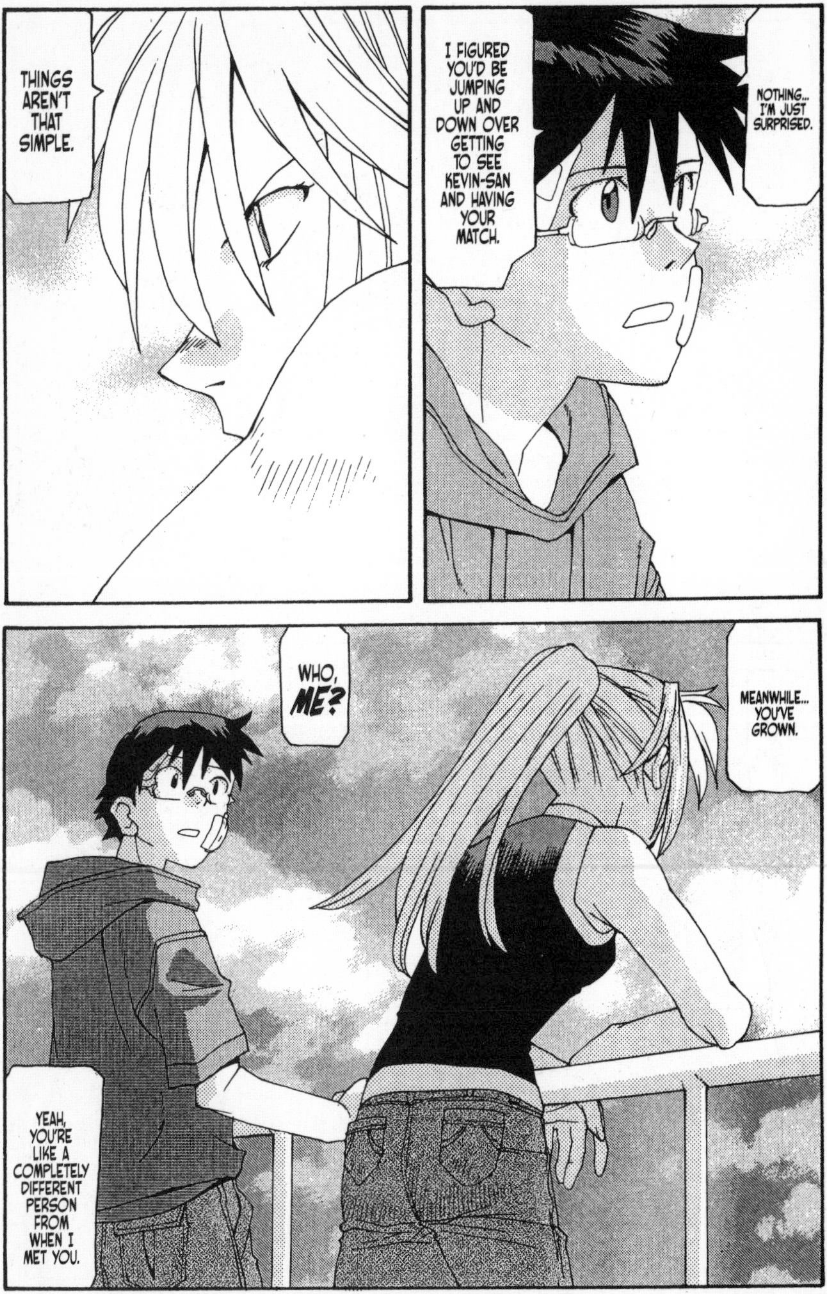
NOTHING... I'M JUST SURPRISED.
I FIGURED YOU'D BE JUMPING UP AND DOWN OVER GETTING TO SEE KEVIN-SAN AND HAVING YOUR MATCH.
THINGS AREN'T THAT SIMPLE.
MEANWHILE... YOU'VE GROWN.
WHO, *ME?*
YEAH, YOU'RE LIKE A COMPLETELY DIFFERENT PERSON FROM WHEN I MET YOU.

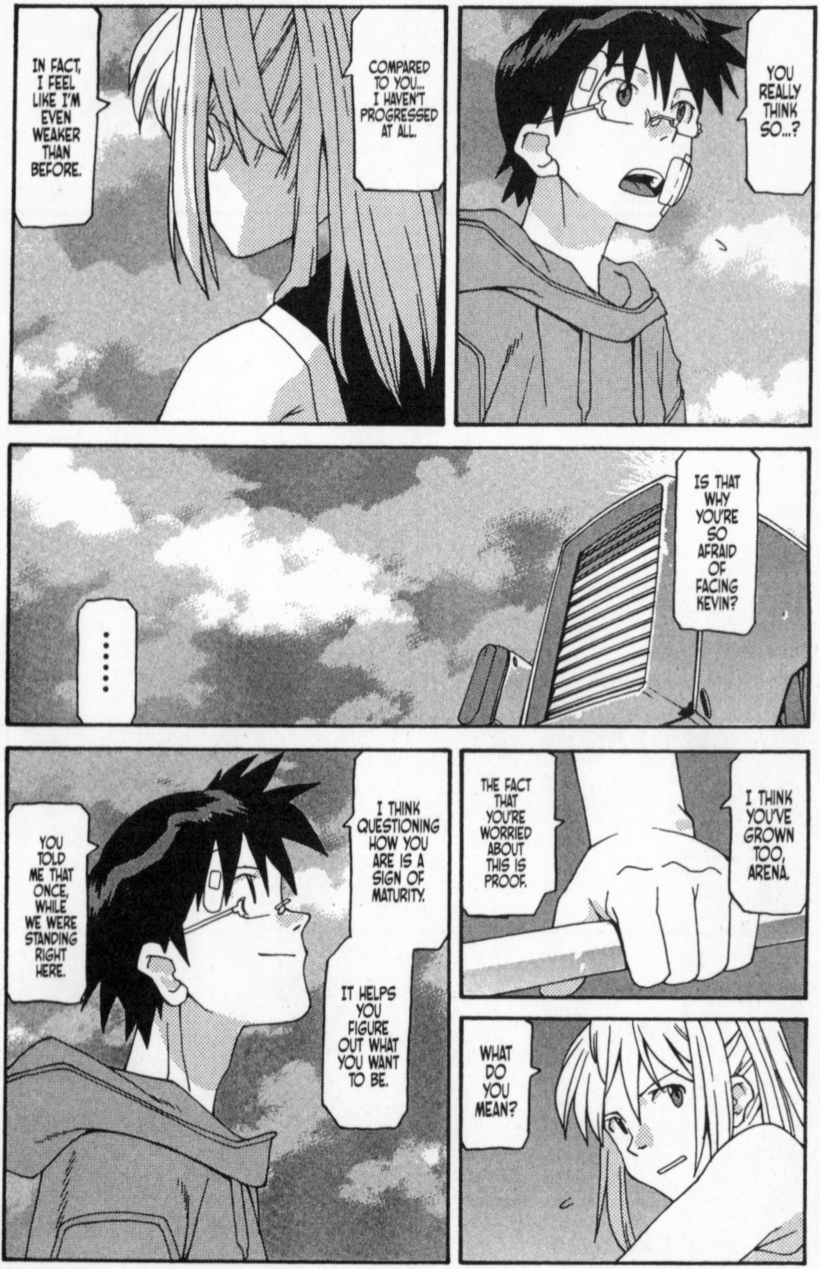
YOU REALLY THINK SO...?
COMPARED TO YOU... I HAVEN'T PROGRESSED AT ALL.
IN FACT, I FEEL LIKE I'M EVEN WEAKER THAN BEFORE.
IS THAT WHY YOU'RE SO AFRAID OF FACING KEVIN?
......
I THINK YOU'VE GROWN TOO, ARENA.
THE FACT THAT YOU'RE WORRIED ABOUT THIS IS PROOF.
WHAT DO YOU MEAN?
I THINK QUESTIONING HOW YOU ARE IS A SIGN OF MATURITY.
IT HELPS YOU FIGURE OUT WHAT YOU WANT TO BE.
YOU TOLD ME THAT ONCE, WHILE WE WERE STANDING RIGHT HERE.

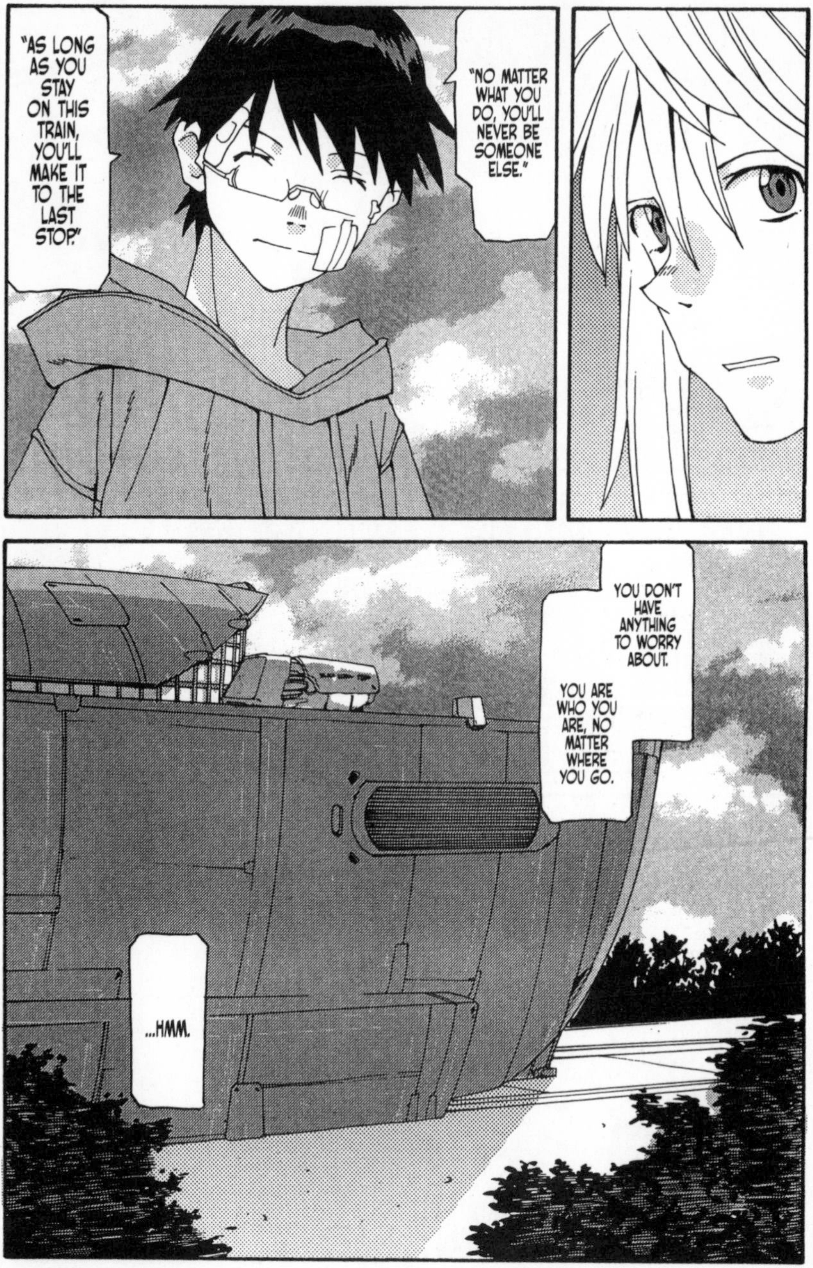
"NO MATTER WHAT YOU DO, YOU'LL NEVER BE SOMEONE ELSE."
"AS LONG AS YOU STAY ON THIS TRAIN, YOU'LL MAKE IT TO THE LAST STOP."
YOU DON'T HAVE ANYTHING TO WORRY ABOUT.
YOU ARE WHO YOU ARE, NO MATTER WHERE YOU GO.
...HMM.

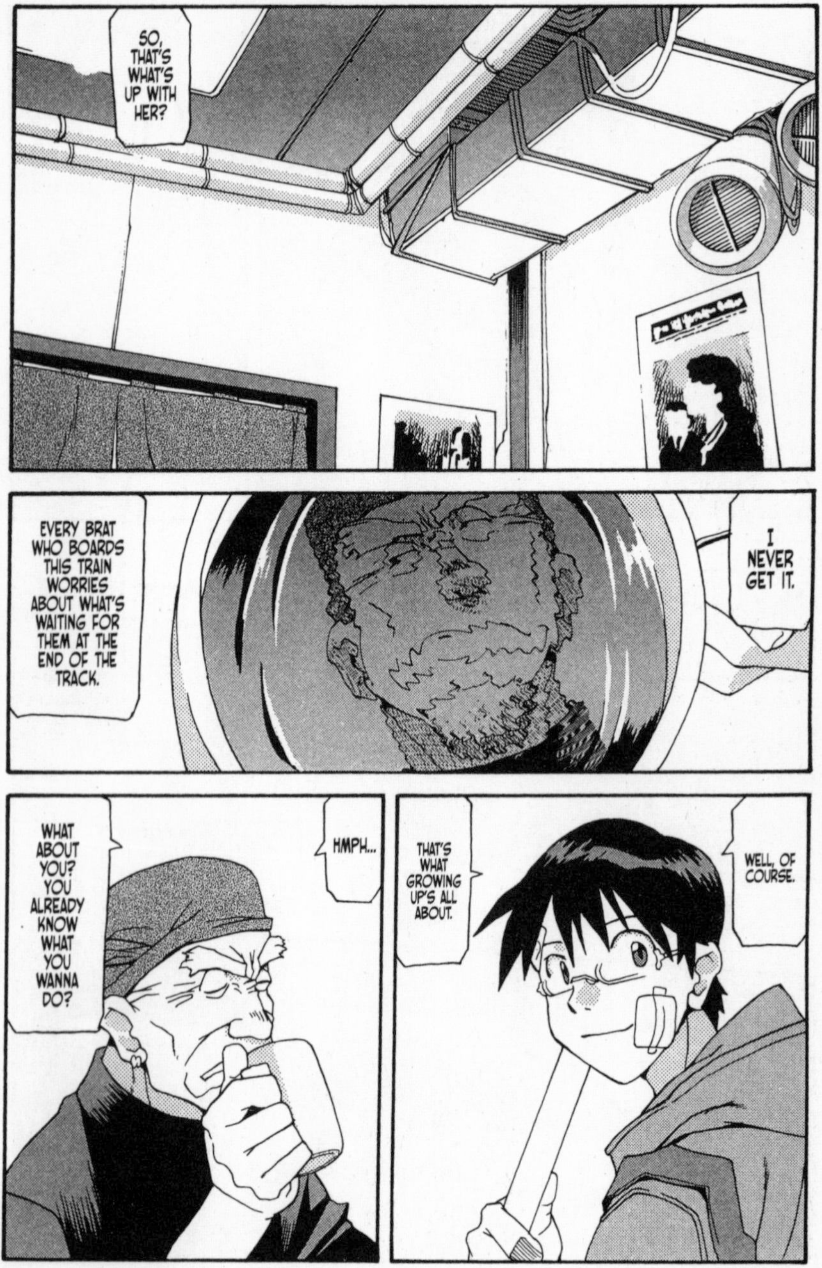
SO, THAT'S WHAT'S UP WITH HER?
I NEVER GET IT.
EVERY BRAT WHO BOARDS THIS TRAIN WORRIES ABOUT WHAT'S WAITING FOR THEM AT THE END OF THE TRACK.
WELL, OF COURSE.
THAT'S WHAT GROWING UP'S ALL ABOUT.
HMPH...
WHAT ABOUT YOU? YOU ALREADY KNOW WHAT YOU WANNA DO?

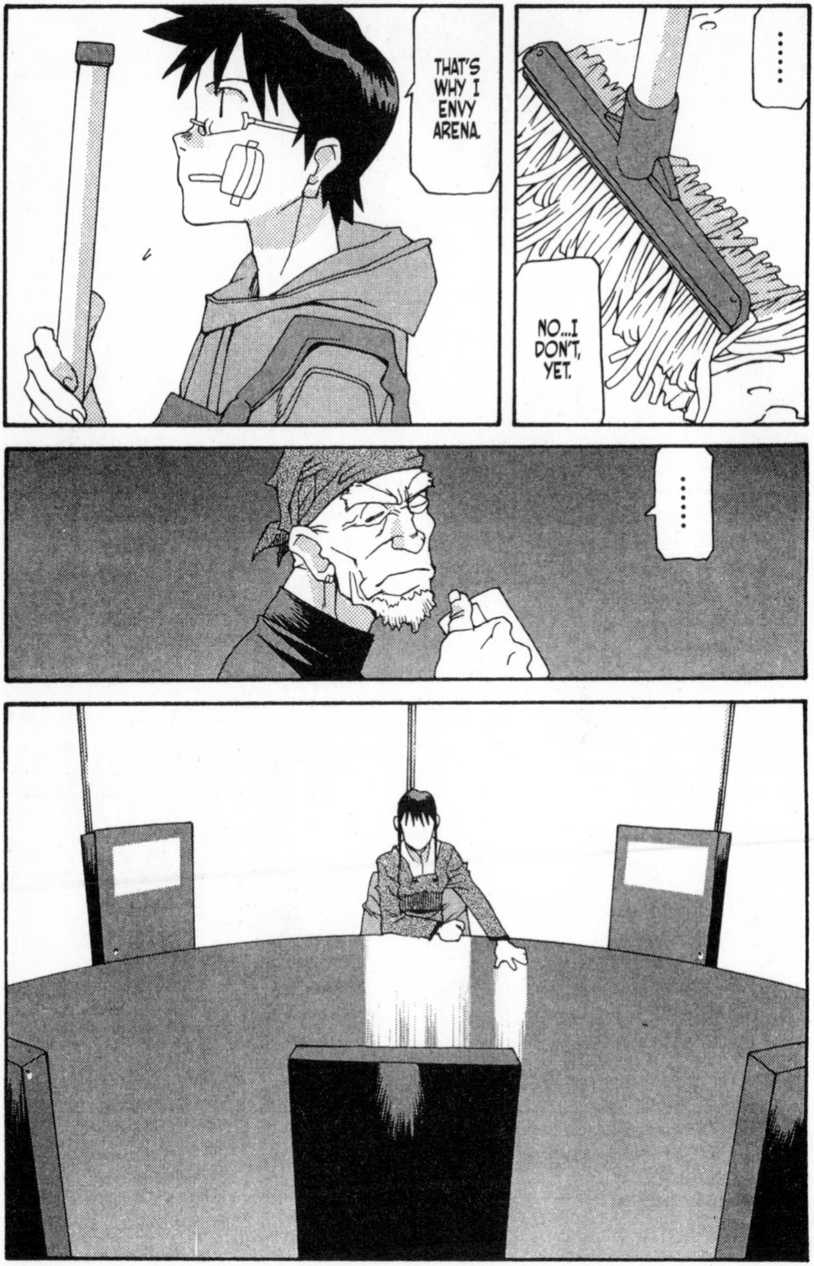
......
NO...I DON'T, YET.
THAT'S WHY I ENVY ARENA.
......

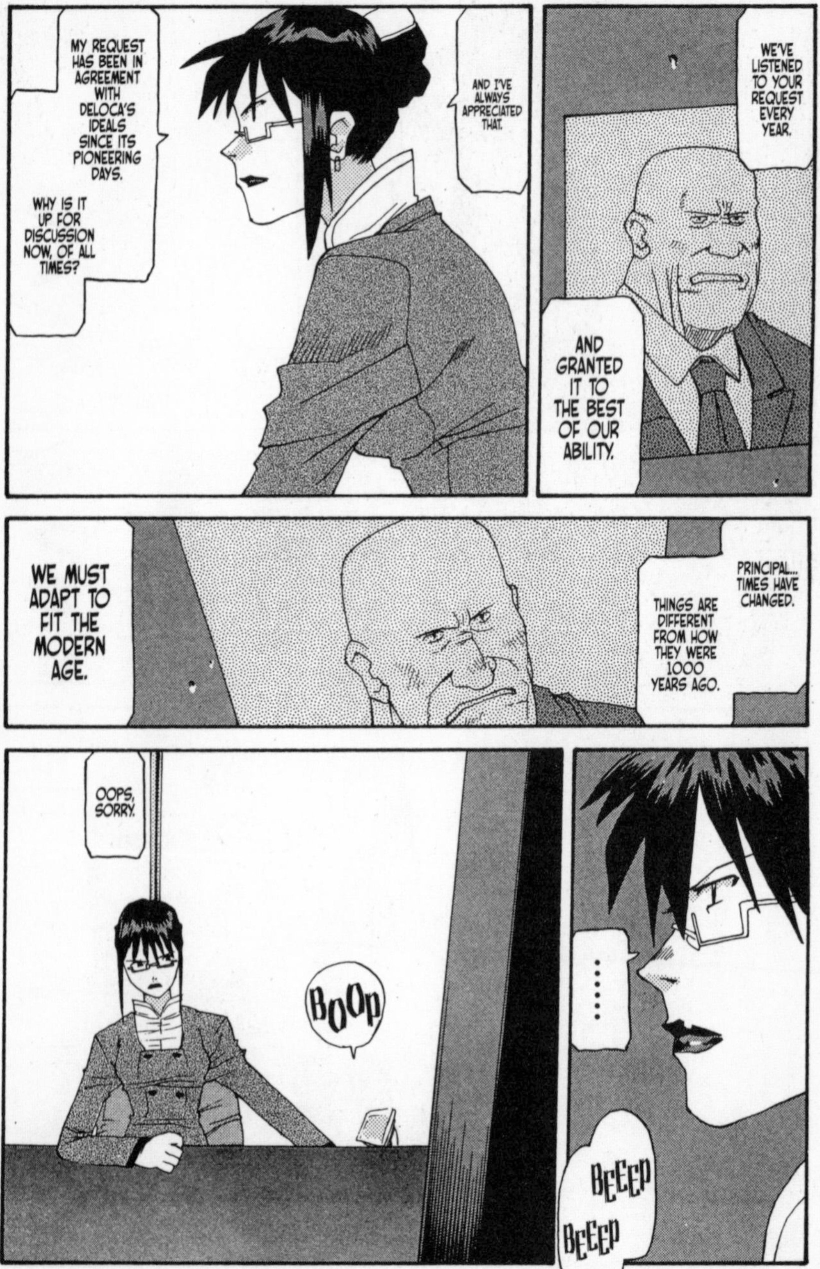
WE'VE LISTENED TO YOUR REQUEST EVERY YEAR.
AND GRANTED IT TO THE BEST OF OUR ABILITY.
AND I'VE ALWAYS APPRECIATED THAT.
MY REQUEST HAS BEEN IN AGREEMENT WITH DELOCA'S IDEALS SINCE ITS PIONEERING DAYS.
WHY IS IT UP FOR DISCUSSION NOW, OF ALL TIMES?
PRINCIPAL... TIMES HAVE CHANGED.
THINGS ARE DIFFERENT FROM HOW THEY WERE 1000 YEARS AGO.
WE MUST ADAPT TO FIT THE MODERN AGE.
......
BEEEP
BEEEP
OOPS, SORRY.
BOOP

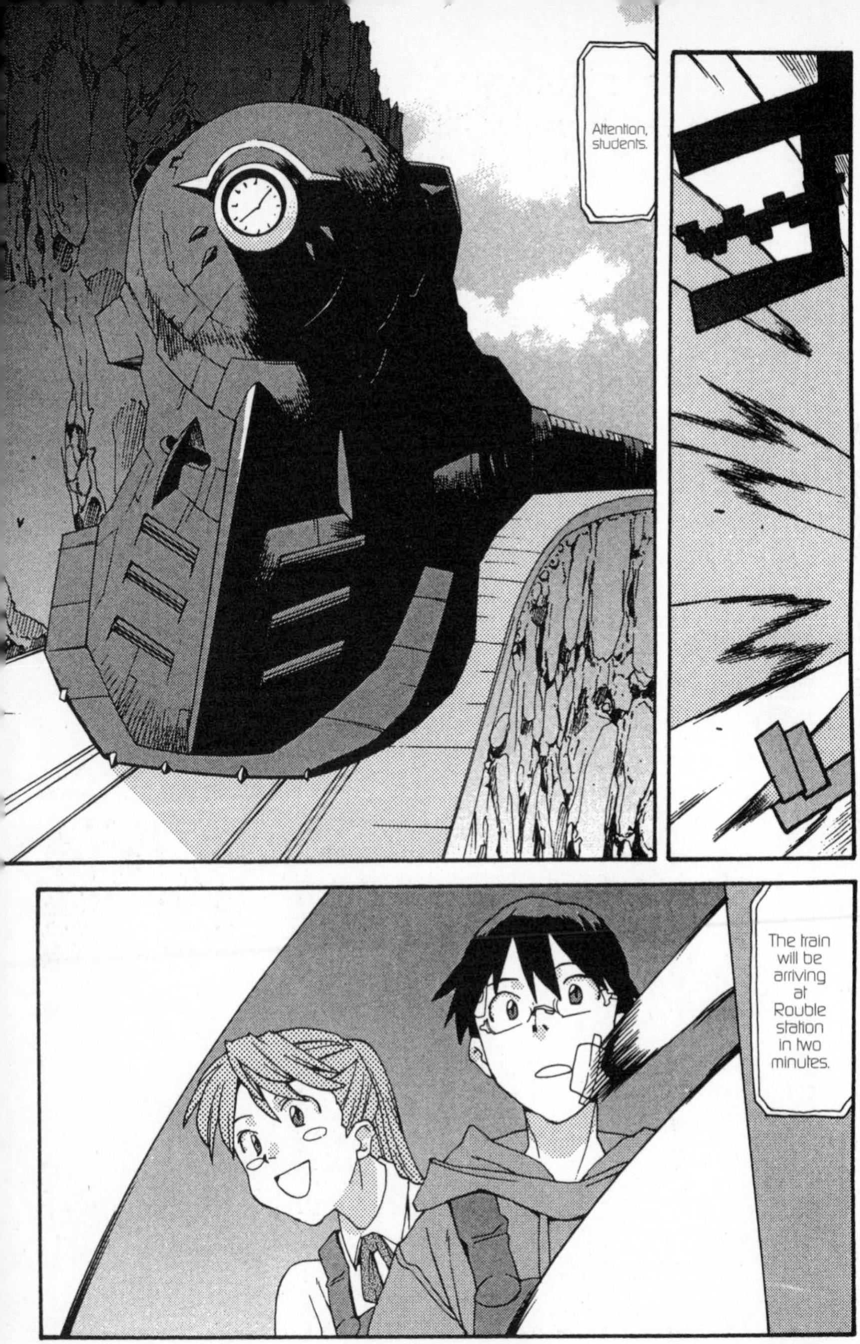
Attention, students.
The train will be arriving at Rouble station in two minutes.

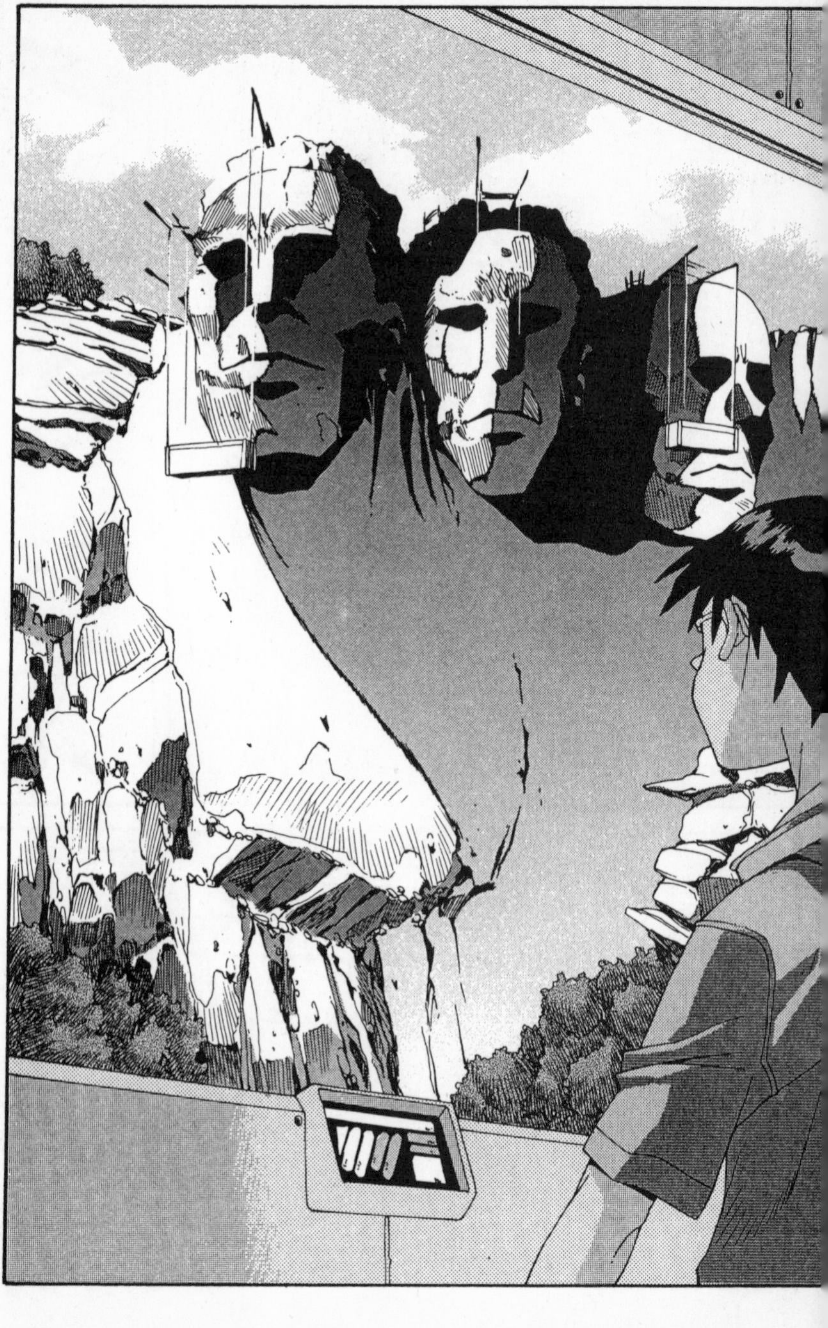

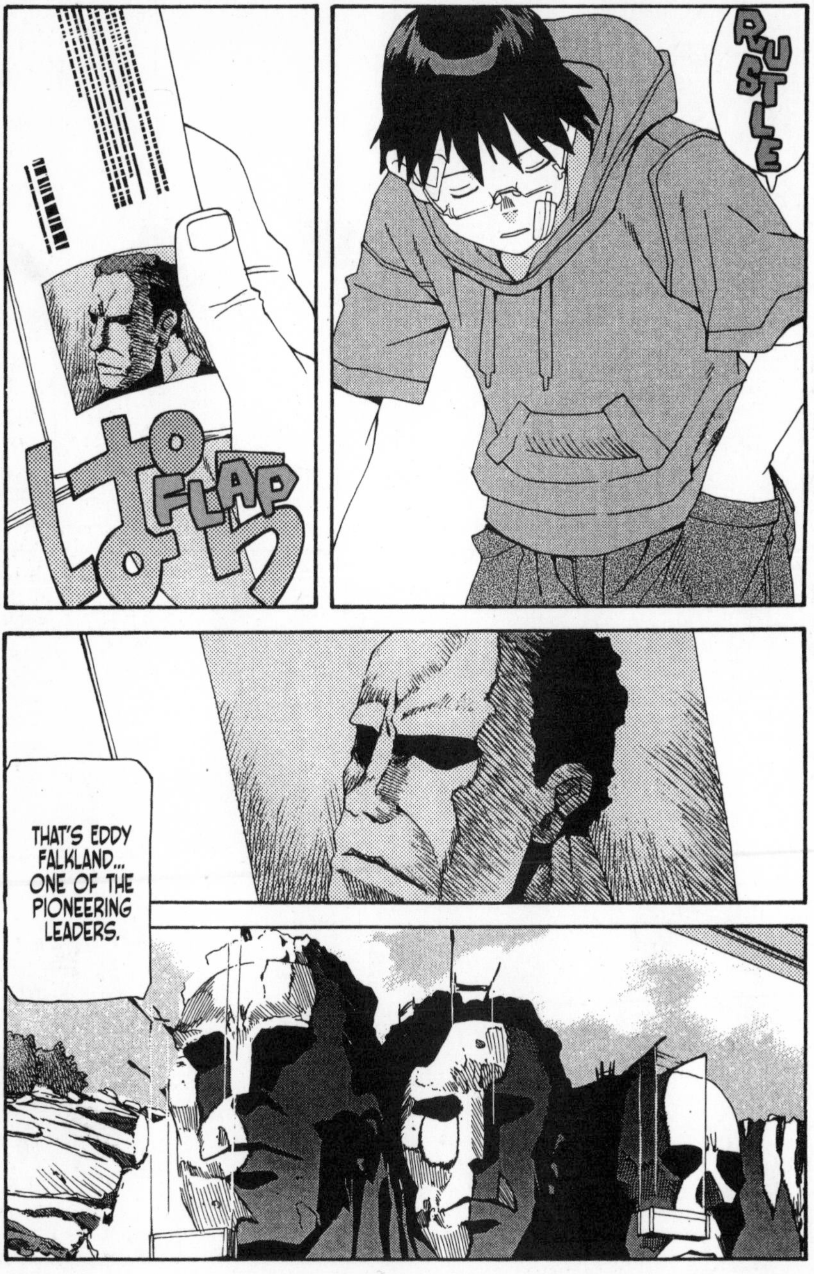
RUSTLE
FLAP
THAT'S EDDY FALKLAND... ONE OF THE PIONEERING LEADERS.

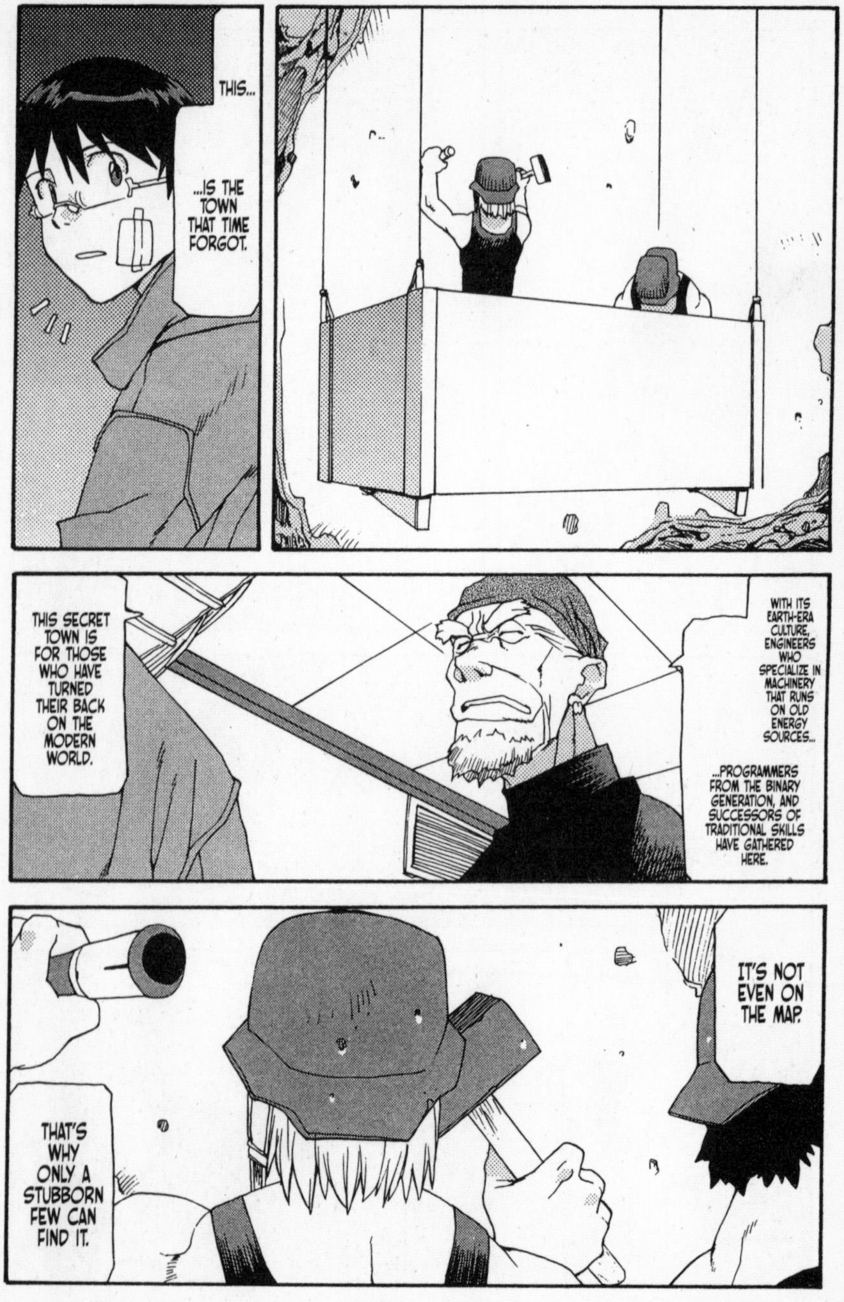
THIS...
...IS THE TOWN THAT TIME FORGOT.
WITH ITS EARTH-ERA CULTURE, ENGINEERS WHO SPECIALIZE IN MACHINERY THAT RUNS ON OLD ENERGY SOURCES...
...PROGRAMMERS FROM THE BINARY GENERATION, AND SUCCESSORS OF TRADITIONAL SKILLS HAVE GATHERED HERE.
THIS SECRET TOWN IS FOR THOSE WHO HAVE TURNED THEIR BACK ON THE MODERN WORLD.
IT'S NOT EVEN ON THE MAP.
THAT'S WHY ONLY A STUBBORN FEW CAN FIND IT.

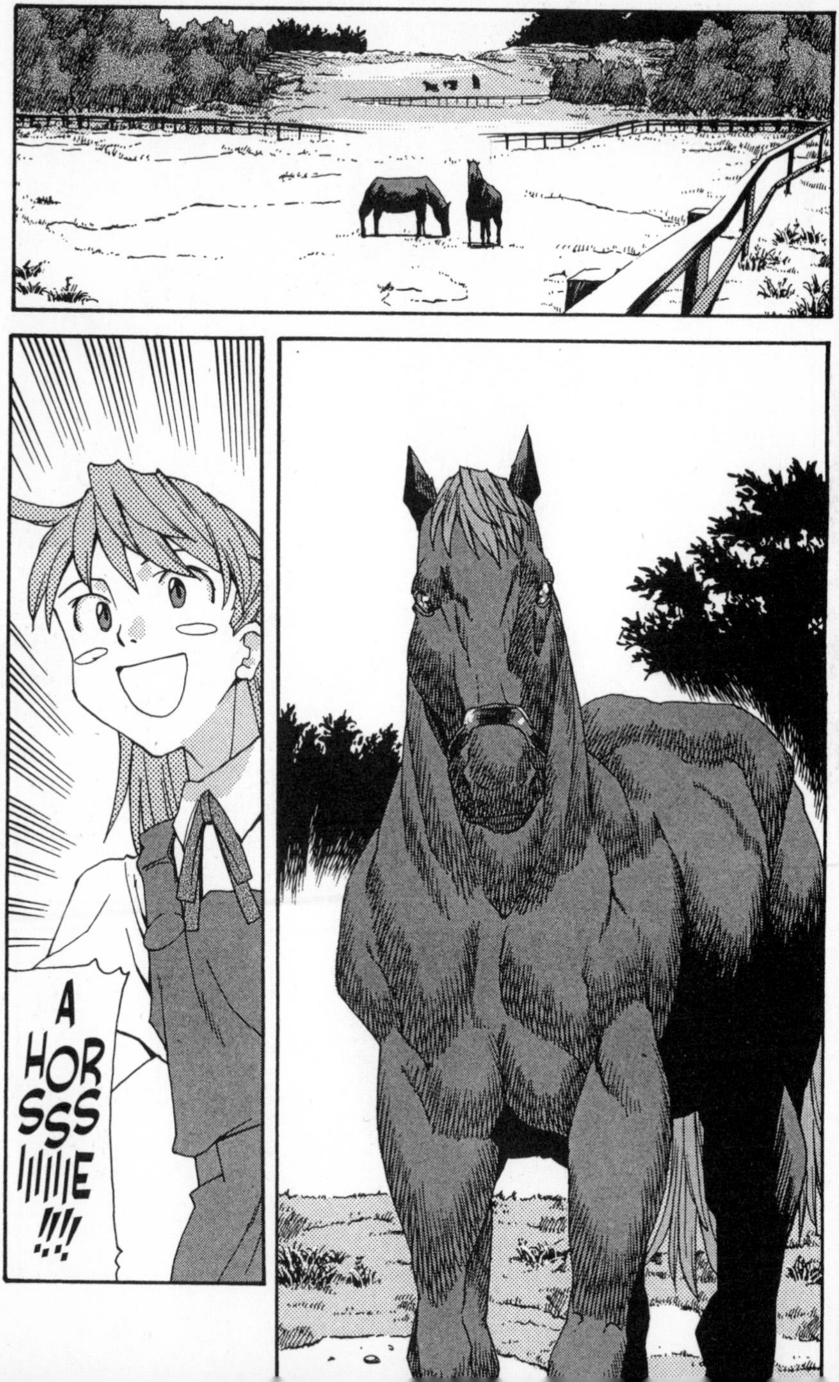
A HORSSSE!!!

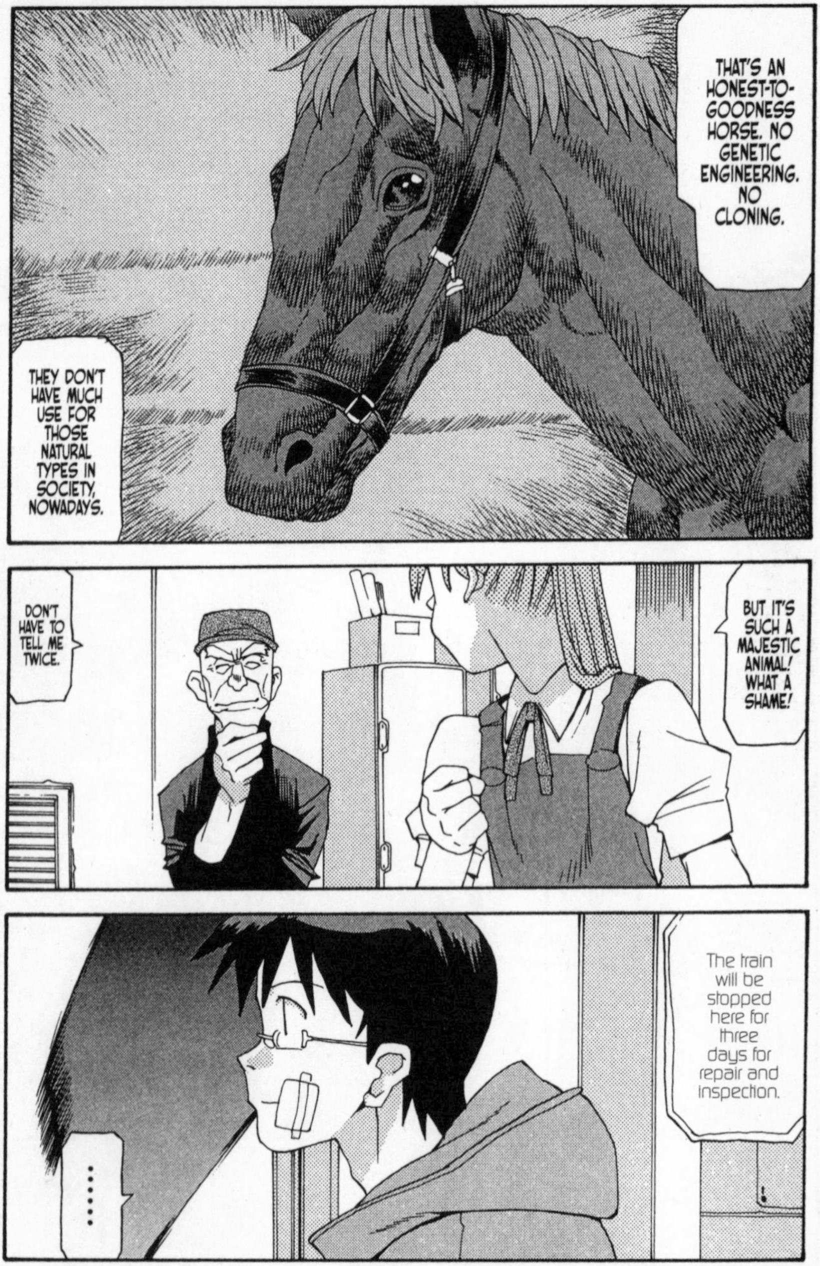
THAT'S AN HONEST-TO-GOODNESS HORSE. NO GENETIC ENGINEERING. NO CLONING.
THEY DON'T HAVE MUCH USE FOR THOSE NATURAL TYPES IN SOCIETY, NOWADAYS.
BUT IT'S SUCH A MAJESTIC ANIMAL! WHAT A SHAME!
DON'T HAVE TO TELL ME TWICE.
The train will be stopped here for three days for repair and inspection.
......

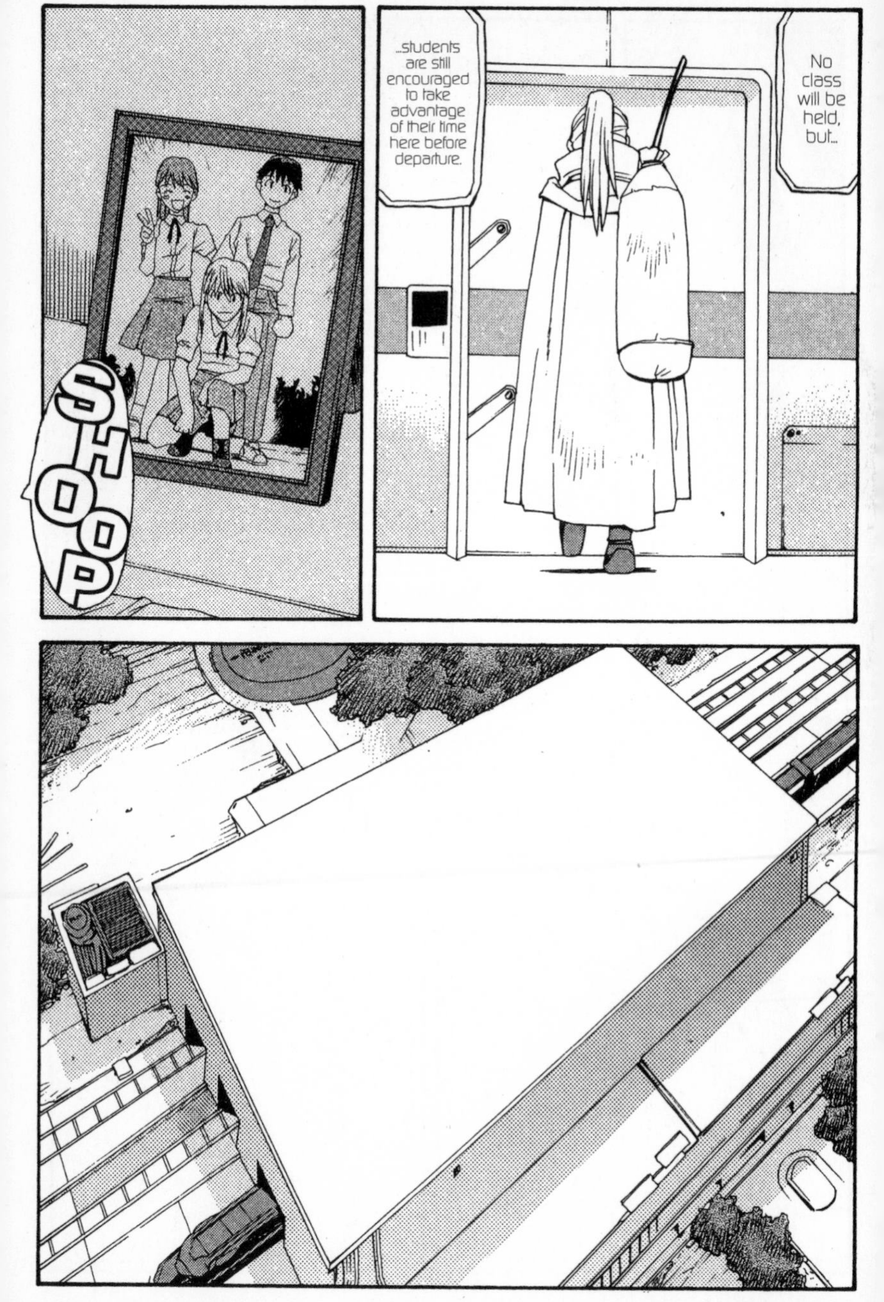
No class will be held, but...
...students are still encouraged to take advantage of their time here before departure.
SHOOP

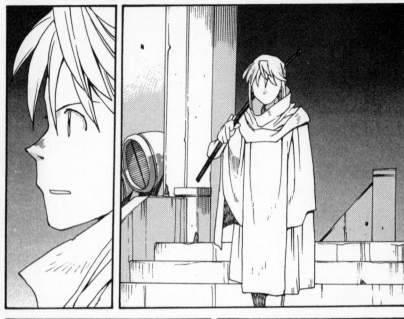

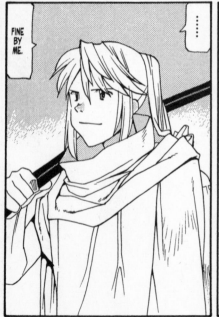

IT'S NOT FAIR TO THE OTHERS, BUT...
...AT LEAST LET ME PERSONALLY SEE YOU OFF.
......
FINE BY ME.

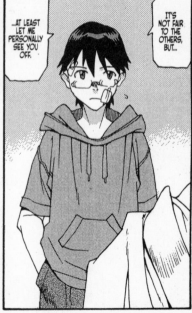

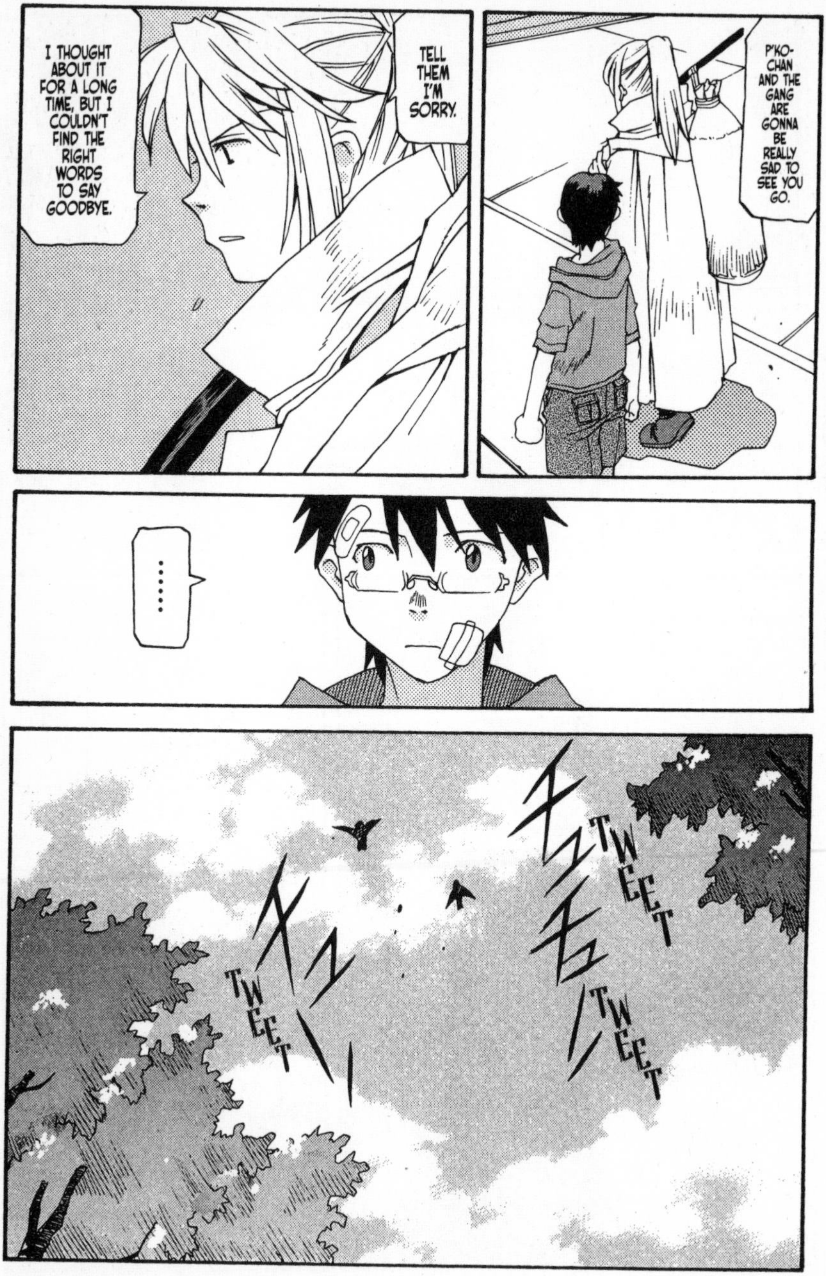
P'KO-CHAN AND THE GANG ARE GONNA BE REALLY SAD TO SEE YOU GO.
TELL THEM I'M SORRY.
I THOUGHT ABOUT IT FOR A LONG TIME, BUT I COULDN'T FIND THE RIGHT WORDS TO SAY GOODBYE.
......
TWEET
TWEET
TWEET

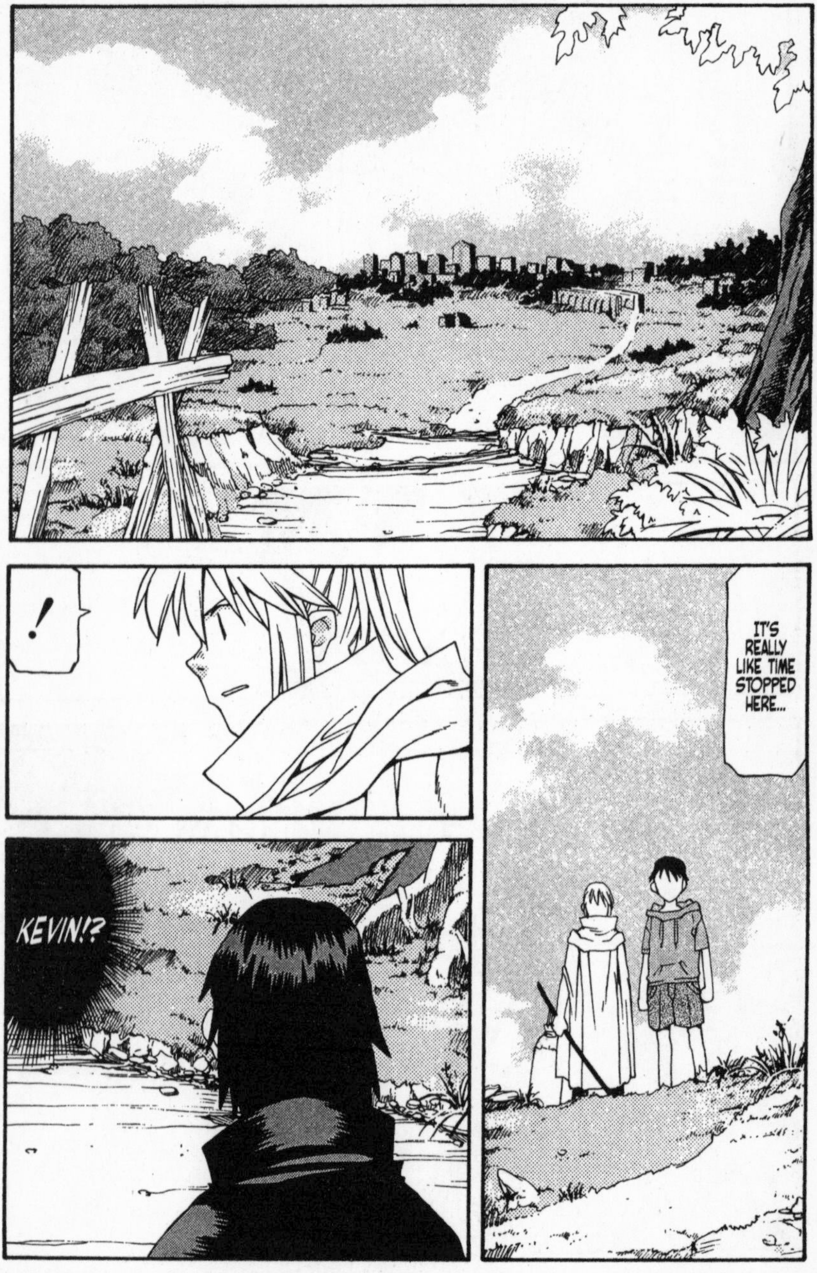
IT'S REALLY LIKE TIME STOPPED HERE...
!
KEVIN!?

ARENA?

WELL...
I GUESS WE
SHOULD TRY
ASKING A
GOVERNMENT
OFFICE OR
POLICE
STATION
WHERE
WE CAN
FIND HIM.

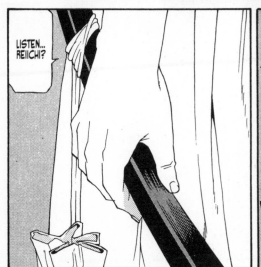

LISTEN...
REIICHI?

はっ

HAAH...

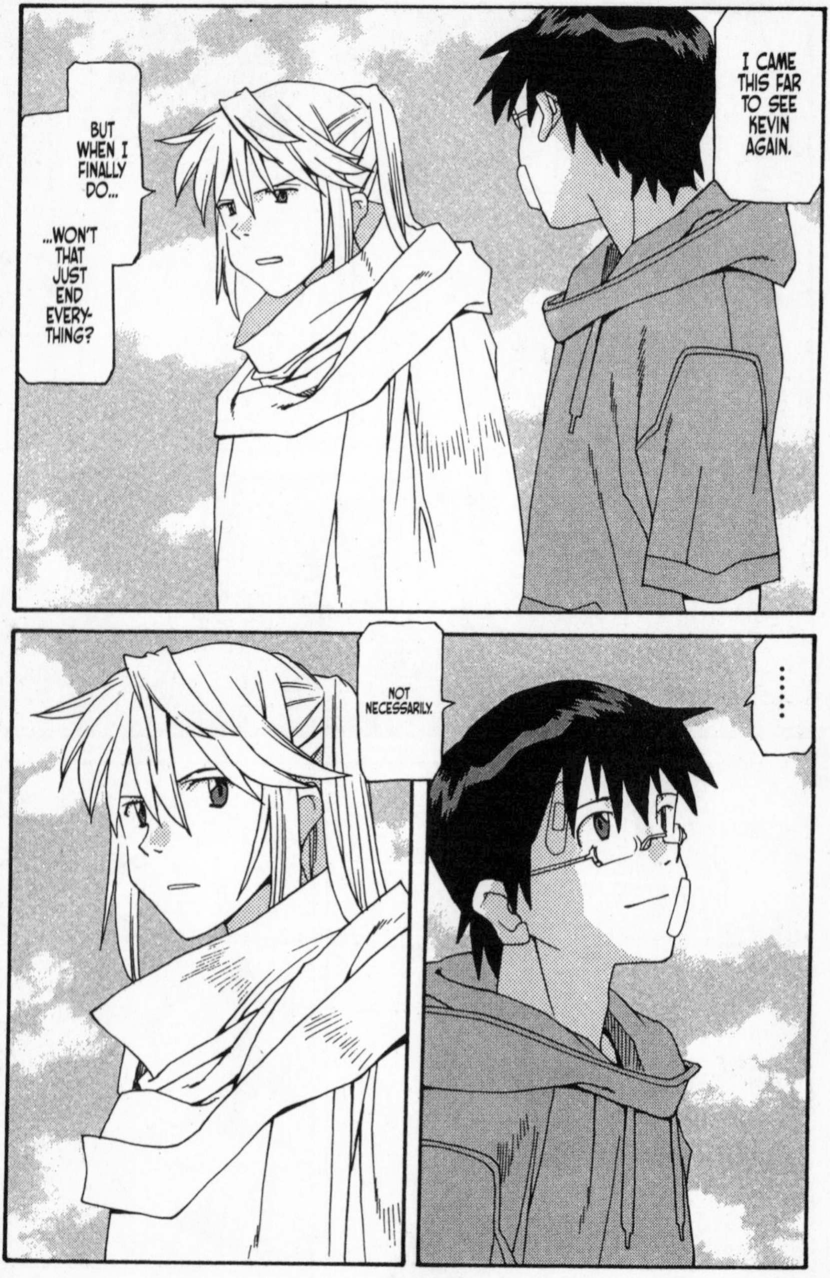
I CAME THIS FAR TO SEE KEVIN AGAIN.
BUT WHEN I FINALLY DO...
...WON'T THAT JUST END EVERYTHING?
......
NOT NECESSARILY.

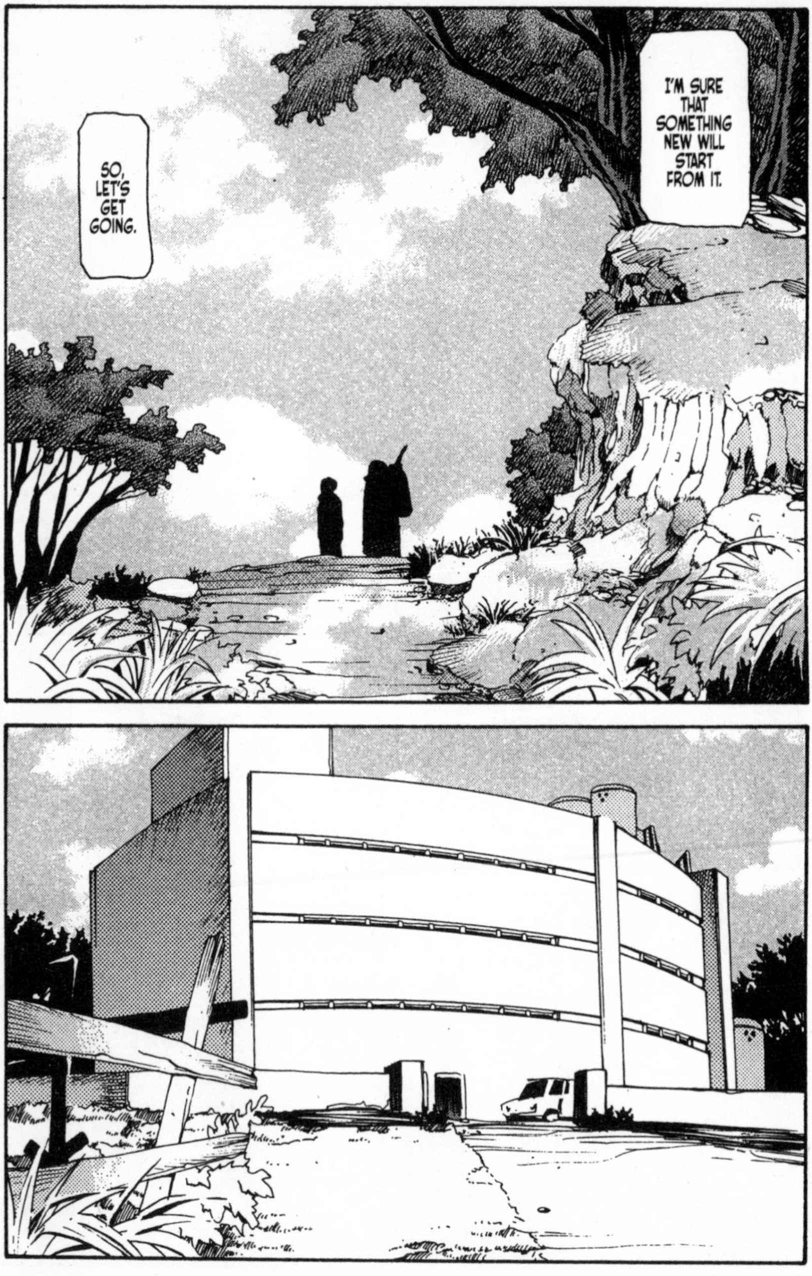
I'M SURE THAT SOMETHING NEW WILL START FROM IT.
SO, LET'S GET GOING.

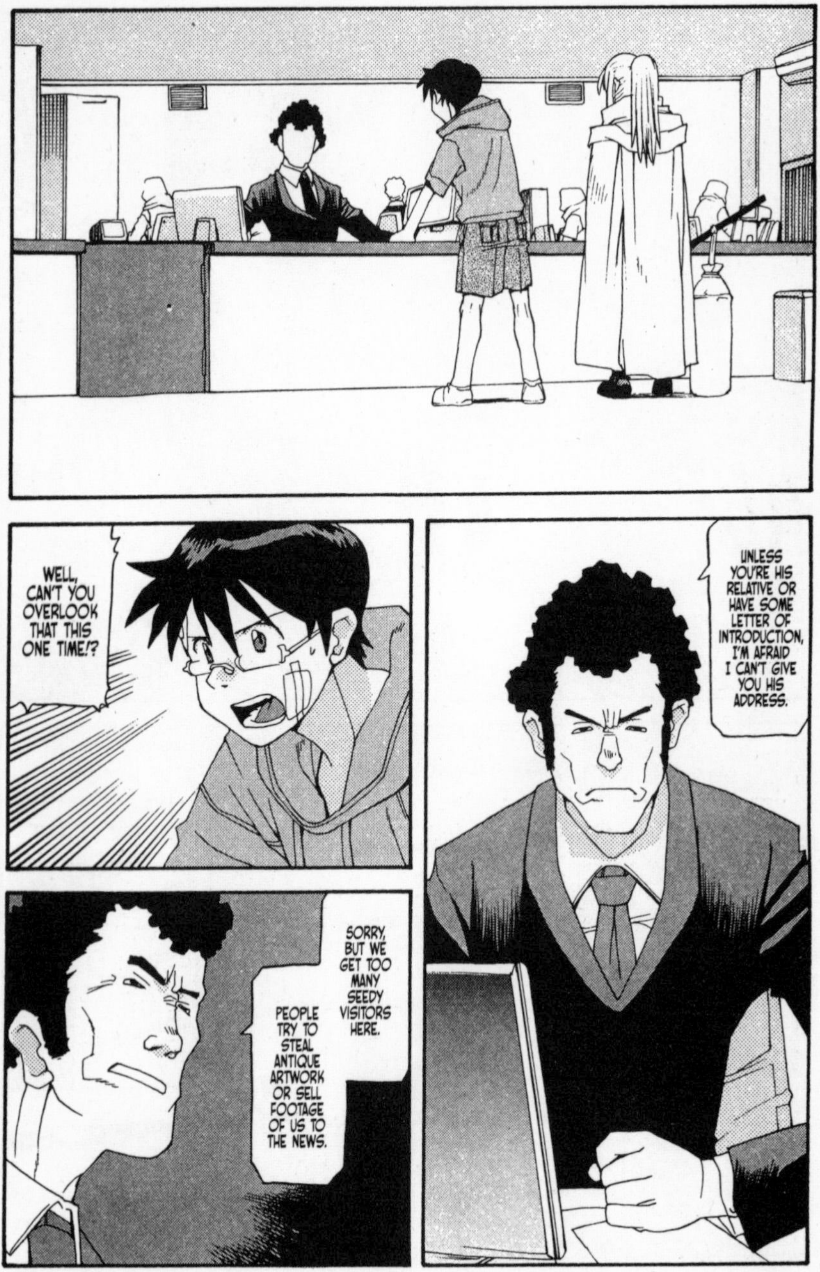
UNLESS YOU'RE HIS RELATIVE OR HAVE SOME LETTER OF INTRODUCTION, I'M AFRAID I CAN'T GIVE YOU HIS ADDRESS.
WELL, CAN'T YOU OVERLOOK THAT THIS ONE TIME!?
SORRY, BUT WE GET TOO MANY SEEDY VISITORS HERE.
PEOPLE TRY TO STEAL ANTIQUE ARTWORK OR SELL FOOTAGE OF US TO THE NEWS.

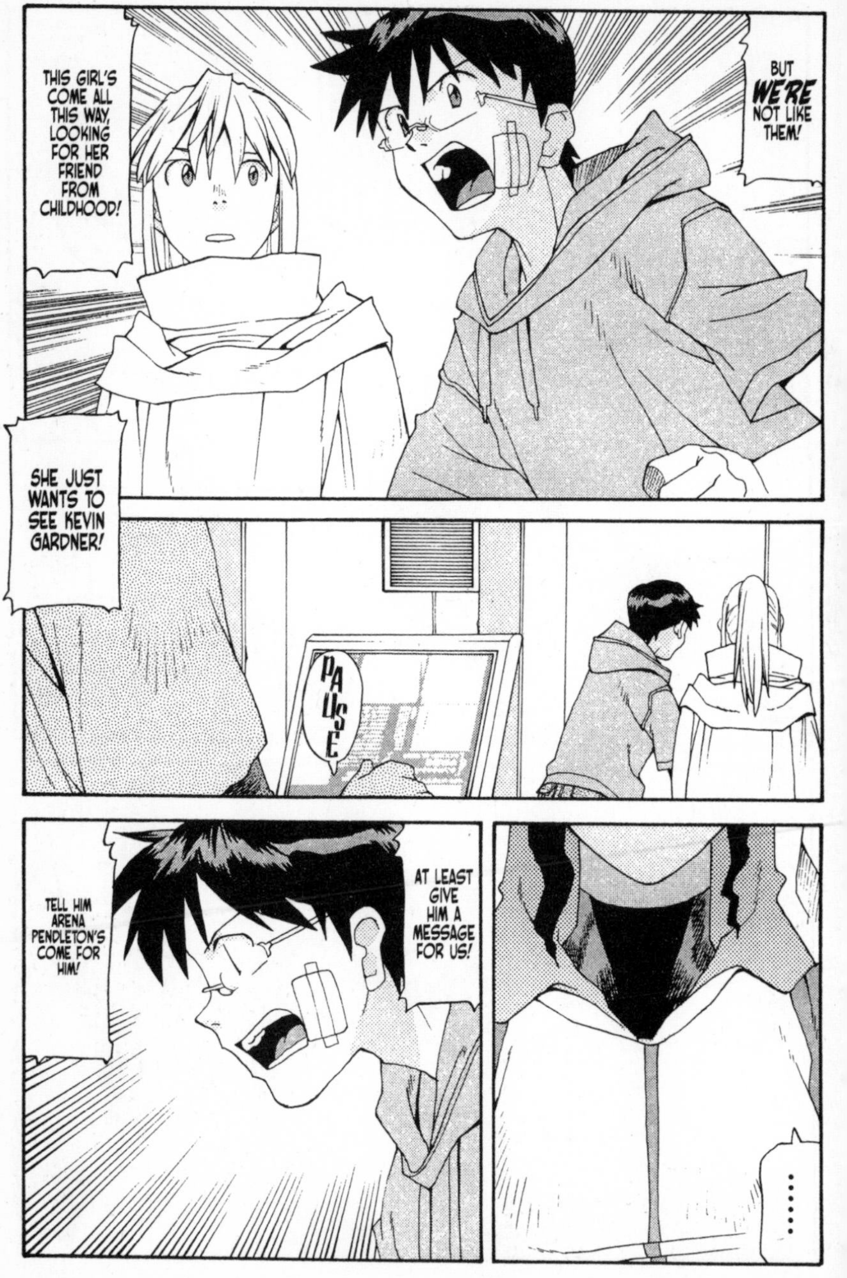
BUT *WE'RE* NOT LIKE THEM!
THIS GIRL'S COME ALL THIS WAY, LOOKING FOR HER FRIEND FROM CHILDHOOD!
SHE JUST WANTS TO SEE KEVIN GARDNER!
PAUSE
......
AT LEAST GIVE HIM A MESSAGE FOR US!
TELL HIM ARENA PENDLETON'S COME FOR HIM!

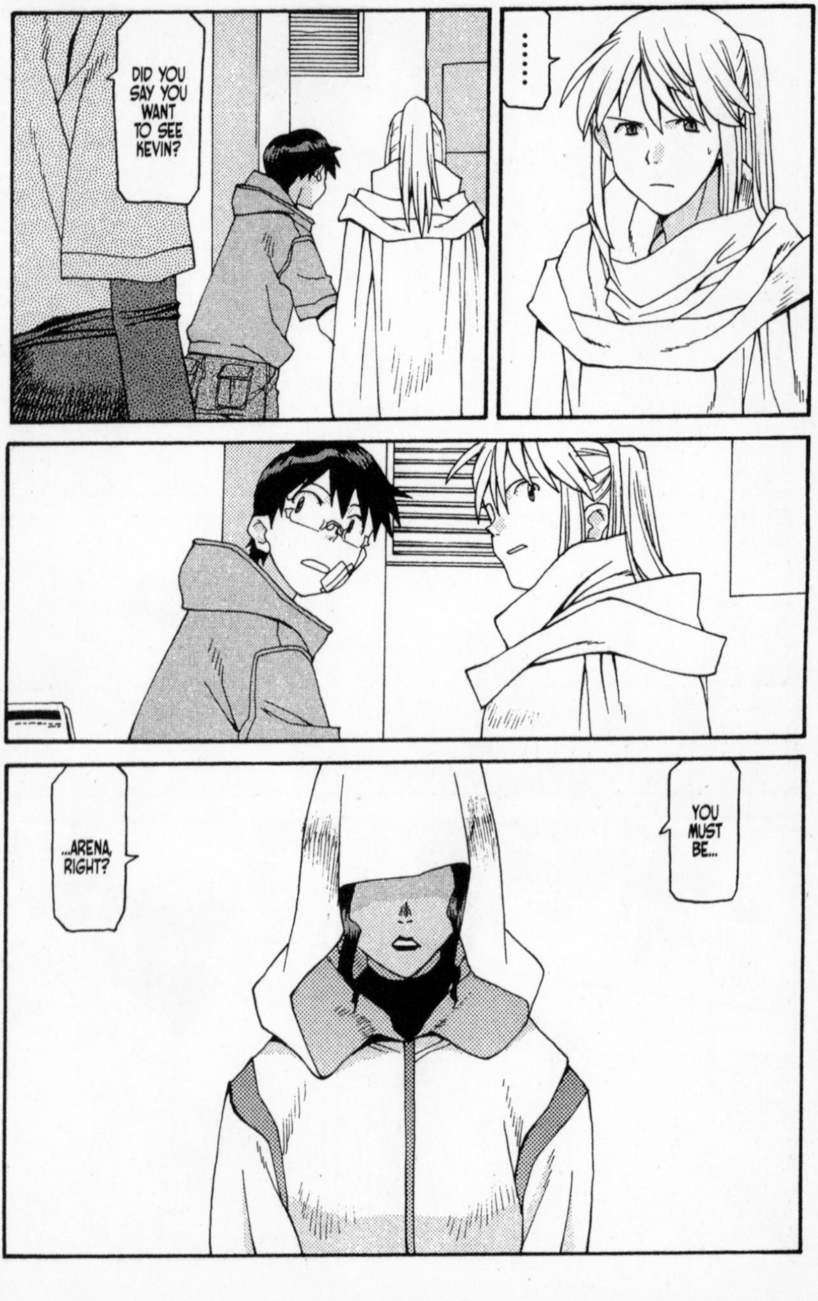
......
DID YOU SAY YOU WANT TO SEE KEVIN?
YOU MUST BE...
...ARENA, RIGHT?

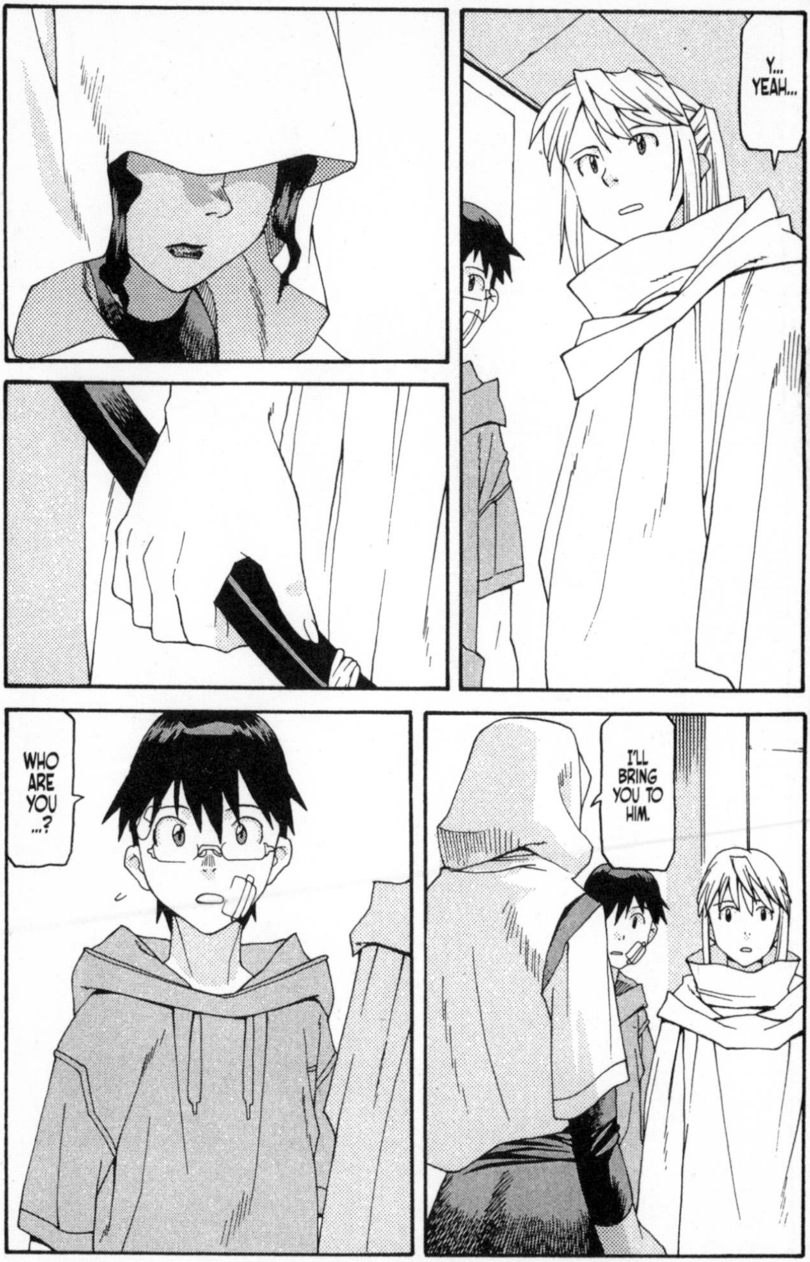
Y... YEAH...
I'LL BRING YOU TO HIM.
WHO ARE YOU ...?

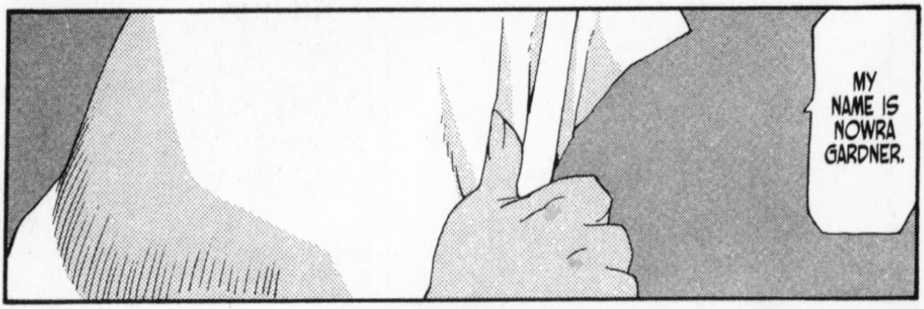
MY NAME IS NOWRA GARDNER.

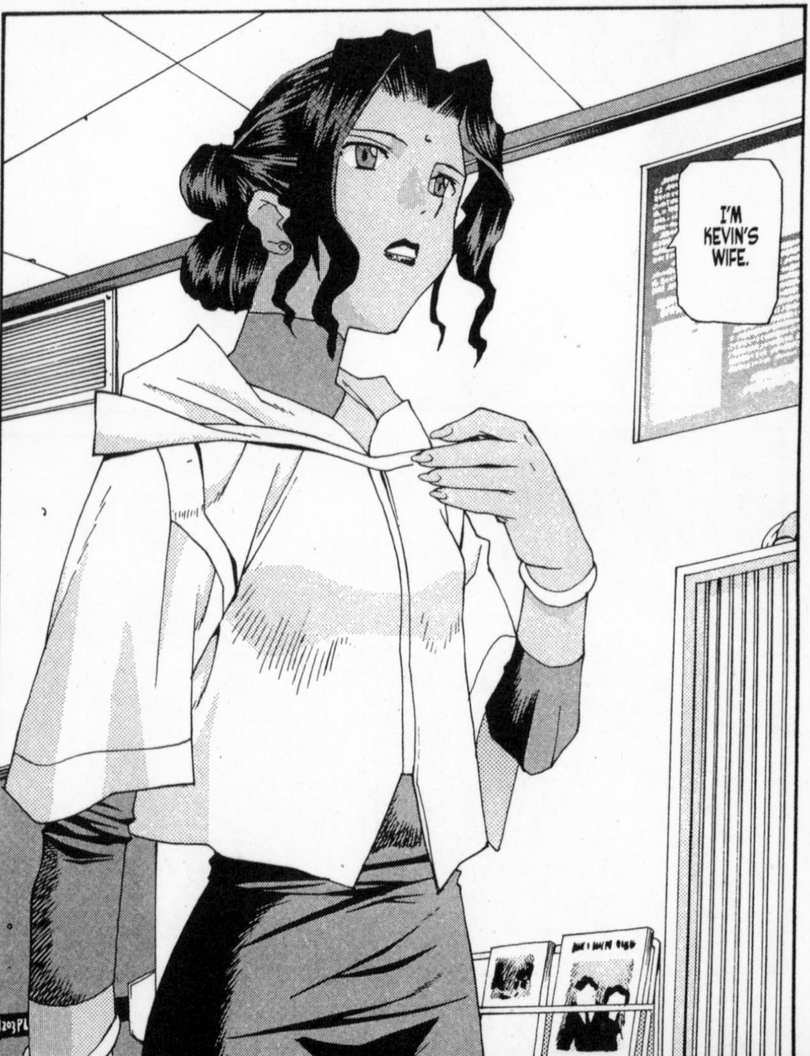
I'M KEVIN'S WIFE.

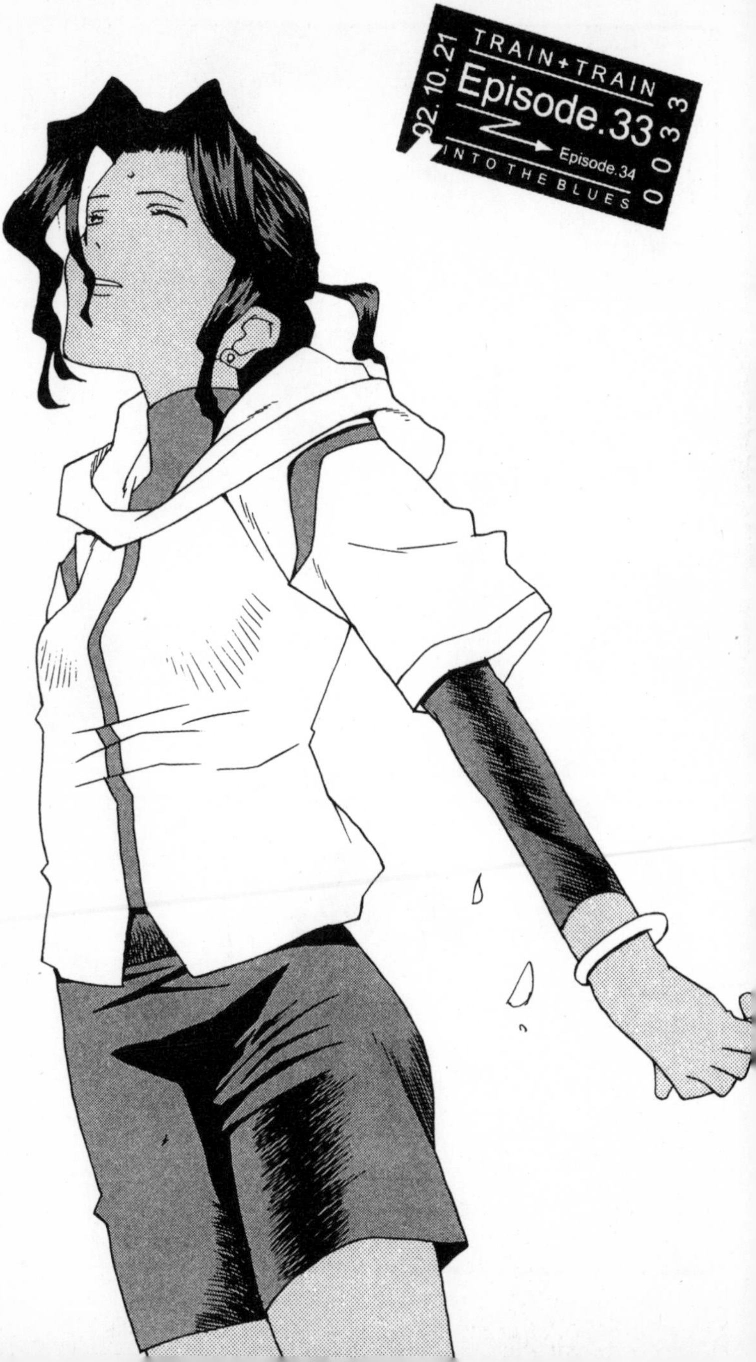

92. 10. 21
TRAIN+TRAIN
Episode.33
Episode.34
INTO THE BLUES
0033

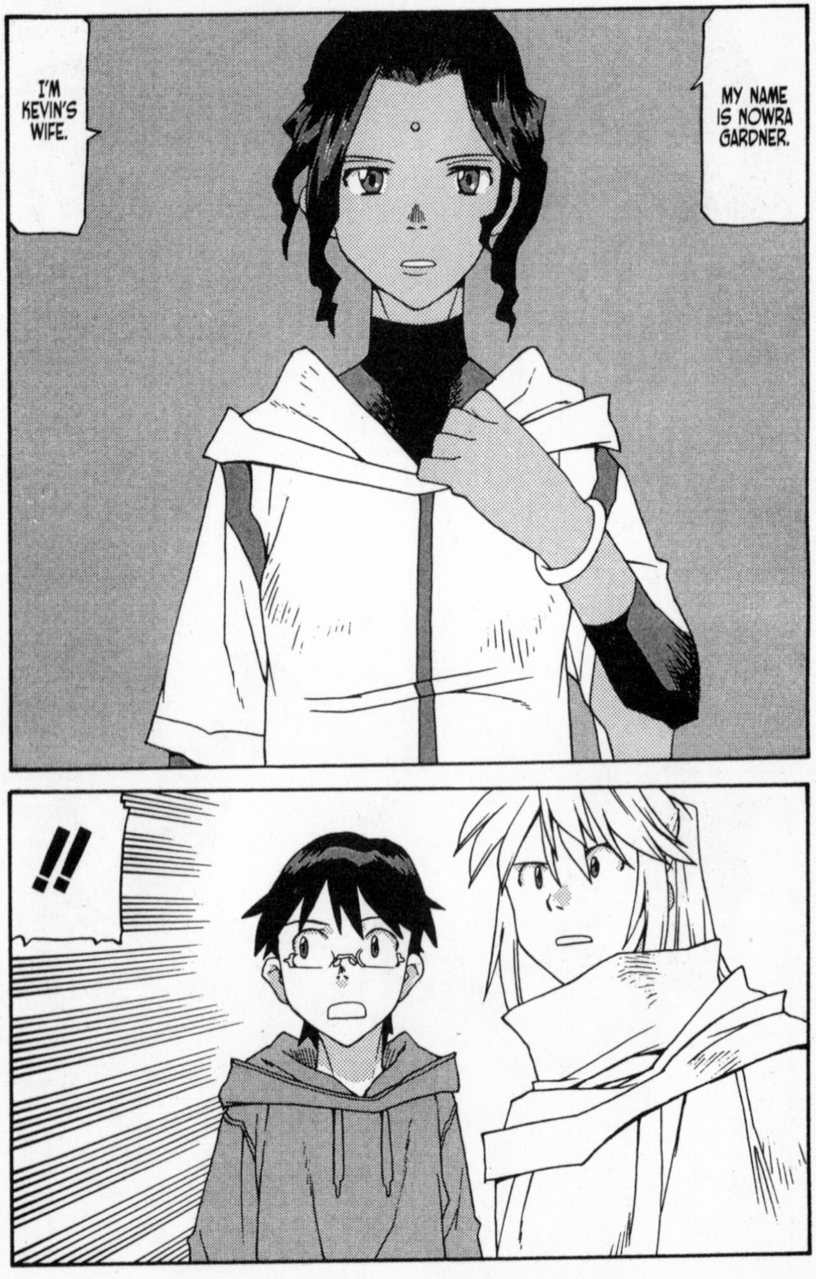
MY NAME IS NOWRA GARDNER.
I'M KEVIN'S WIFE.
!!

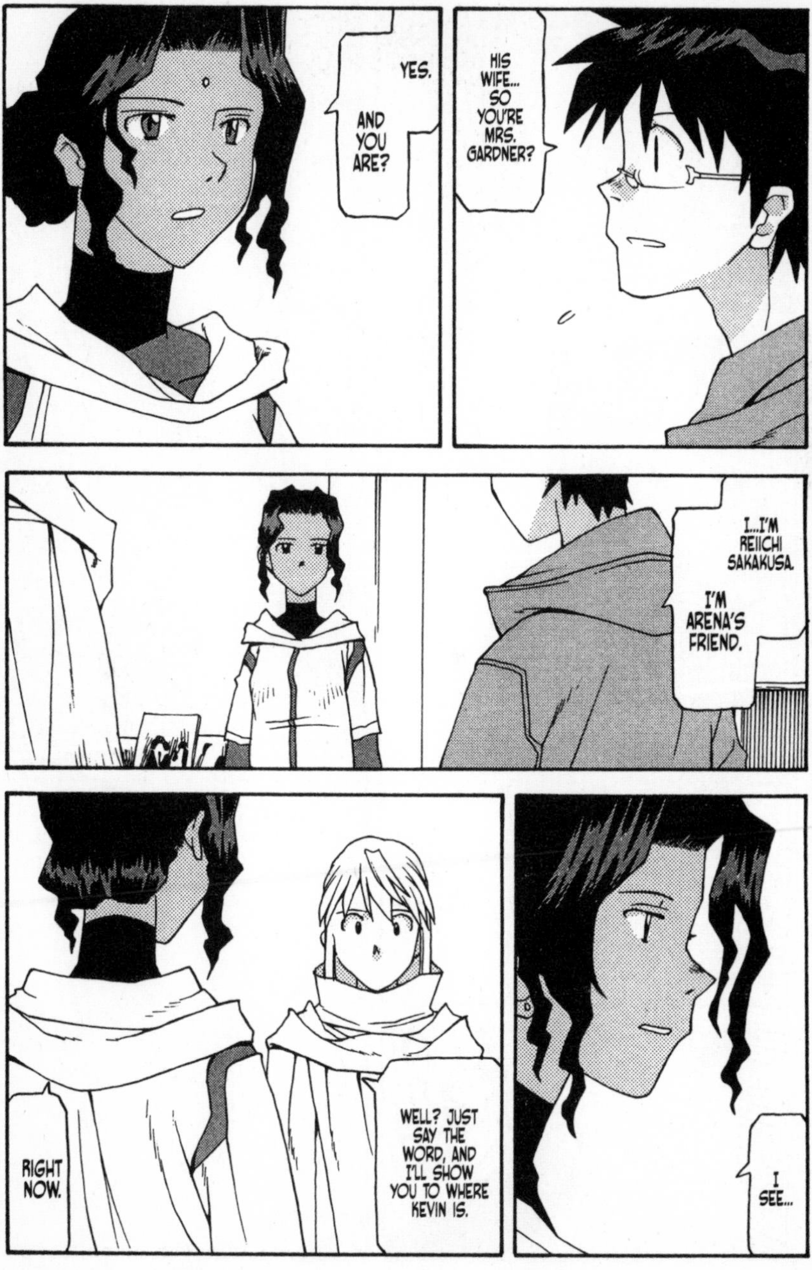
HIS WIFE... SO YOU'RE MRS. GARDNER?
YES.
AND YOU ARE?
I...I'M REIICHI SAKAKUSA.
I'M ARENA'S FRIEND.
I SEE...
WELL? JUST SAY THE WORD, AND I'LL SHOW YOU TO WHERE KEVIN IS.
RIGHT NOW.

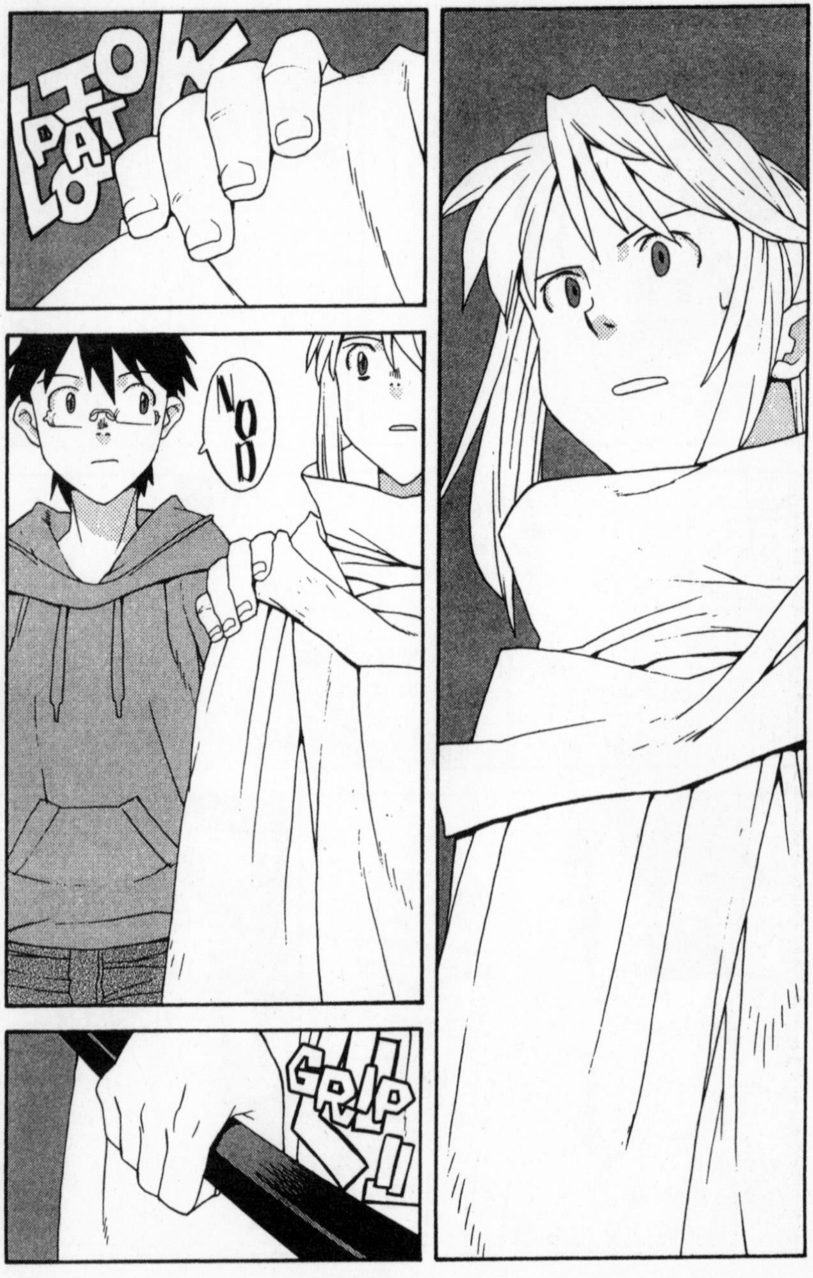
PAT
NOD
GRIP

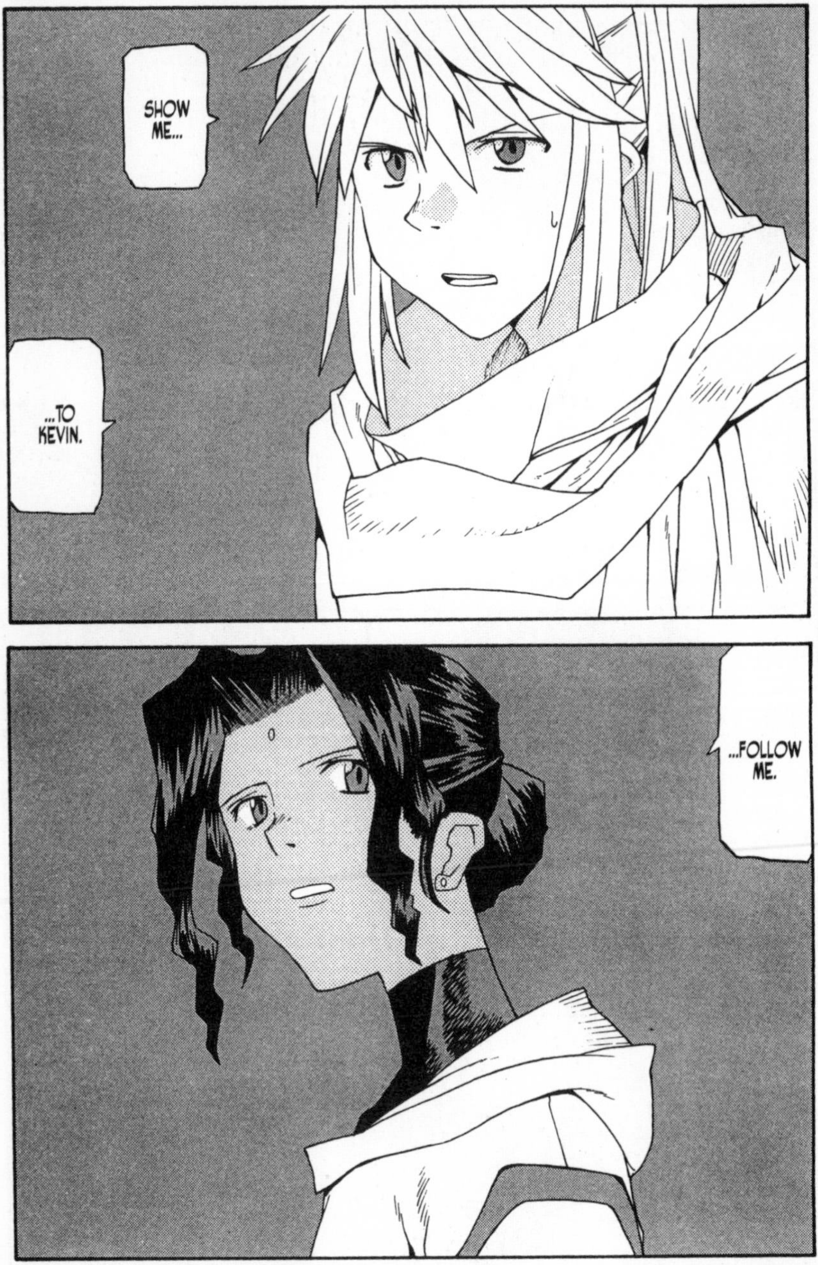
SHOW ME...
...TO KEVIN.
...FOLLOW ME.

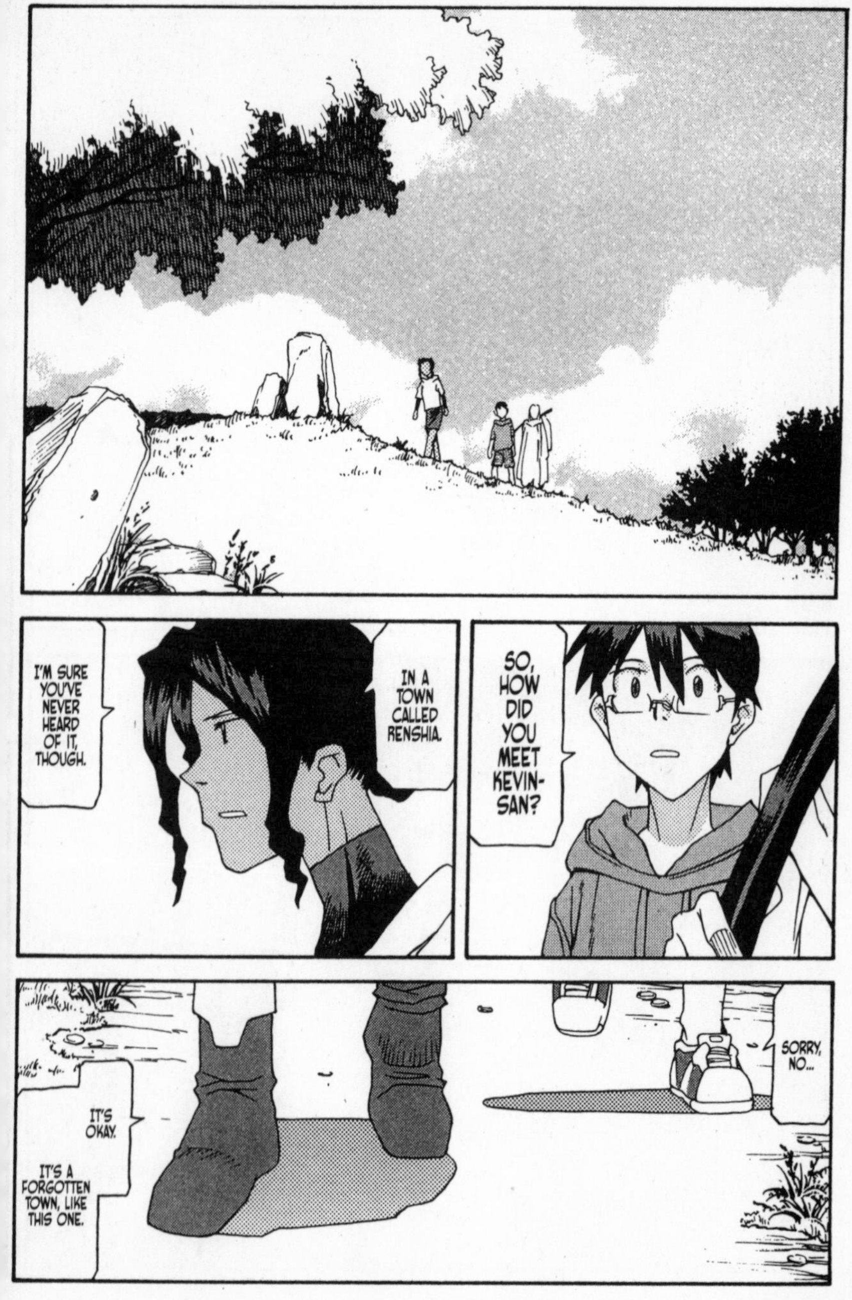
SO, HOW DID YOU MEET KEVIN-SAN?
IN A TOWN CALLED RENSHIA.
I'M SURE YOU'VE NEVER HEARD OF IT, THOUGH.
SORRY, NO...
IT'S OKAY.
IT'S A FORGOTTEN TOWN, LIKE THIS ONE.

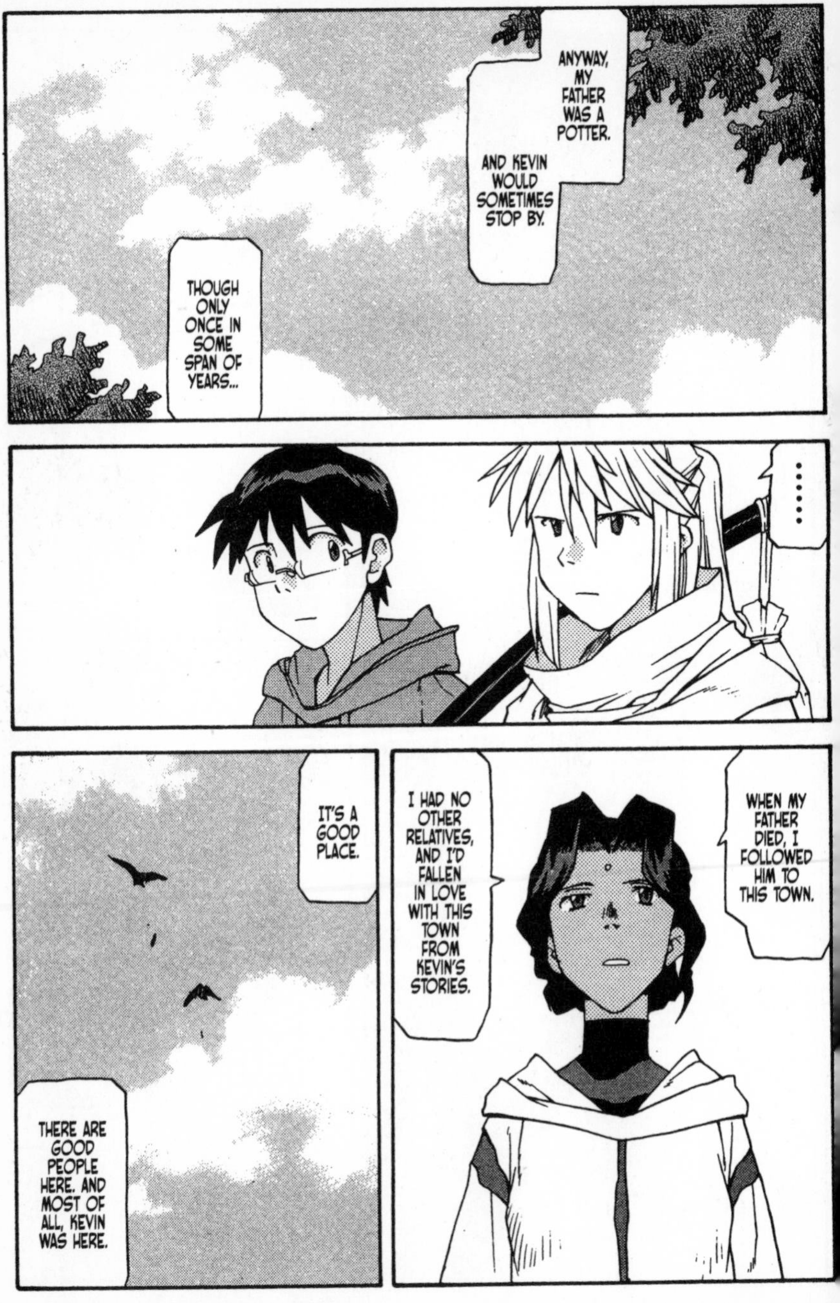
ANYWAY, MY FATHER WAS A POTTER.
AND KEVIN WOULD SOMETIMES STOP BY.
THOUGH ONLY ONCE IN SOME SPAN OF YEARS...
......
WHEN MY FATHER DIED, I FOLLOWED HIM TO THIS TOWN.
I HAD NO OTHER RELATIVES, AND I'D FALLEN IN LOVE WITH THIS TOWN FROM KEVIN'S STORIES.
IT'S A GOOD PLACE.
THERE ARE GOOD PEOPLE HERE. AND MOST OF ALL, KEVIN WAS HERE.

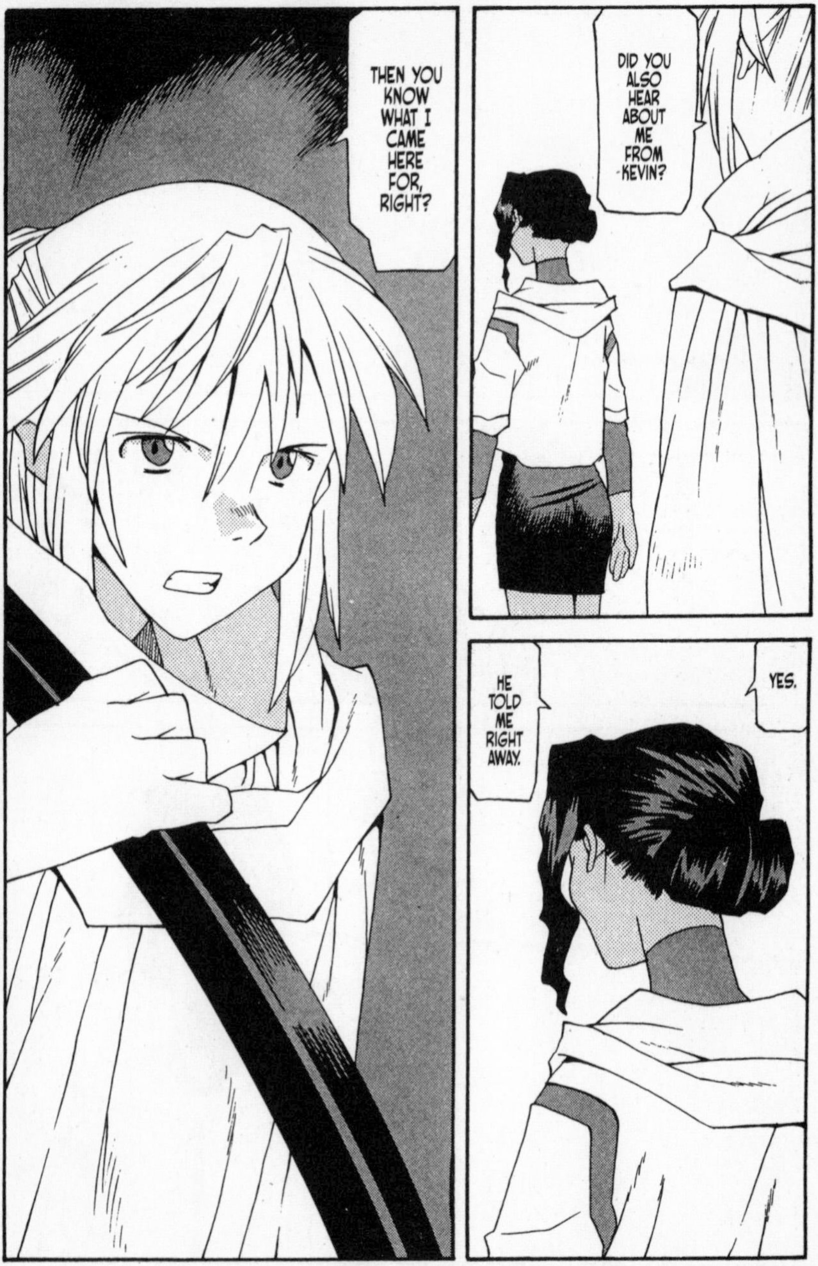
DID YOU ALSO HEAR ABOUT ME FROM KEVIN?
YES.
HE TOLD ME RIGHT AWAY.
THEN YOU KNOW WHAT I CAME HERE FOR, RIGHT?

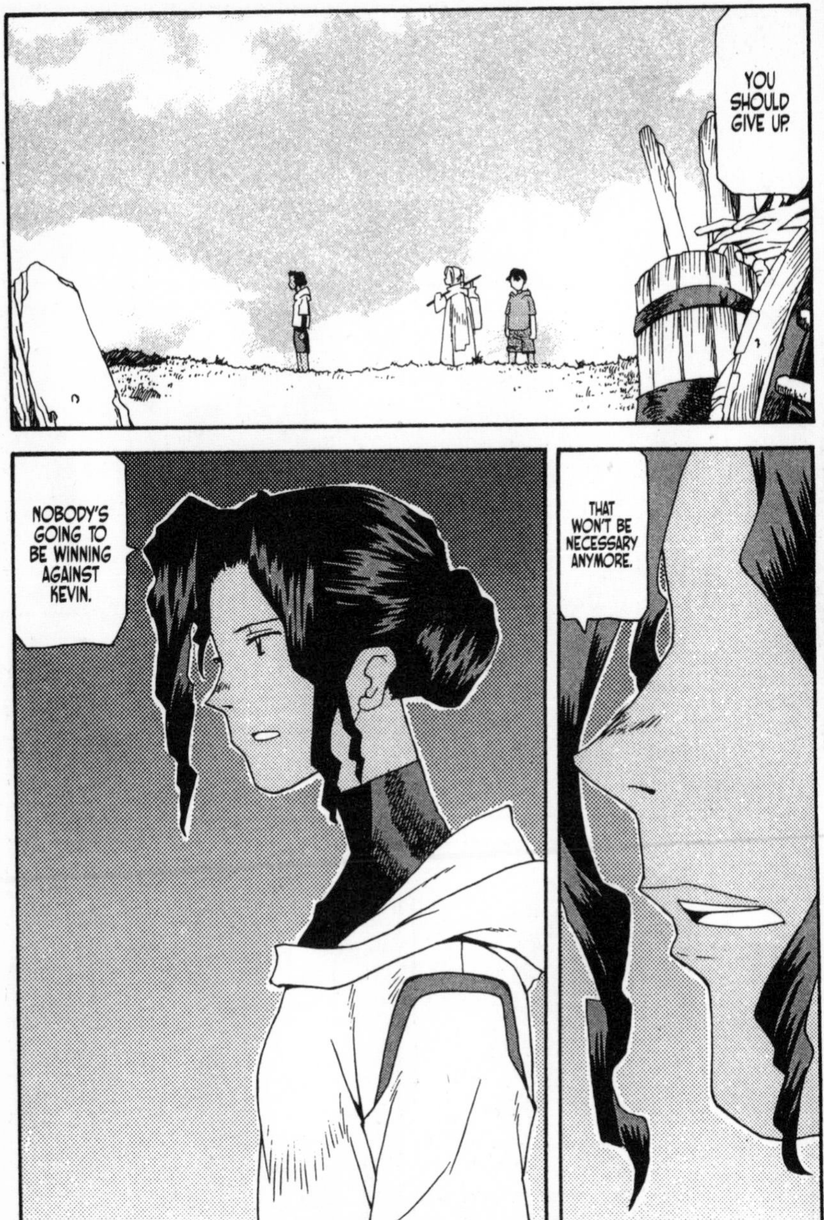
YOU SHOULD GIVE UP.
THAT WON'T BE NECESSARY ANYMORE.
NOBODY'S GOING TO BE WINNING AGAINST KEVIN.

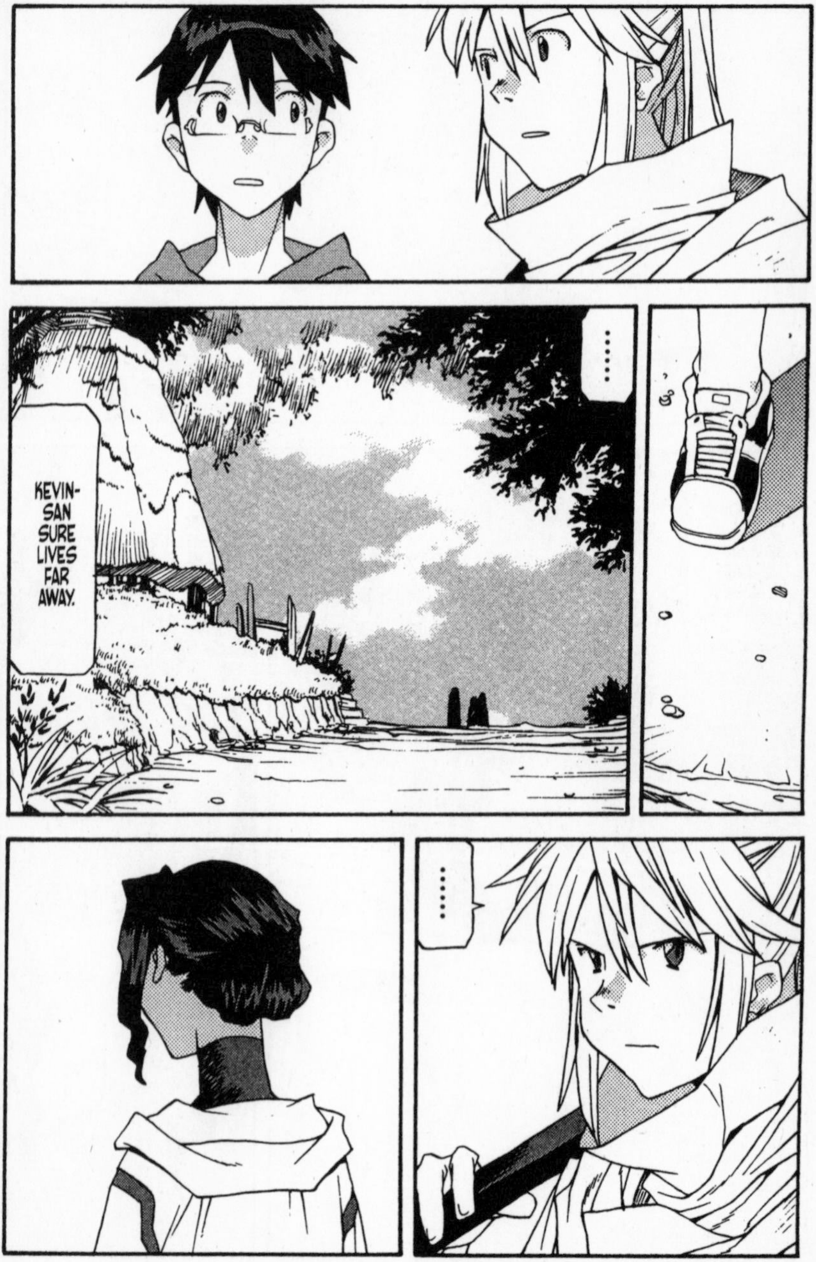
......
KEVIN-SAN SURE LIVES FAR AWAY.
......

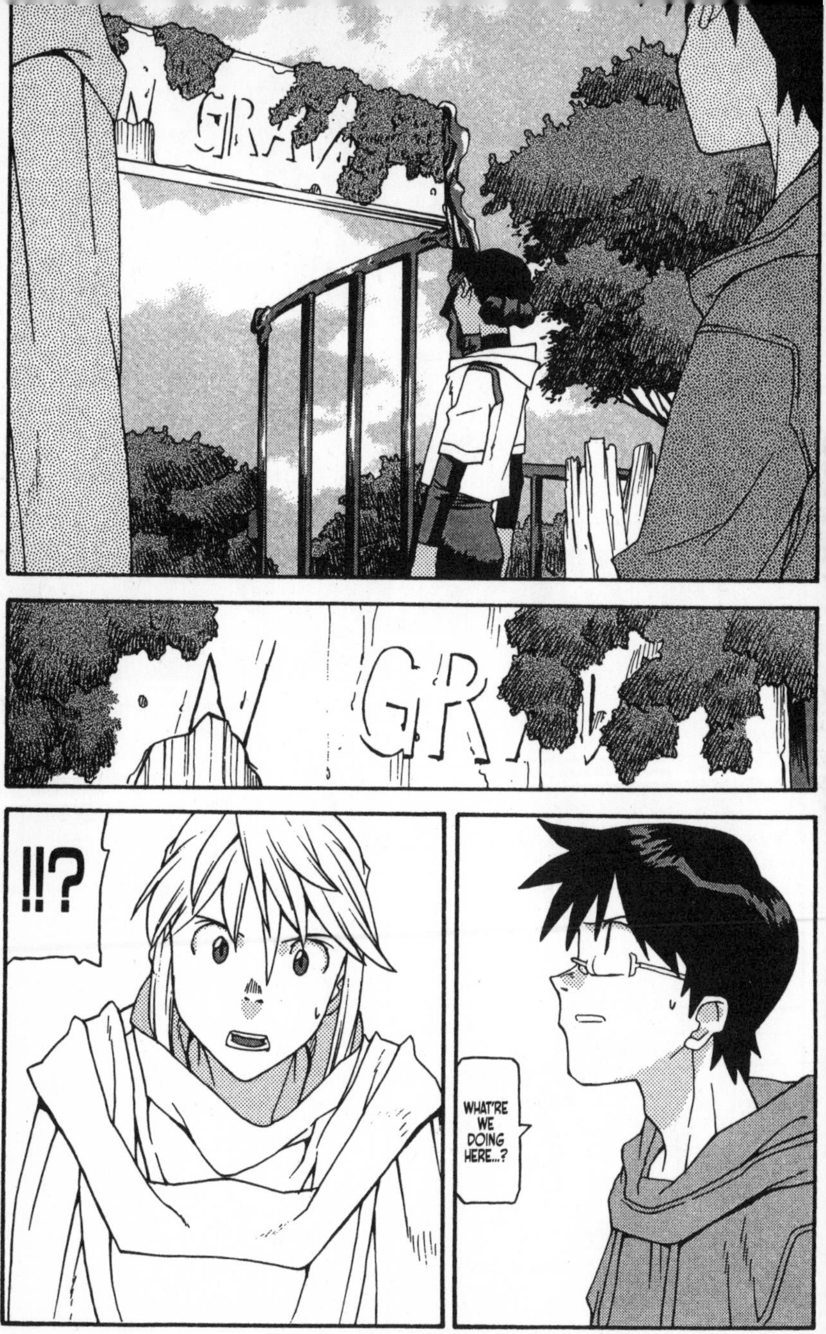
WHAT'RE WE DOING HERE...?
!!?

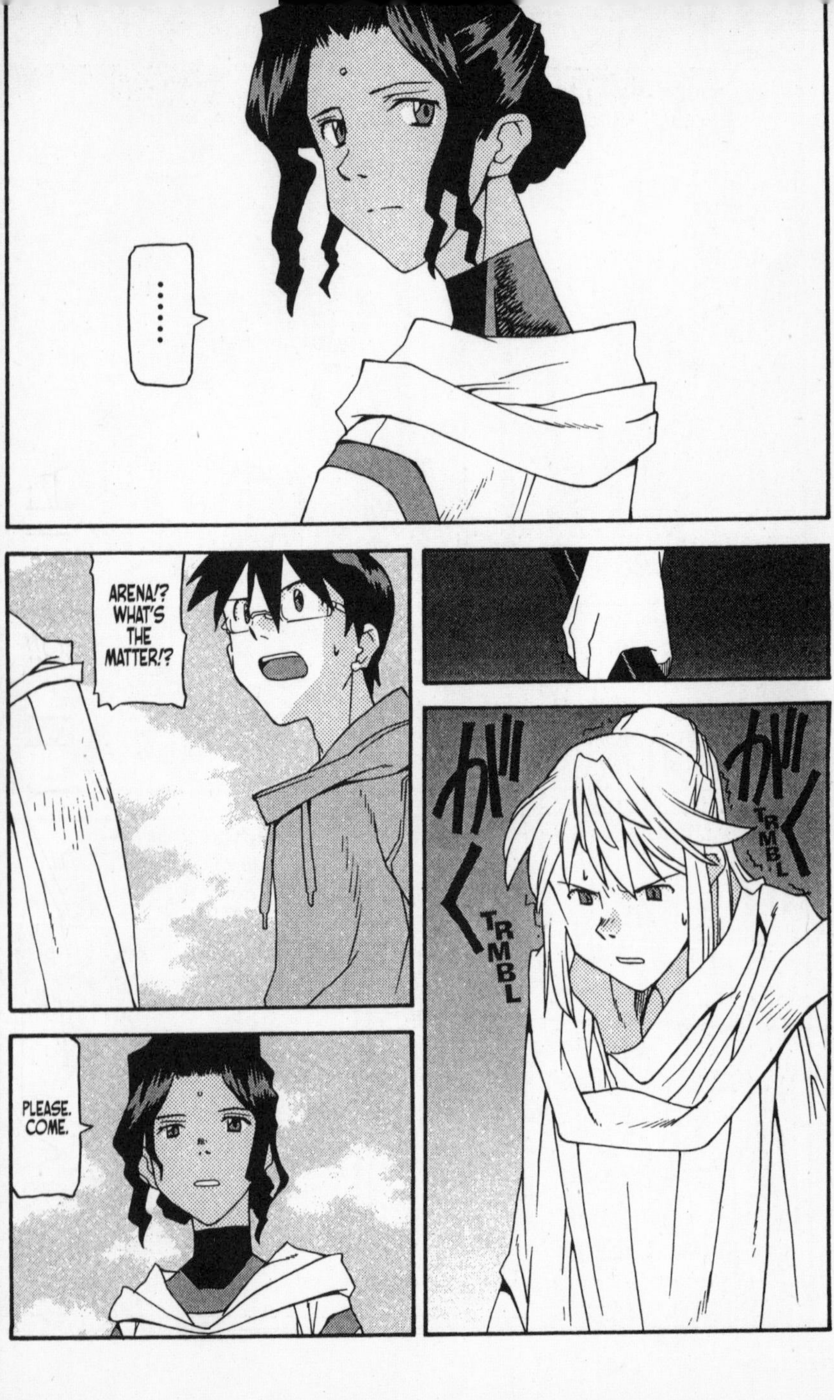
......
TRMBL
TRMBL
ARENA!? WHAT'S THE MATTER!?
PLEASE. COME.

ARENA!?

N...
NO...

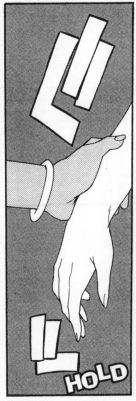

HOLD

IT CAN'T BE...!

NO...!
NO!!

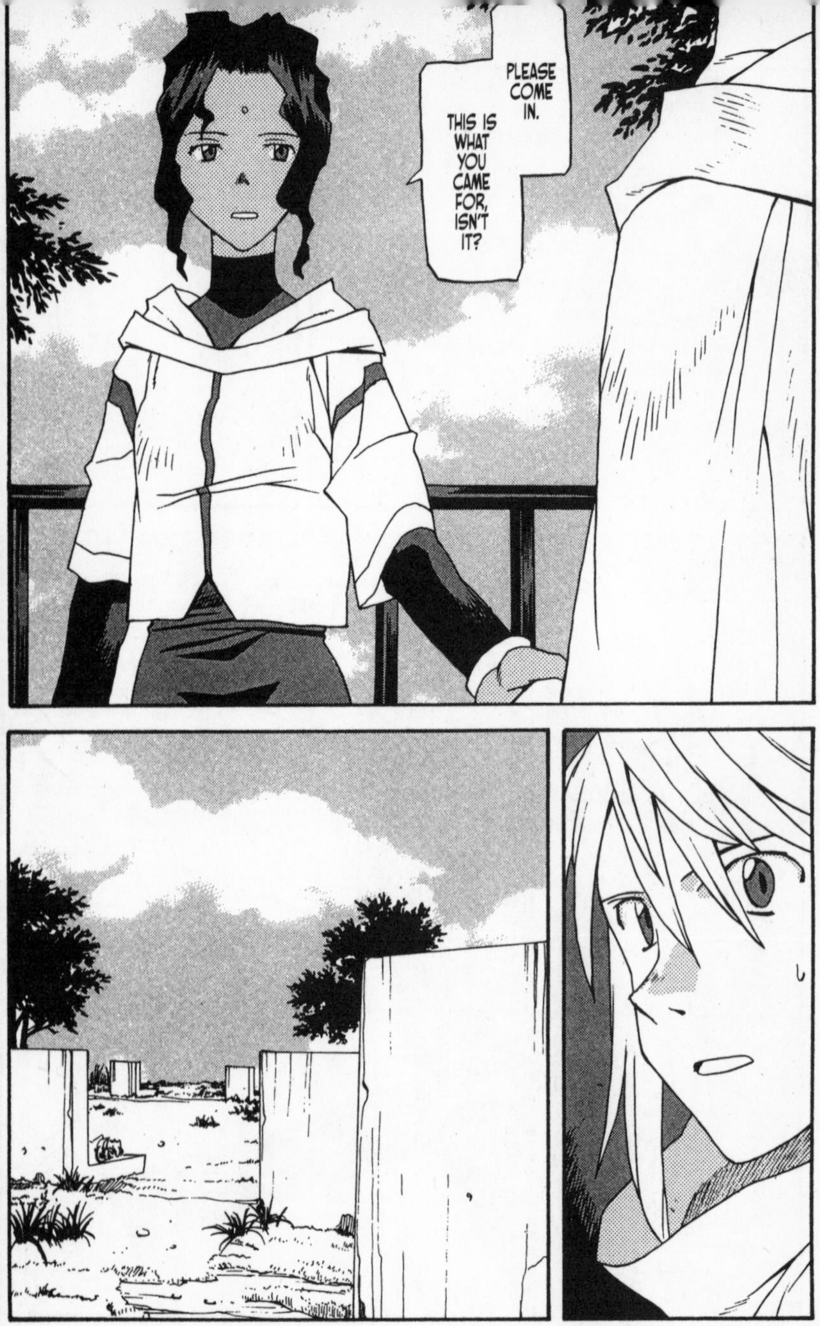
PLEASE COME IN.
THIS IS WHAT YOU CAME FOR, ISN'T IT?

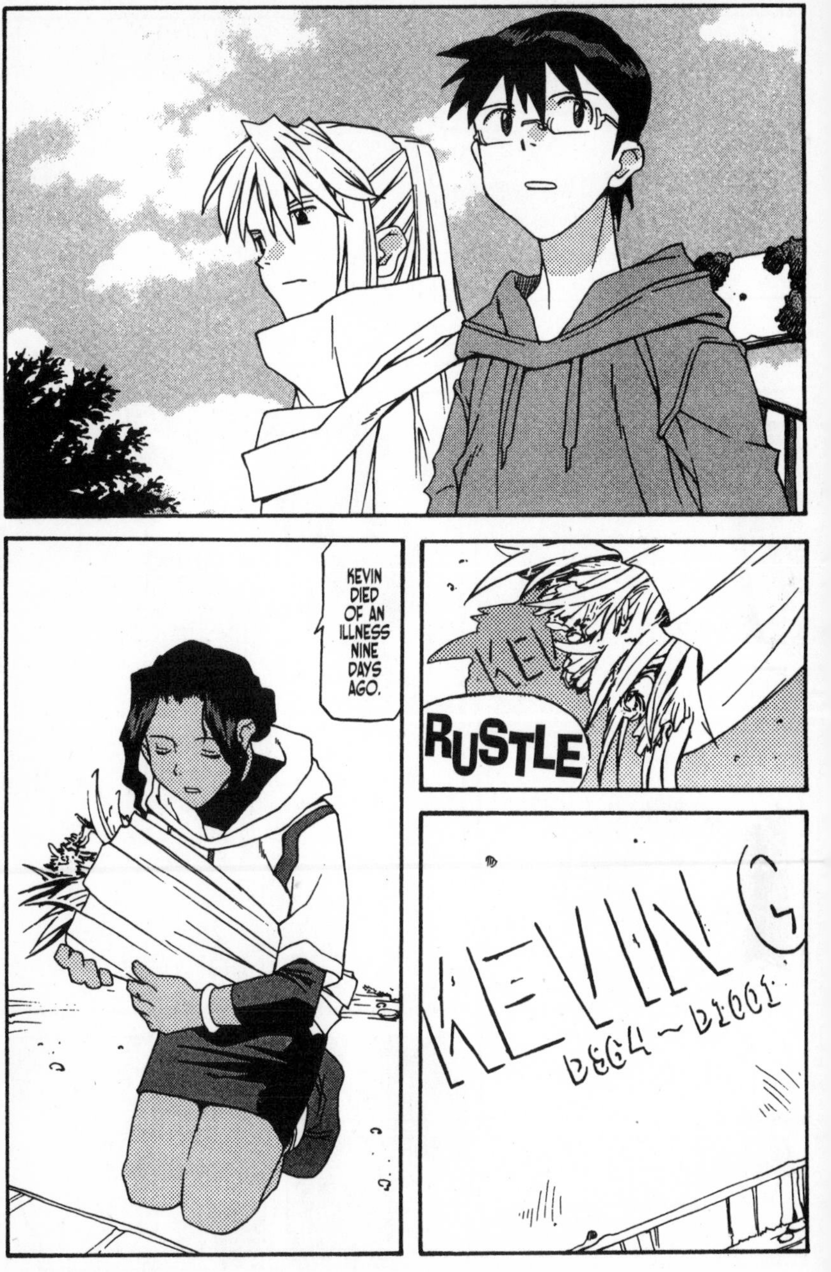
RUSTLE
KEVIN G
KEVIN DIED OF AN ILLNESS NINE DAYS AGO.

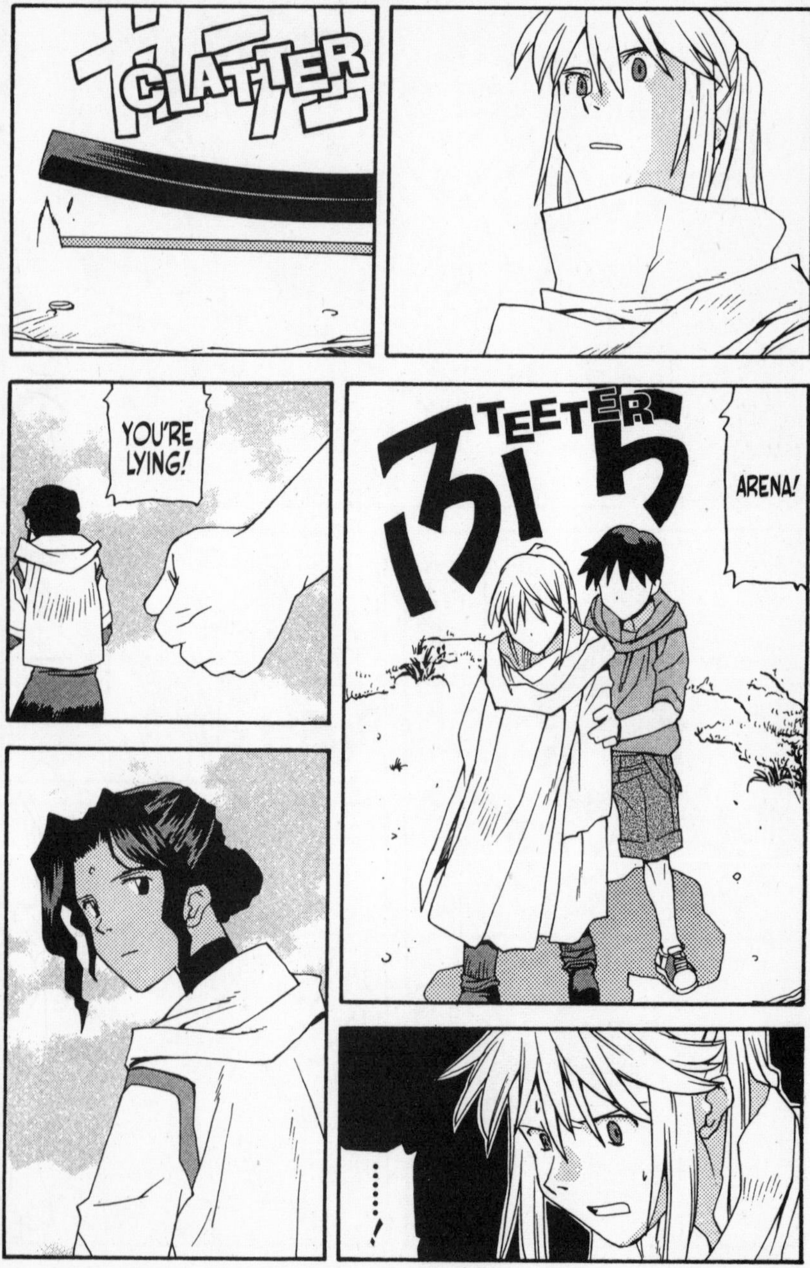
CLATTER
TEETER
ARENA!
YOU'RE LYING!
......!

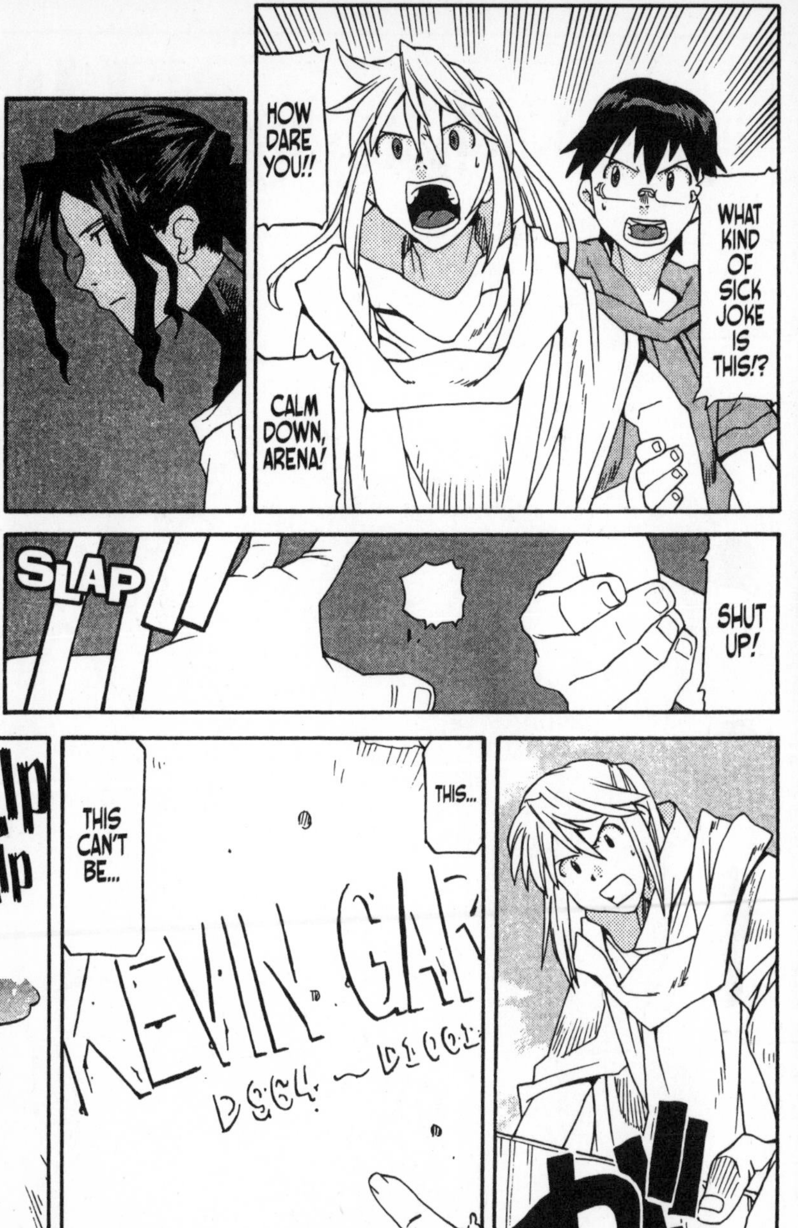
HOW DARE YOU!!
WHAT KIND OF SICK JOKE IS THIS!?
CALM DOWN, ARENA!
SHUT UP!
SLAP
GRAB
THIS...
THIS CAN'T BE...
PLIP PLIP

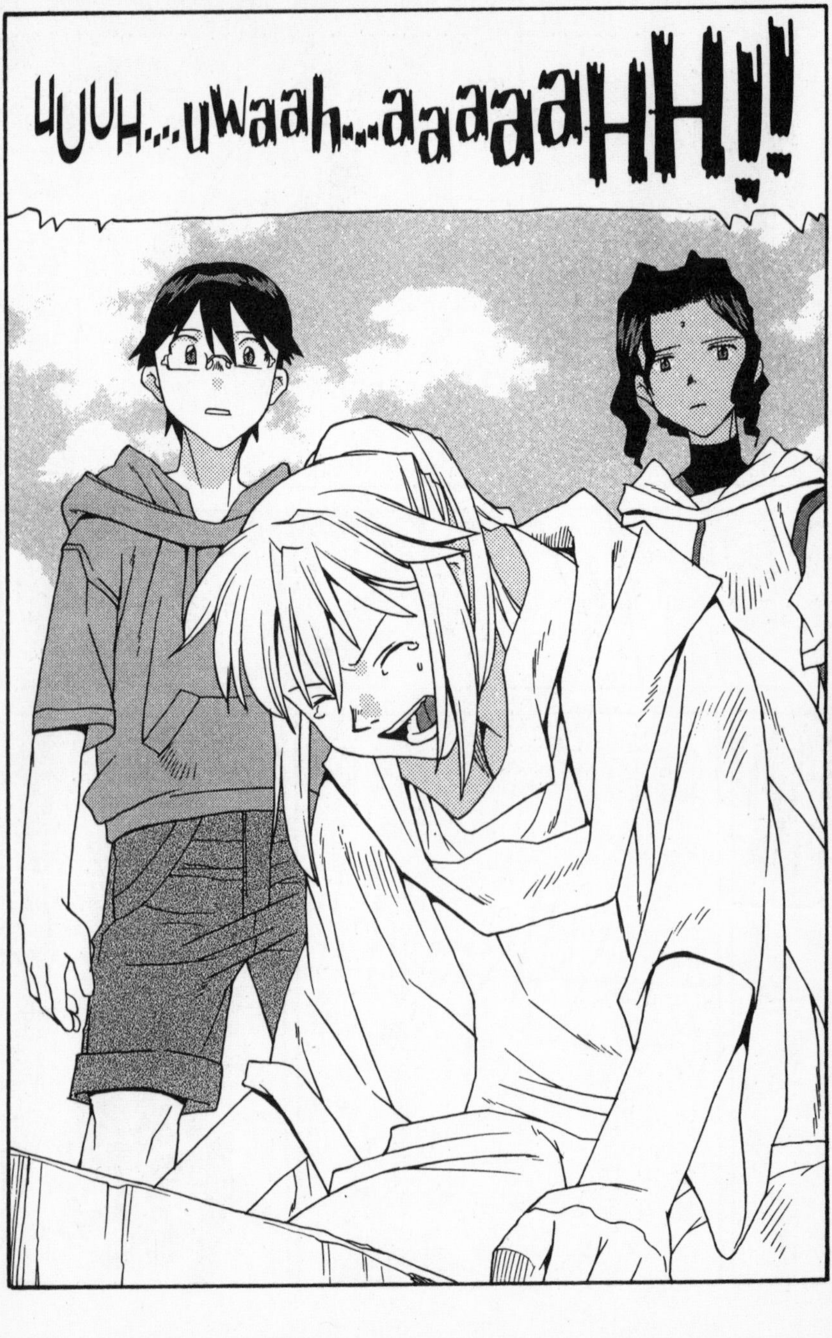
UUUH...UWAAH...AAAAAAHH!!

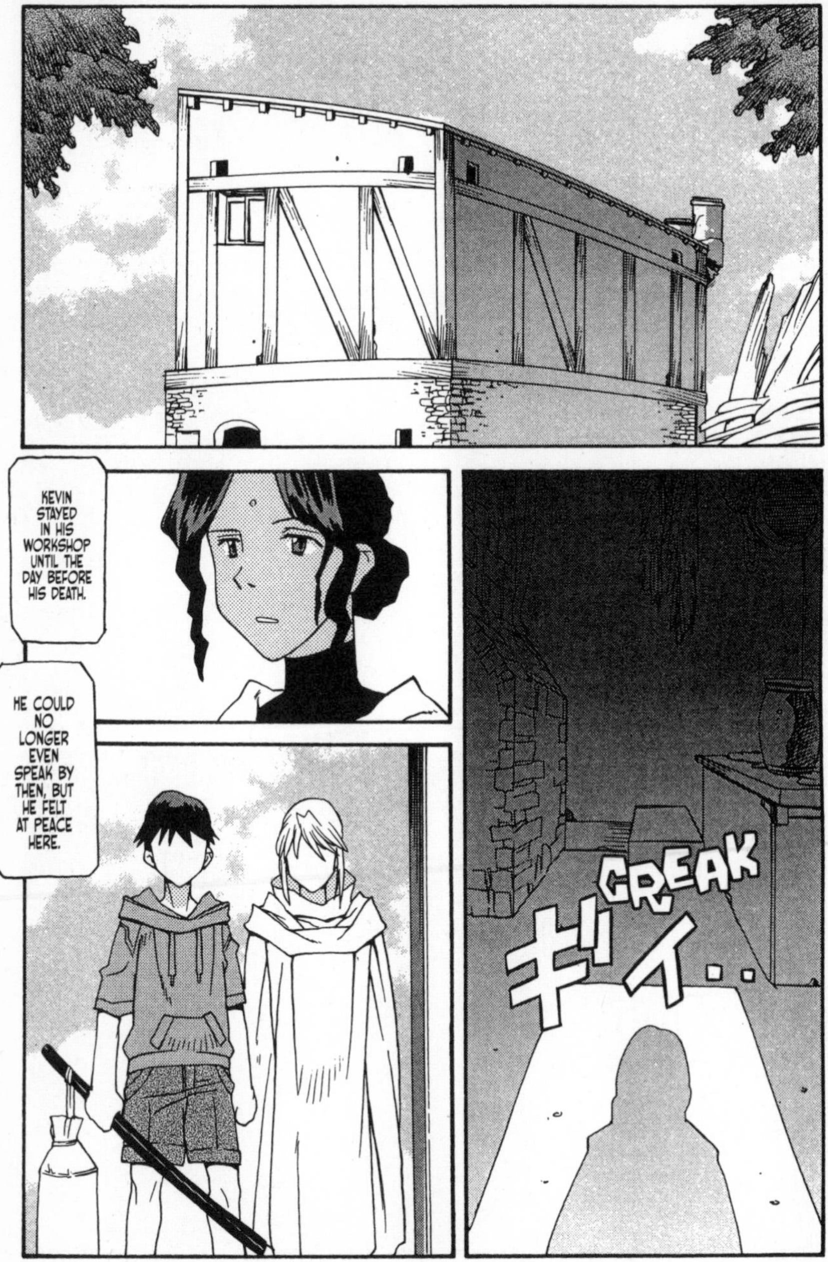
KEVIN STAYED IN HIS WORKSHOP UNTIL THE DAY BEFORE HIS DEATH.
HE COULD NO LONGER EVEN SPEAK BY THEN, BUT HE FELT AT PEACE HERE.
CREAK
ギリイ..

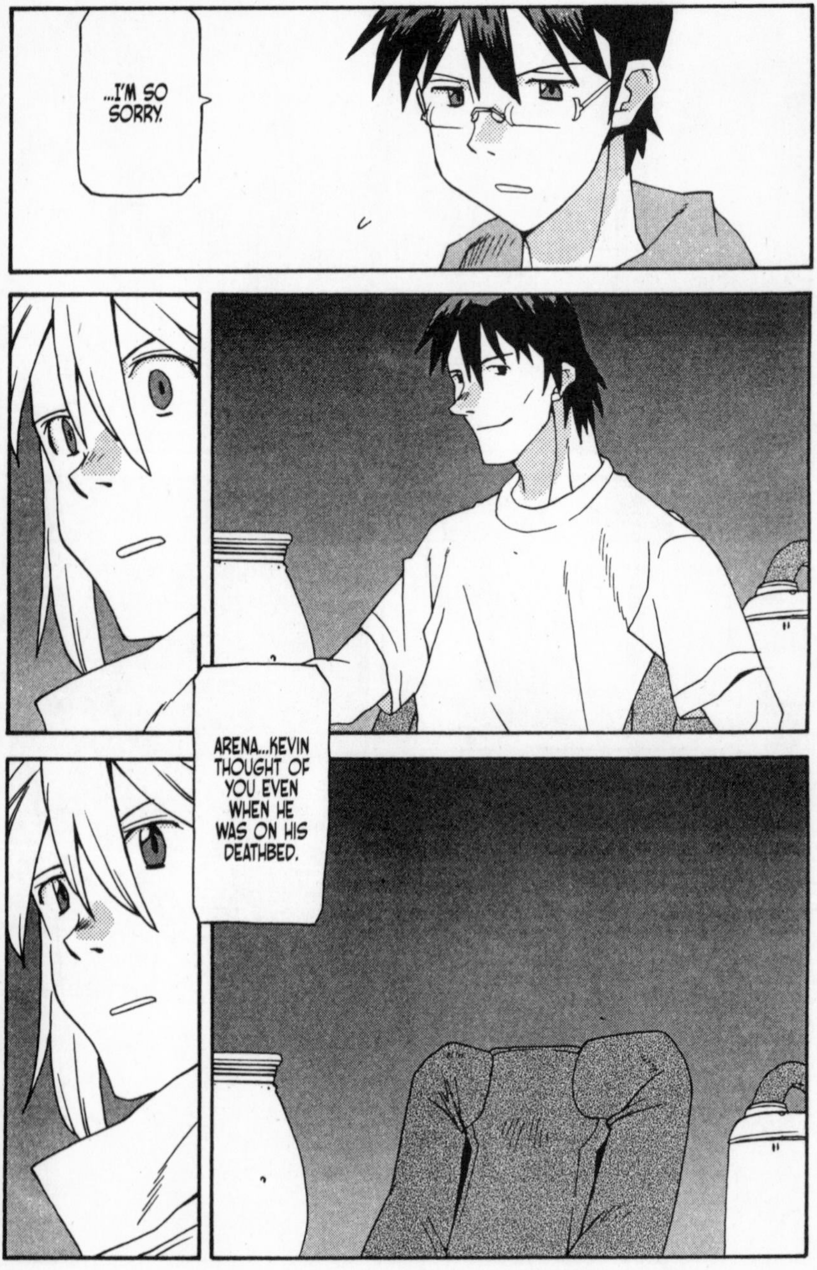
...I'M SO SORRY.
ARENA...KEVIN THOUGHT OF YOU EVEN WHEN HE WAS ON HIS DEATHBED.

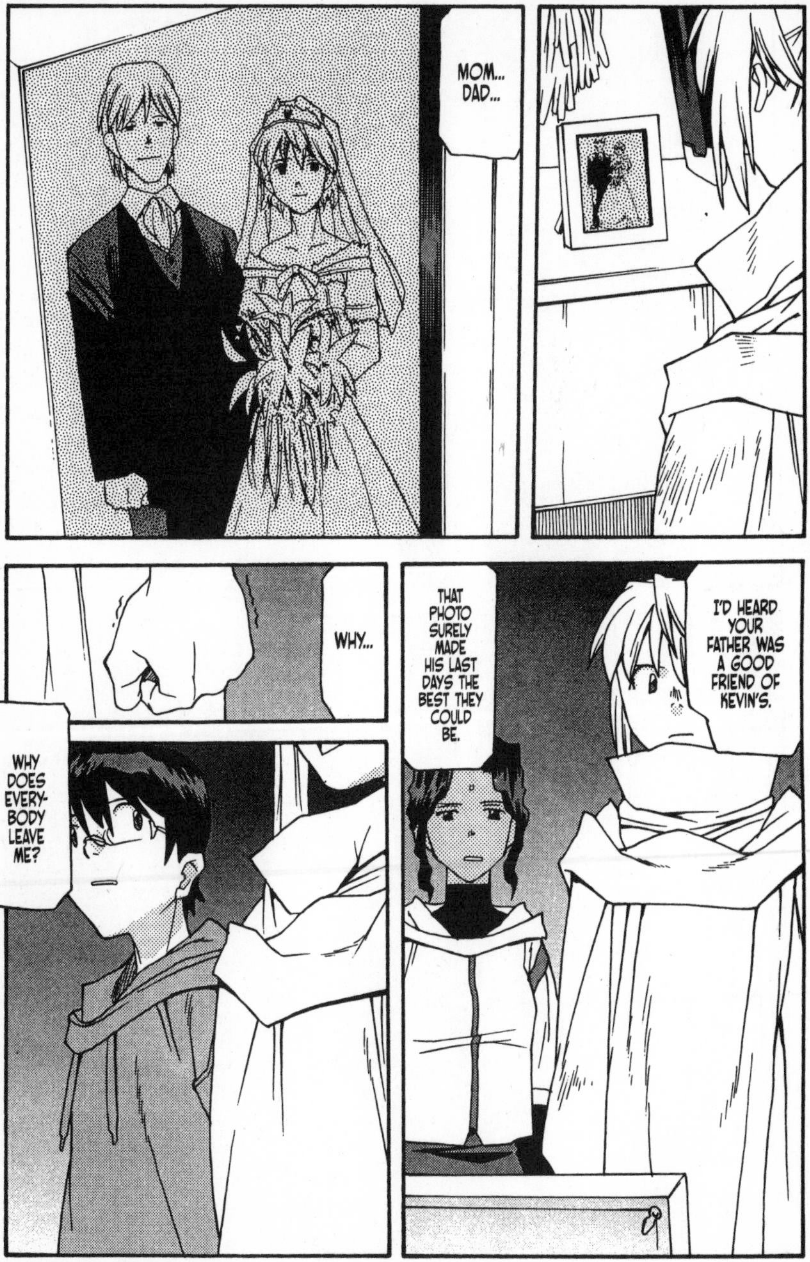
MOM... DAD...
I'D HEARD YOUR FATHER WAS A GOOD FRIEND OF KEVIN'S.
THAT PHOTO SURELY MADE HIS LAST DAYS THE BEST THEY COULD BE.
WHY...
WHY DOES EVERY-BODY LEAVE ME?

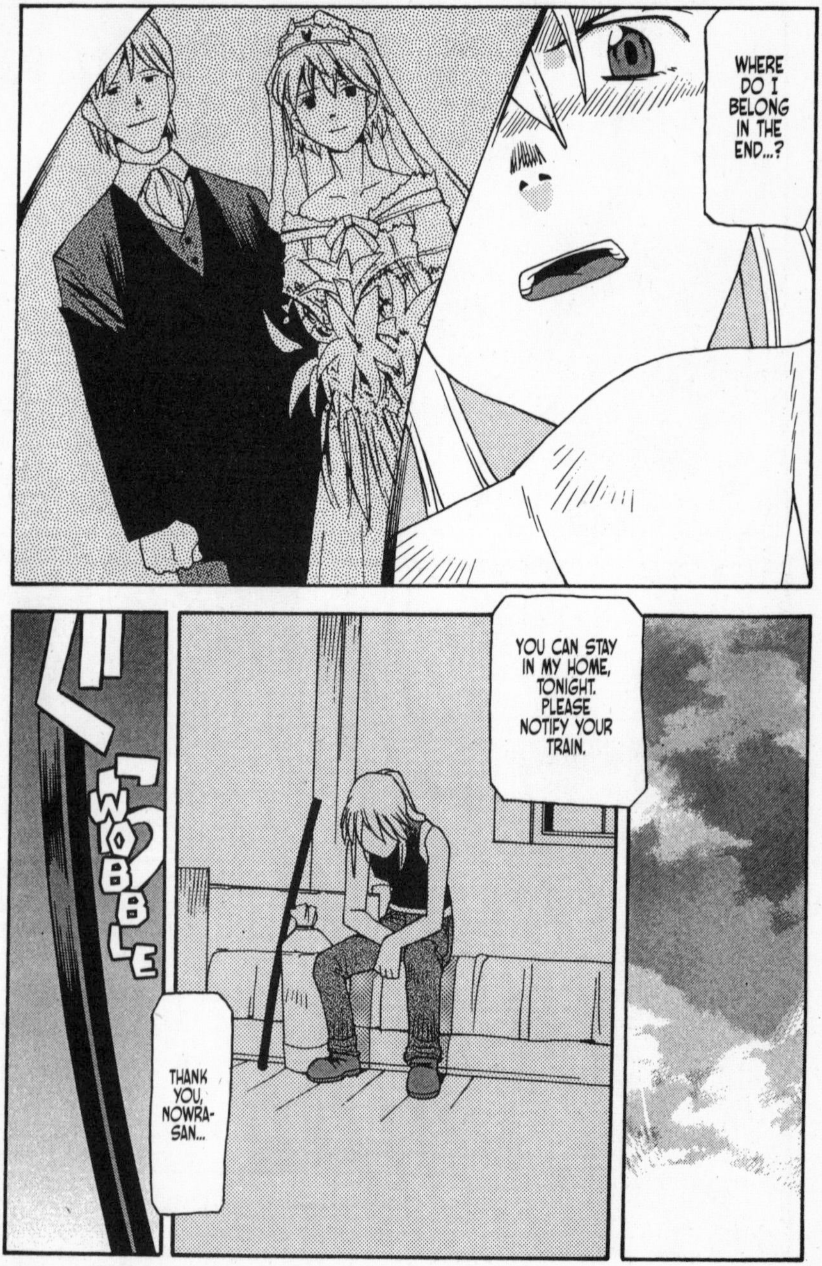
WHERE DO I BELONG IN THE END...?
YOU CAN STAY IN MY HOME, TONIGHT. PLEASE NOTIFY YOUR TRAIN.
THANK YOU, NOWRA-SAN...
WOBBLE

CLACK

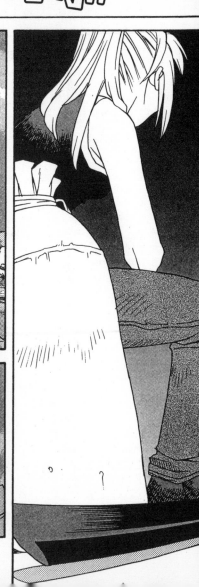

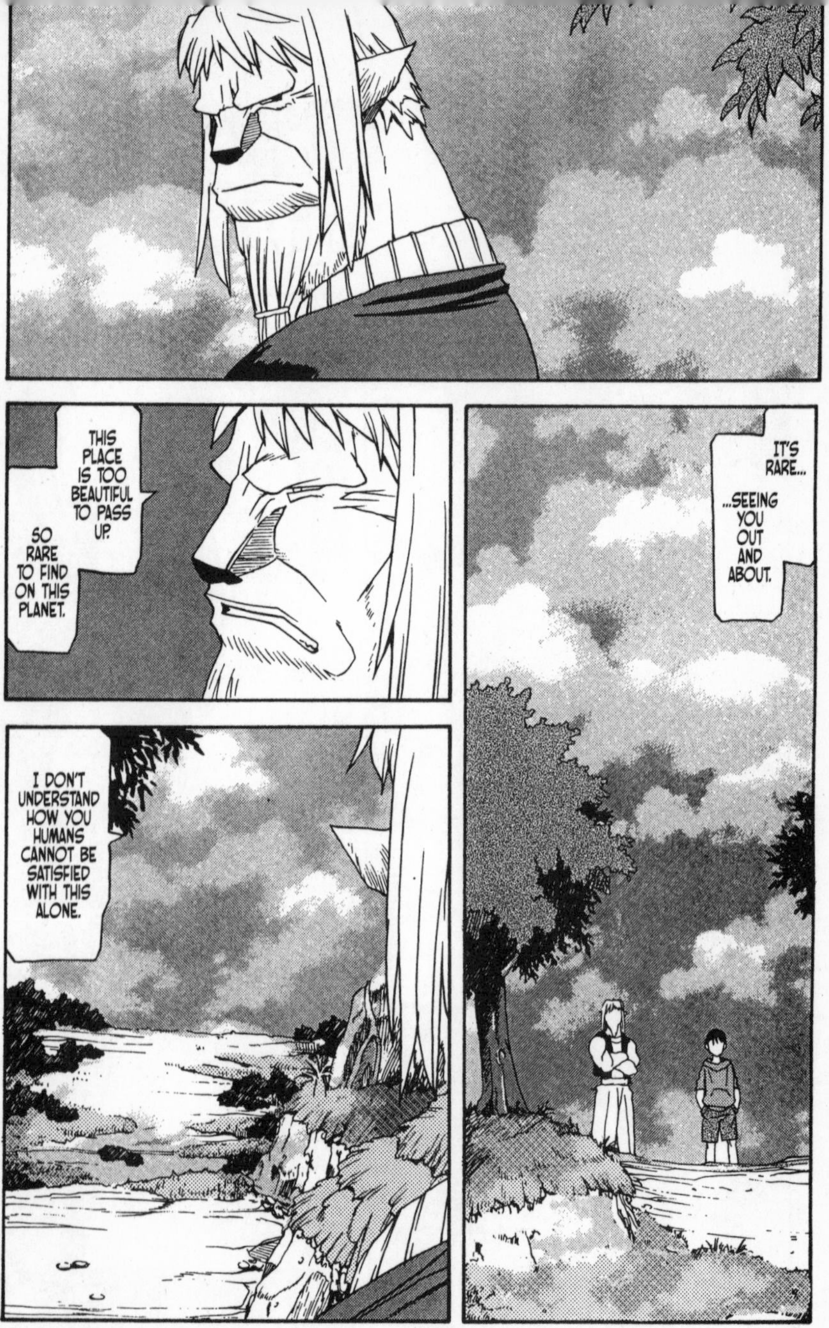
IT'S RARE...
...SEEING YOU OUT AND ABOUT.
THIS PLACE IS TOO BEAUTIFUL TO PASS UP.
SO RARE TO FIND ON THIS PLANET.
I DON'T UNDERSTAND HOW YOU HUMANS CANNOT BE SATISFIED WITH THIS ALONE.

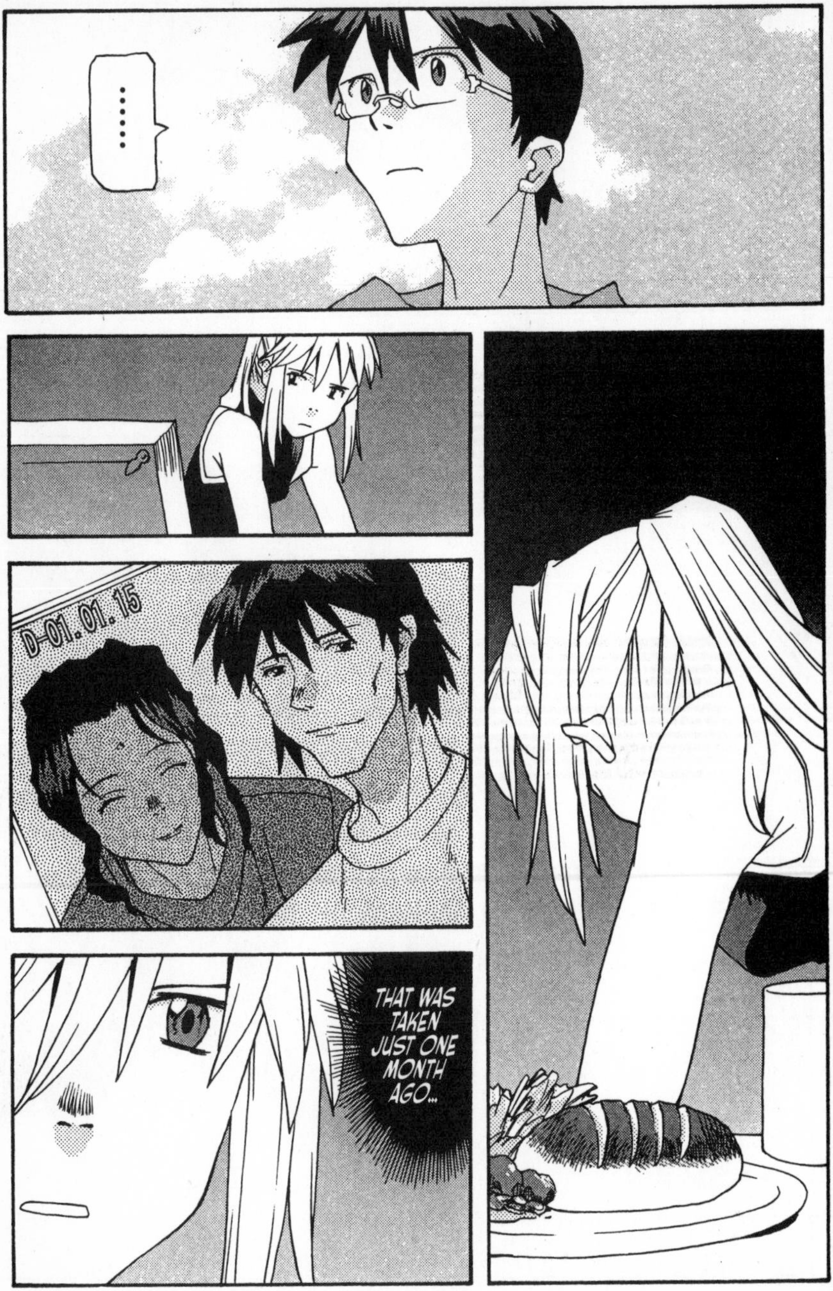
……
D-01. 01. 15
THAT WAS TAKEN JUST ONE MONTH AGO...

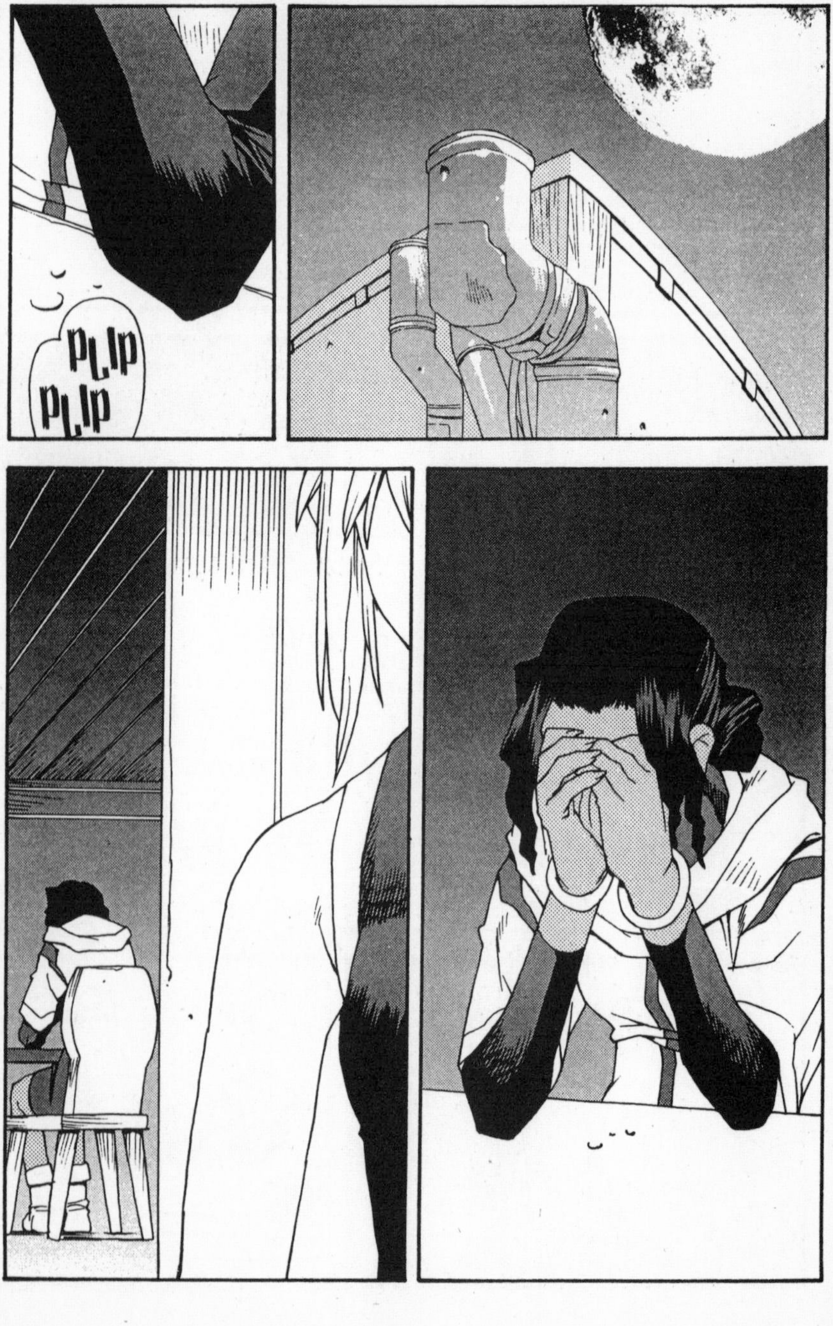
PLIP
PLIP

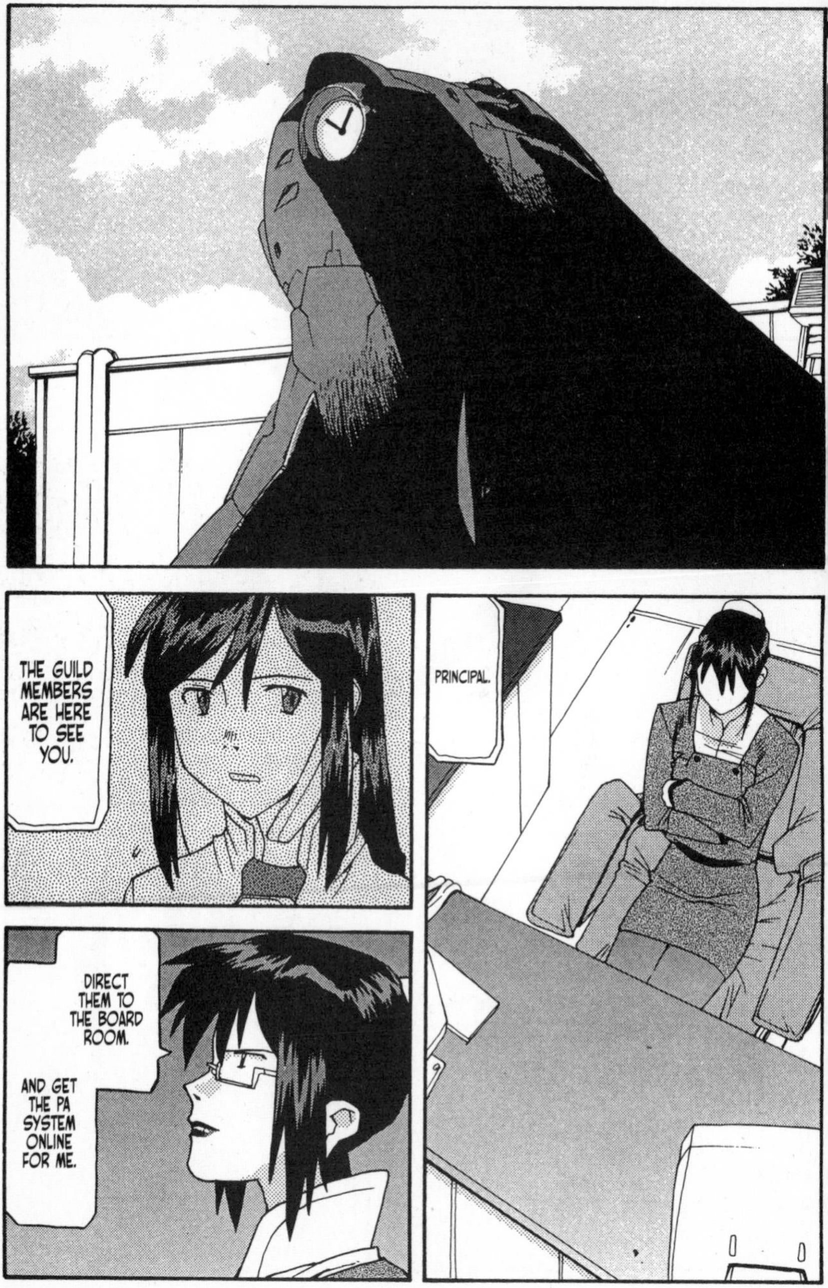
PRINCIPAL.
THE GUILD MEMBERS ARE HERE TO SEE YOU.
DIRECT THEM TO THE BOARD ROOM.
AND GET THE PA SYSTEM ONLINE FOR ME.

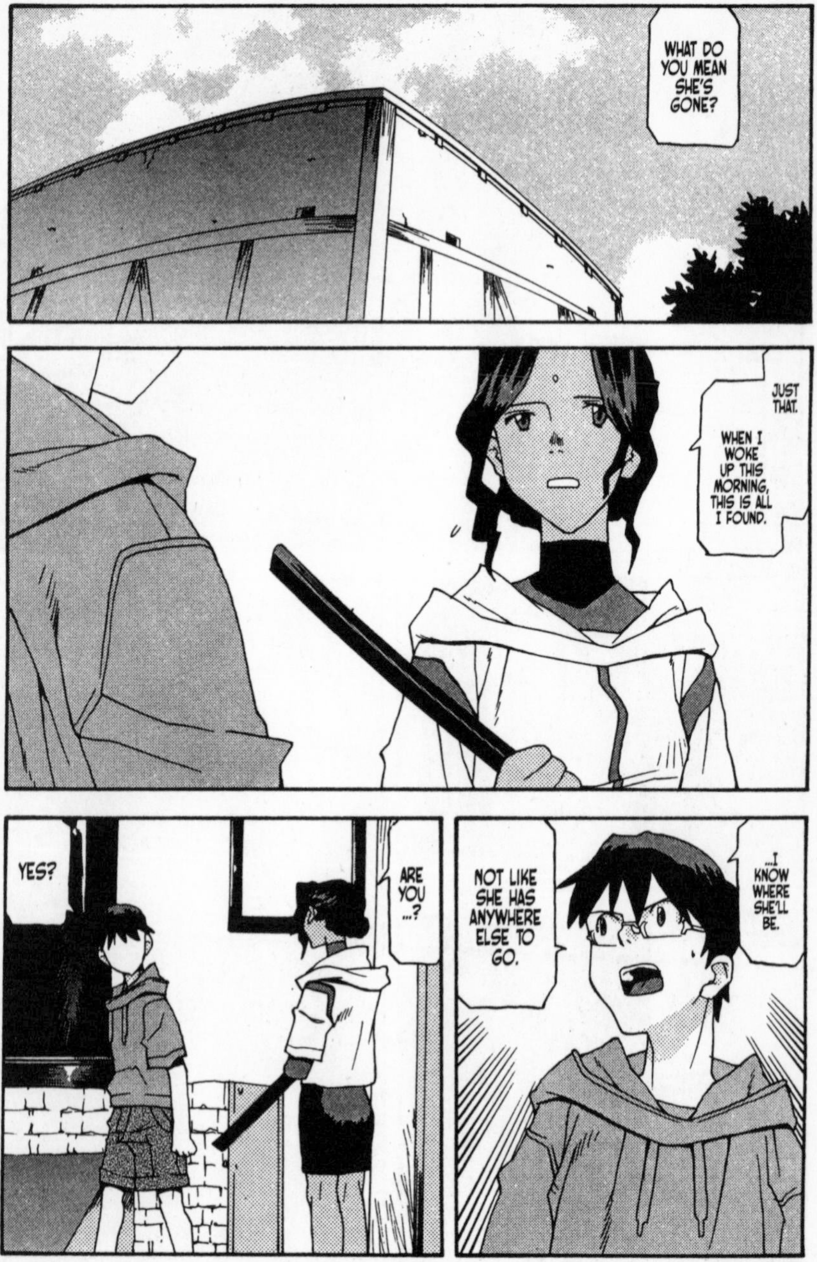
WHAT DO YOU MEAN SHE'S GONE?
JUST THAT.
WHEN I WOKE UP THIS MORNING, THIS IS ALL I FOUND.
...I KNOW WHERE SHE'LL BE.
NOT LIKE SHE HAS ANYWHERE ELSE TO GO.
ARE YOU ...?
YES?

NEVER MIND.

· · · · ·

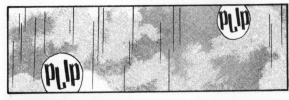

PLIP

PLIP

SSSHHH

EXCUSE ME, BUT...

...I'LL BE RIGHT BACK.

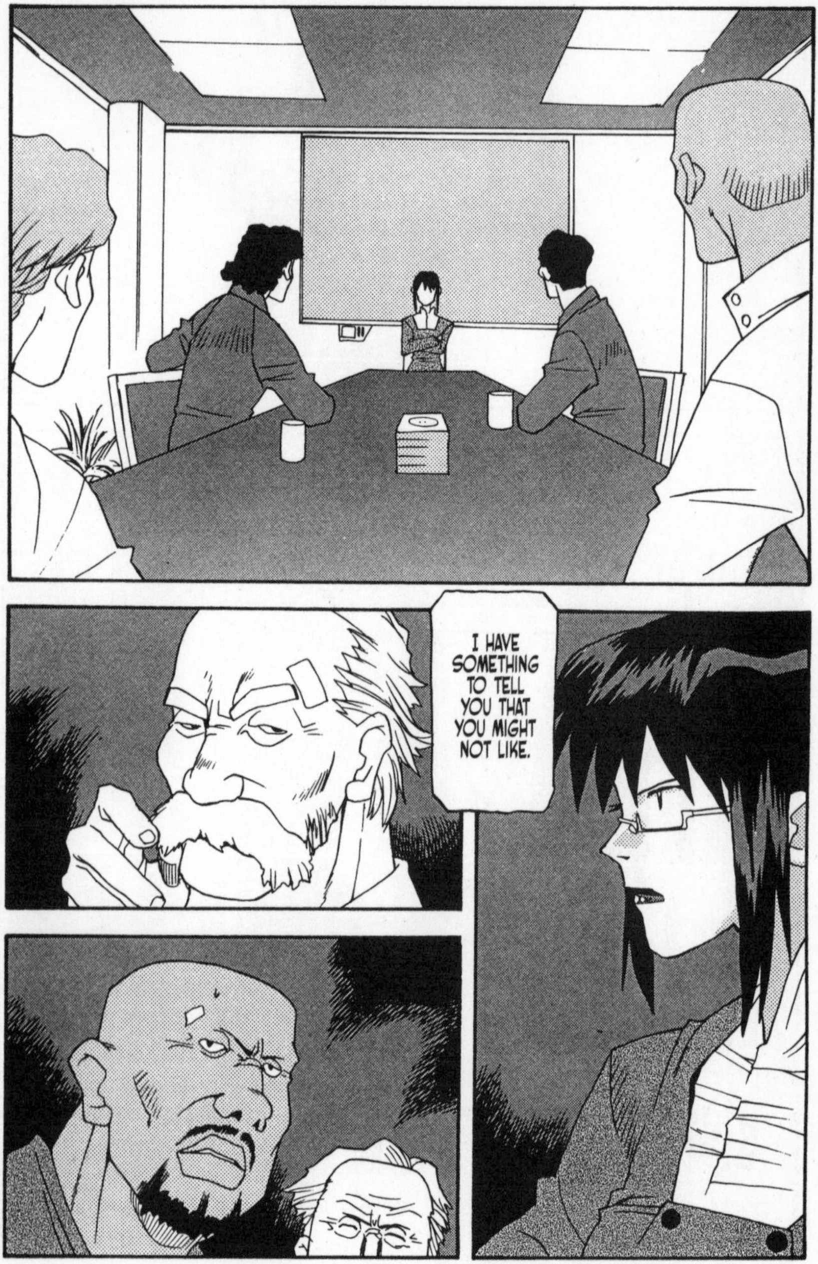
I HAVE SOMETHING TO TELL YOU THAT YOU MIGHT NOT LIKE.

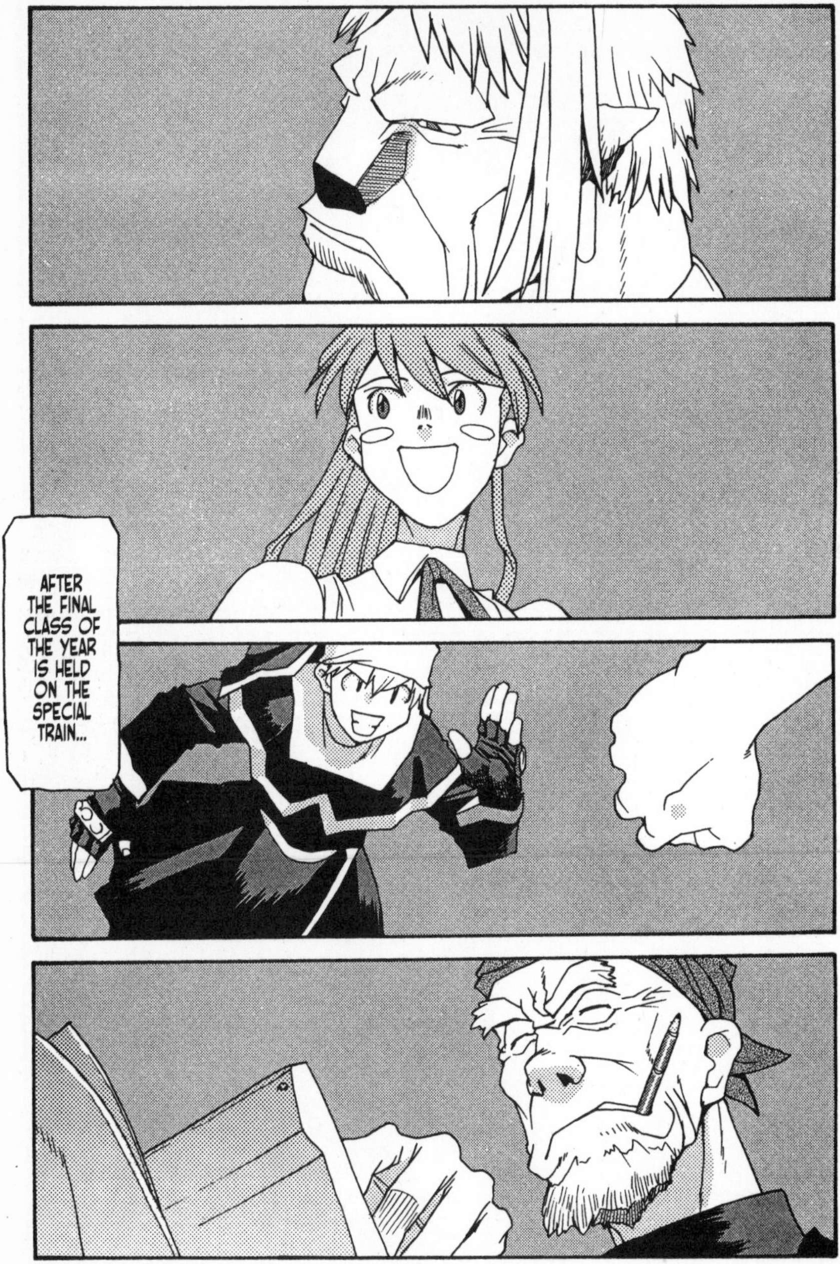
AFTER THE FINAL CLASS OF THE YEAR IS HELD ON THE SPECIAL TRAIN...

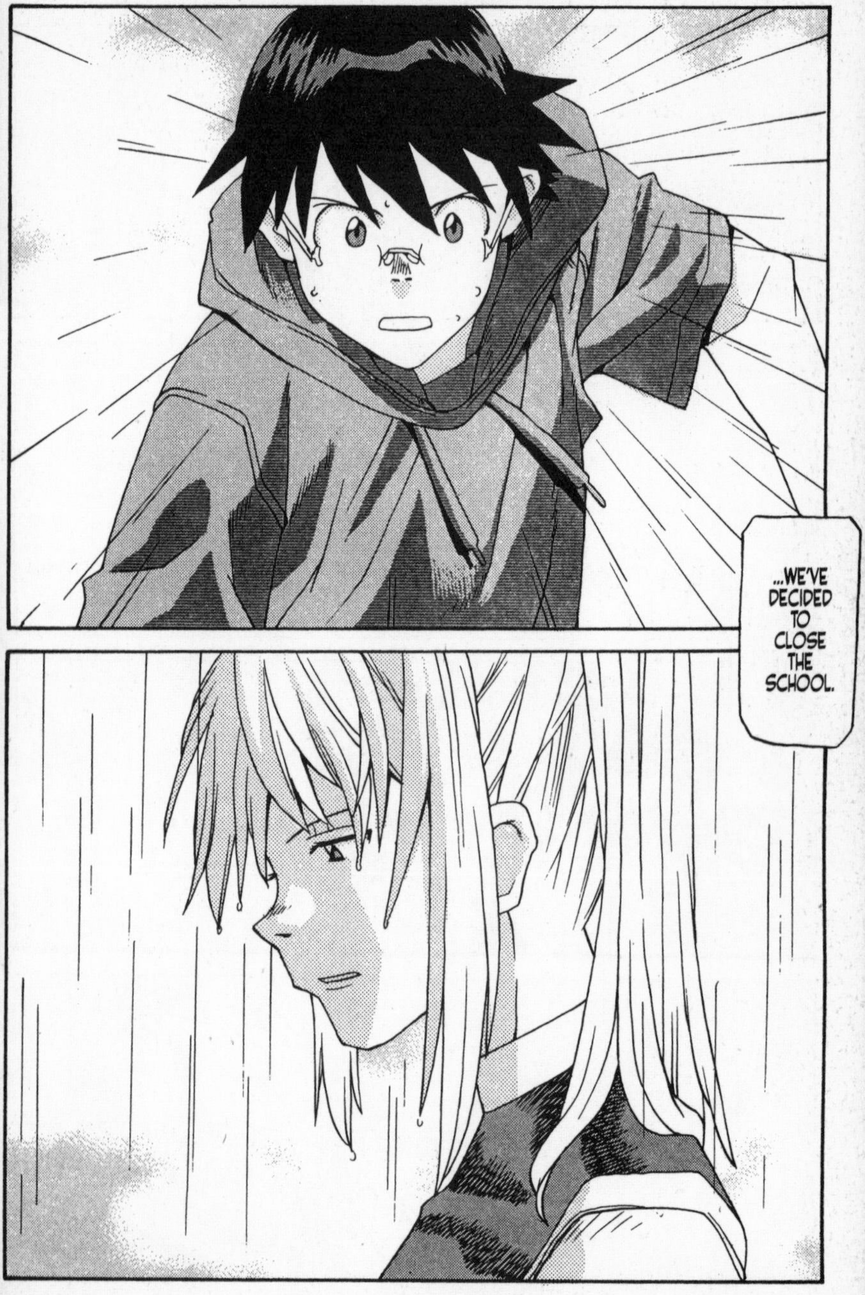
...WE'VE DECIDED TO CLOSE THE SCHOOL.

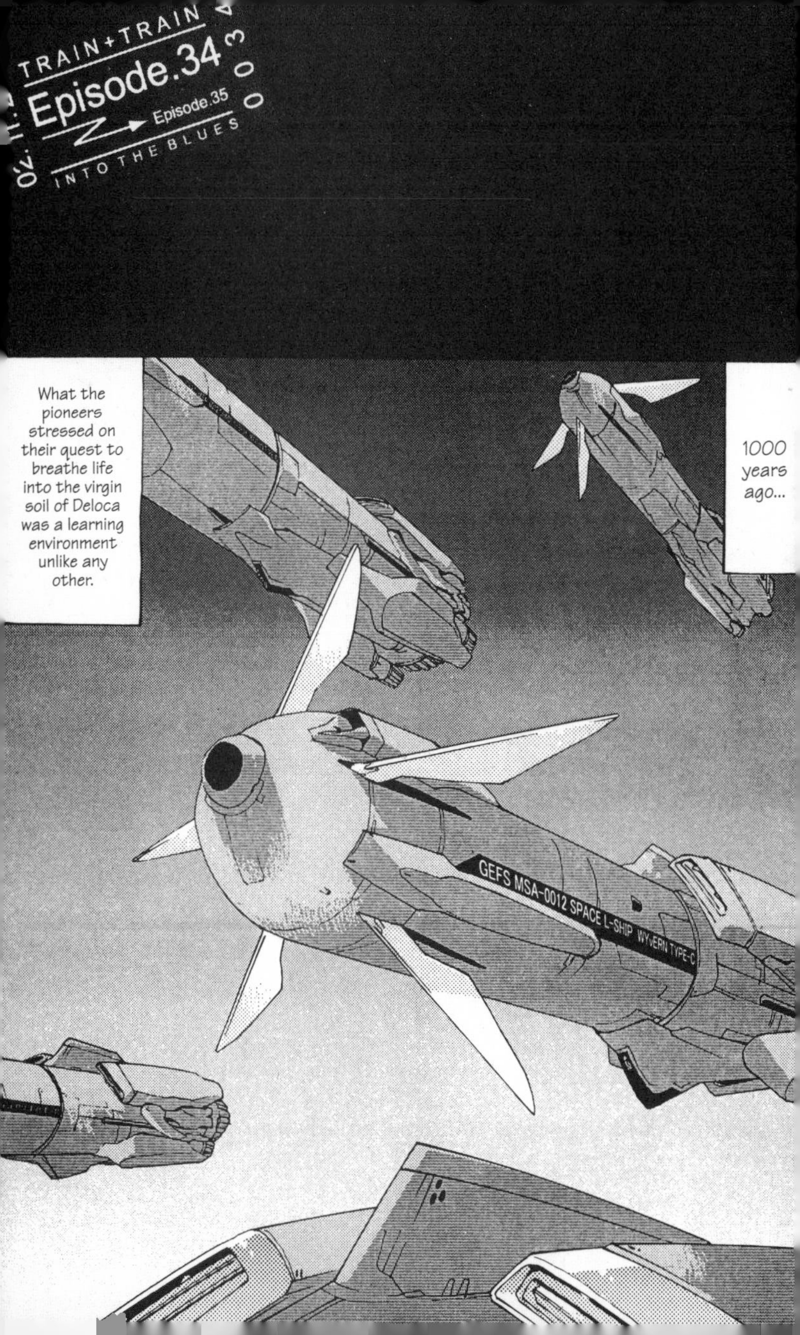
TRAIN+TRAIN
Episode.34
Episode.35
INTO THE BLUES
1000 years ago...
What the pioneers stressed on their quest to breathe life into the virgin soil of Deloca was a learning environment unlike any other.
GEFS MSA-0012 SPACE L-SHIP WYVERN TYPE-C

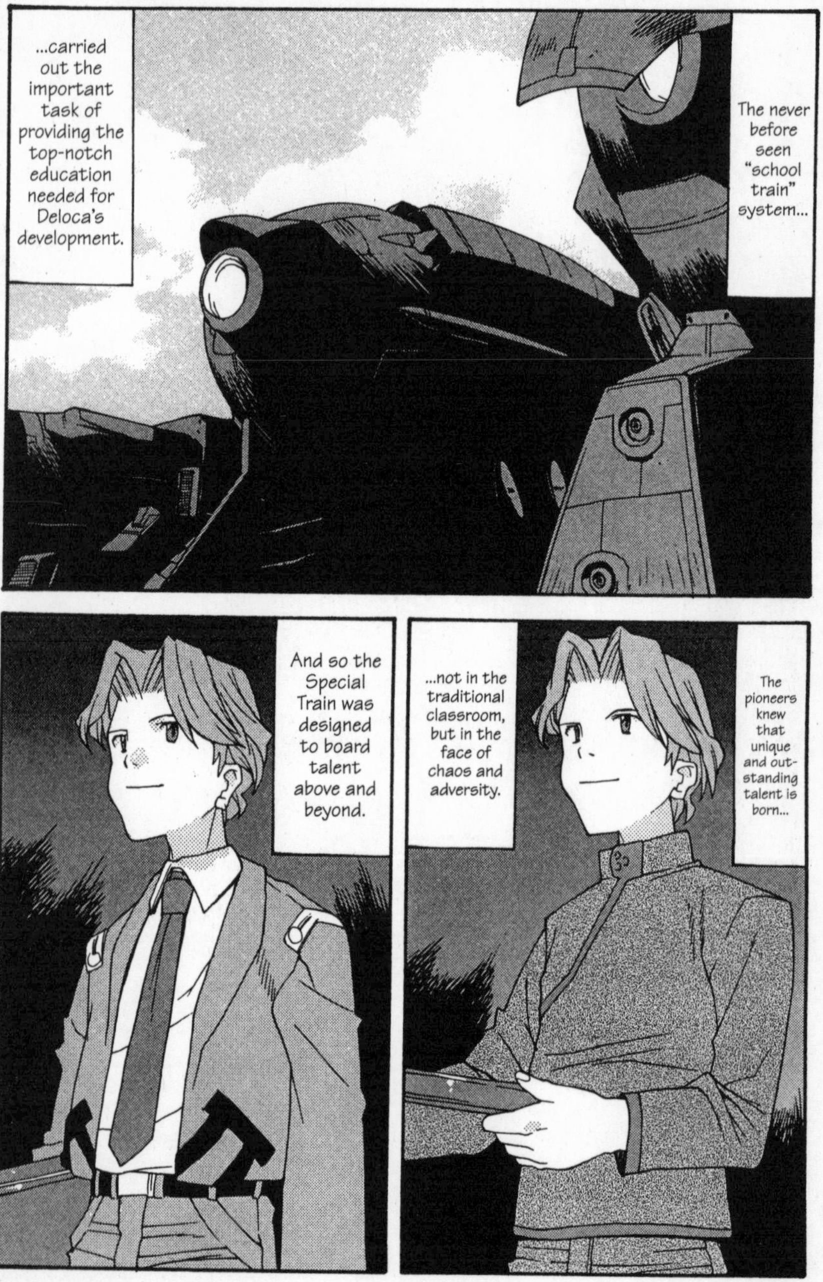
The never before seen "school train" system...
...carried out the important task of providing the top-notch education needed for Deloca's development.
The pioneers knew that unique and out-standing talent is born...
...not in the traditional classroom, but in the face of chaos and adversity.
And so the Special Train was designed to board talent above and beyond.

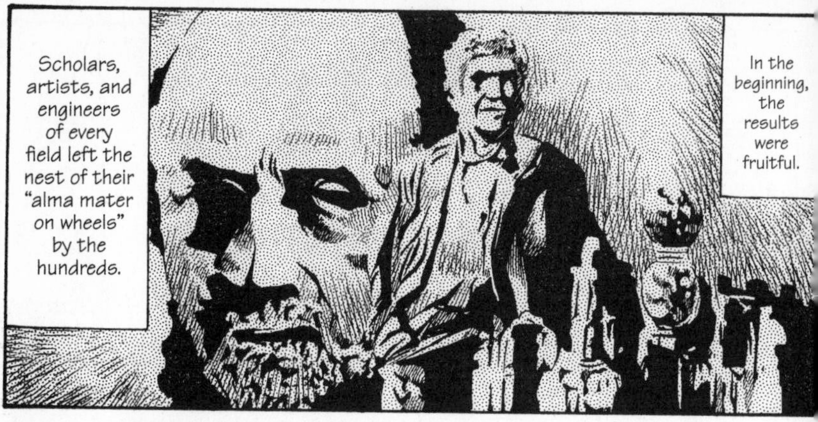
In the beginning, the results were fruitful.
Scholars, artists, and engineers of every field left the nest of their "alma mater on wheels" by the hundreds.

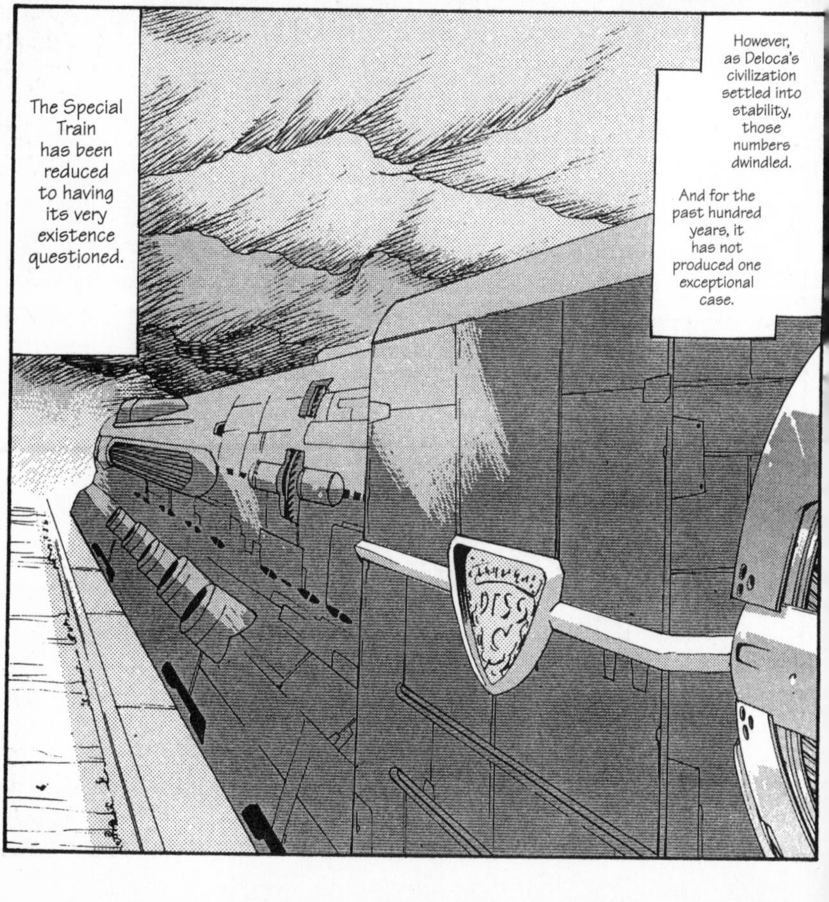
However, as Deloca's civilization settled into stability, those numbers dwindled.
And for the past hundred years, it has not produced one exceptional case.
The Special Train has been reduced to having its very existence questioned.

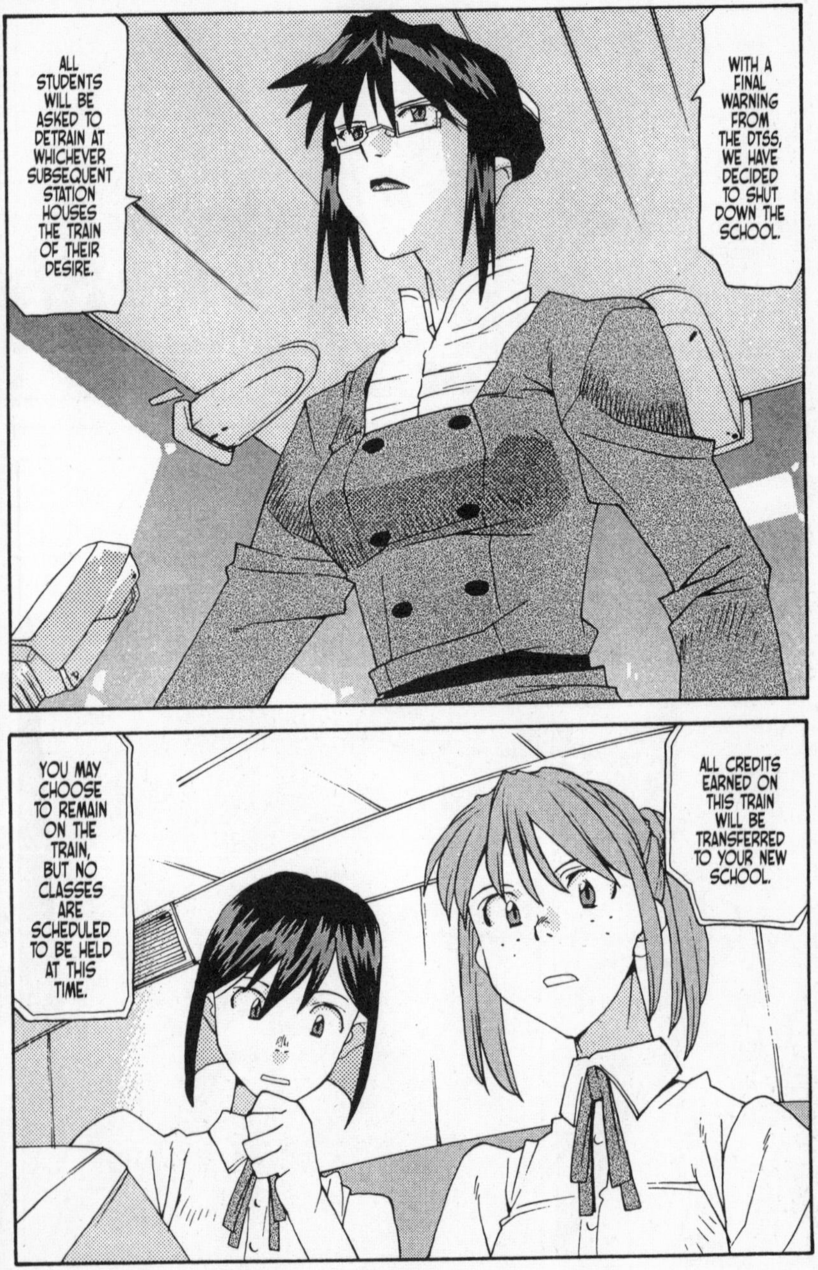
WITH A FINAL WARNING FROM THE DTSS, WE HAVE DECIDED TO SHUT DOWN THE SCHOOL.
ALL STUDENTS WILL BE ASKED TO DETRAIN AT WHICHEVER SUBSEQUENT STATION HOUSES THE TRAIN OF THEIR DESIRE.
ALL CREDITS EARNED ON THIS TRAIN WILL BE TRANSFERRED TO YOUR NEW SCHOOL.
YOU MAY CHOOSE TO REMAIN ON THE TRAIN, BUT NO CLASSES ARE SCHEDULED TO BE HELD AT THIS TIME.

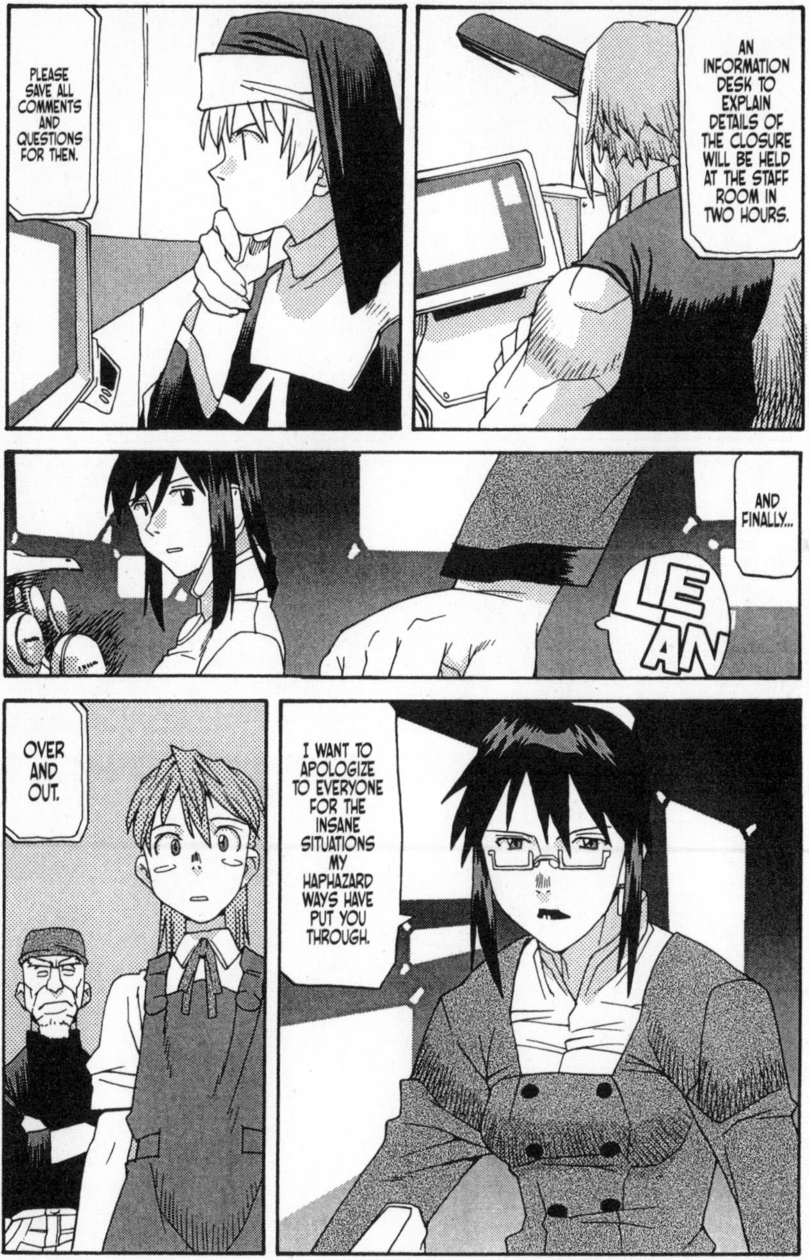
AN INFORMATION DESK TO EXPLAIN DETAILS OF THE CLOSURE WILL BE HELD AT THE STAFF ROOM IN TWO HOURS.
PLEASE SAVE ALL COMMENTS AND QUESTIONS FOR THEN.
AND FINALLY...
LEAN
I WANT TO APOLOGIZE TO EVERYONE FOR THE INSANE SITUATIONS MY HAPHAZARD WAYS HAVE PUT YOU THROUGH.
OVER AND OUT.

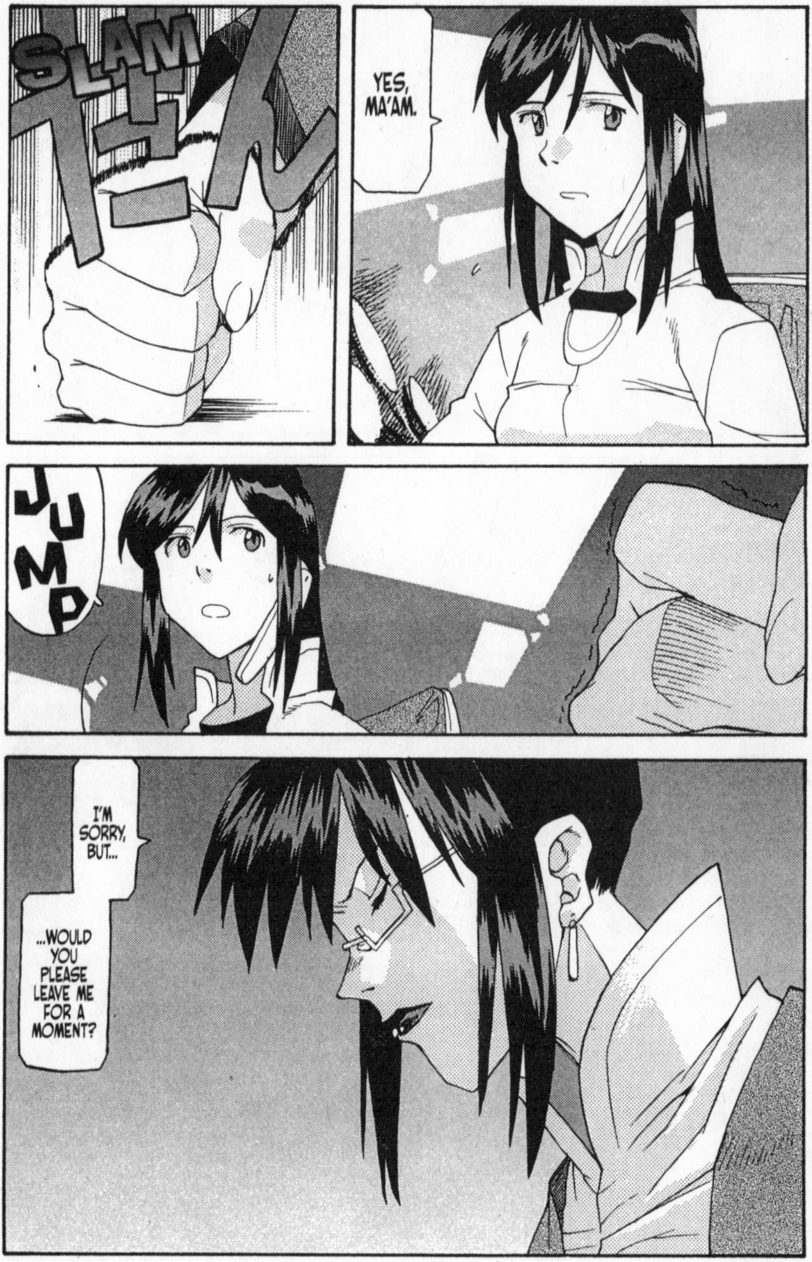
YES, MA'AM.
SLAM
JUMP
I'M SORRY, BUT...
...WOULD YOU PLEASE LEAVE ME FOR A MOMENT?

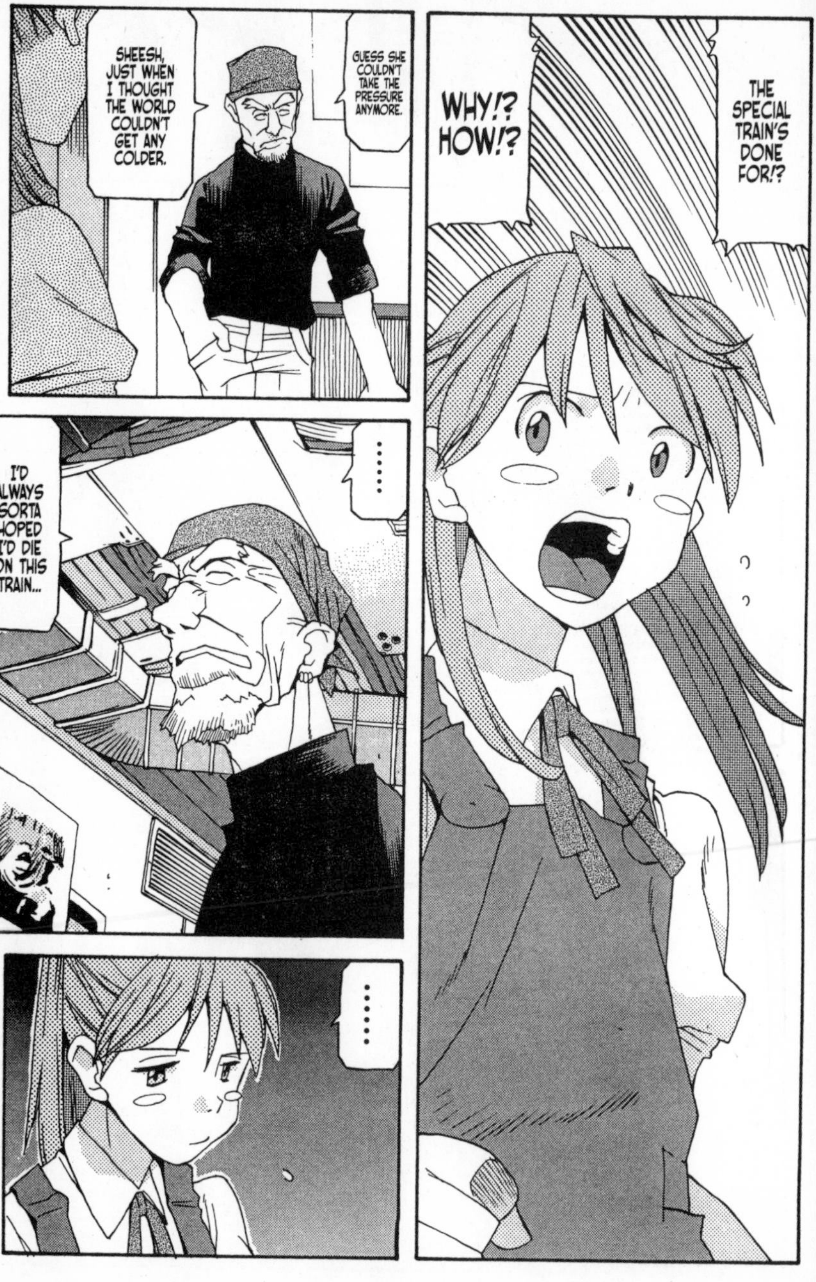
THE SPECIAL TRAIN'S DONE FOR!?
WHY!? HOW!?
GUESS SHE COULDN'T TAKE THE PRESSURE ANYMORE.
SHEESH, JUST WHEN I THOUGHT THE WORLD COULDN'T GET ANY COLDER.
……
I'D ALWAYS SORTA HOPED I'D DIE ON THIS TRAIN...
……

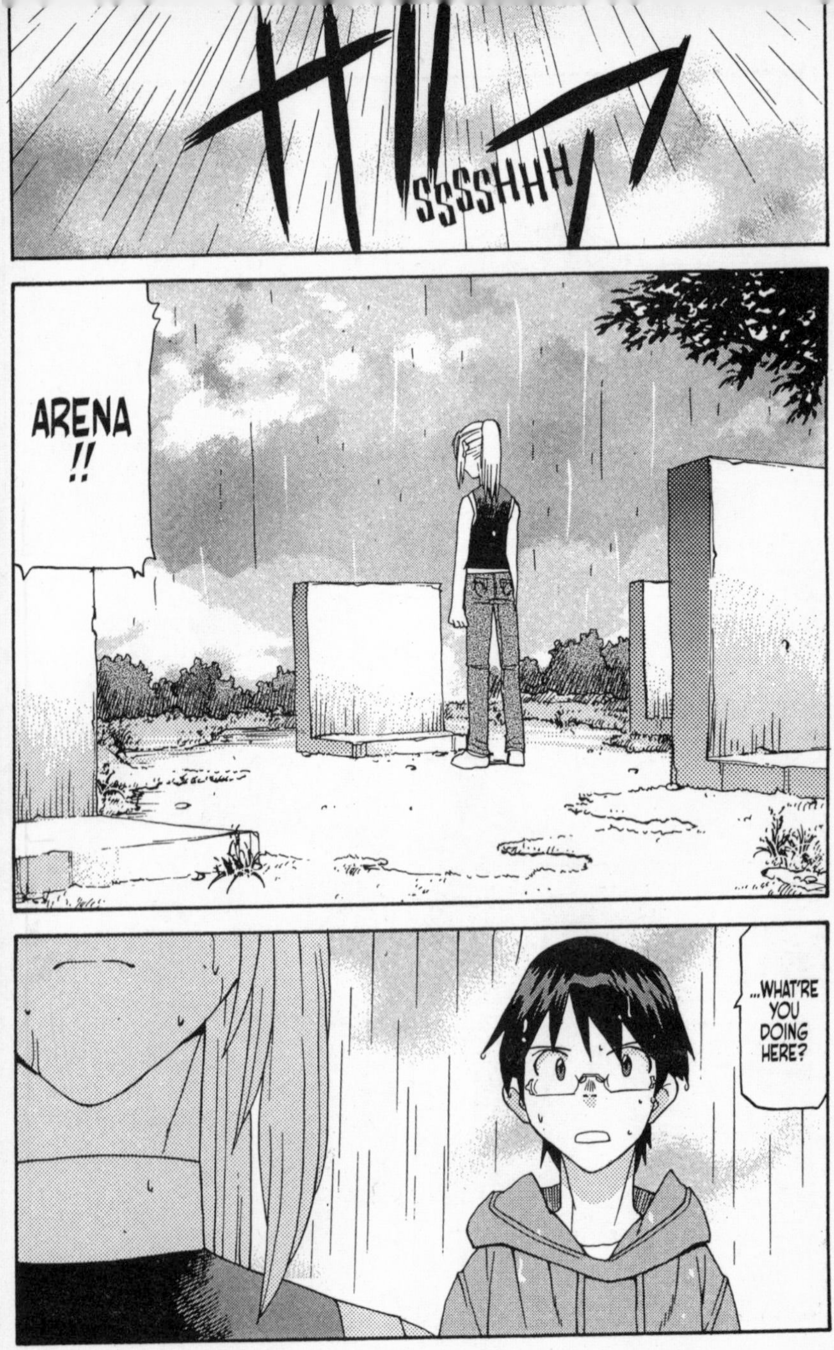
SSSSHHH
ARENA !!
...WHAT'RE YOU DOING HERE?

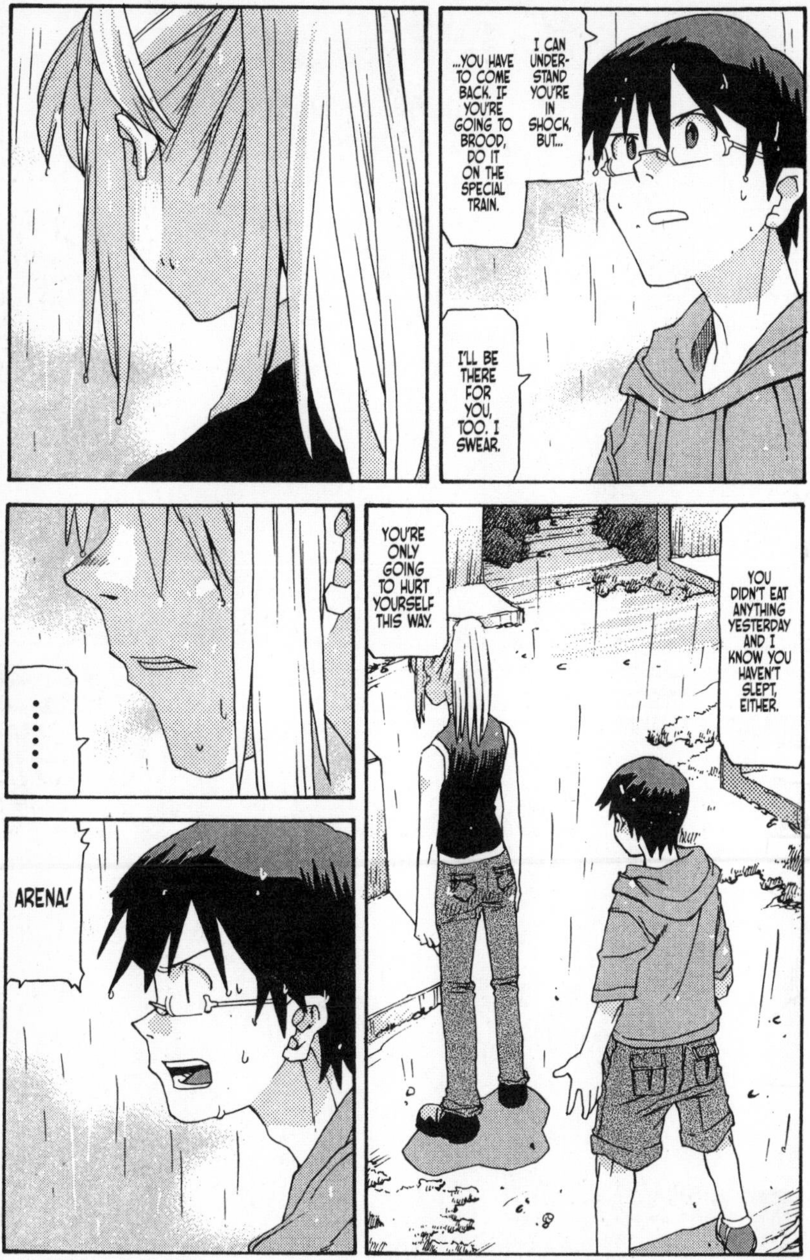
I CAN UNDER-STAND YOU'RE IN SHOCK, BUT...
...YOU HAVE TO COME BACK. IF YOU'RE GOING TO BROOD, DO IT ON THE SPECIAL TRAIN.
I'LL BE THERE FOR YOU, TOO. I SWEAR.
YOU DIDN'T EAT ANYTHING YESTERDAY AND I KNOW YOU HAVEN'T SLEPT, EITHER.
YOU'RE ONLY GOING TO HURT YOURSELF THIS WAY.
......
ARENA!

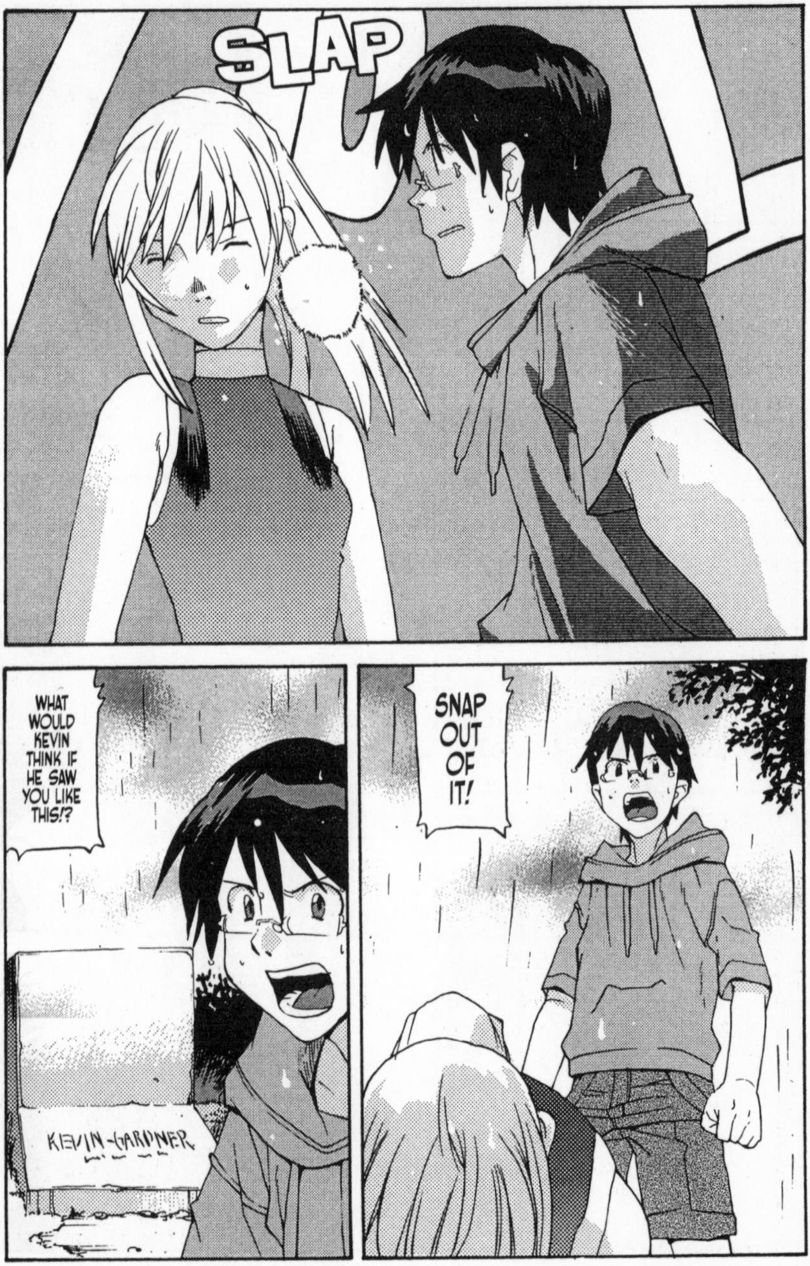
SLAP
SNAP OUT OF IT!
WHAT WOULD KEVIN THINK IF HE SAW YOU LIKE THIS!?
KEVIN GARDNER

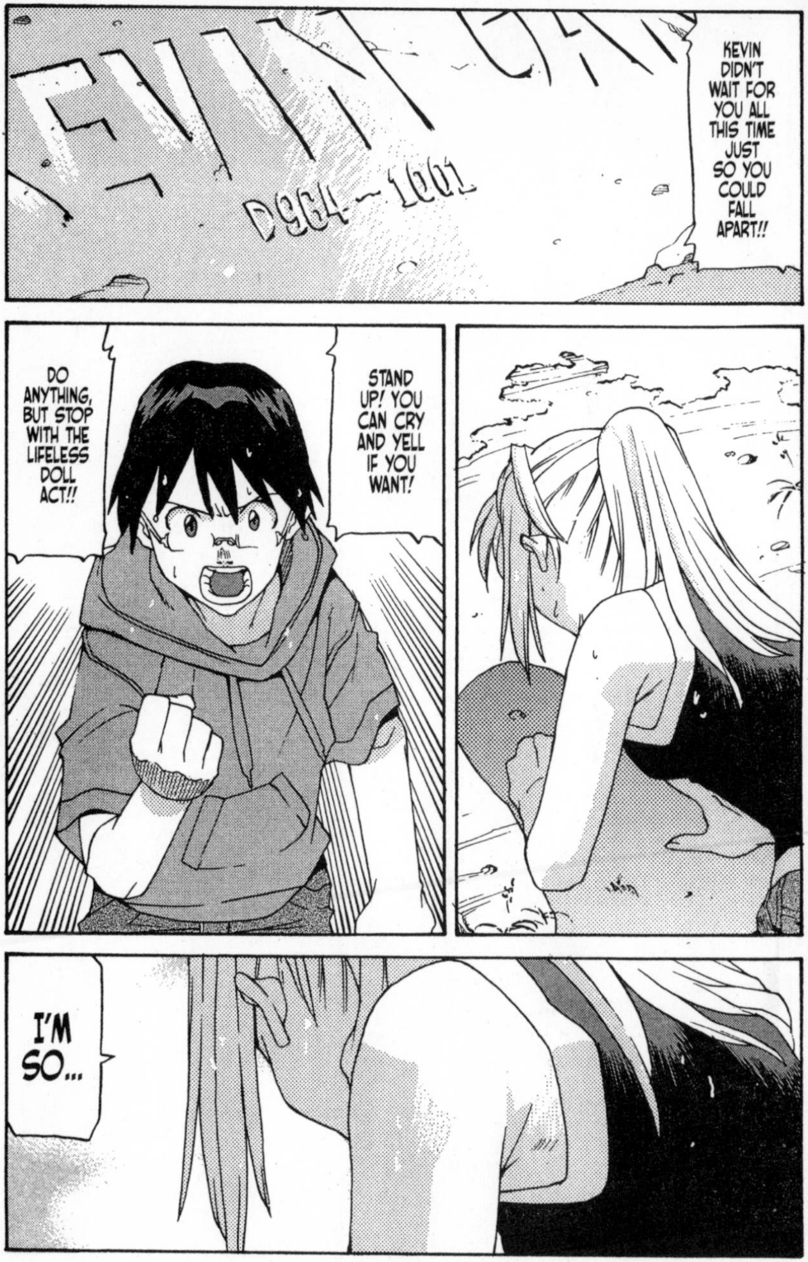
KEVIN DIDN'T WAIT FOR YOU ALL THIS TIME JUST SO YOU COULD FALL APART!!
STAND UP! YOU CAN CRY AND YELL IF YOU WANT!
DO ANYTHING, BUT STOP WITH THE LIFELESS DOLL ACT!!
I'M SO...

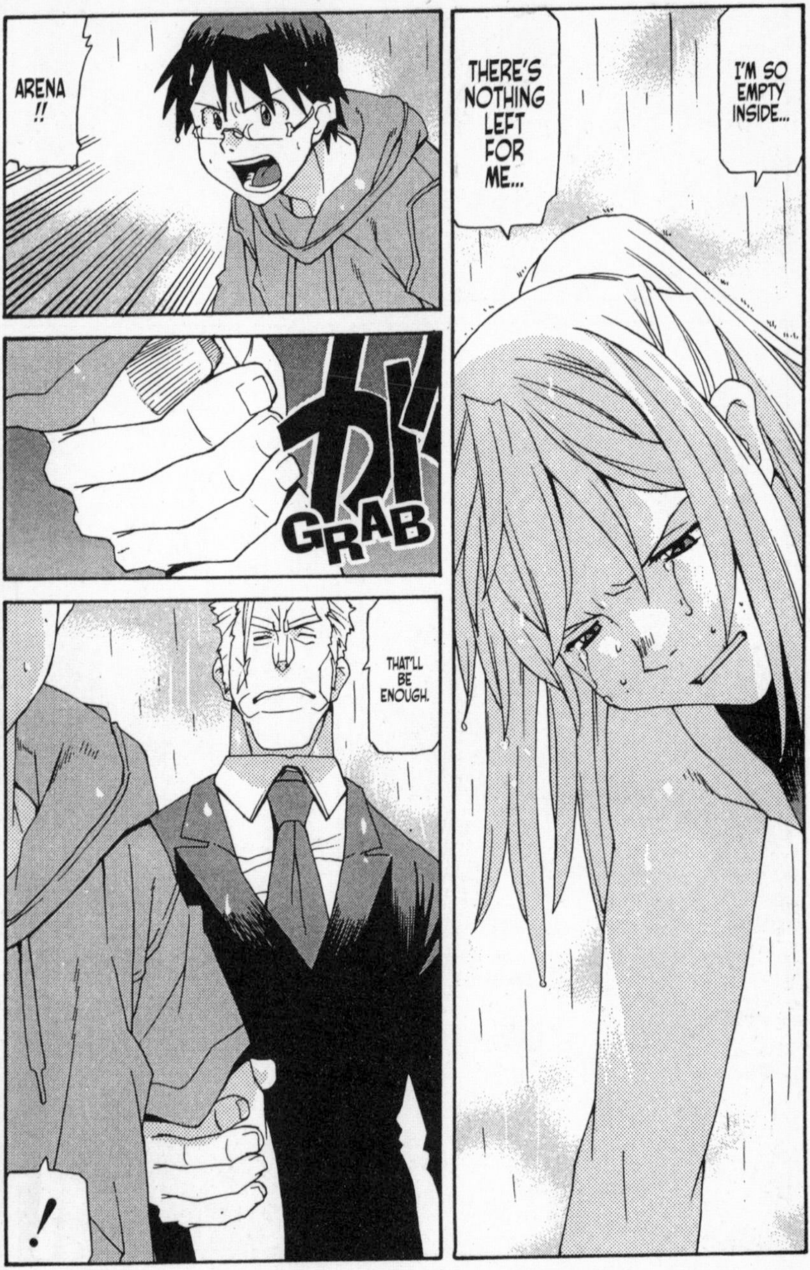
I'M SO EMPTY INSIDE...
THERE'S NOTHING LEFT FOR ME...
ARENA !!
GRAB
THAT'LL BE ENOUGH.
!

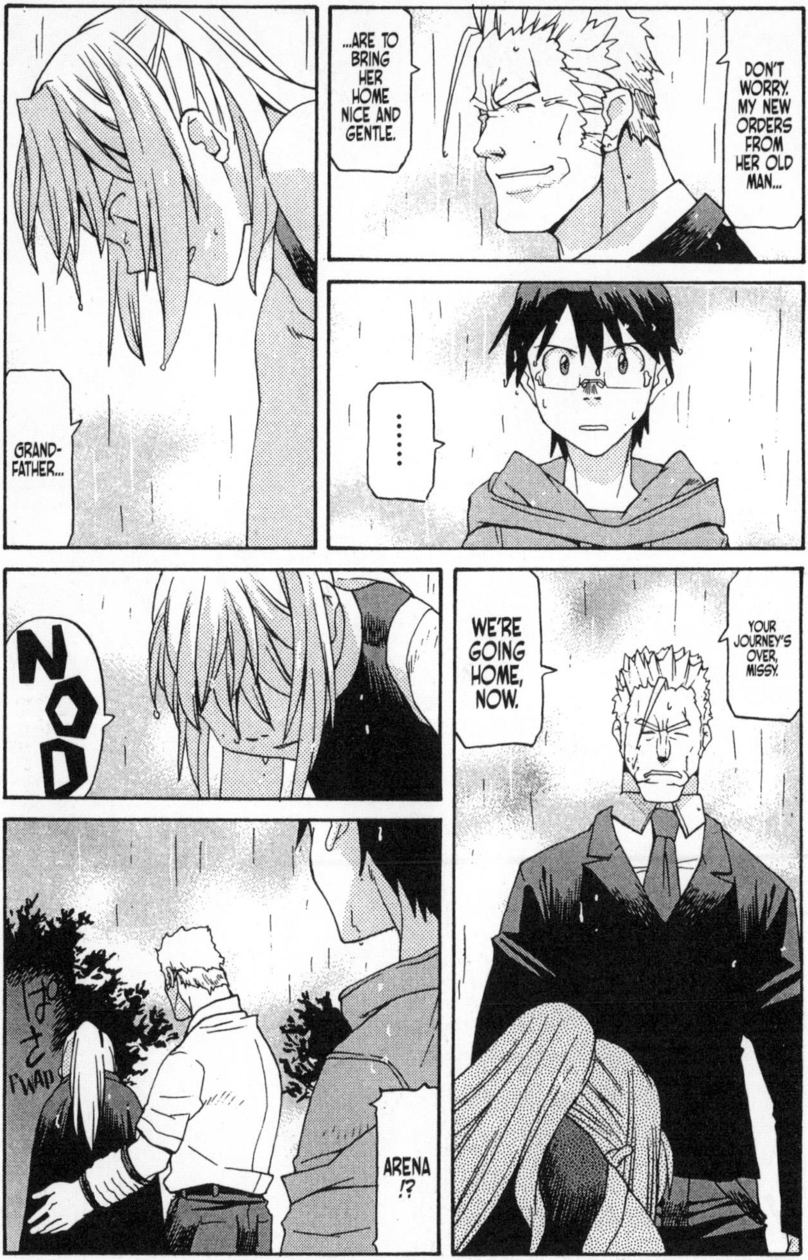
DON'T WORRY. MY NEW ORDERS FROM HER OLD MAN...
...ARE TO BRING HER HOME NICE AND GENTLE.
......
GRAND-FATHER...
YOUR JOURNEY'S OVER, MISSY.
WE'RE GOING HOME, NOW.
NOD
ARENA!?
ぱさ
FWAP

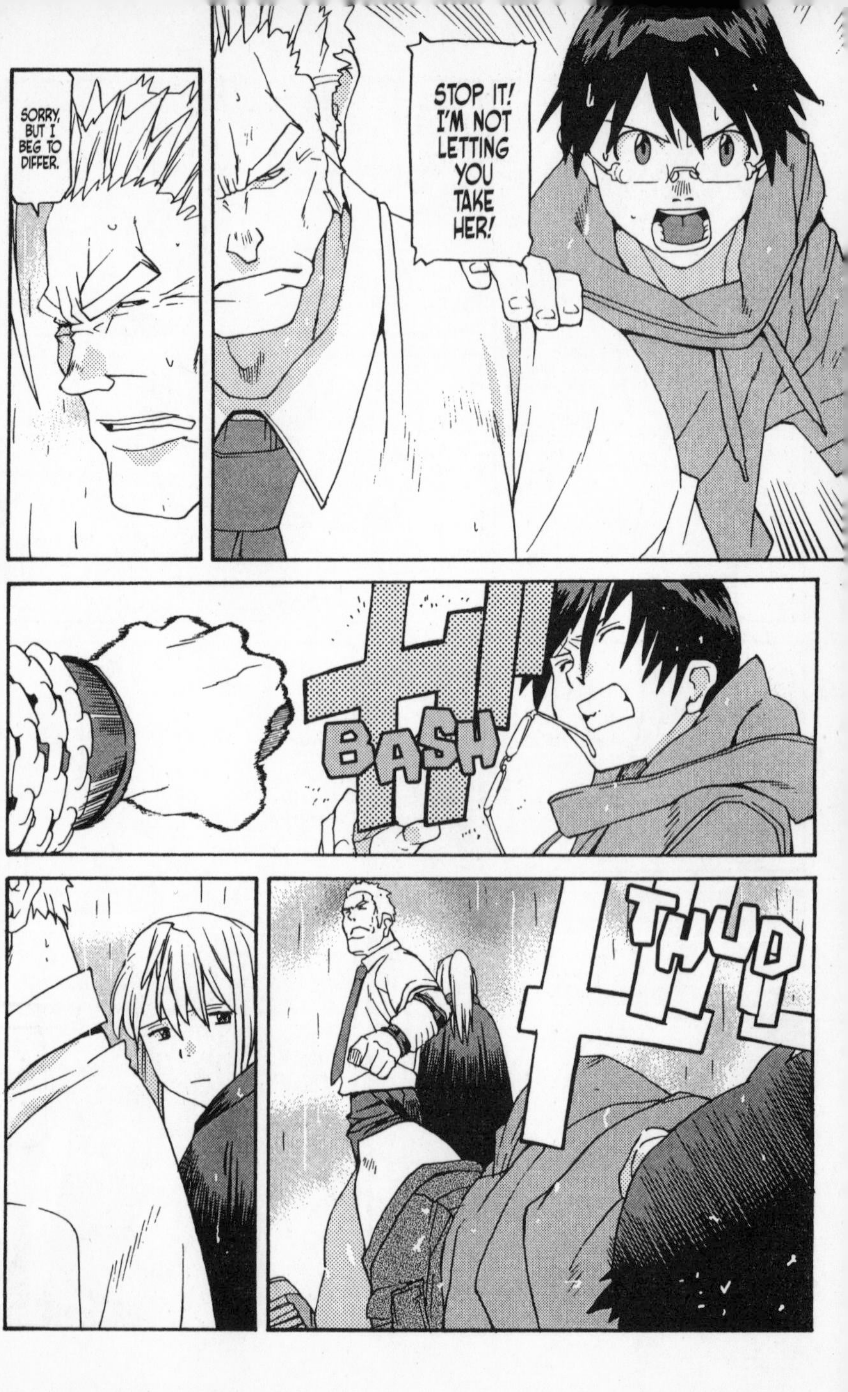
STOP IT! I'M NOT LETTING YOU TAKE HER!
SORRY, BUT I BEG TO DIFFER.
BASH
THUD

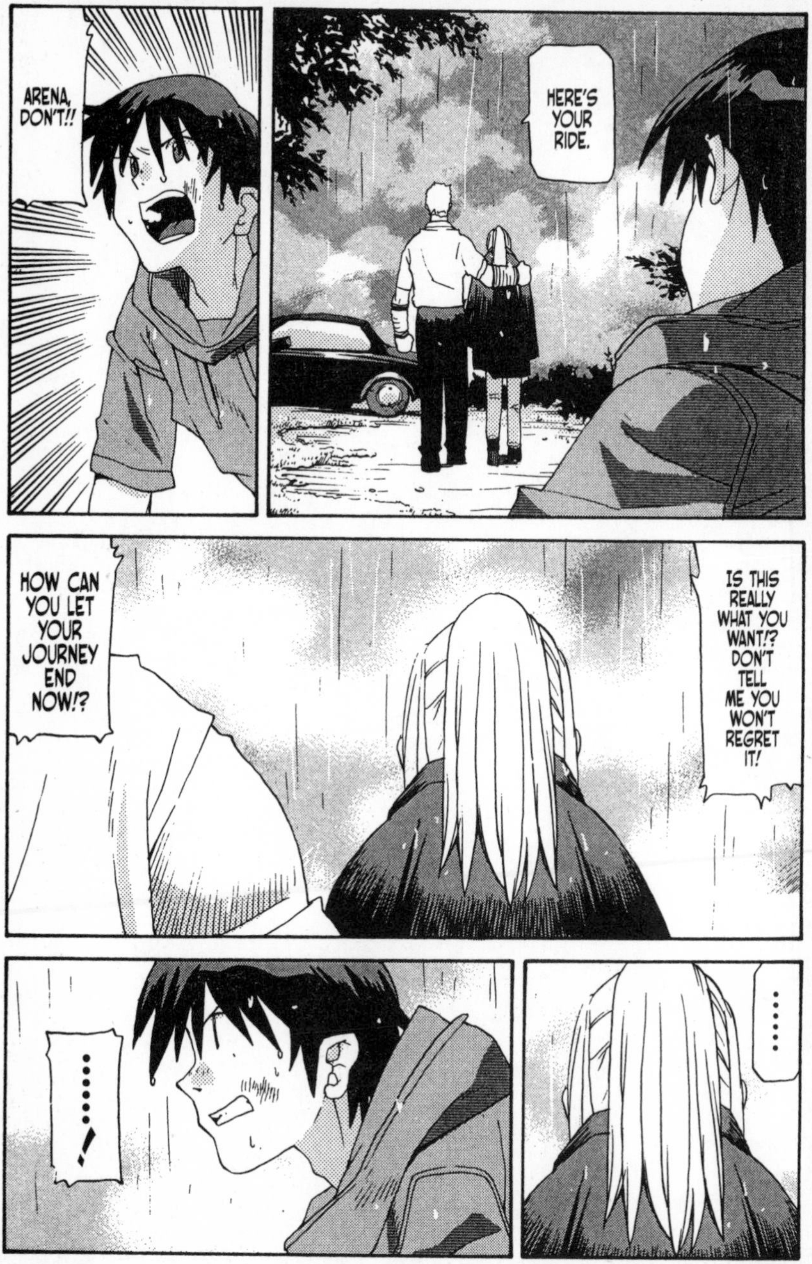
HERE'S YOUR RIDE.
ARENA, DON'T!!
IS THIS REALLY WHAT YOU WANT!? DON'T TELL ME YOU WON'T REGRET IT!
HOW CAN YOU LET YOUR JOURNEY END NOW!?
......
......!

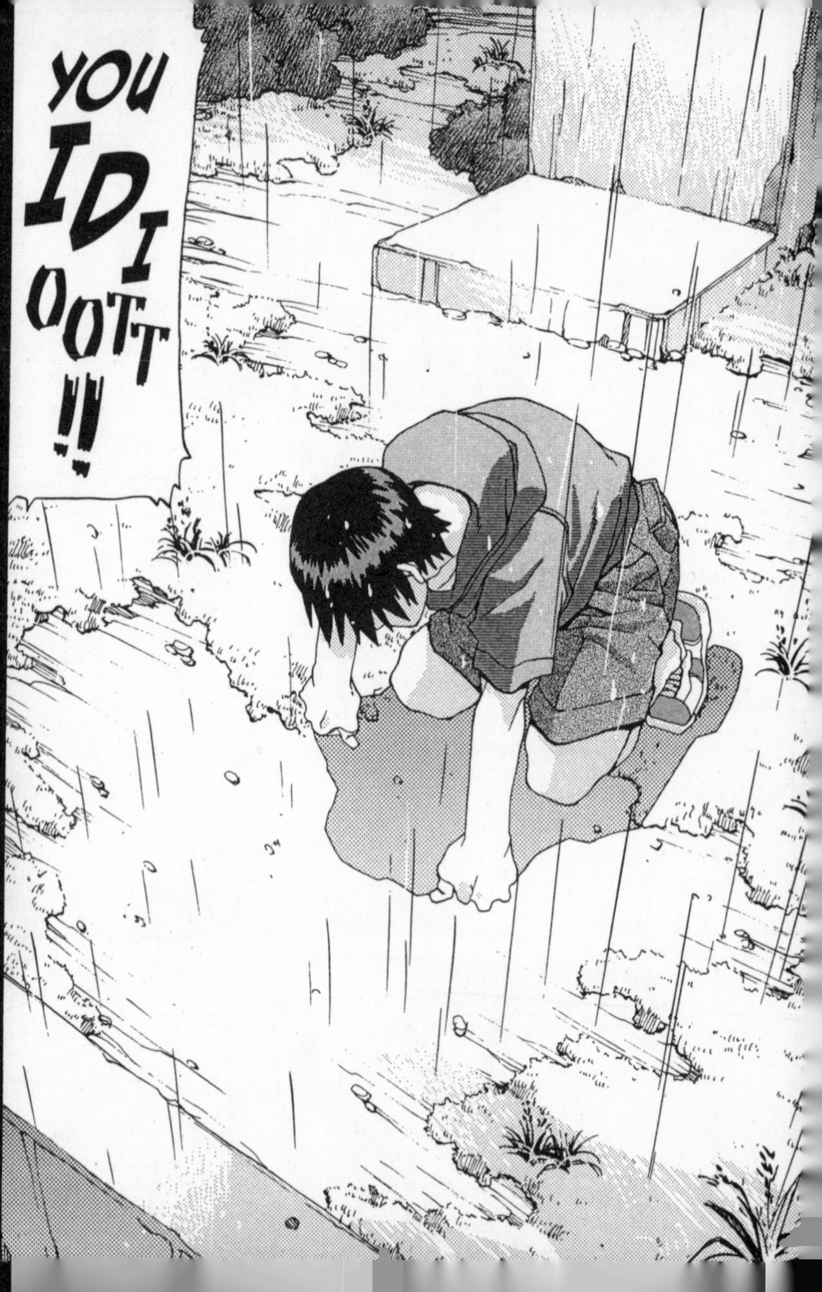
YOU IDIOOTTT!!

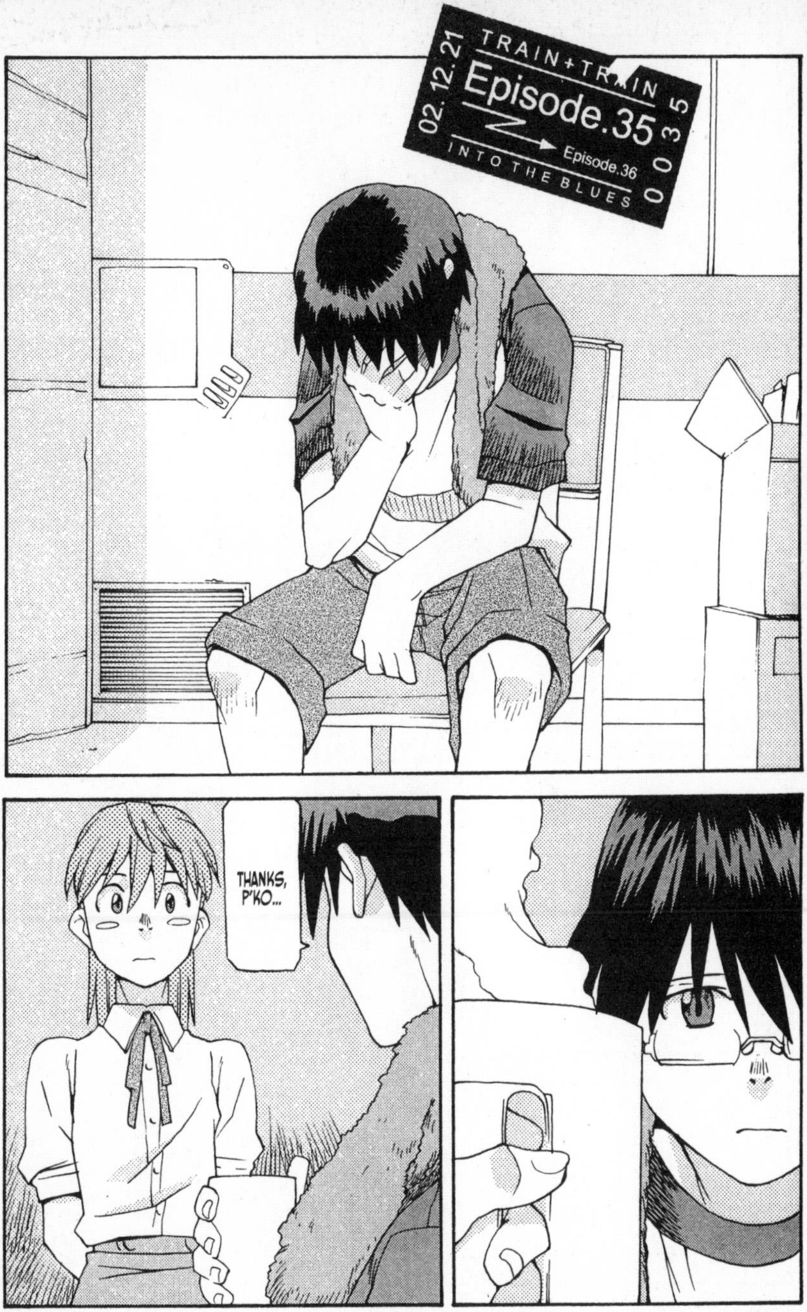
TRAIN+TRAIN
Episode.35
Episode.36
INTO THE BLUES
02. 12. 21
0035
THANKS, P'KO...

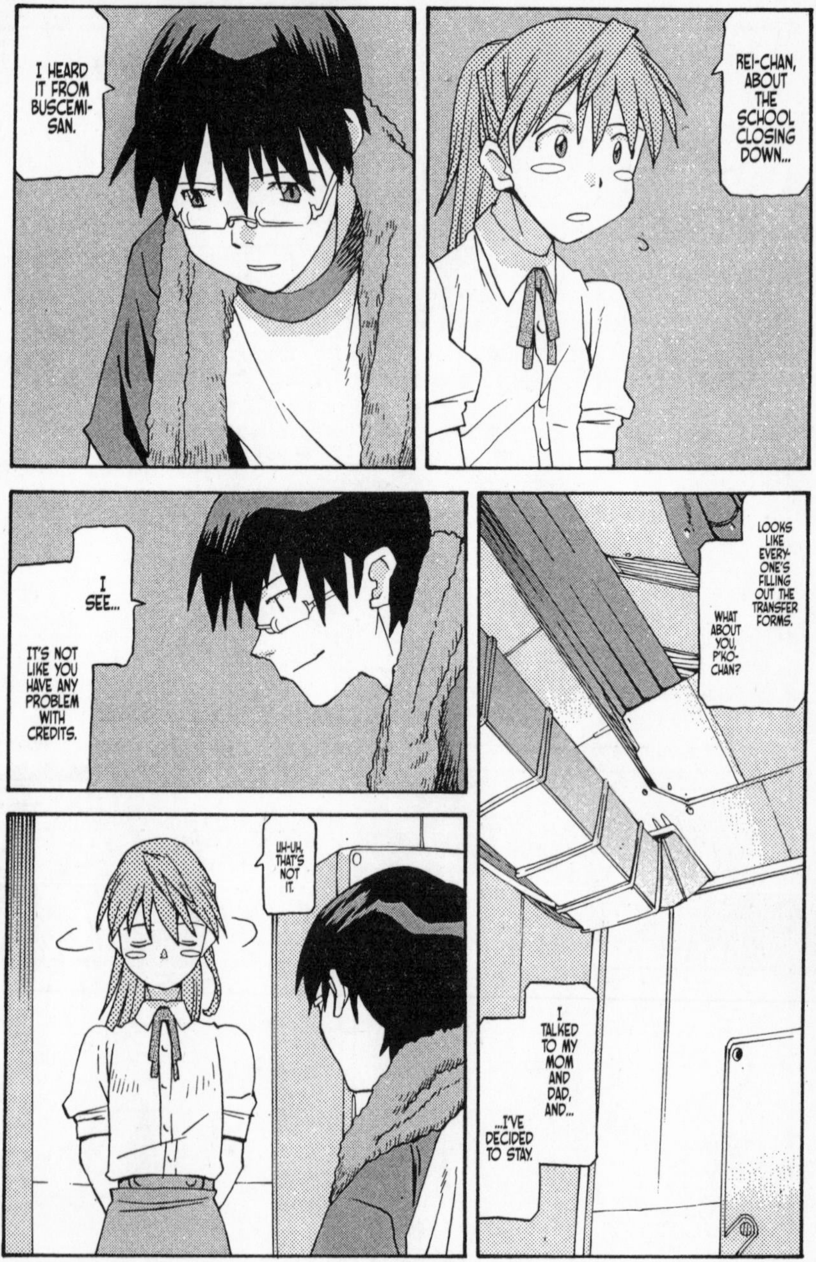
REI-CHAN, ABOUT THE SCHOOL CLOSING DOWN...
I HEARD IT FROM BUSCEMI-SAN.
LOOKS LIKE EVERY-ONE'S FILLING OUT THE TRANSFER FORMS.
WHAT ABOUT YOU, P'KO-CHAN?
I SEE...
IT'S NOT LIKE YOU HAVE ANY PROBLEM WITH CREDITS.
I TALKED TO MY MOM AND DAD, AND...
...I'VE DECIDED TO STAY.
UH-UH, THAT'S NOT IT.

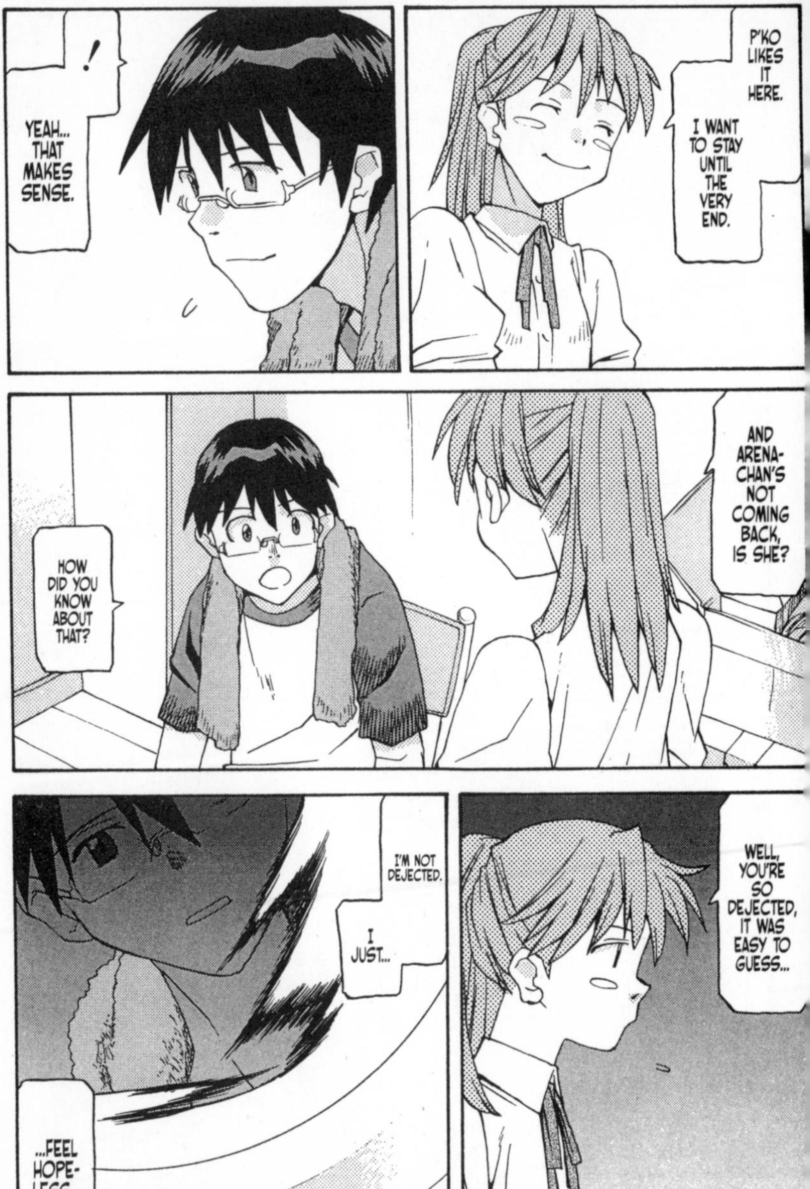
P'KO LIKES IT HERE.
I WANT TO STAY UNTIL THE VERY END.
!
YEAH... THAT MAKES SENSE.
AND ARENA-CHAN'S NOT COMING BACK, IS SHE?
HOW DID YOU KNOW ABOUT THAT?
WELL, YOU'RE SO DEJECTED, IT WAS EASY TO GUESS...
I'M NOT DEJECTED.
I JUST...
...FEEL HOPE-LESS...

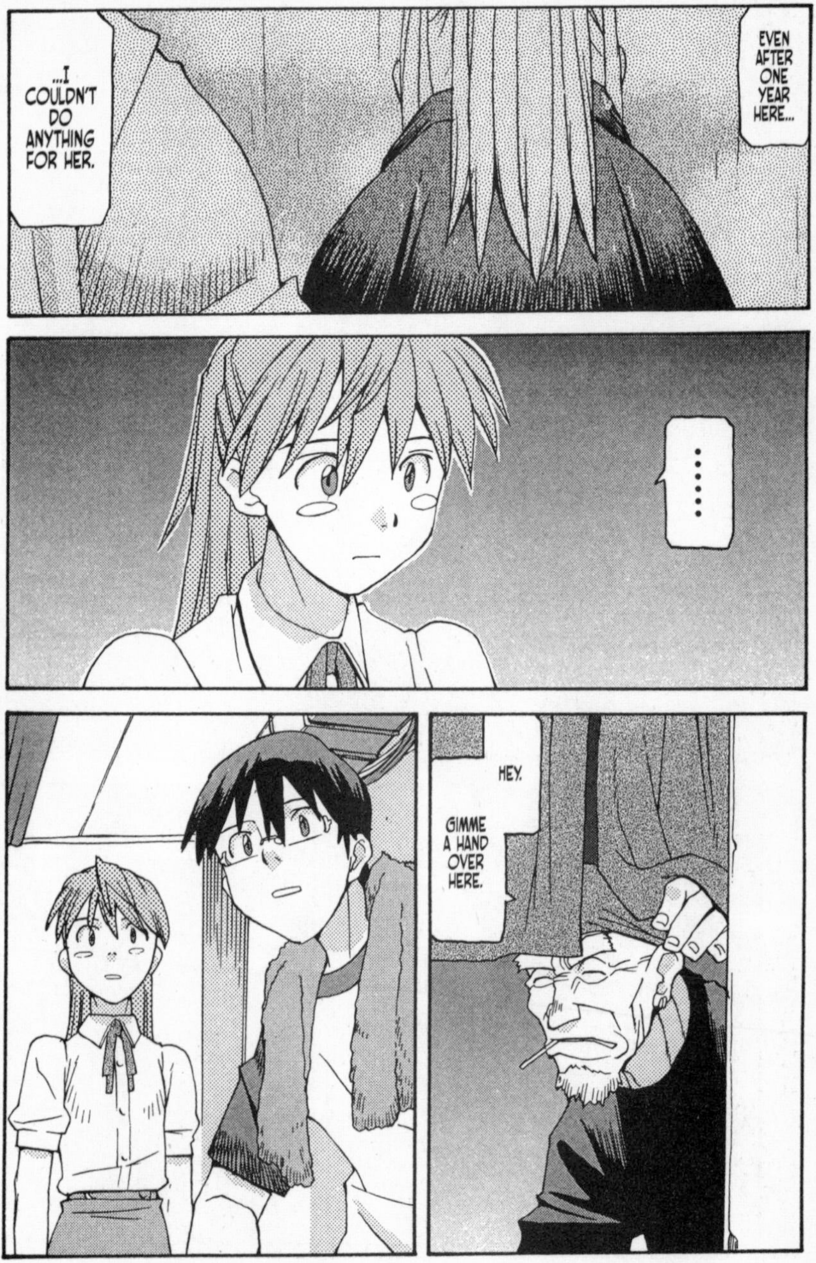
EVEN AFTER ONE YEAR HERE...
...I COULDN'T DO ANYTHING FOR HER.
......
HEY.
GIMME A HAND OVER HERE.

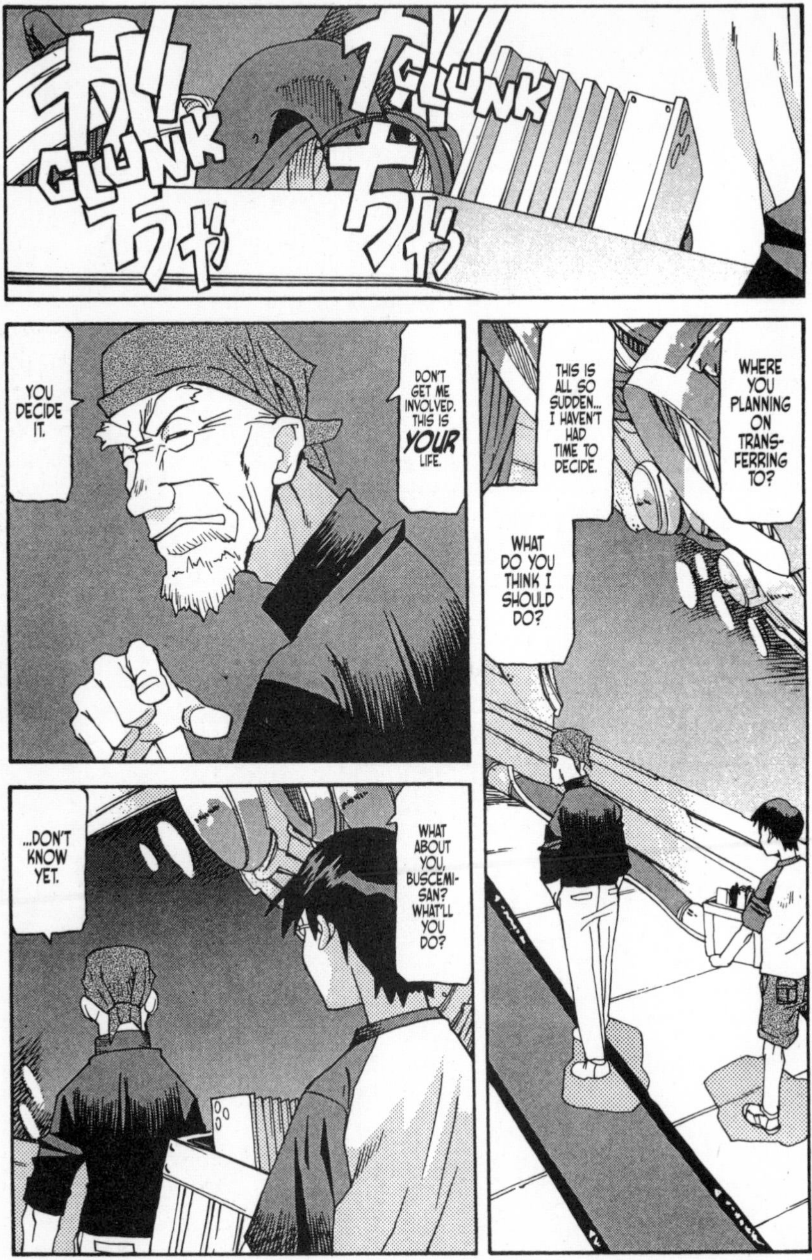
CLUNK
CLUNK
WHERE YOU PLANNING ON TRANS-FERRING TO?
THIS IS ALL SO SUDDEN... I HAVEN'T HAD TIME TO DECIDE.
WHAT DO YOU THINK I SHOULD DO?
DON'T GET ME INVOLVED. THIS IS **YOUR** LIFE.
YOU DECIDE IT.
WHAT ABOUT YOU, BUSCEMI-SAN? WHAT'LL YOU DO?
...DON'T KNOW YET.

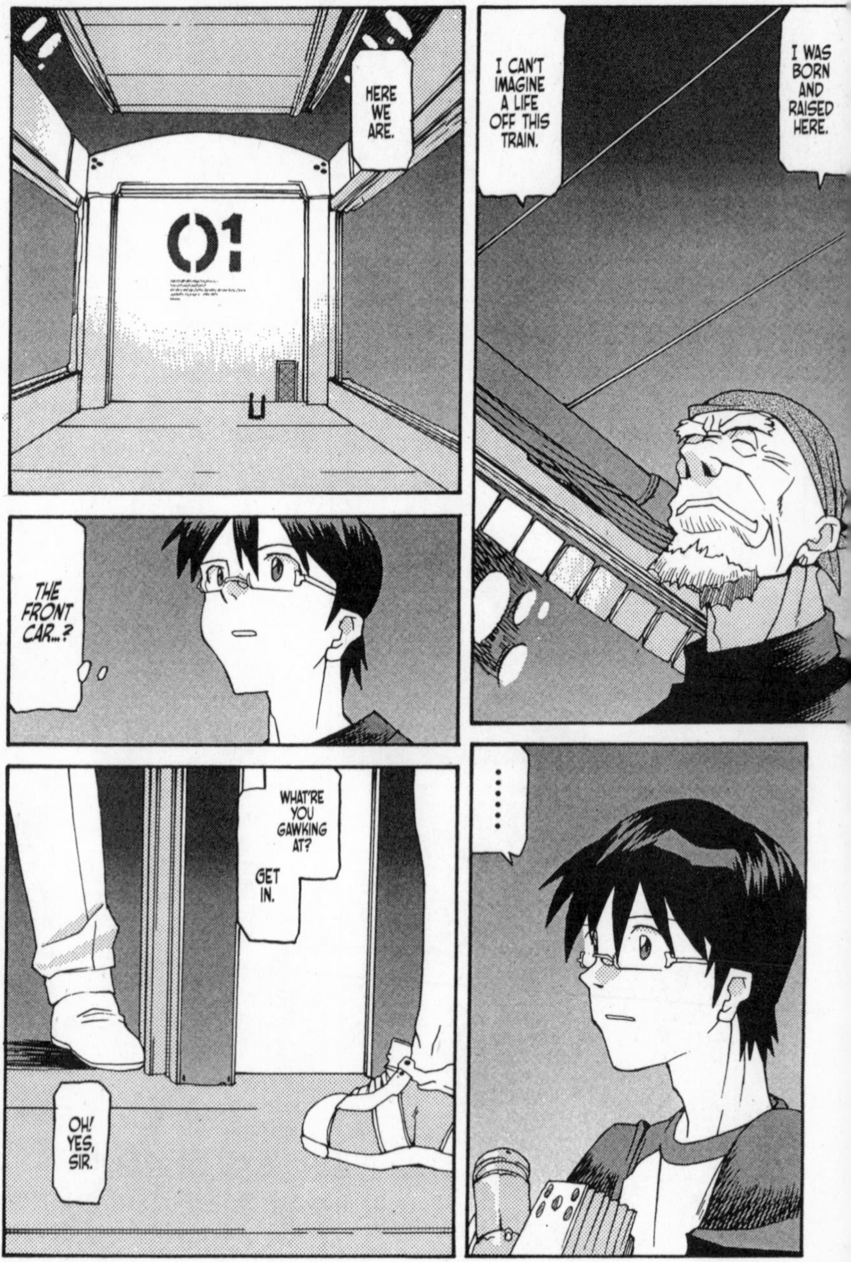
I WAS BORN AND RAISED HERE.
I CAN'T IMAGINE A LIFE OFF THIS TRAIN.
HERE WE ARE.
01
THE FRONT CAR...?
......
WHAT'RE YOU GAWKING AT?
GET IN.
OH! YES, SIR.

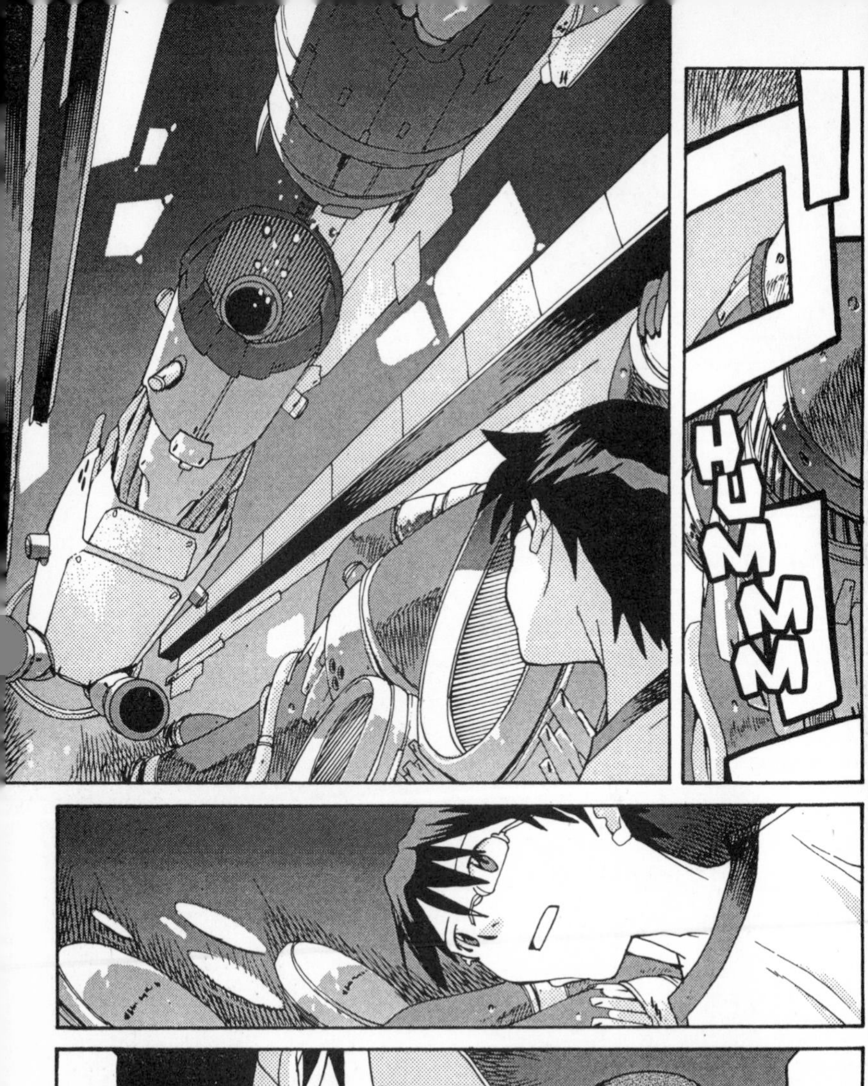
HUMMMM
WHAT? NEVER SEEN AN ENGINE ROOM BEFORE?
NO, NEVER...

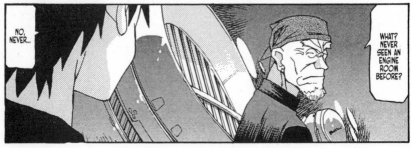

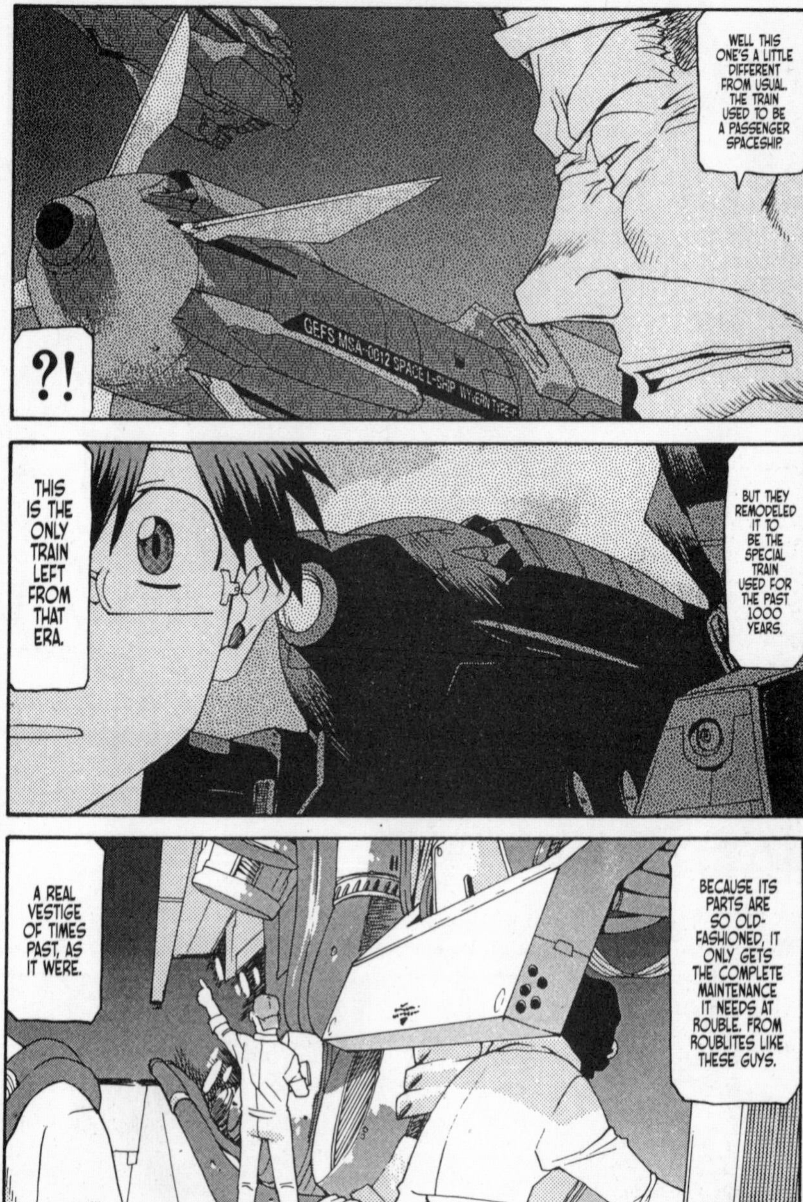
WELL THIS ONE'S A LITTLE DIFFERENT FROM USUAL. THE TRAIN USED TO BE A PASSENGER SPACESHIP.
GEFS MSA-0012 SPACE L-SHIP WYVERN TYPE-C
?!
BUT THEY REMODELED IT TO BE THE SPECIAL TRAIN USED FOR THE PAST 1000 YEARS.
THIS IS THE ONLY TRAIN LEFT FROM THAT ERA.
BECAUSE ITS PARTS ARE SO OLD-FASHIONED, IT ONLY GETS THE COMPLETE MAINTENANCE IT NEEDS AT ROUBLE. FROM ROUBLITES LIKE THESE GUYS.
A REAL VESTIGE OF TIMES PAST, AS IT WERE.

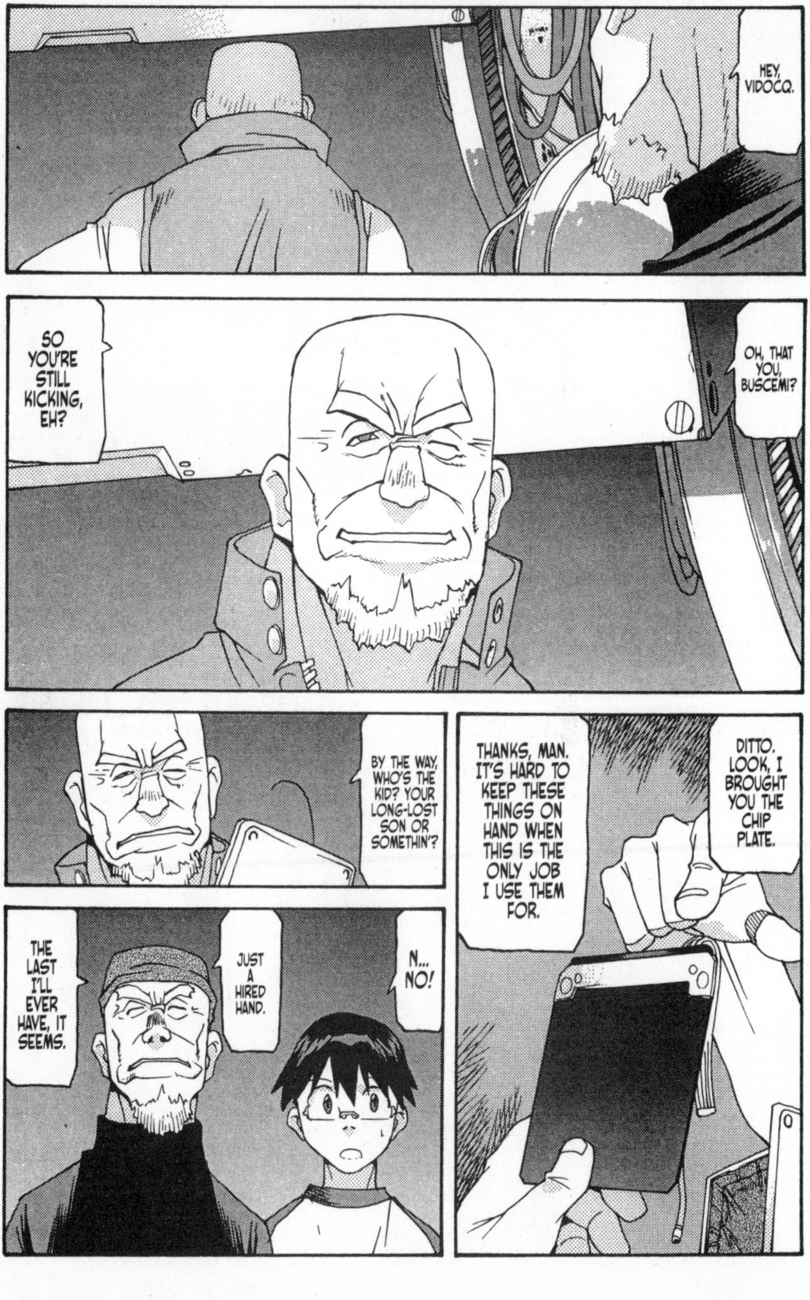
HEY, VIDOCQ.
OH, THAT YOU, BUSCEMI?
SO YOU'RE STILL KICKING, EH?
DITTO. LOOK, I BROUGHT YOU THE CHIP PLATE.
THANKS, MAN. IT'S HARD TO KEEP THESE THINGS ON HAND WHEN THIS IS THE ONLY JOB I USE THEM FOR.
BY THE WAY, WHO'S THE KID? YOUR LONG-LOST SON OR SOMETHIN'?
N... NO!
JUST A HIRED HAND.
THE LAST I'LL EVER HAVE, IT SEEMS.

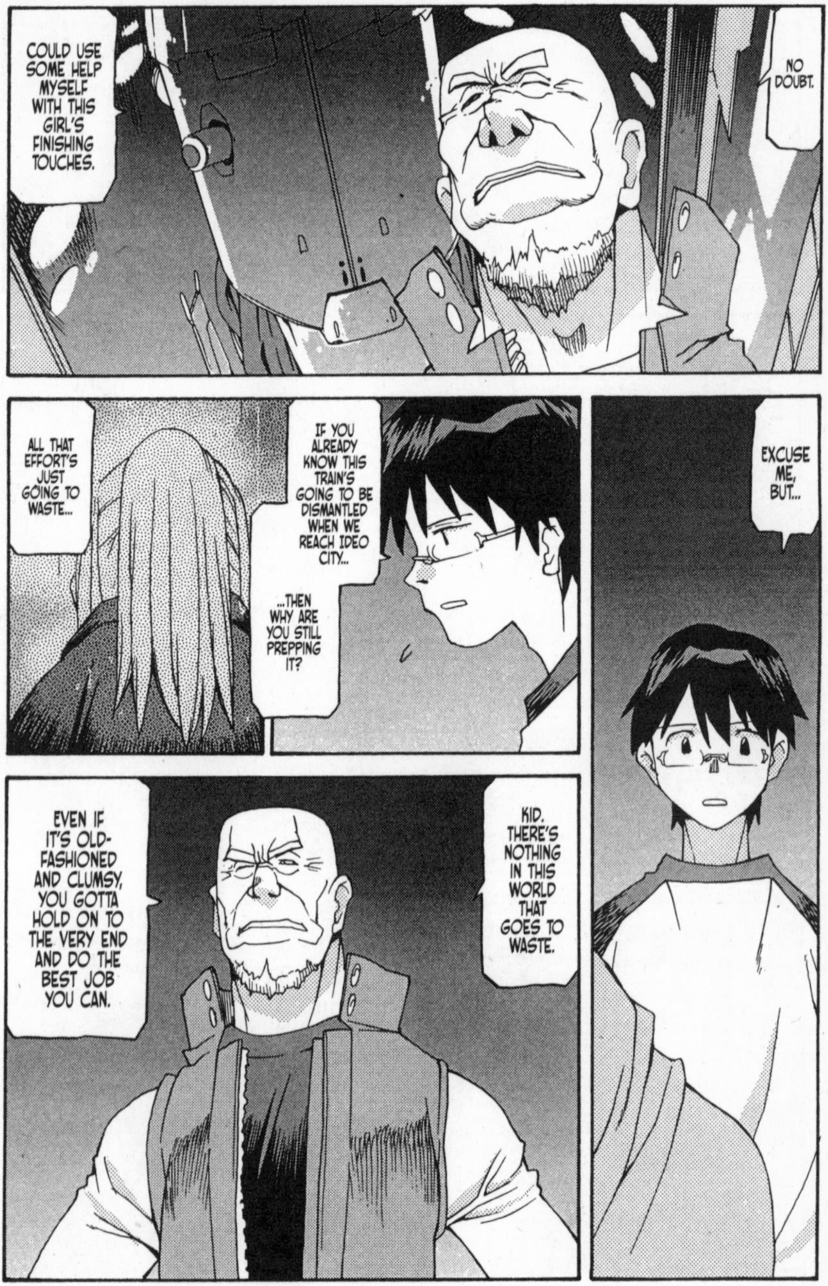
NO DOUBT.
COULD USE SOME HELP MYSELF WITH THIS GIRL'S FINISHING TOUCHES.
EXCUSE ME, BUT...
IF YOU ALREADY KNOW THIS TRAIN'S GOING TO BE DISMANTLED WHEN WE REACH IDEO CITY...
...THEN WHY ARE YOU STILL PREPPING IT?
ALL THAT EFFORT'S JUST GOING TO WASTE...
KID. THERE'S NOTHING IN THIS WORLD THAT GOES TO WASTE.
EVEN IF IT'S OLD-FASHIONED AND CLUMSY, YOU GOTTA HOLD ON TO THE VERY END AND DO THE BEST JOB YOU CAN.

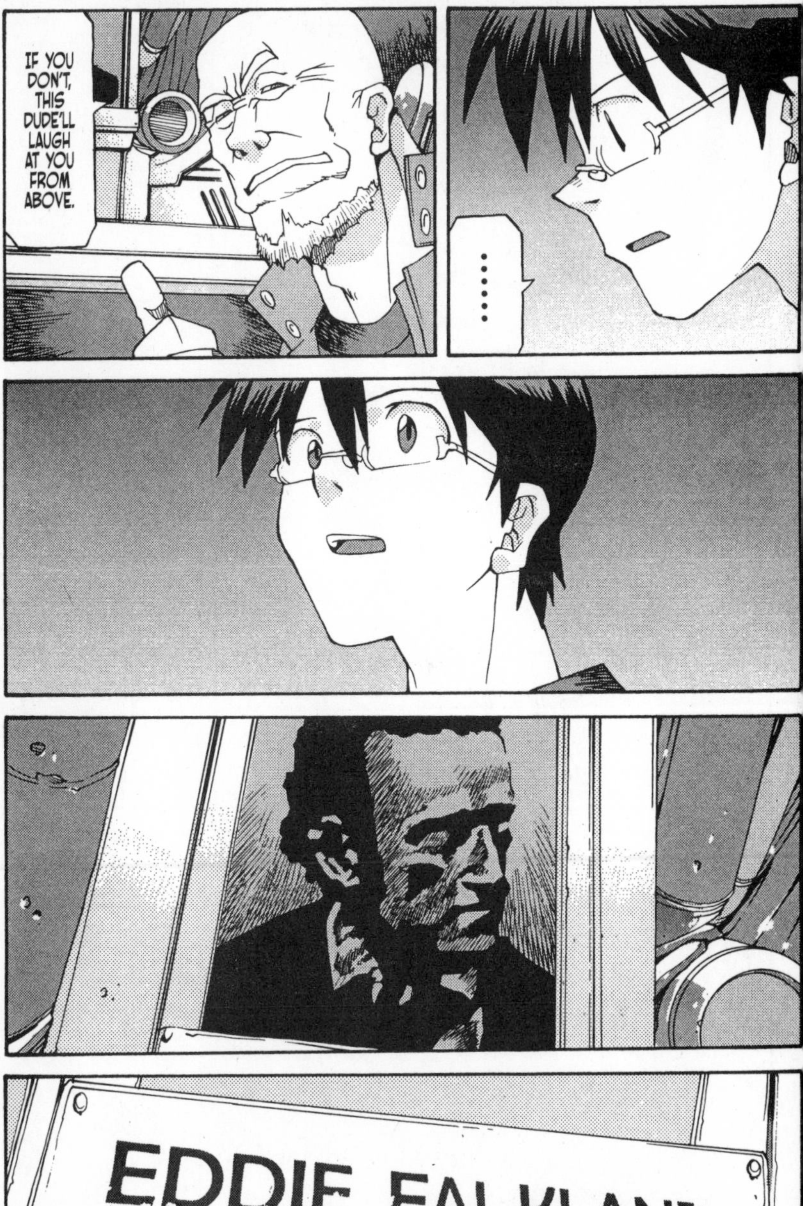
......
IF YOU DON'T, THIS DUDE'LL LAUGH AT YOU FROM ABOVE.
EDDIE FALKLAND

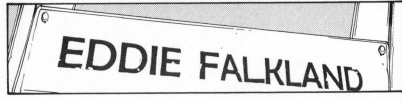

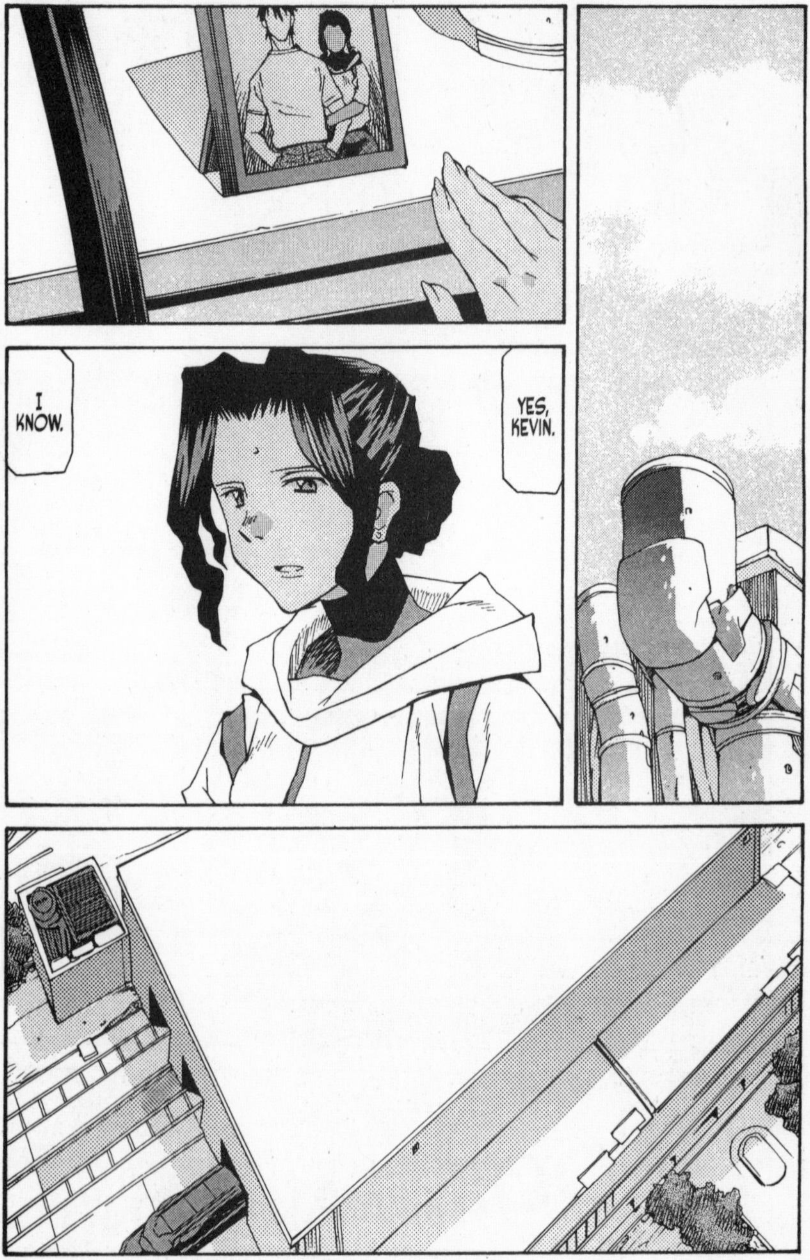
YES, KEVIN.
I KNOW.

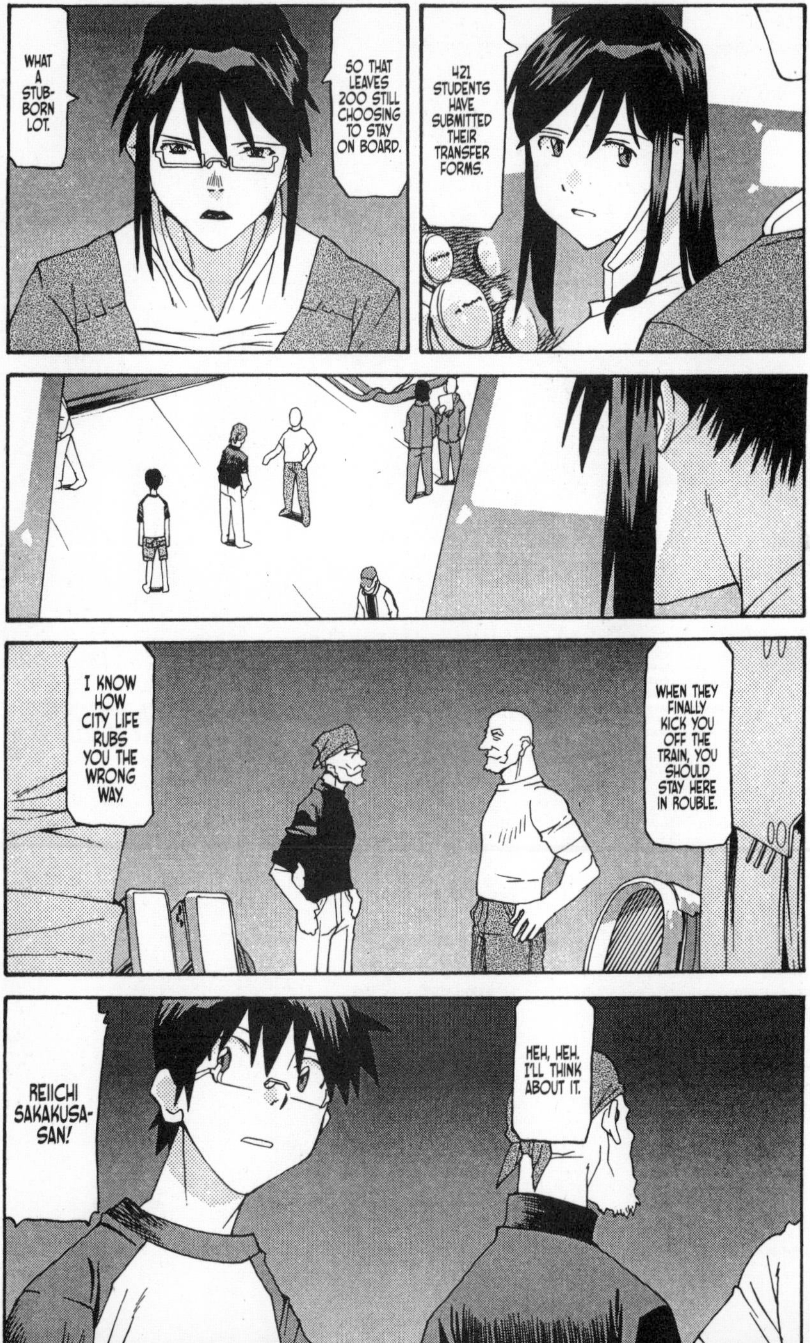
421 STUDENTS HAVE SUBMITTED THEIR TRANSFER FORMS.
SO THAT LEAVES 200 STILL CHOOSING TO STAY ON BOARD.
WHAT A STUBBORN LOT.
WHEN THEY FINALLY KICK YOU OFF THE TRAIN, YOU SHOULD STAY HERE IN ROUBLE.
I KNOW HOW CITY LIFE RUBS YOU THE WRONG WAY.
HEH, HEH. I'LL THINK ABOUT IT.
REIICHI SAKAKUSA-SAN!

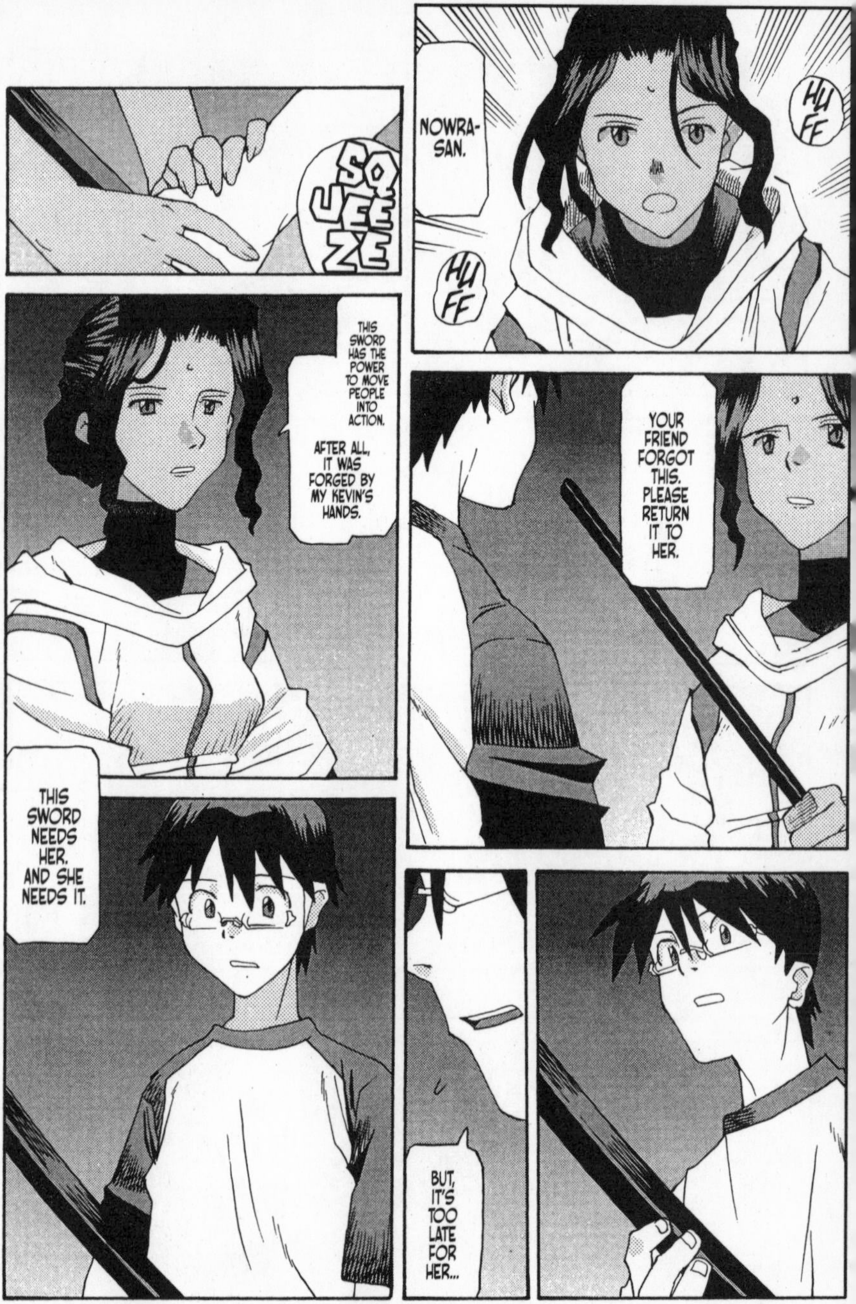
HUFF
NOWRA-SAN.
HUFF
SQUEEZE
YOUR FRIEND FORGOT THIS. PLEASE RETURN IT TO HER.
THIS SWORD HAS THE POWER TO MOVE PEOPLE INTO ACTION.
AFTER ALL, IT WAS FORGED BY MY KEVIN'S HANDS.
THIS SWORD NEEDS HER. AND SHE NEEDS IT.
BUT, IT'S TOO LATE FOR HER...

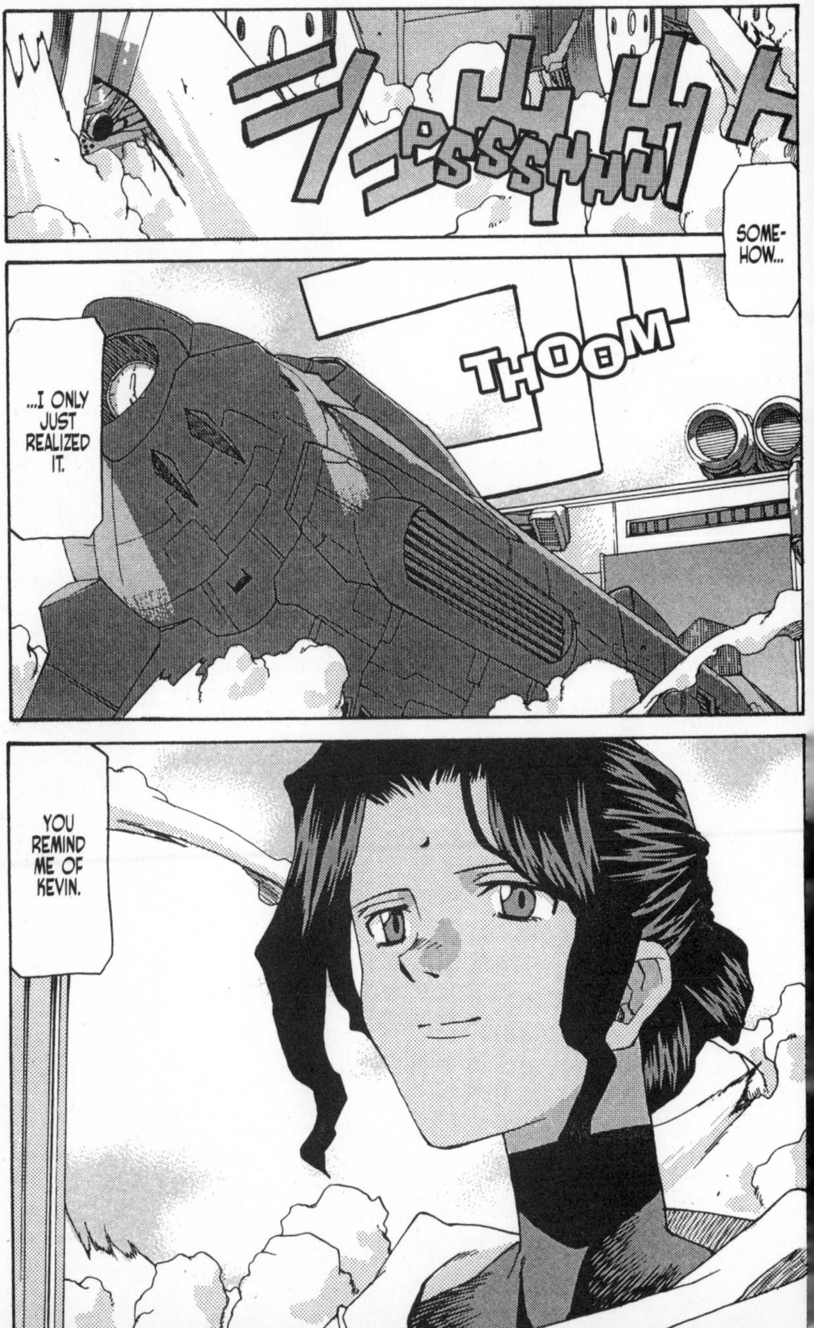
PSSSHHH!
SOME-HOW...
THOOOM
...I ONLY JUST REALIZED IT.
YOU REMIND ME OF KEVIN.

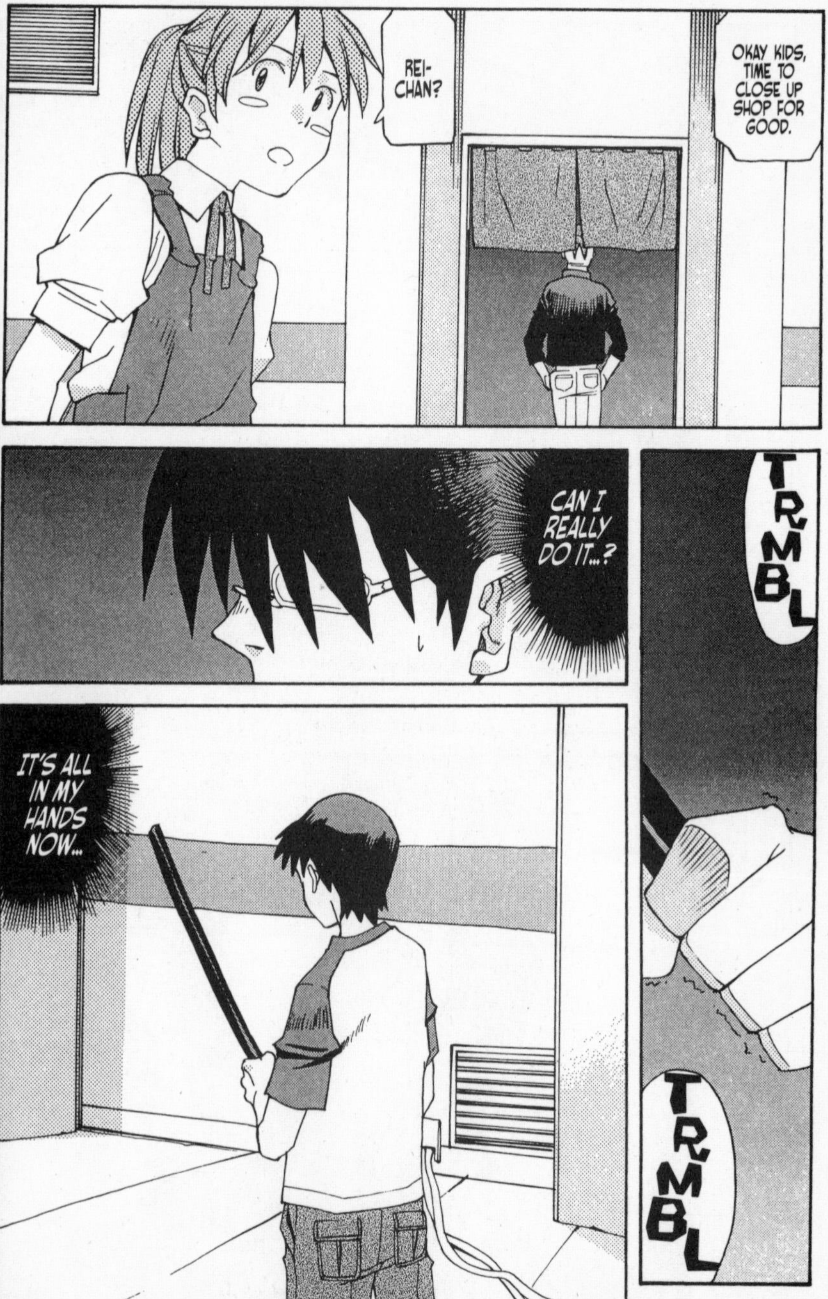
OKAY KIDS, TIME TO CLOSE UP SHOP FOR GOOD.
REI-CHAN?
TRMBL
CAN I REALLY DO IT...?
TRMBL
IT'S ALL IN MY HANDS NOW...

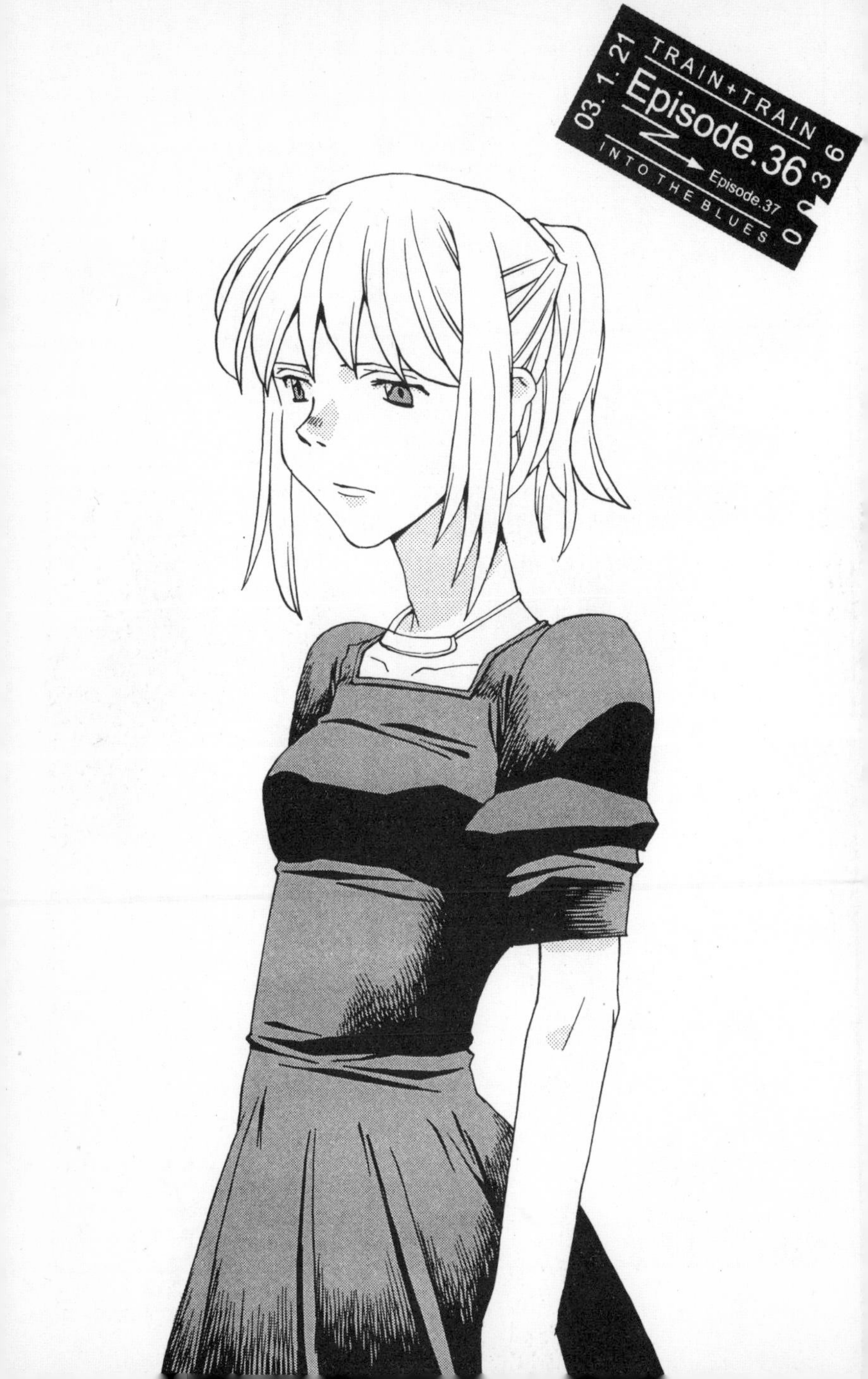
03. 1. 21
TRAIN+TRAIN
Episode.36
Episode.37
INTO THE BLUES
036

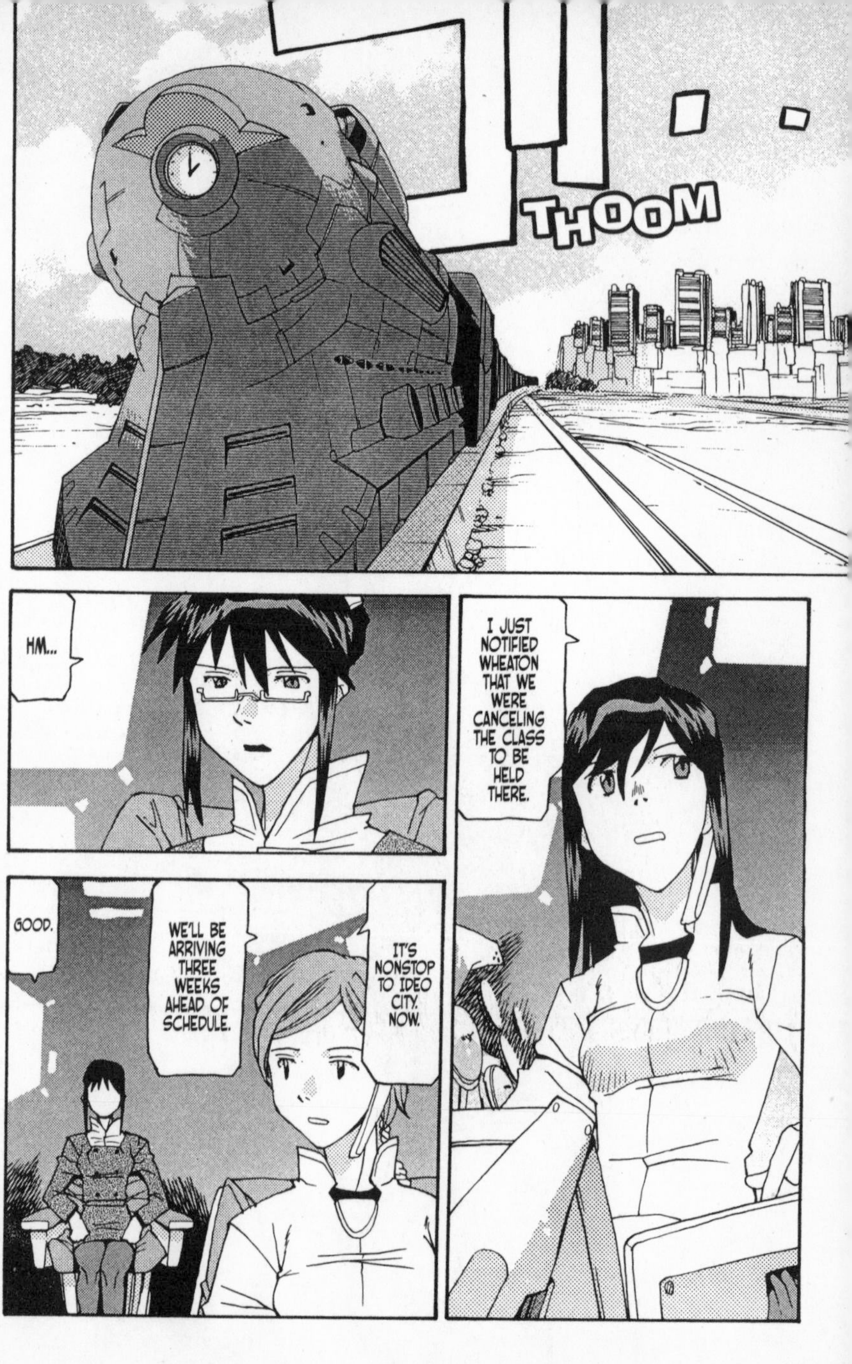
THOOM
I JUST NOTIFIED WHEATON THAT WE WERE CANCELING THE CLASS TO BE HELD THERE.
HM...
IT'S NONSTOP TO IDEO CITY. NOW.
WE'LL BE ARRIVING THREE WEEKS AHEAD OF SCHEDULE.
GOOD.

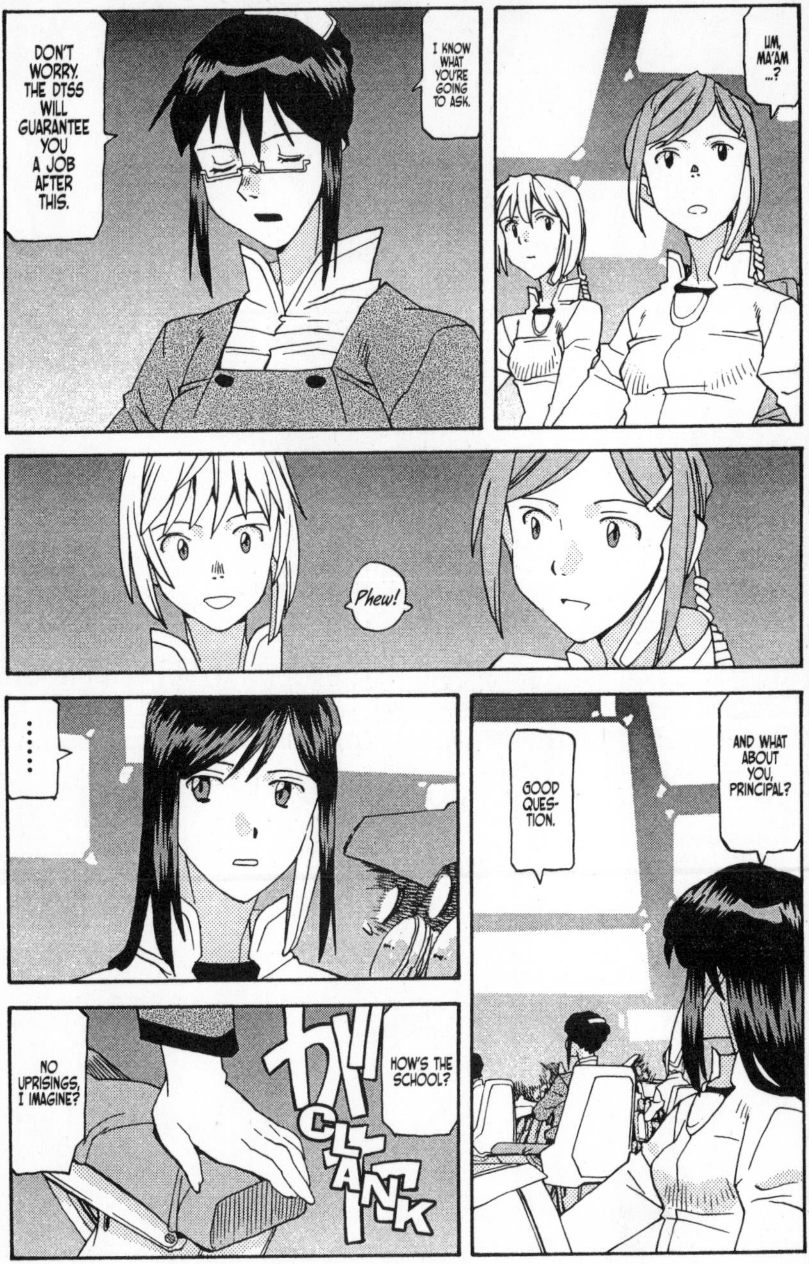
UM, MA'AM ...?
I KNOW WHAT YOU'RE GOING TO ASK.
DON'T WORRY. THE DTSS WILL GUARANTEE YOU A JOB AFTER THIS.
Phew!
AND WHAT ABOUT YOU, PRINCIPAL?
GOOD QUESTION.
......
CLANK
HOW'S THE SCHOOL?
NO UPRISINGS, I IMAGINE?

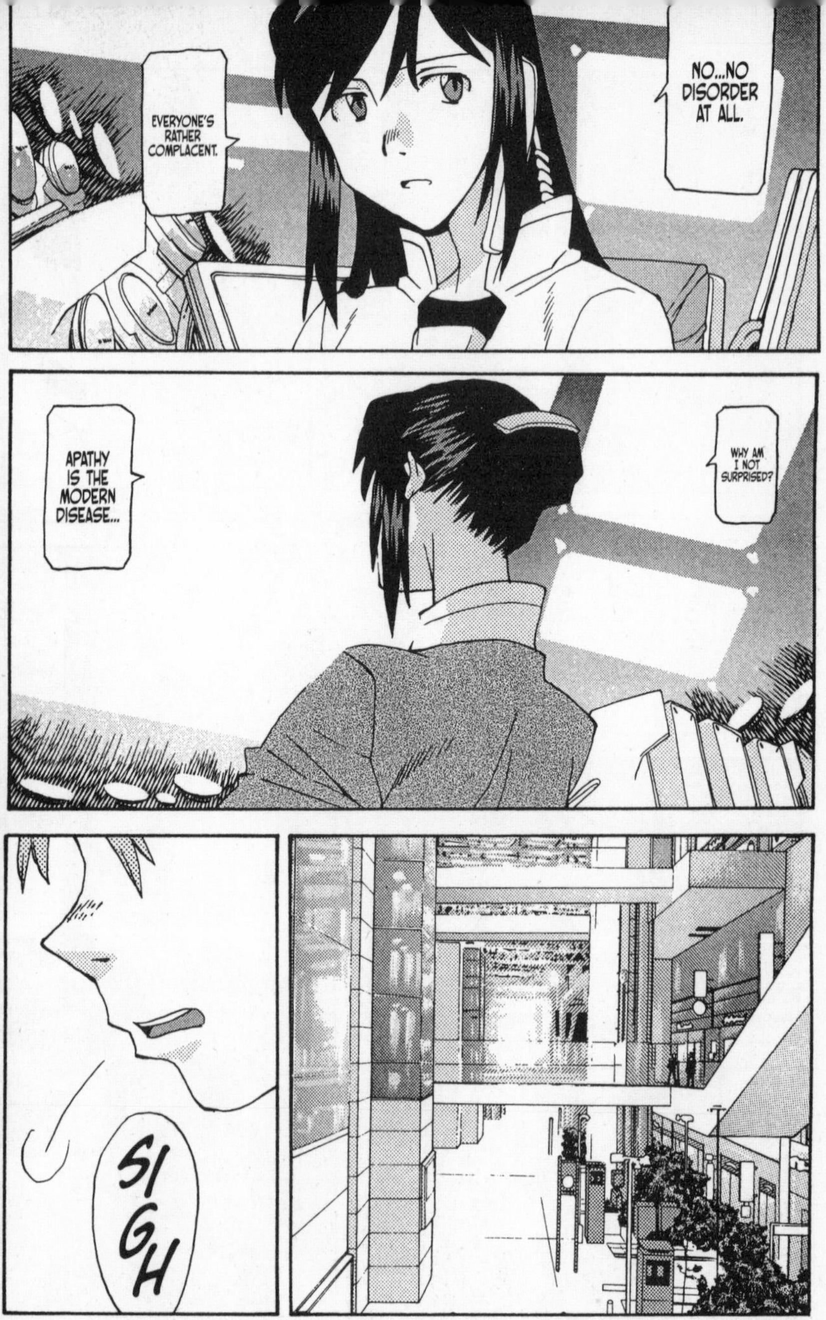
NO...NO DISORDER AT ALL.
EVERYONE'S RATHER COMPLACENT.
WHY AM I NOT SURPRISED?
APATHY IS THE MODERN DISEASE...
SIGH

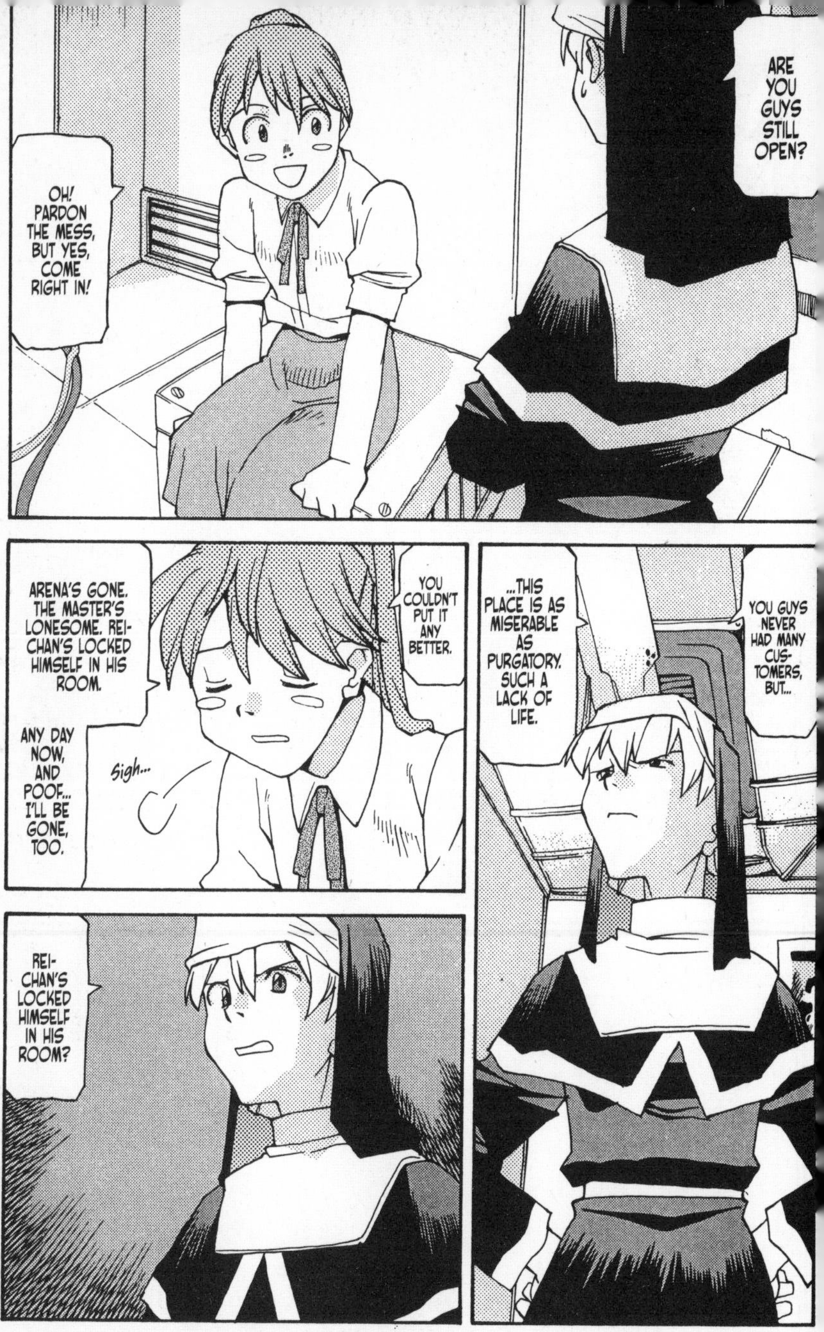
ARE YOU GUYS STILL OPEN?
OH! PARDON THE MESS, BUT YES, COME RIGHT IN!
YOU GUYS NEVER HAD MANY CUS-TOMERS, BUT...
...THIS PLACE IS AS MISERABLE AS PURGATORY. SUCH A LACK OF LIFE.
YOU COULDN'T PUT IT ANY BETTER.
ARENA'S GONE. THE MASTER'S LONESOME. REI-CHAN'S LOCKED HIMSELF IN HIS ROOM.
Sigh...
ANY DAY NOW, AND POOF... I'LL BE GONE, TOO.
REI-CHAN'S LOCKED HIMSELF IN HIS ROOM?

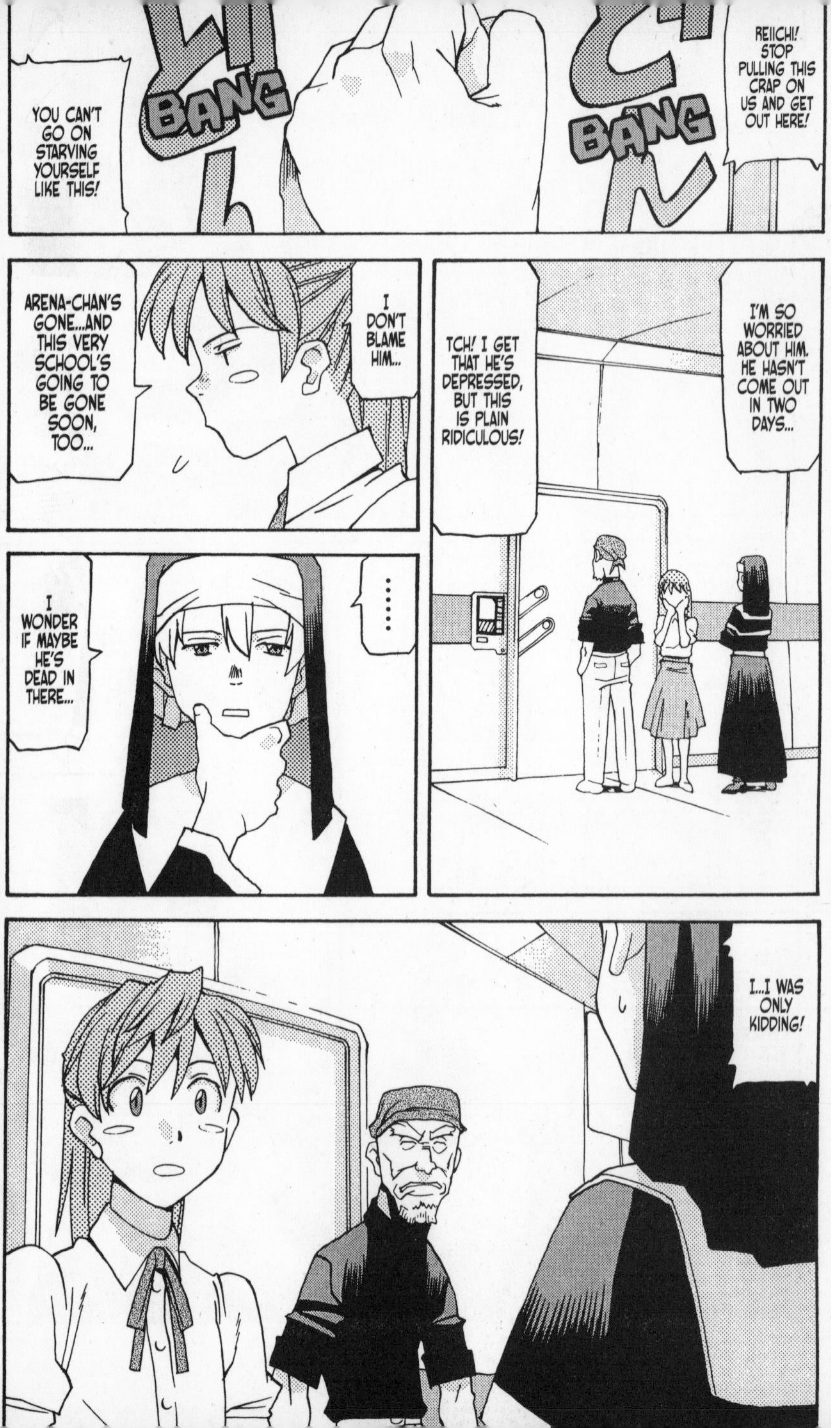

REIICHI! STOP PULLING THIS CRAP ON US AND GET OUT HERE!
BANG
BANG
YOU CAN'T GO ON STARVING YOURSELF LIKE THIS!
I'M SO WORRIED ABOUT HIM. HE HASN'T COME OUT IN TWO DAYS...
TCH! I GET THAT HE'S DEPRESSED, BUT THIS IS PLAIN RIDICULOUS!
I DON'T BLAME HIM...
ARENA-CHAN'S GONE...AND THIS VERY SCHOOL'S GOING TO BE GONE SOON, TOO...
......
I WONDER IF MAYBE HE'S DEAD IN THERE...
I...I WAS ONLY KIDDING!

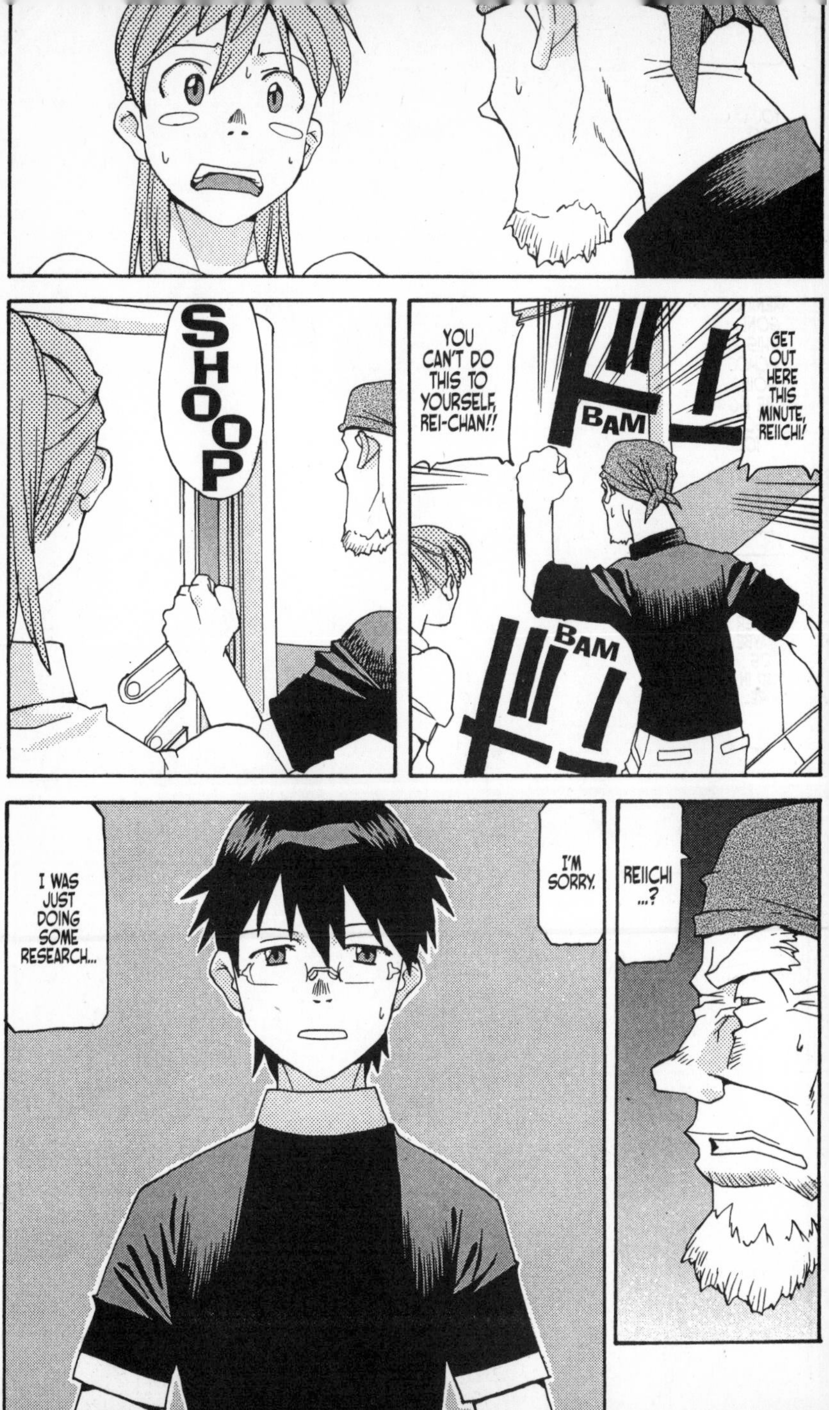
GET OUT HERE THIS MINUTE, REIICHI!
BAM
YOU CAN'T DO THIS TO YOURSELF, REI-CHAN!!
BAM
SHOOP
REIICHI ...?
I'M SORRY.
I WAS JUST DOING SOME RESEARCH...

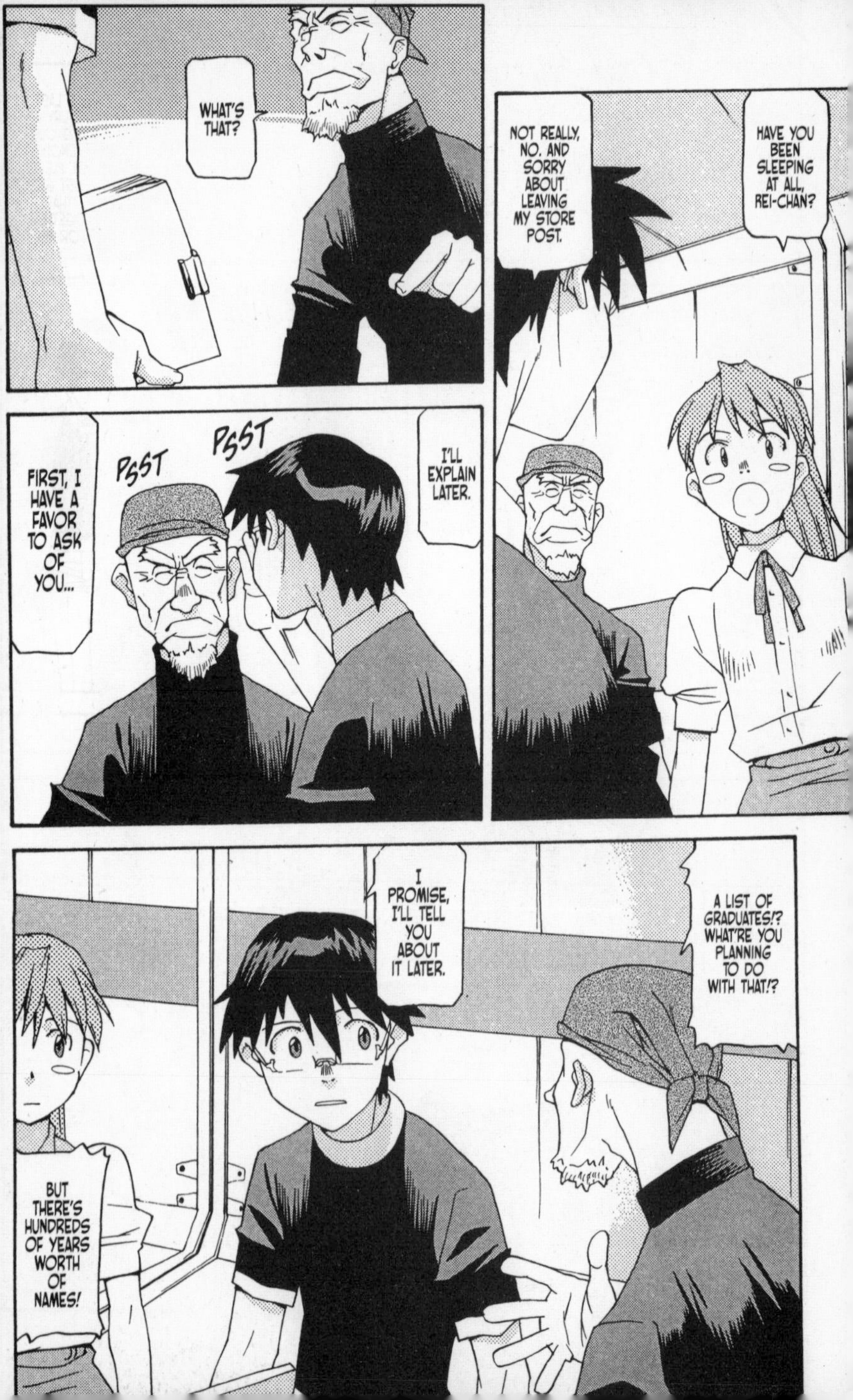
HAVE YOU BEEN SLEEPING AT ALL, REI-CHAN?
NOT REALLY, NO. AND SORRY ABOUT LEAVING MY STORE POST.
WHAT'S THAT?
I'LL EXPLAIN LATER.
PSST
PSST
FIRST, I HAVE A FAVOR TO ASK OF YOU...
A LIST OF GRADUATES!? WHAT'RE YOU PLANNING TO DO WITH THAT!?
I PROMISE, I'LL TELL YOU ABOUT IT LATER.
BUT THERE'S HUNDREDS OF YEARS WORTH OF NAMES!

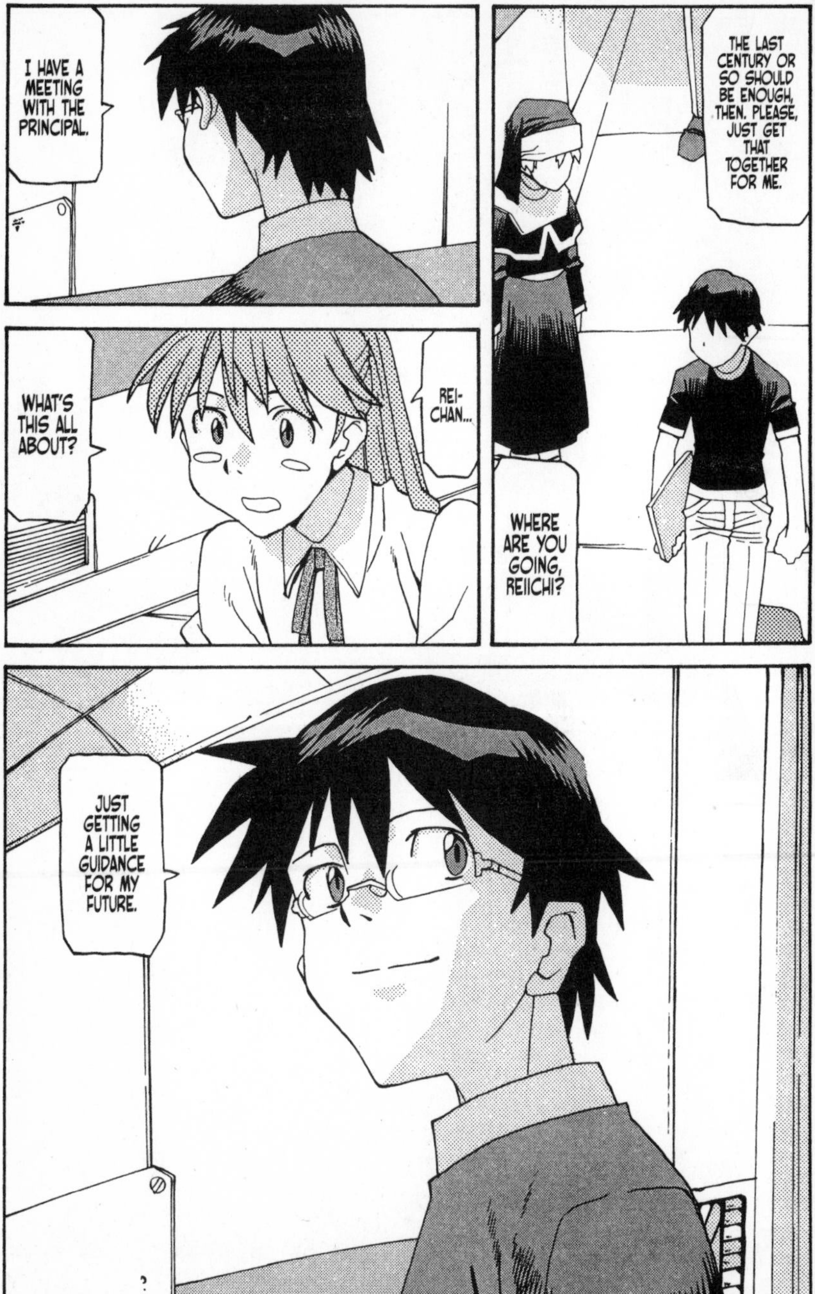
THE LAST CENTURY OR SO SHOULD BE ENOUGH, THEN. PLEASE, JUST GET THAT TOGETHER FOR ME.
WHERE ARE YOU GOING, REIICHI?
I HAVE A MEETING WITH THE PRINCIPAL.
REI-CHAN...
WHAT'S THIS ALL ABOUT?
JUST GETTING A LITTLE GUIDANCE FOR MY FUTURE.

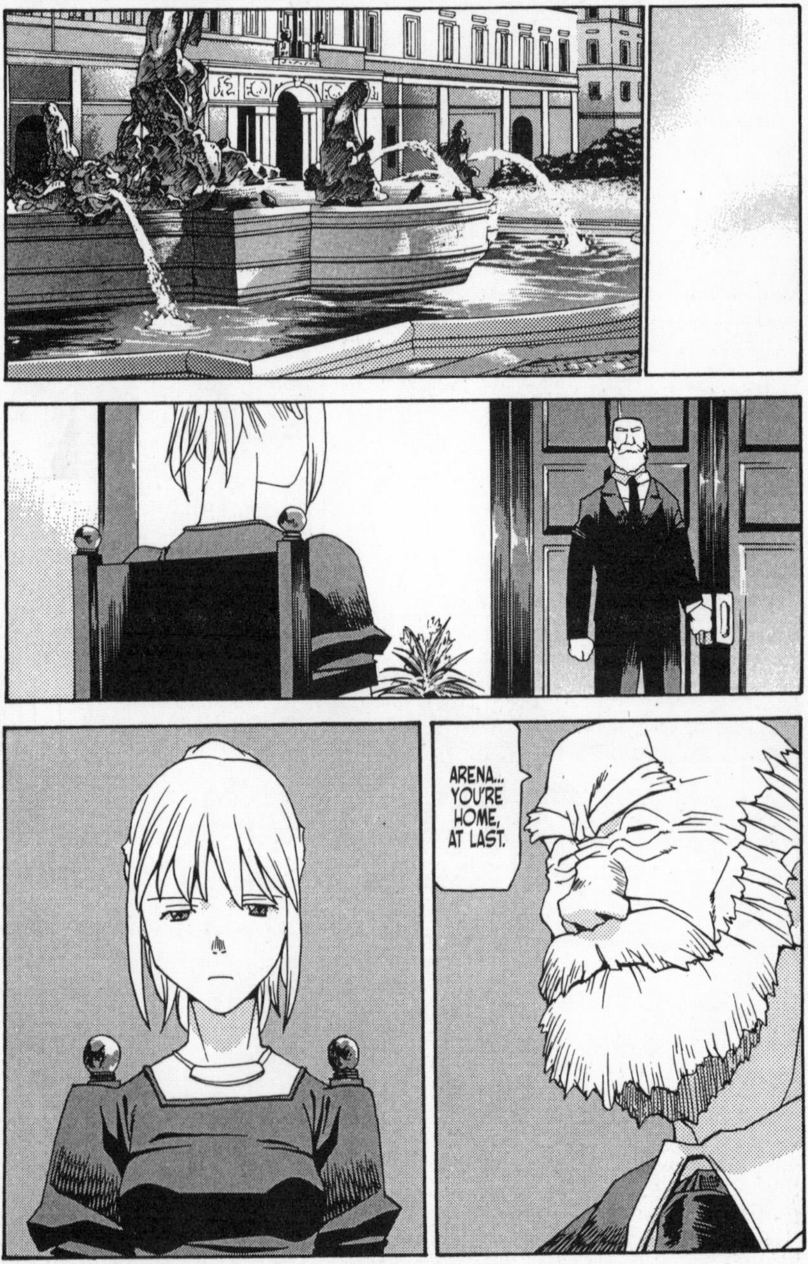
ARENA... YOU'RE HOME, AT LAST.

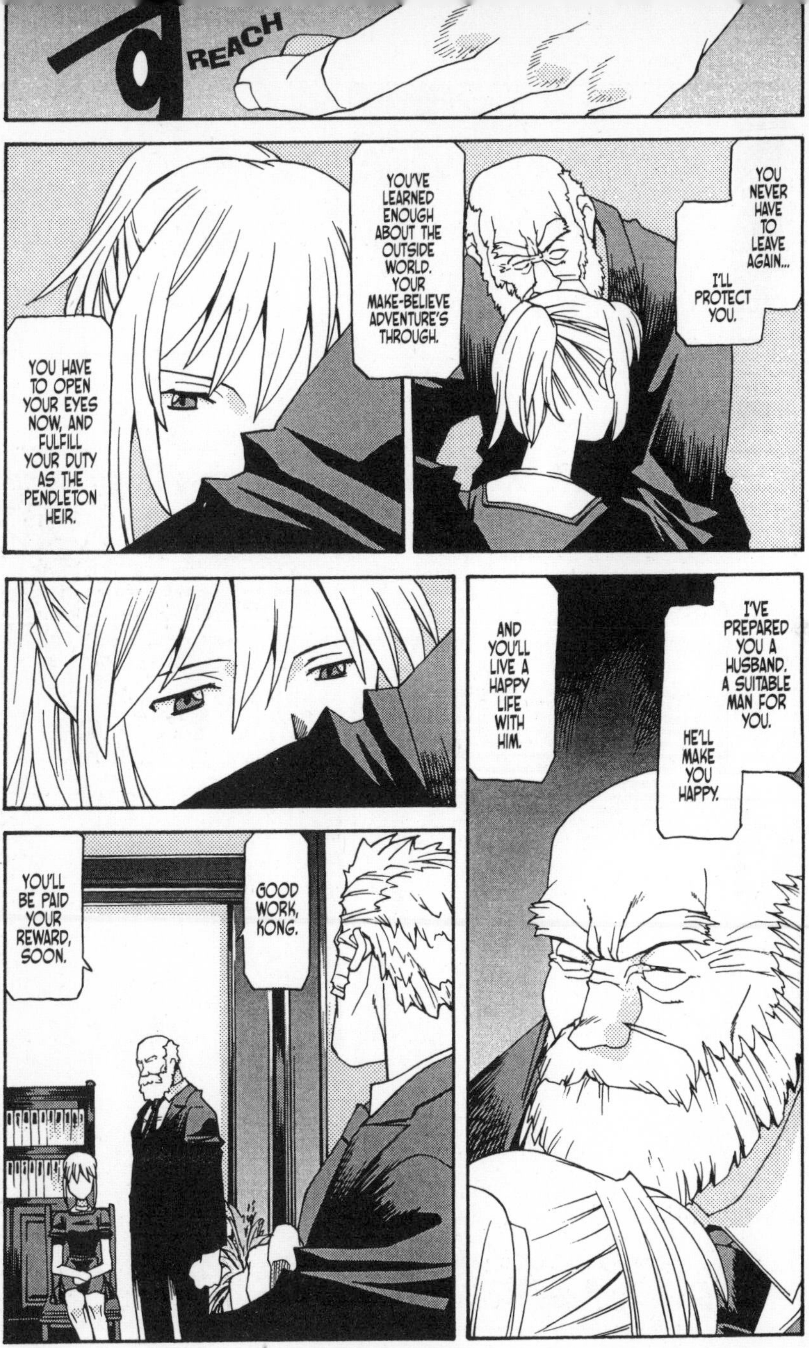
REACH
YOU NEVER HAVE TO LEAVE AGAIN...
I'LL PROTECT YOU.
YOU'VE LEARNED ENOUGH ABOUT THE OUTSIDE WORLD. YOUR MAKE-BELIEVE ADVENTURE'S THROUGH.
YOU HAVE TO OPEN YOUR EYES NOW, AND FULFILL YOUR DUTY AS THE PENDLETON HEIR.
I'VE PREPARED YOU A HUSBAND. A SUITABLE MAN FOR YOU.
HE'LL MAKE YOU HAPPY.
AND YOU'LL LIVE A HAPPY LIFE WITH HIM.
GOOD WORK, KONG.
YOU'LL BE PAID YOUR REWARD, SOON.

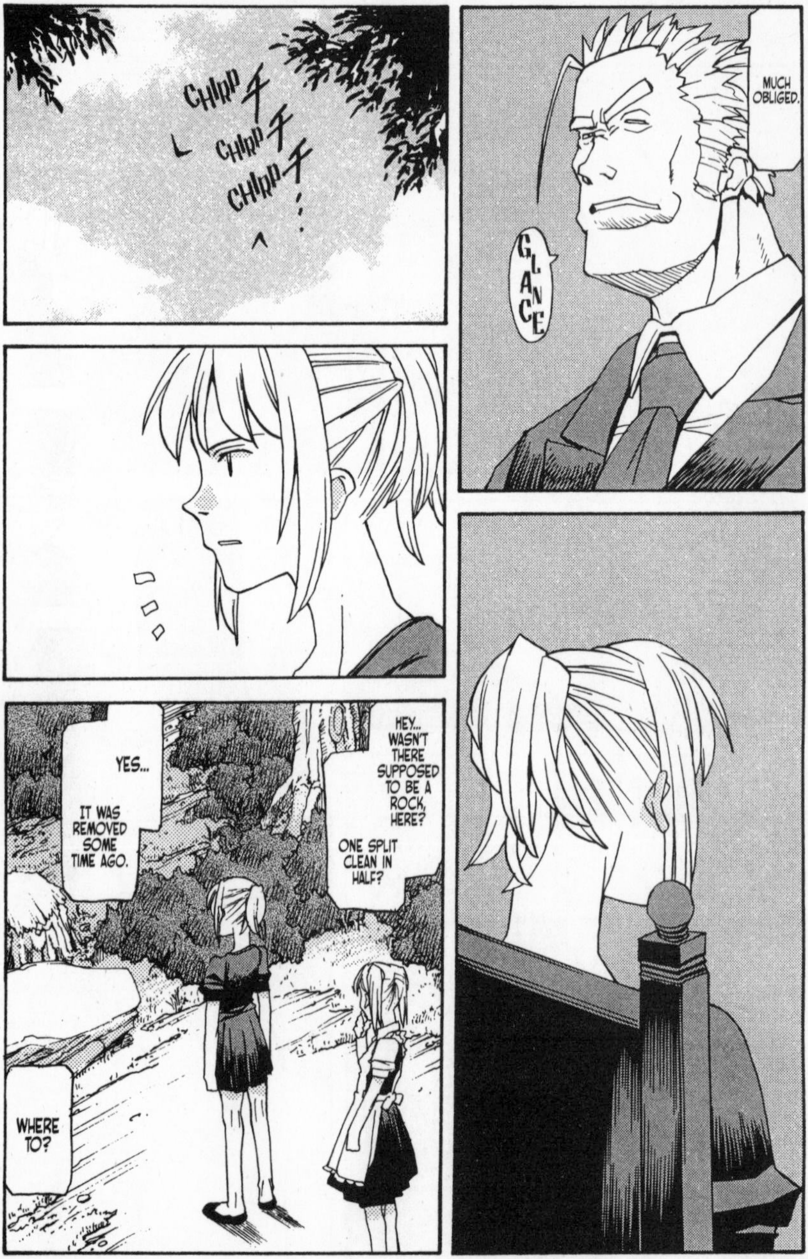
MUCH OBLIGED.
GLANCE
CHIRP CHIRP CHIRP
HEY... WASN'T THERE SUPPOSED TO BE A ROCK, HERE?
ONE SPLIT CLEAN IN HALF?
YES...
IT WAS REMOVED SOME TIME AGO.
WHERE TO?

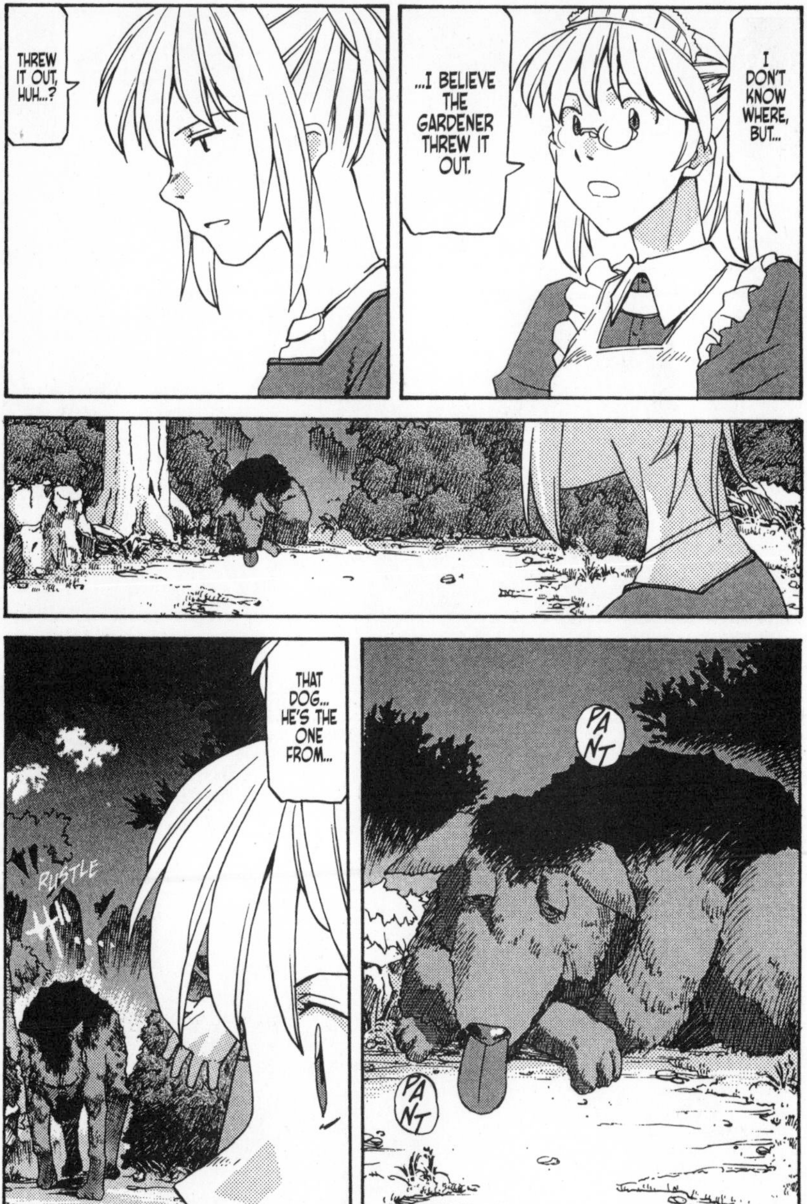
I DON'T KNOW WHERE, BUT...
...I BELIEVE THE GARDENER THREW IT OUT.
THREW IT OUT, HUH...?
PANT
PANT
THAT DOG... HE'S THE ONE FROM...
RUSTLE

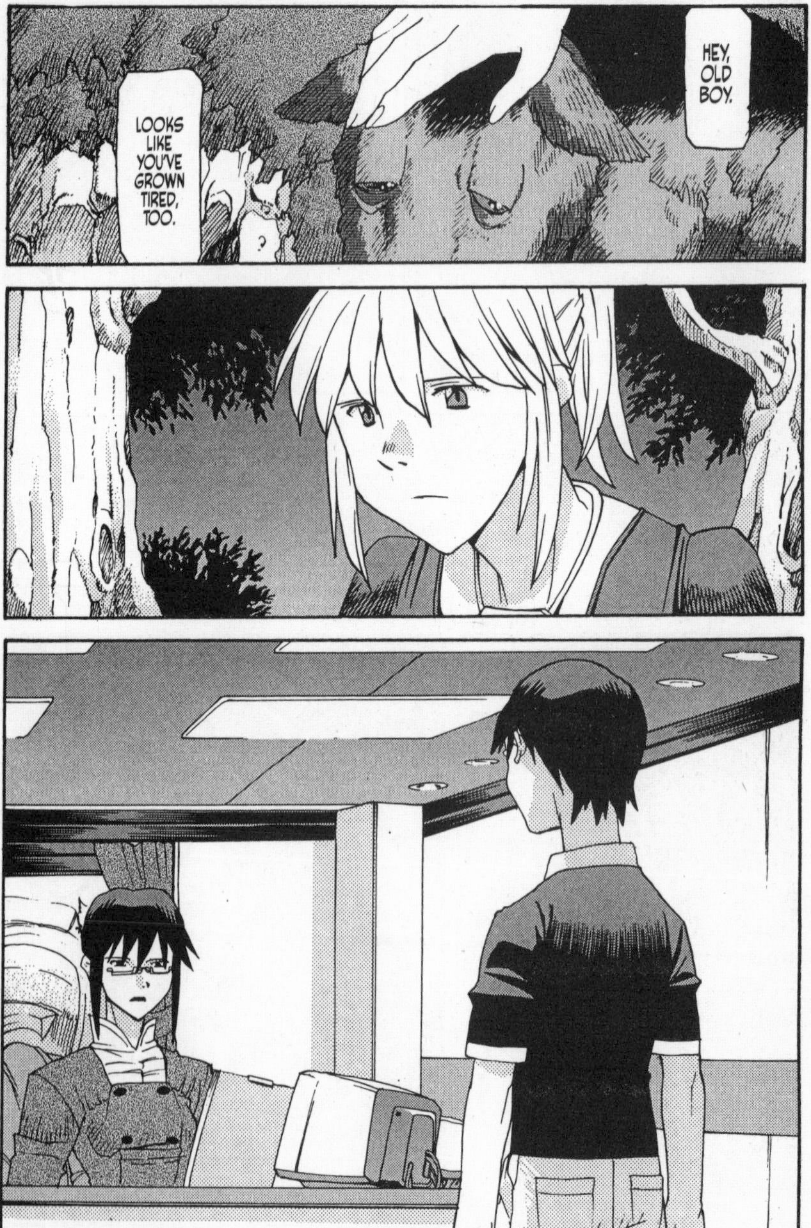
HEY, OLD BOY.
LOOKS LIKE YOU'VE GROWN TIRED, TOO.

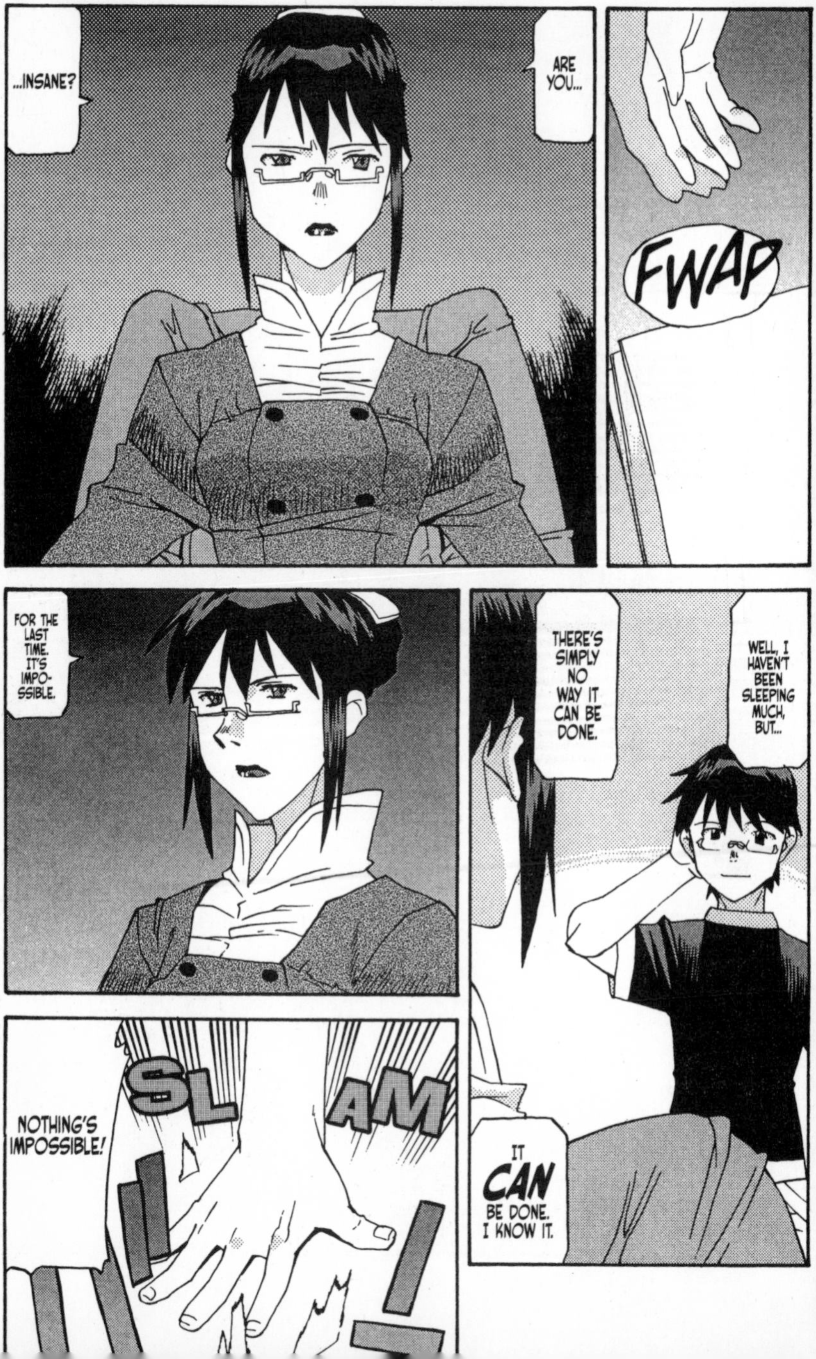
FWAP
ARE YOU...
...INSANE?
WELL, I HAVEN'T BEEN SLEEPING MUCH, BUT...
THERE'S SIMPLY NO WAY IT CAN BE DONE.
IT CAN BE DONE. I KNOW IT.
FOR THE LAST TIME. IT'S IMPO-SSIBLE.
SLAM
NOTHING'S IMPOSSIBLE!

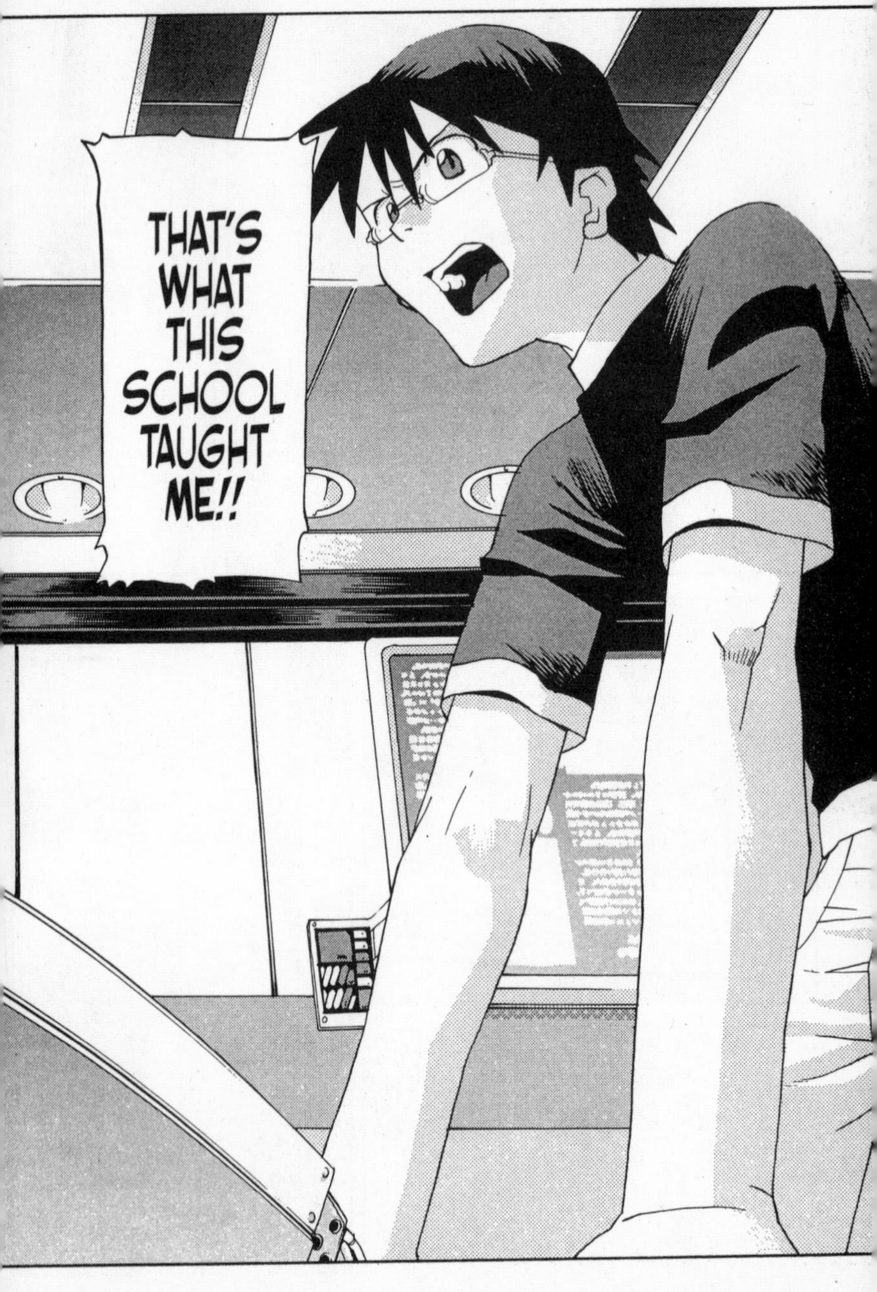
THAT'S WHAT THIS SCHOOL TAUGHT ME!!

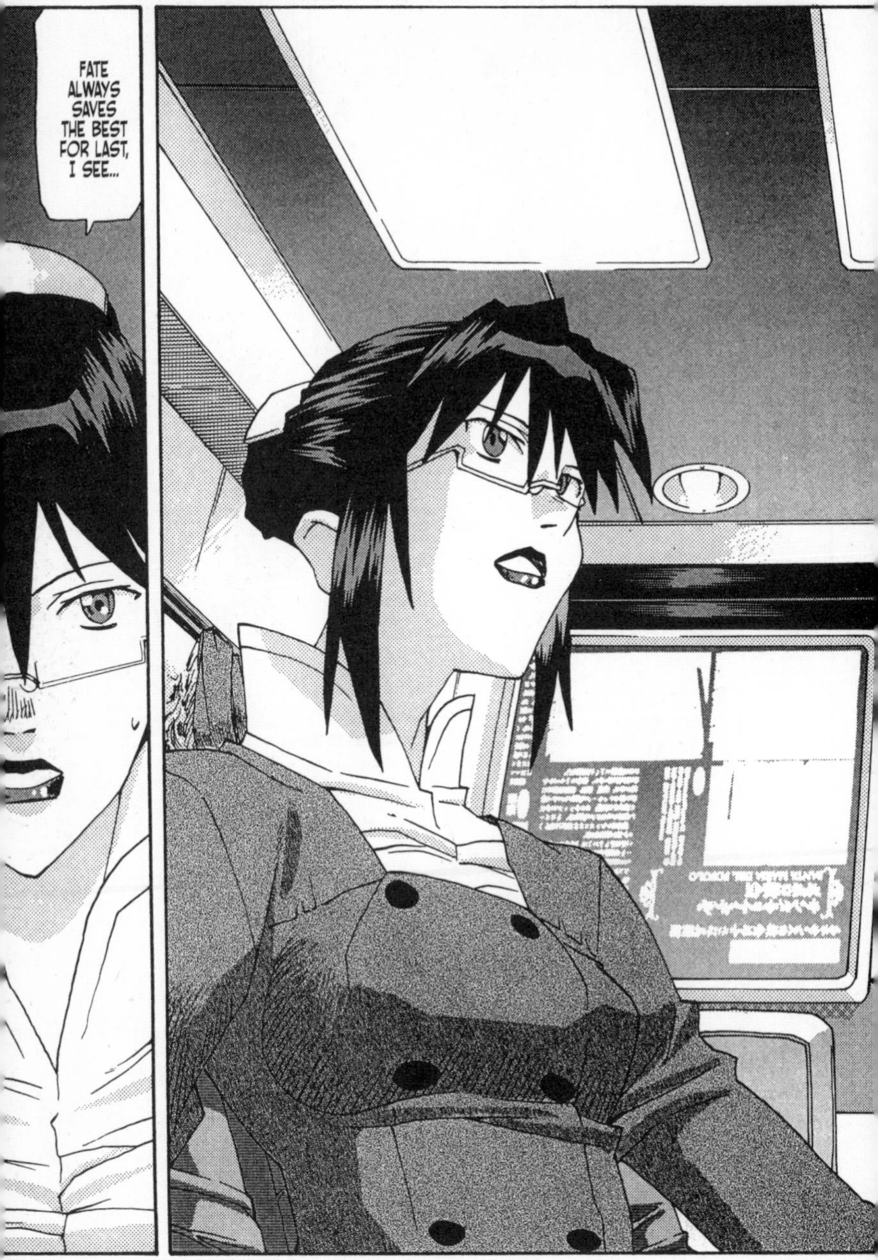
FATE ALWAYS SAVES THE BEST FOR LAST, I SEE...

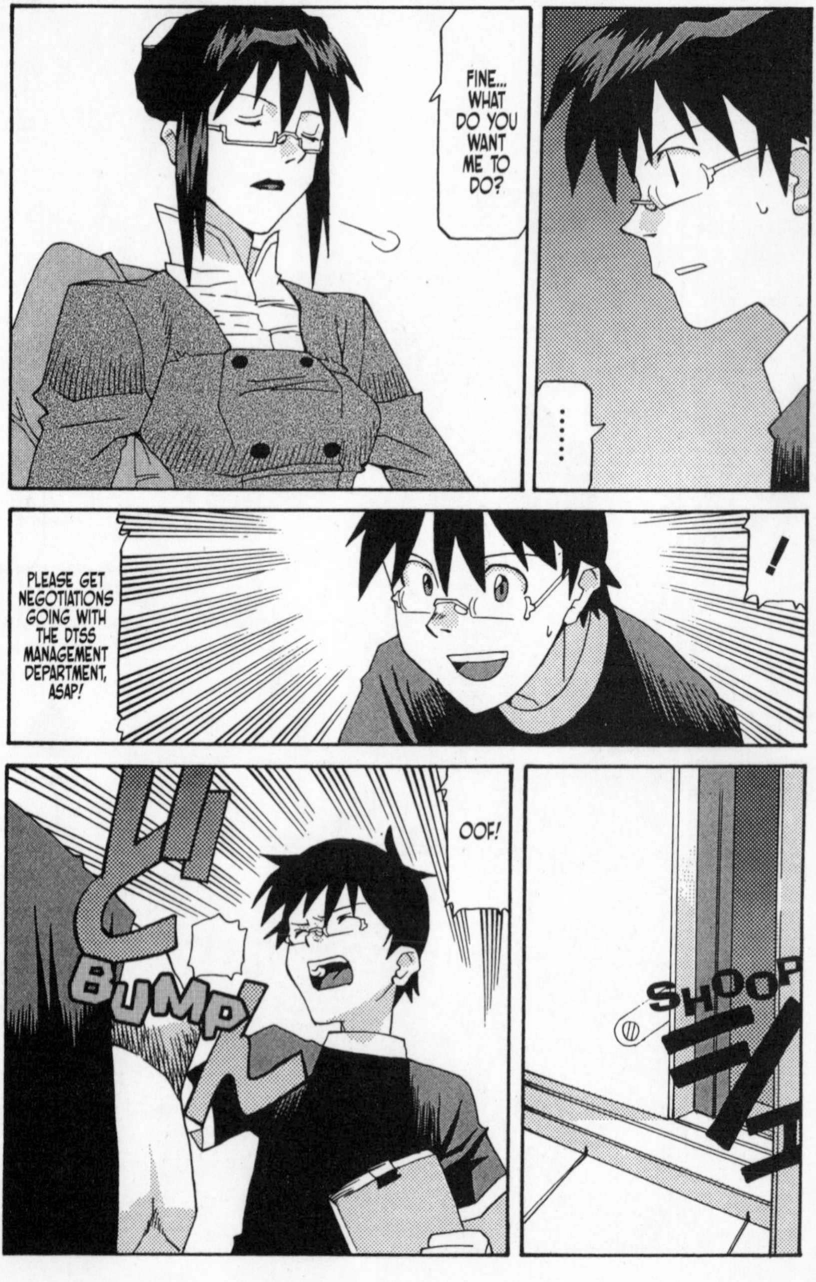
……
FINE... WHAT DO YOU WANT ME TO DO?
!
PLEASE GET NEGOTIATIONS GOING WITH THE DTSS MANAGEMENT DEPARTMENT, ASAP!
SHOOP
OOF!
BUMP!

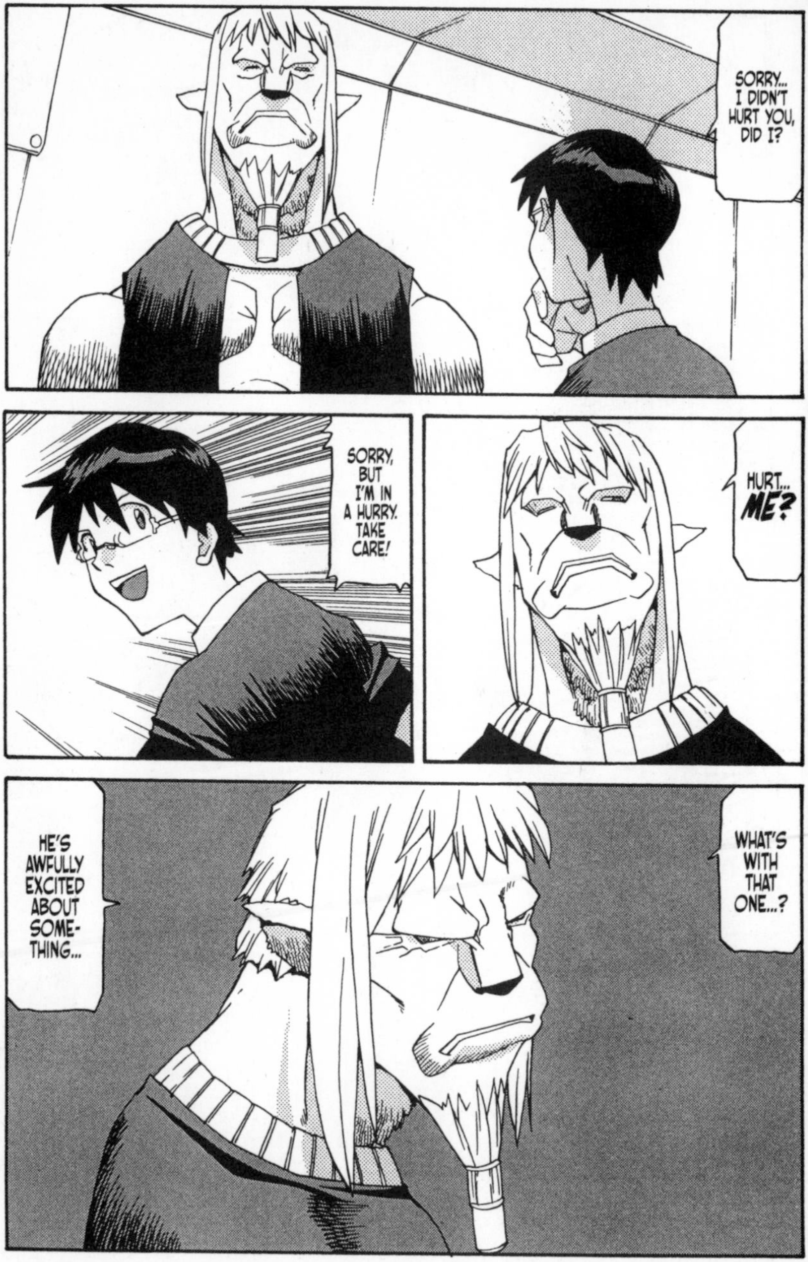
SORRY... I DIDN'T HURT YOU, DID I?
HURT... ***ME?***
SORRY, BUT I'M IN A HURRY. TAKE CARE!
WHAT'S WITH THAT ONE...?
HE'S AWFULLY EXCITED ABOUT SOME-THING...

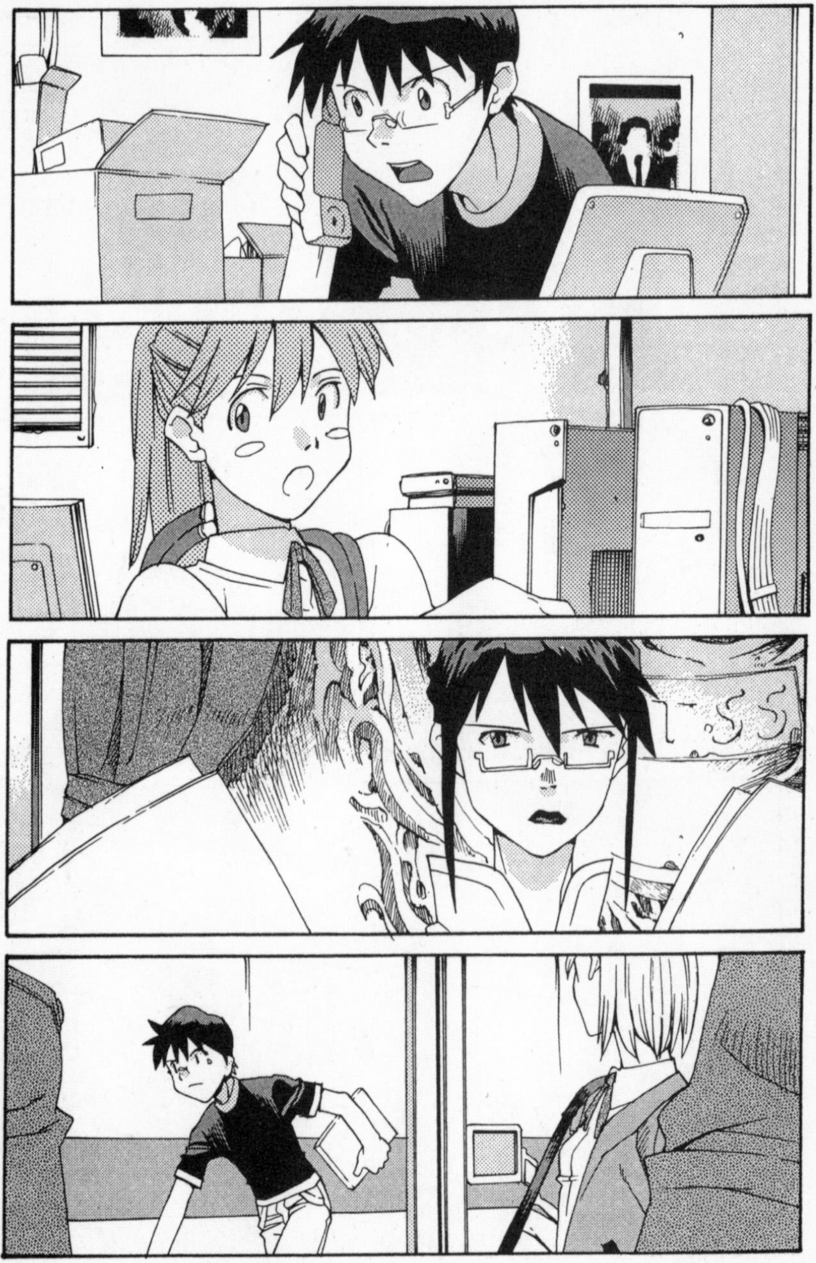

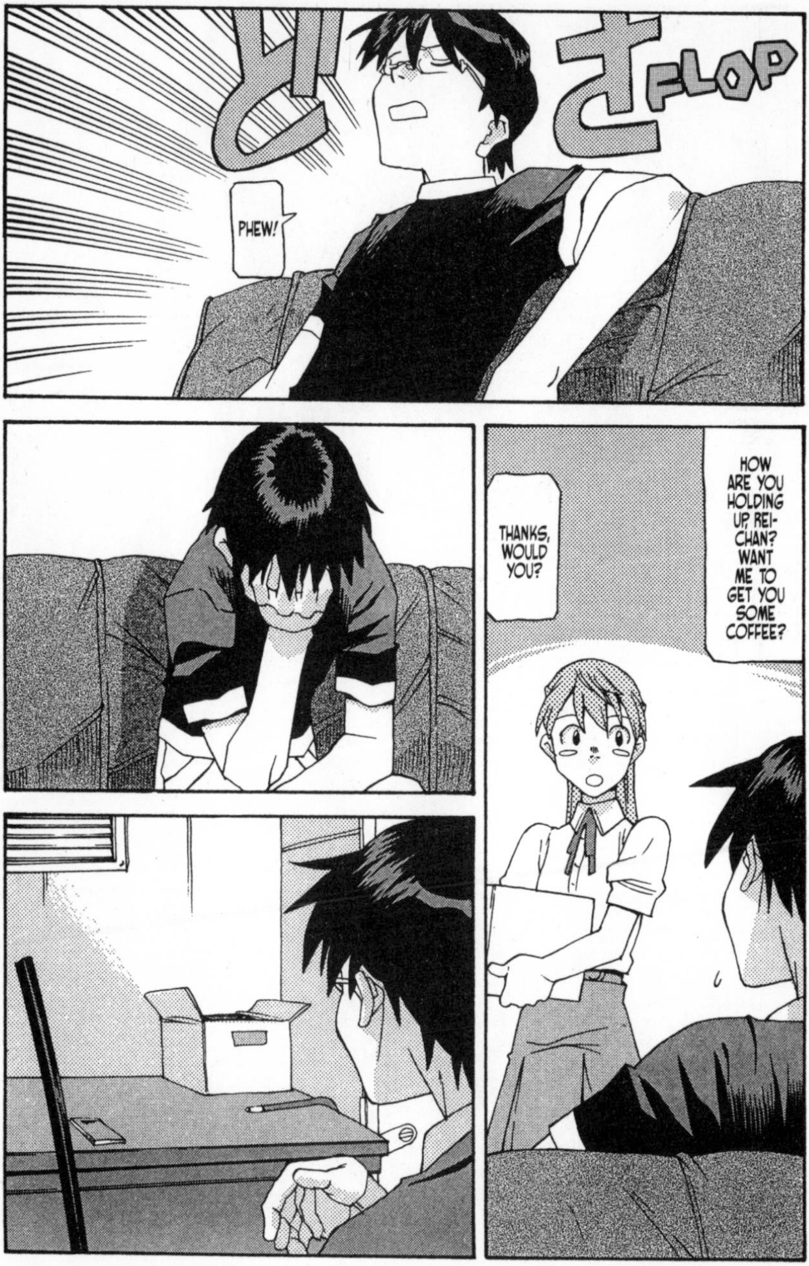
どさ
FLOP
PHEW!
HOW ARE YOU HOLDING UP, REI-CHAN? WANT ME TO GET YOU SOME COFFEE?
THANKS, WOULD YOU?

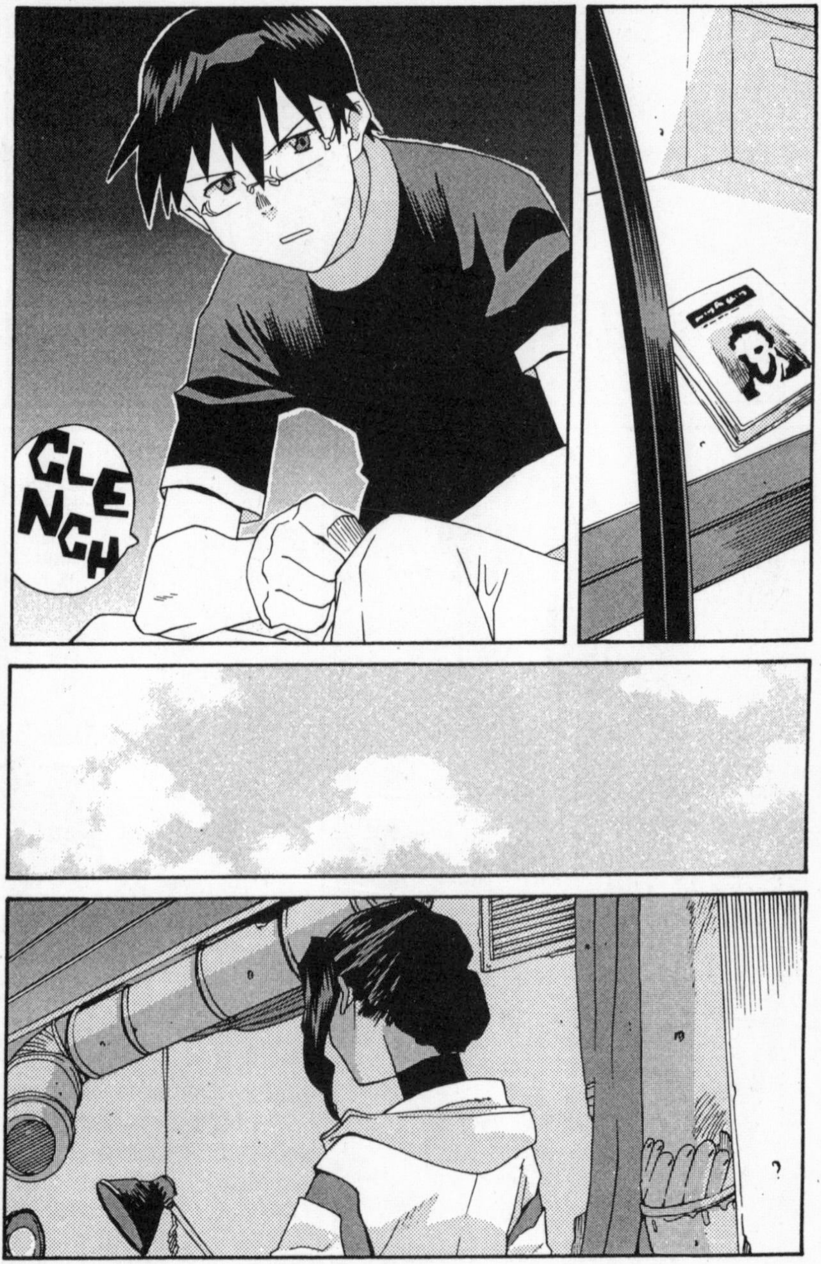
CLENCH

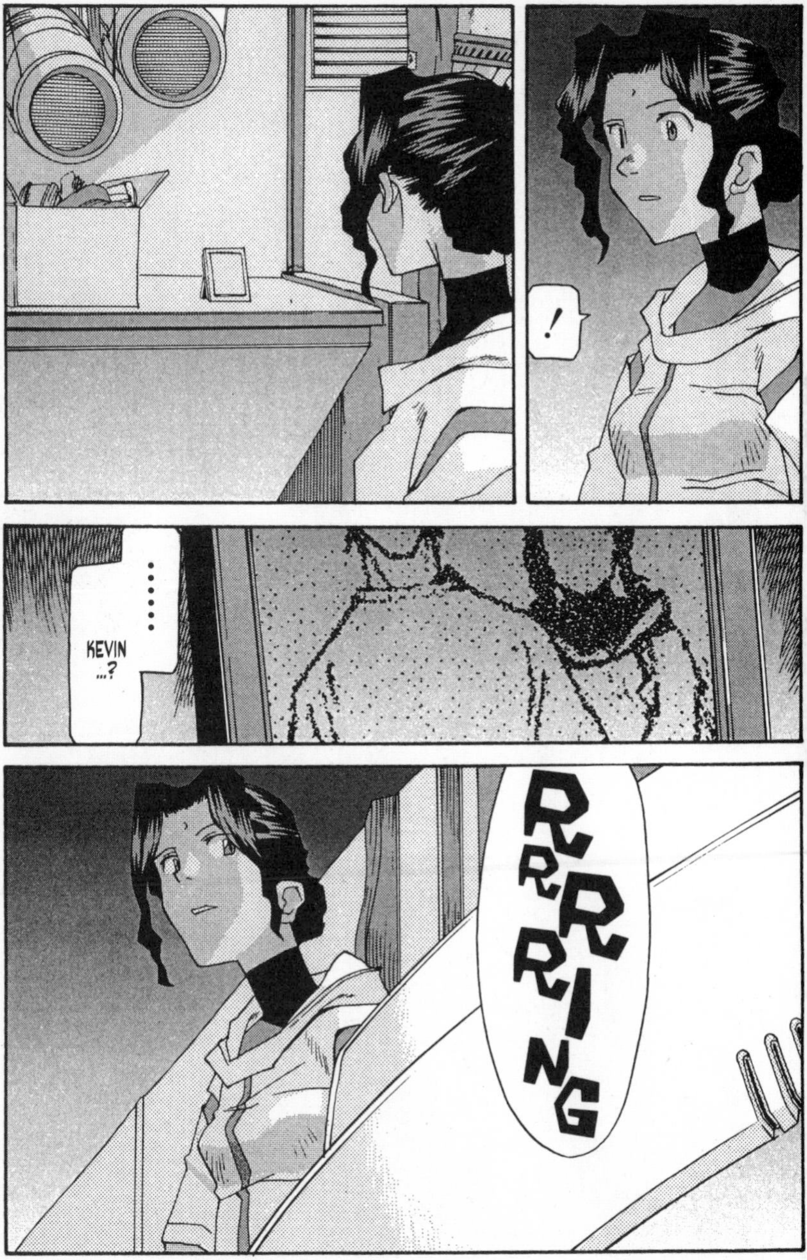
!
......
KEVIN ...?
RRRRRING

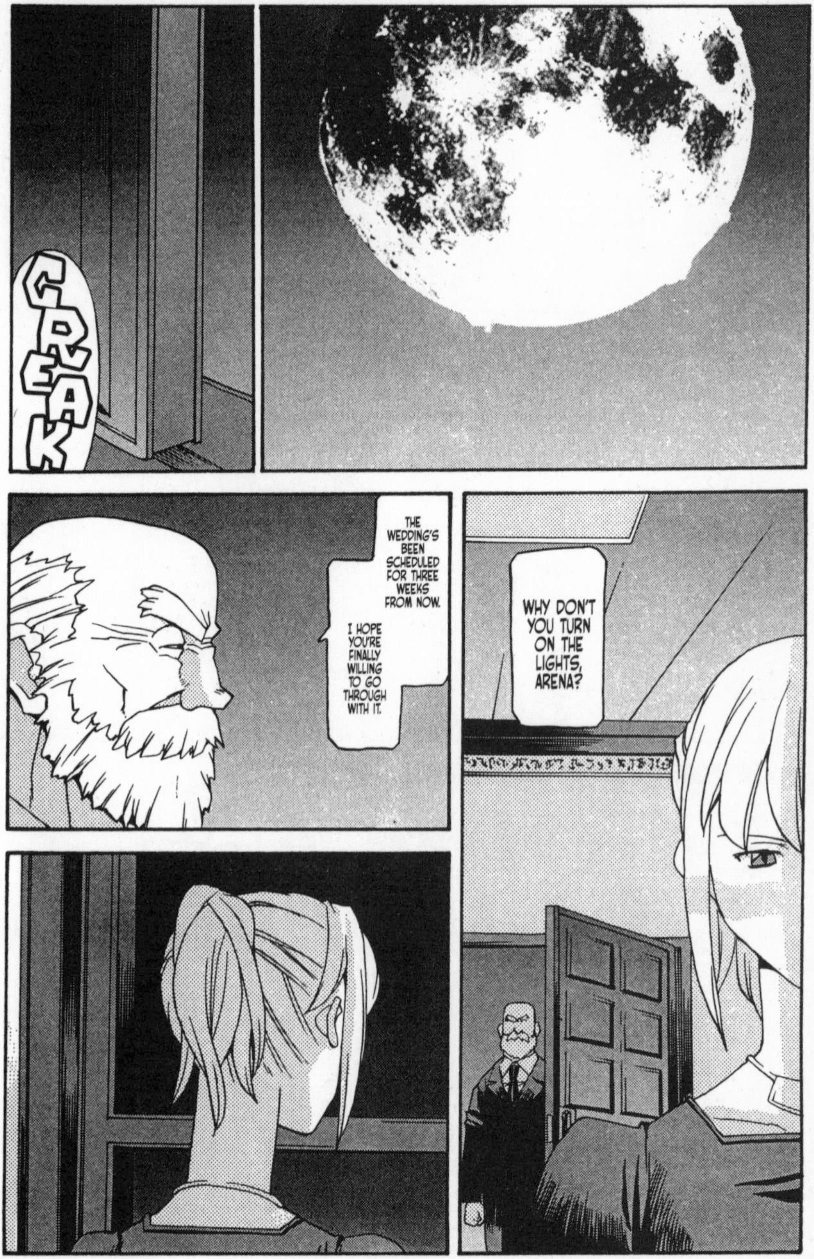
CREAK
WHY DON'T YOU TURN ON THE LIGHTS, ARENA?
THE WEDDING'S BEEN SCHEDULED FOR THREE WEEKS FROM NOW.
I HOPE YOU'RE FINALLY WILLING TO GO THROUGH WITH IT.

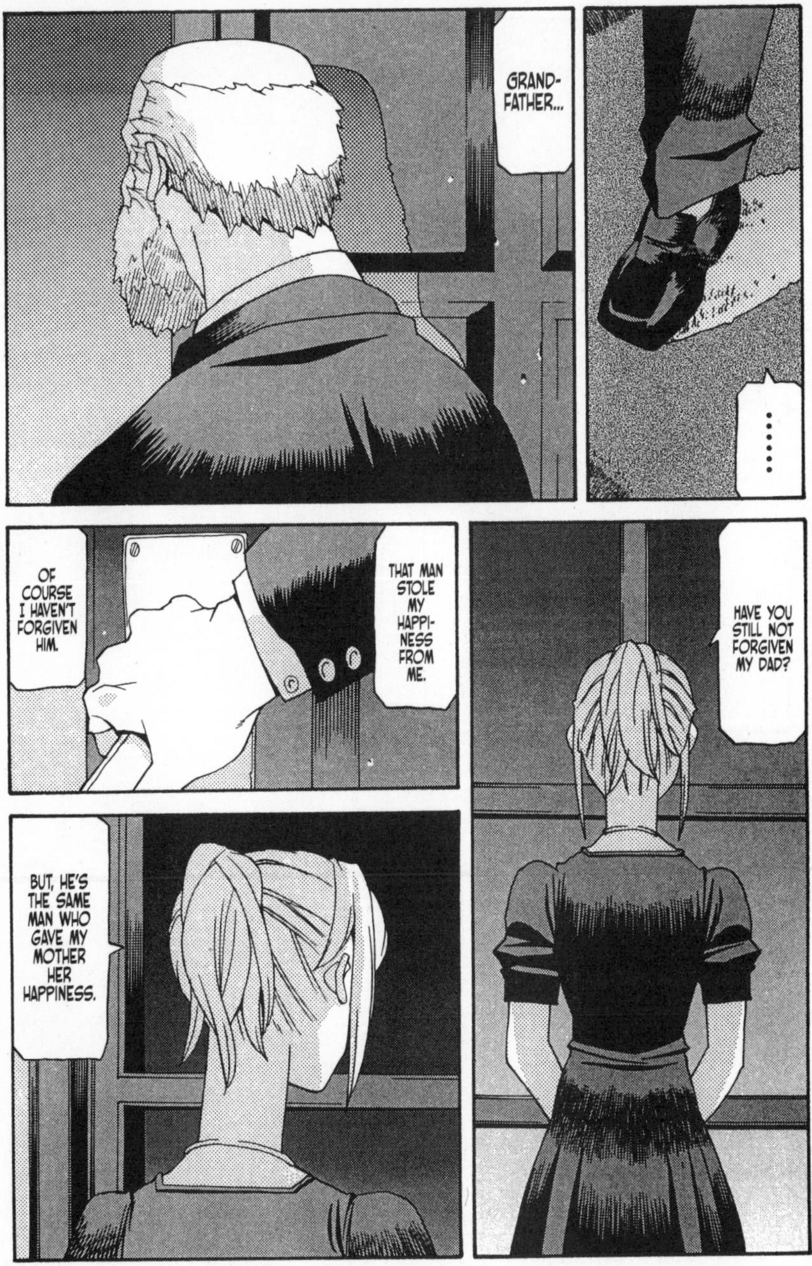
......
GRAND-FATHER...
HAVE YOU STILL NOT FORGIVEN MY DAD?
THAT MAN STOLE MY HAPPI-NESS FROM ME.
OF COURSE I HAVEN'T FORGIVEN HIM.
BUT, HE'S THE SAME MAN WHO GAVE MY MOTHER HER HAPPINESS.

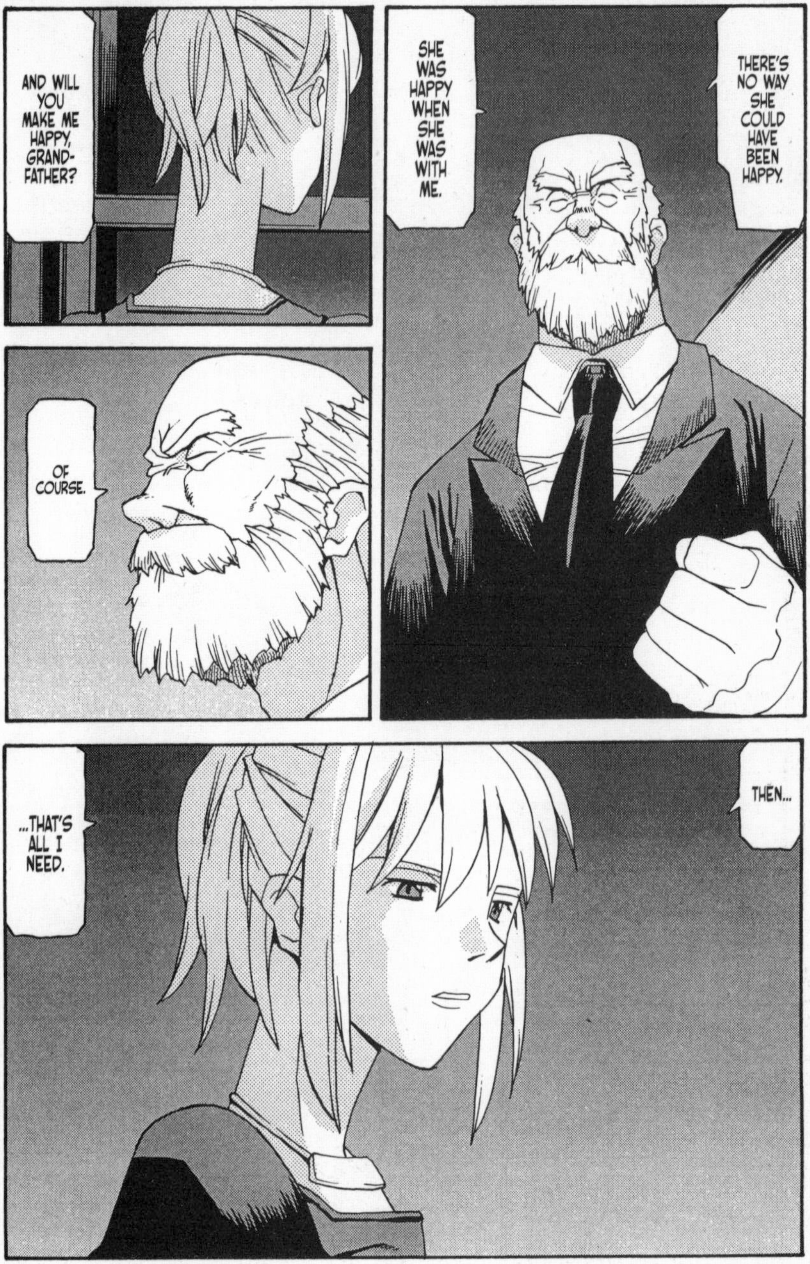
THERE'S NO WAY SHE COULD HAVE BEEN HAPPY.
SHE WAS HAPPY WHEN SHE WAS WITH ME.
AND WILL YOU MAKE ME HAPPY, GRAND-FATHER?
OF COURSE.
THEN...
...THAT'S ALL I NEED.

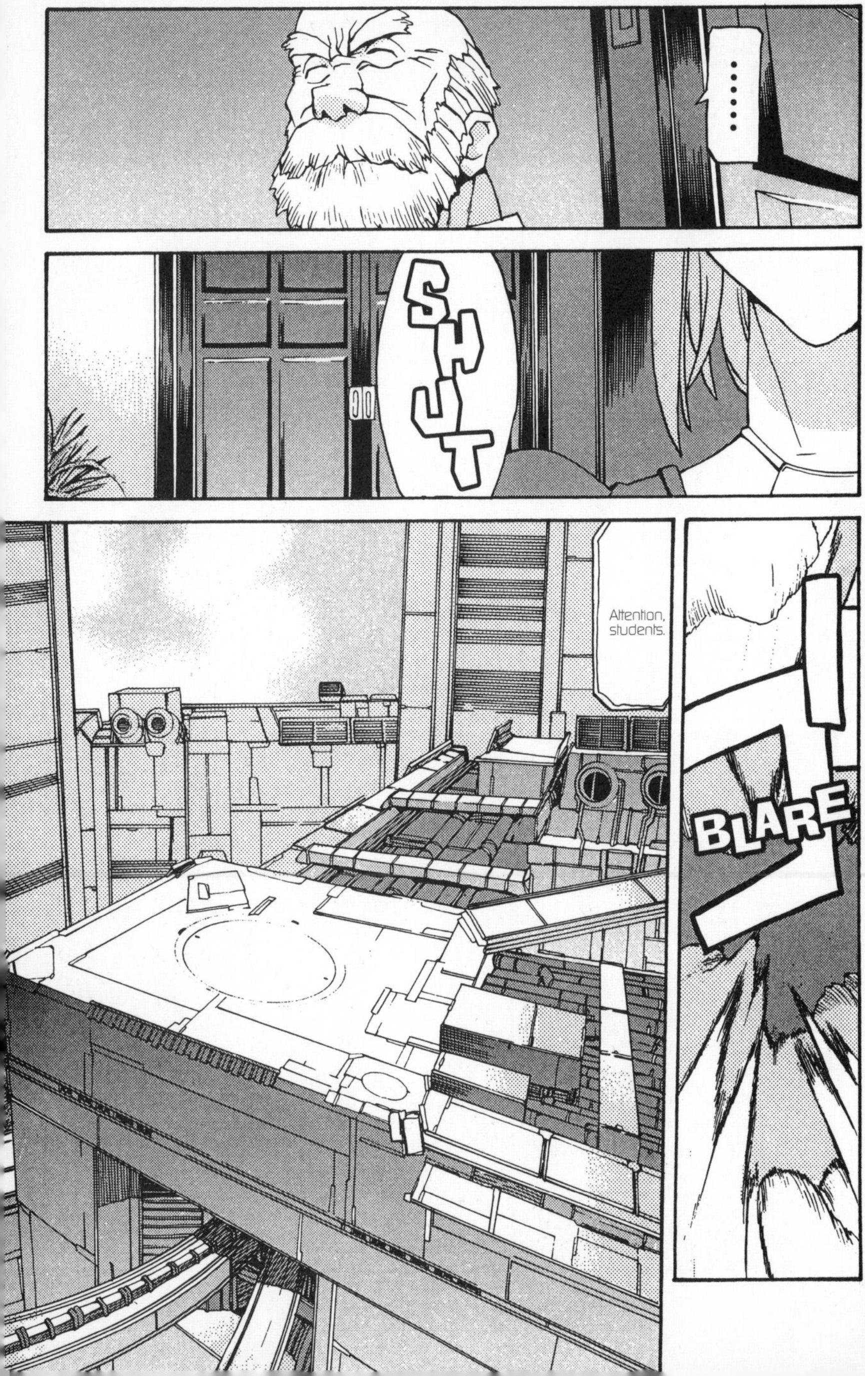
......
SHUT
BLARE
Attention, students.

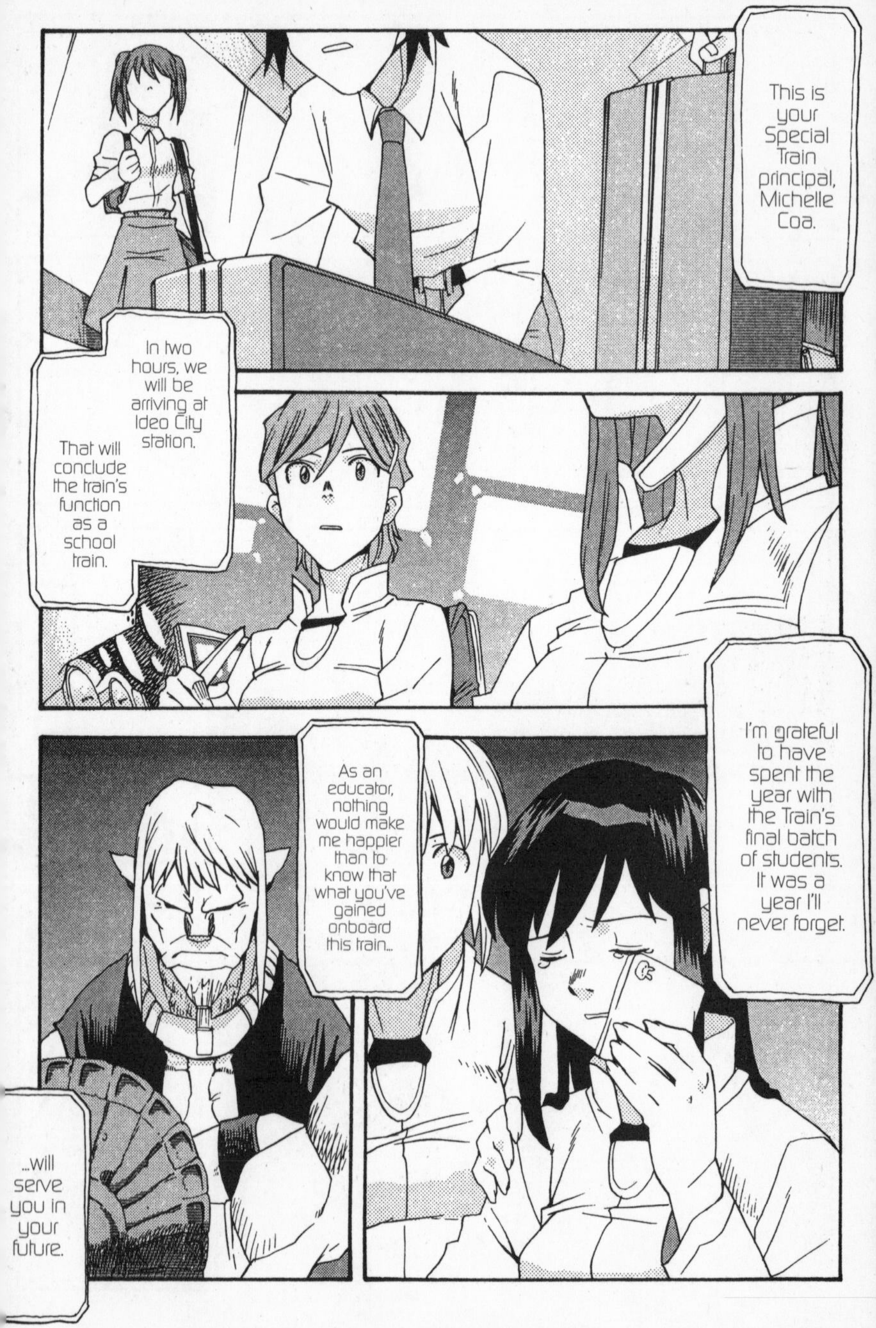
This is your Special Train principal, Michelle Coa.
In two hours, we will be arriving at Ideo City station.
That will conclude the train's function as a school train.
I'm grateful to have spent the year with the Train's final batch of students. It was a year I'll never forget.
As an educator, nothing would make me happier than to know that what you've gained onboard this train...
...will serve you in your future.

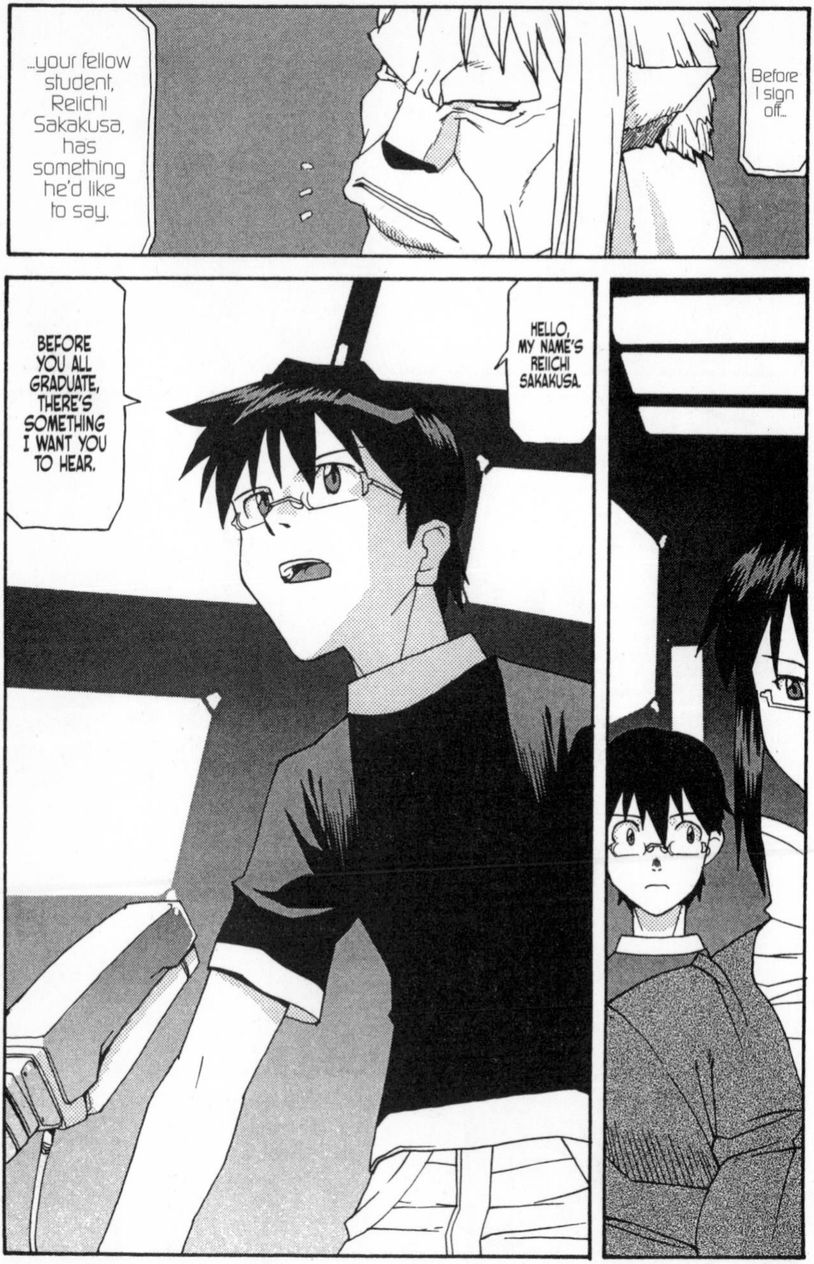
Before I sign off...
...your fellow student, Reiichi Sakakusa, has something he'd like to say.
HELLO, MY NAME'S REIICHI SAKAKUSA.
BEFORE YOU ALL GRADUATE, THERE'S SOMETHING I WANT YOU TO HEAR.

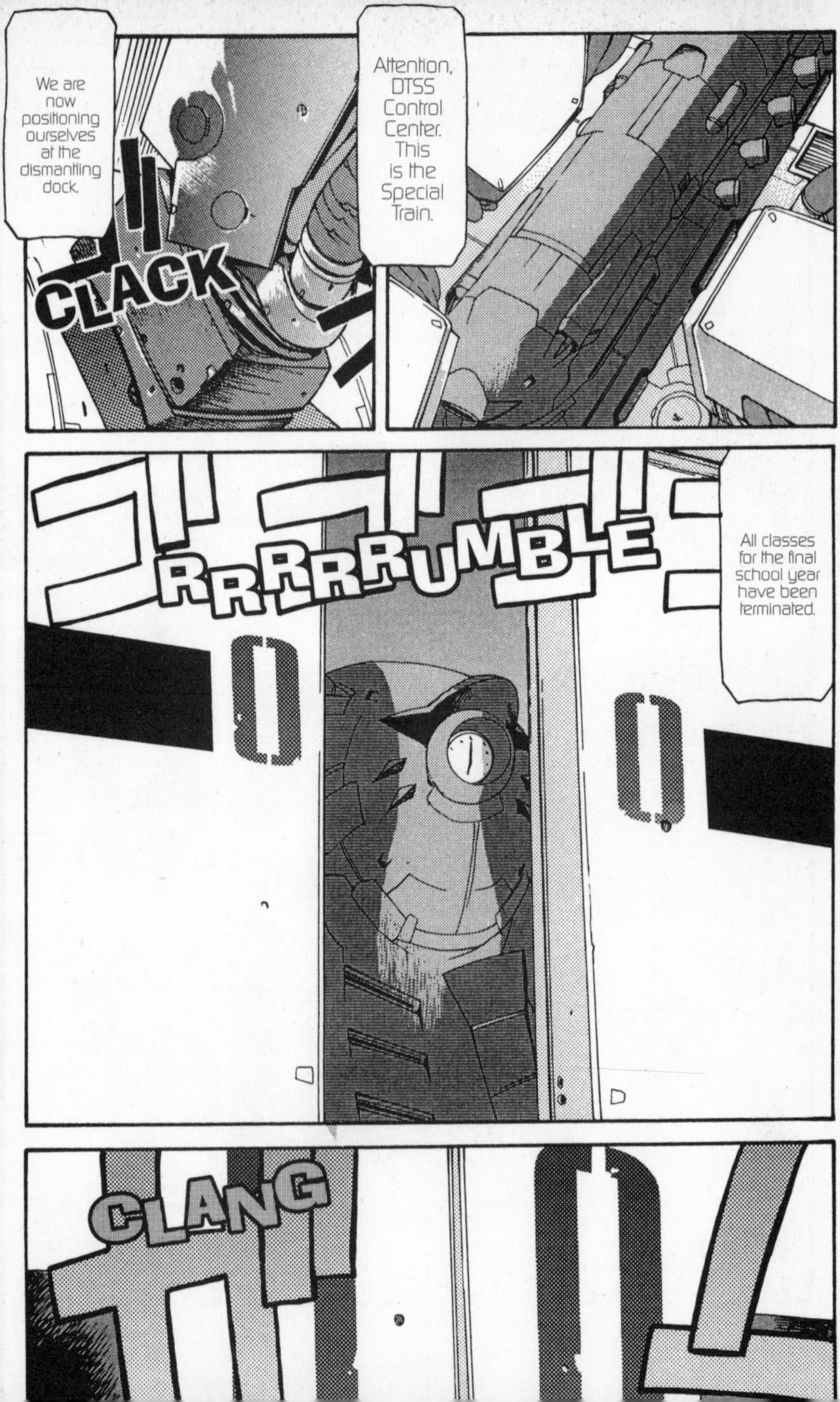
Attention, DTSS Control Center. This is the Special Train.
We are now positioning ourselves at the dismantling dock.
CLACK
All classes for the final school year have been terminated.
RRRRRUMBLE
CLANG

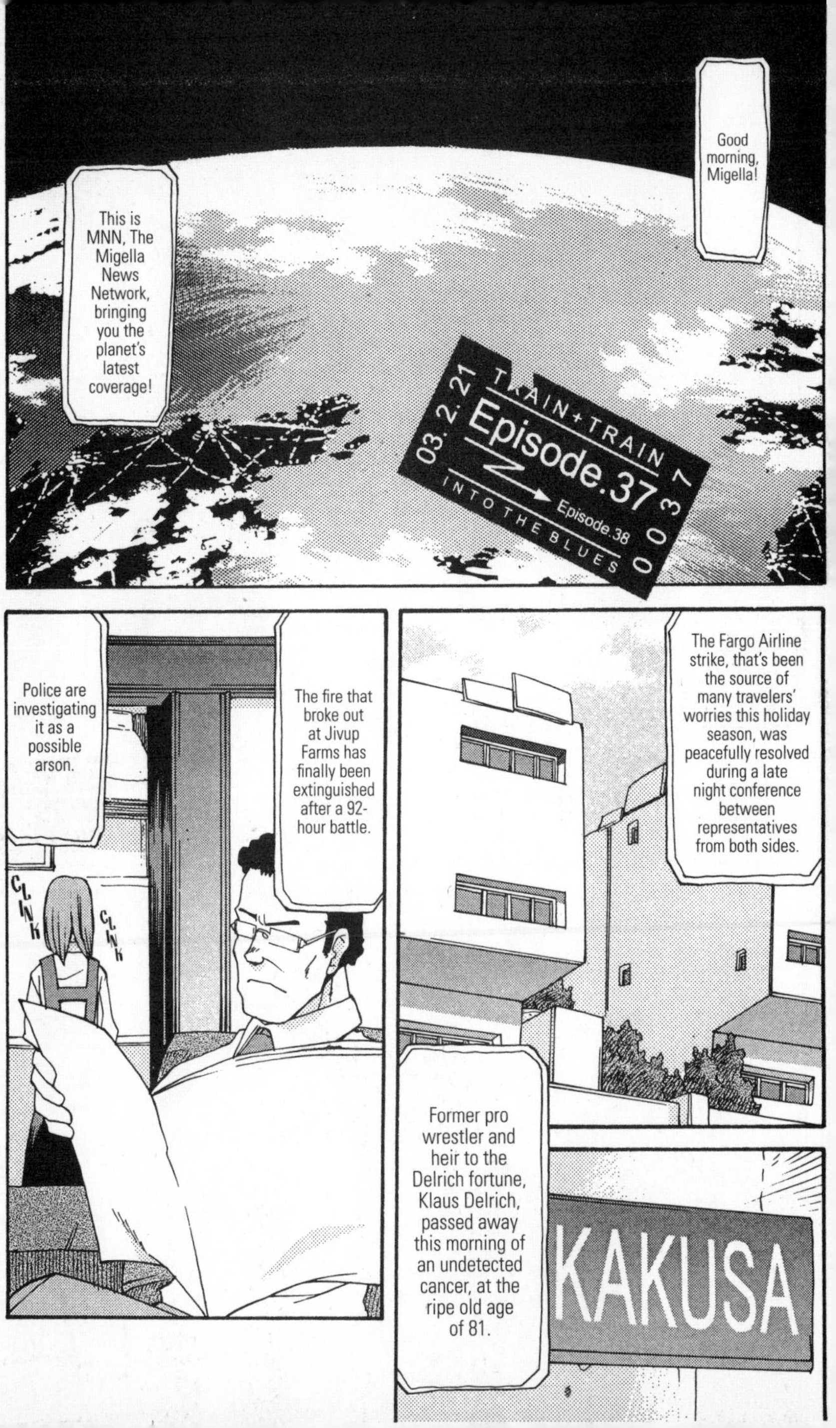
Good morning, Migella!
This is MNN, The Migella News Network, bringing you the planet's latest coverage!
TRAIN+TRAIN
03.2.21
Episode.37
Episode.38
INTO THE BLUES
0037
The Fargo Airline strike, that's been the source of many travelers' worries this holiday season, was peacefully resolved during a late night conference between representatives from both sides.
Former pro wrestler and heir to the Delrich fortune, Klaus Delrich, passed away this morning of an undetected cancer, at the ripe old age of 81.
KAKUSA
The fire that broke out at Jivup Farms has finally been extinguished after a 92-hour battle.
Police are investigating it as a possible arson.
CLINK
CLINK

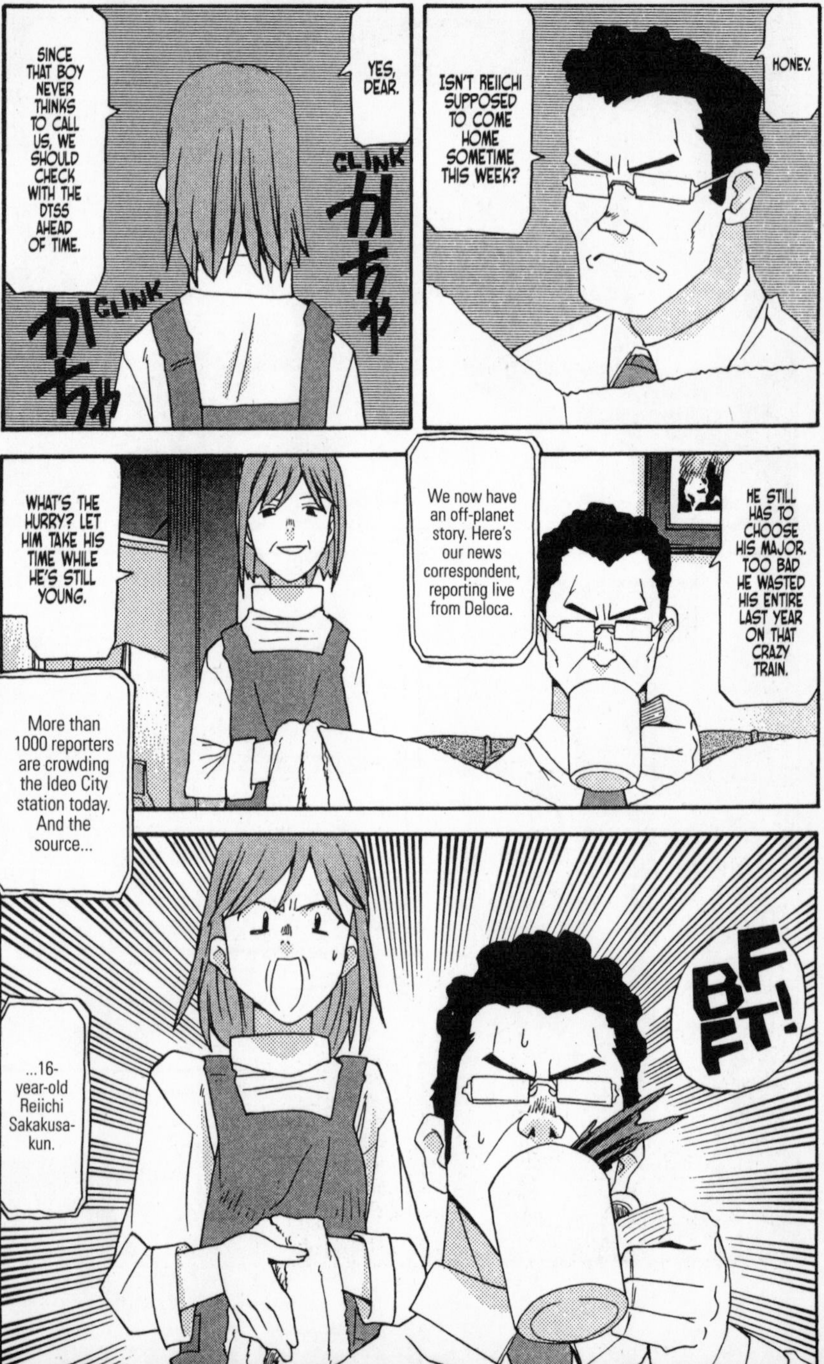
HONEY.
ISN'T REIICHI SUPPOSED TO COME HOME SOMETIME THIS WEEK?
YES, DEAR.
CLINK カチャ
SINCE THAT BOY NEVER THINKS TO CALL US, WE SHOULD CHECK WITH THE DTSS AHEAD OF TIME.
カチャ CLINK
HE STILL HAS TO CHOOSE HIS MAJOR. TOO BAD HE WASTED HIS ENTIRE LAST YEAR ON THAT CRAZY TRAIN.
We now have an off-planet story. Here's our news correspondent, reporting live from Deloca.
WHAT'S THE HURRY? LET HIM TAKE HIS TIME WHILE HE'S STILL YOUNG.
More than 1000 reporters are crowding the Ideo City station today. And the source...
BFFT!
...16-year-old Reiichi Sakakusa-kun.

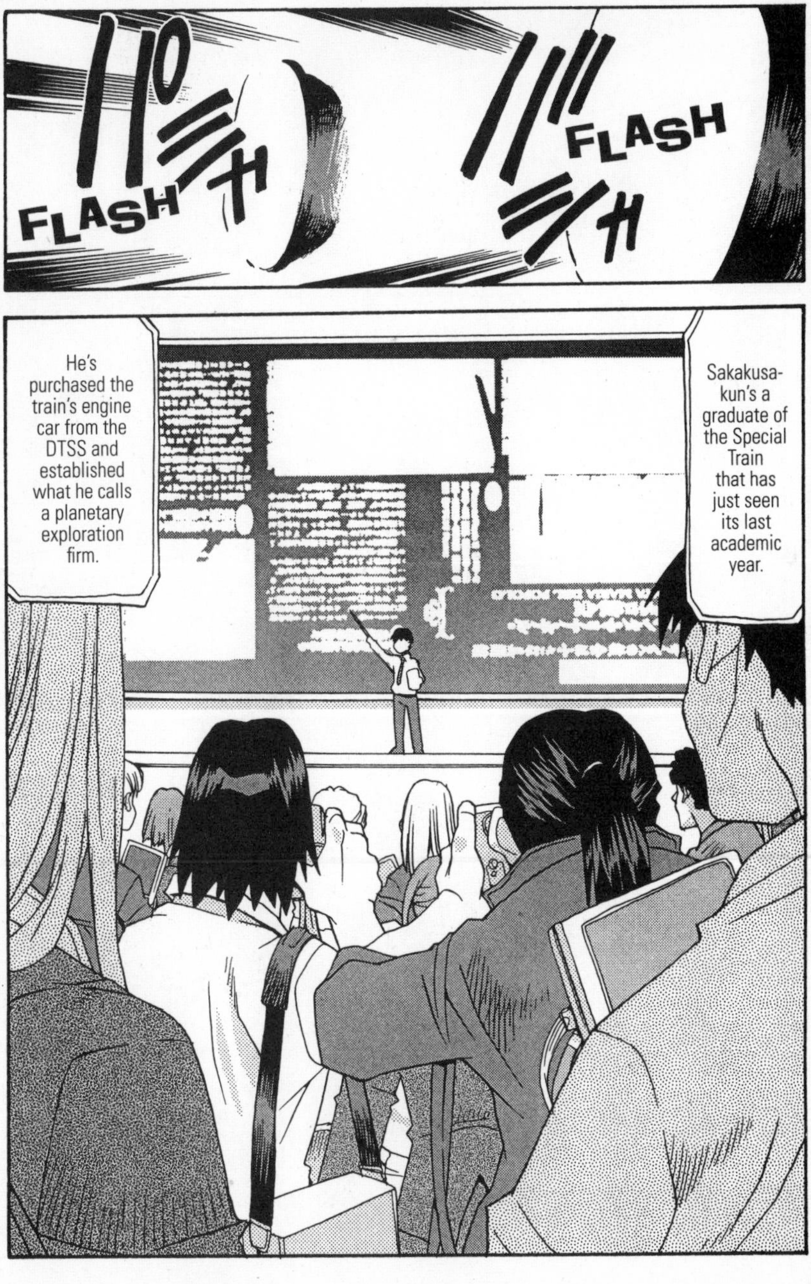
バシャ
FLASH
パシャ
FLASH
Sakakusa-kun's a graduate of the Special Train that has just seen its last academic year.
He's purchased the train's engine car from the DTSS and established what he calls a planetary exploration firm.

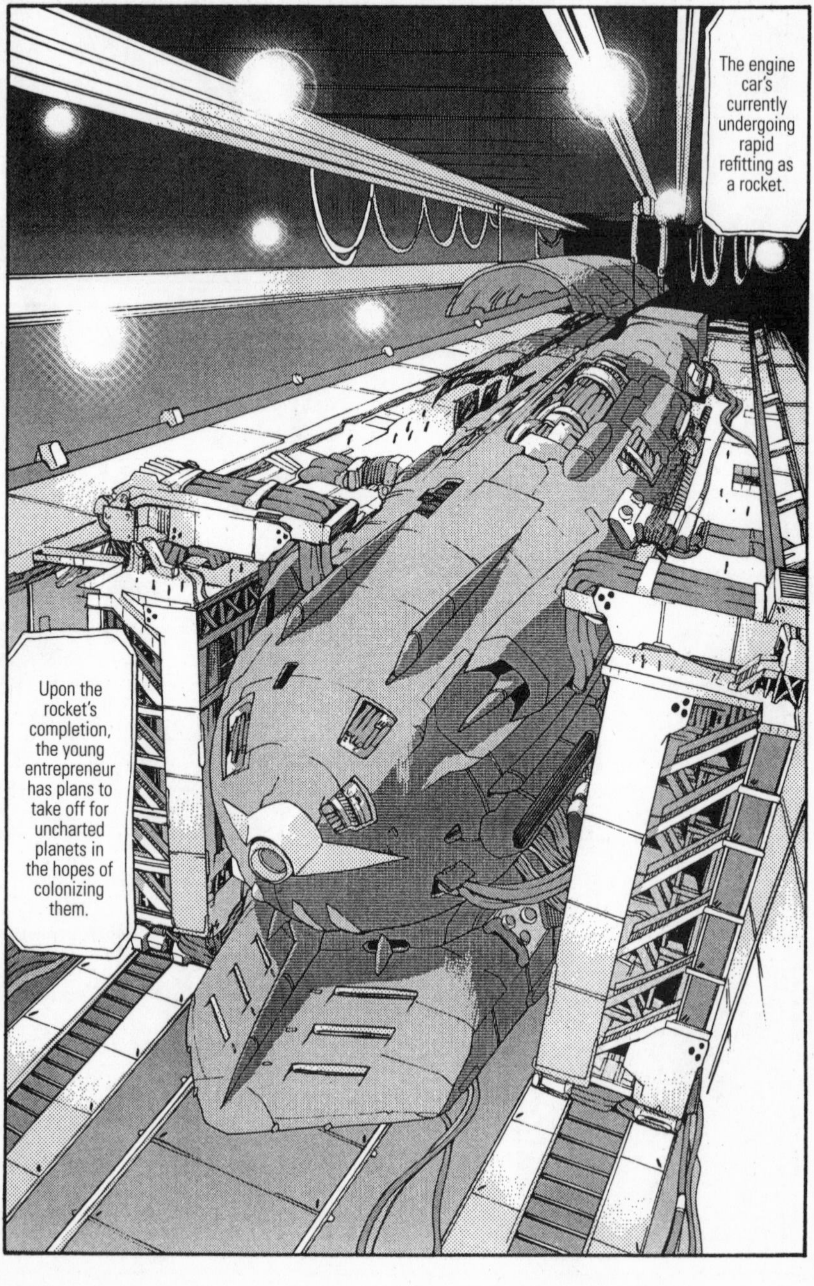
The engine car's currently undergoing rapid refitting as a rocket.
Upon the rocket's completion, the young entrepreneur has plans to take off for uncharted planets in the hopes of colonizing them.

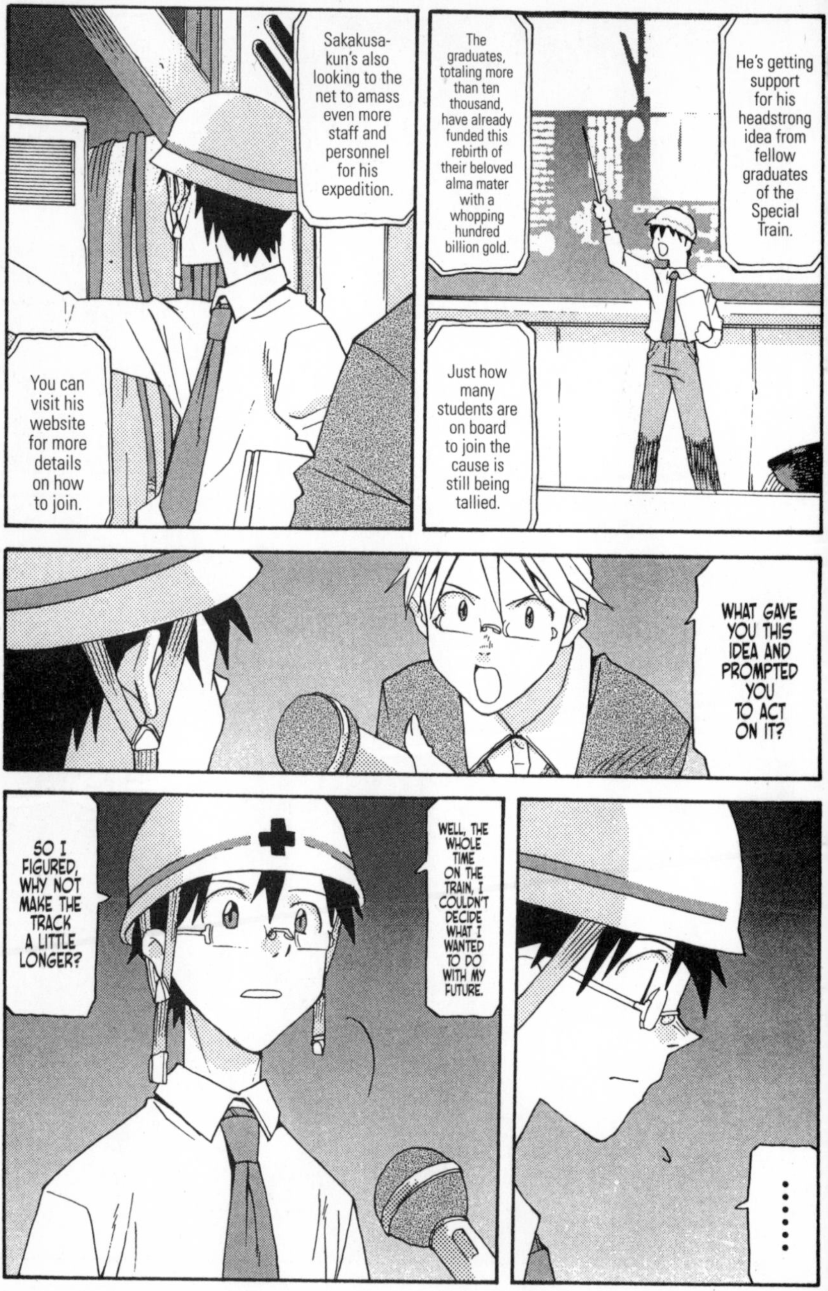
He's getting support for his headstrong idea from fellow graduates of the Special Train.
The graduates, totaling more than ten thousand, have already funded this rebirth of their beloved alma mater with a whopping hundred billion gold.
Just how many students are on board to join the cause is still being tallied.
Sakakusa-kun's also looking to the net to amass even more staff and personnel for his expedition.
You can visit his website for more details on how to join.
WHAT GAVE YOU THIS IDEA AND PROMPTED YOU TO ACT ON IT?
......
WELL, THE WHOLE TIME ON THE TRAIN, I COULDN'T DECIDE WHAT I WANTED TO DO WITH MY FUTURE.
SO I FIGURED, WHY NOT MAKE THE TRACK A LITTLE LONGER?

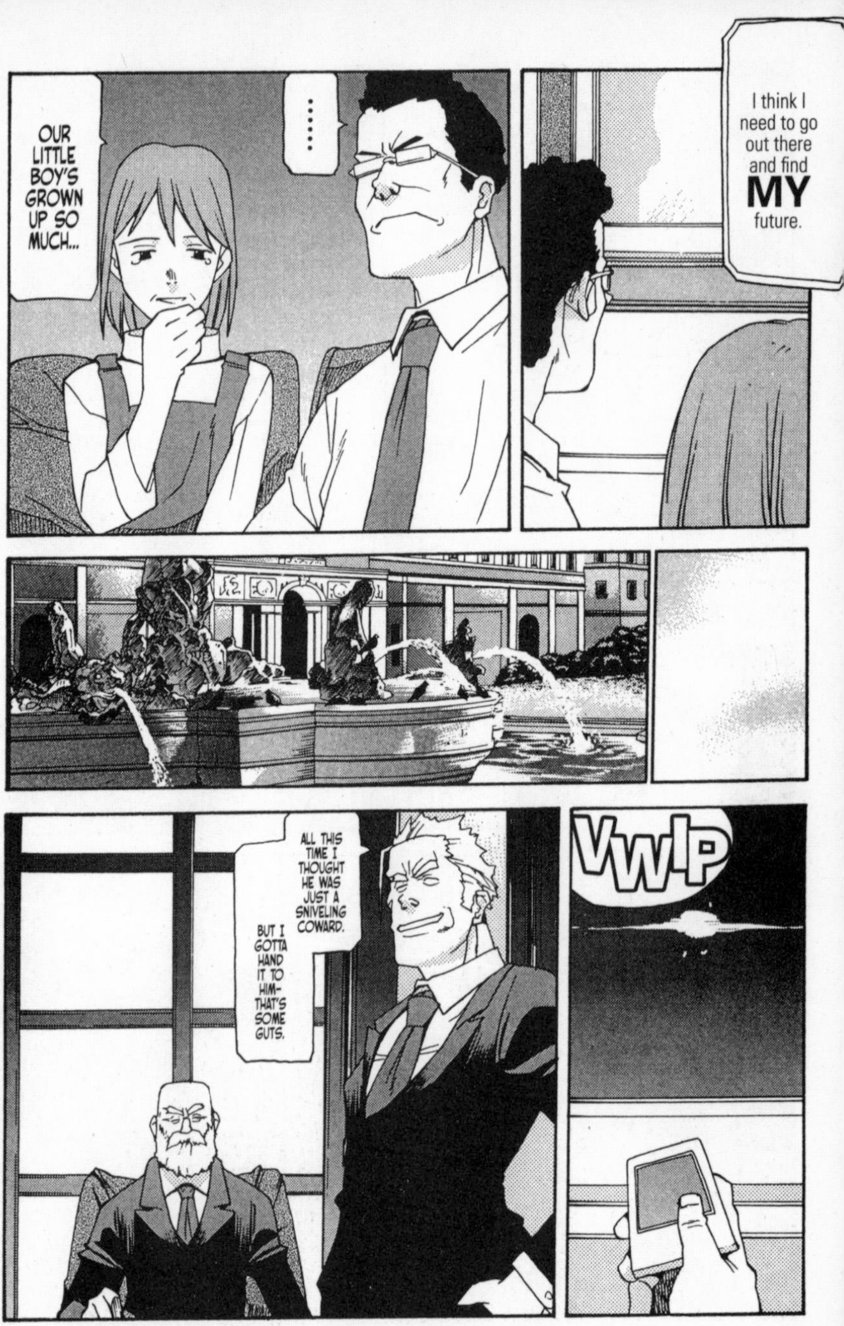
I think I need to go out there and find MY future.
......
OUR LITTLE BOY'S GROWN UP SO MUCH...
VWIP
ALL THIS TIME I THOUGHT HE WAS JUST A SNIVELING COWARD.
BUT I GOTTA HAND IT TO HIM-THAT'S SOME GUTS.

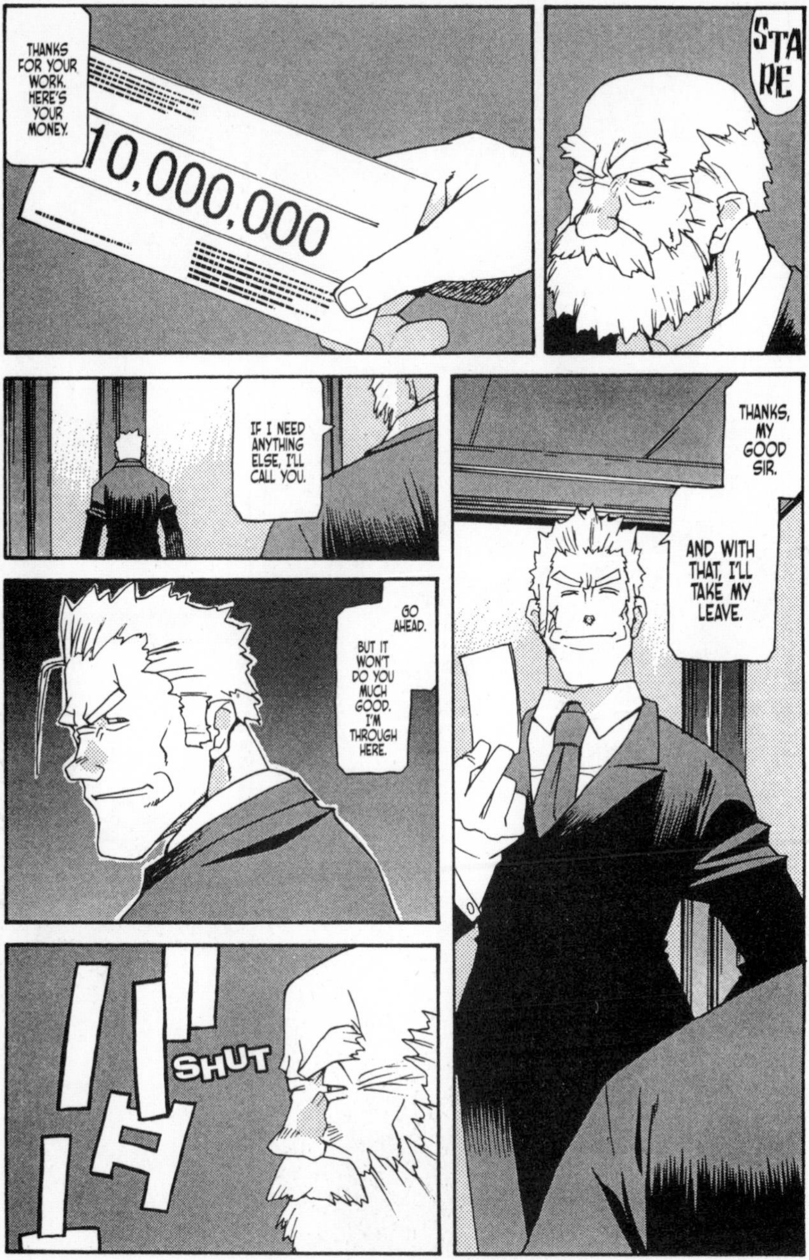
STARE
THANKS FOR YOUR WORK. HERE'S YOUR MONEY.
10,000,000
THANKS, MY GOOD SIR.
AND WITH THAT, I'LL TAKE MY LEAVE.
IF I NEED ANYTHING ELSE, I'LL CALL YOU.
GO AHEAD.
BUT IT WON'T DO YOU MUCH GOOD. I'M THROUGH HERE.
SHUT

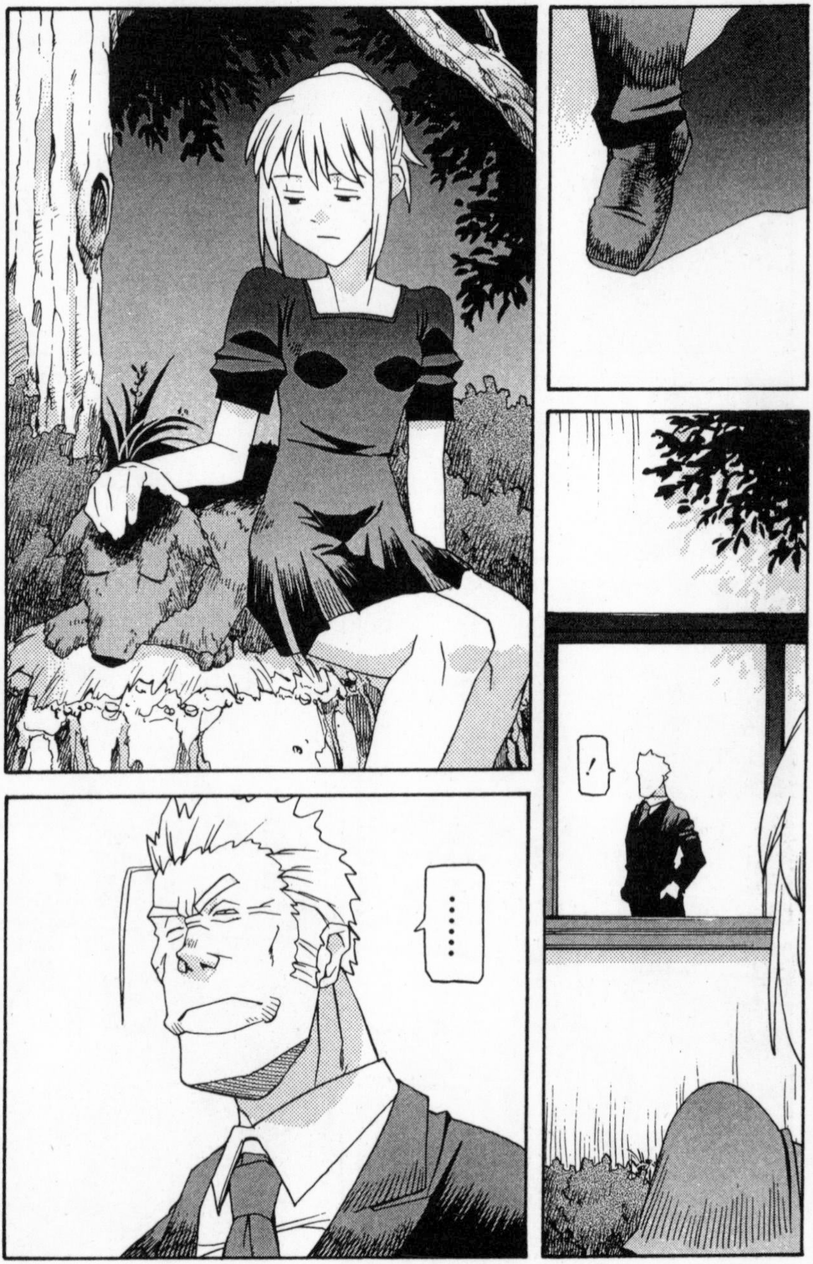
!
……

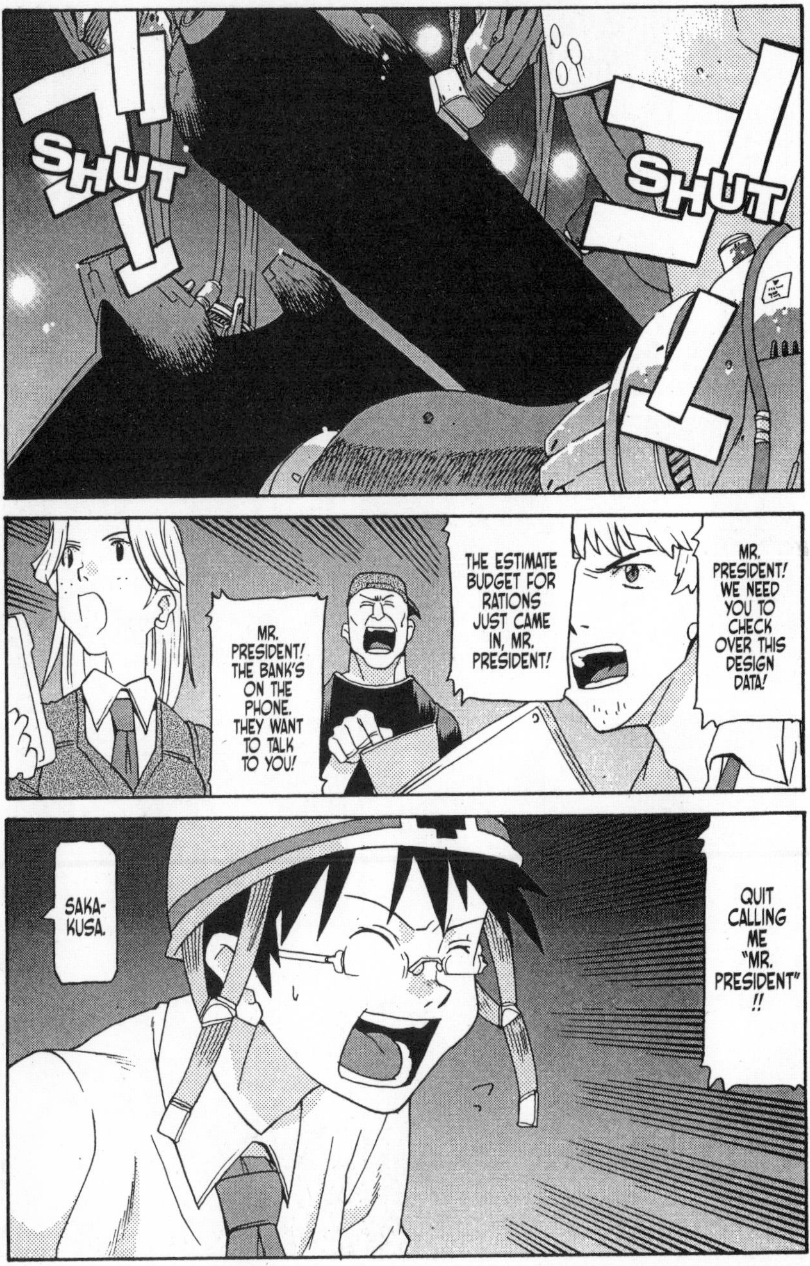
SHUT
SHUT
MR. PRESIDENT! WE NEED YOU TO CHECK OVER THIS DESIGN DATA!
THE ESTIMATE BUDGET FOR RATIONS JUST CAME IN, MR. PRESIDENT!
MR. PRESIDENT! THE BANK'S ON THE PHONE. THEY WANT TO TALK TO YOU!
QUIT CALLING ME "MR. PRESIDENT" !!
SAKA-KUSA.

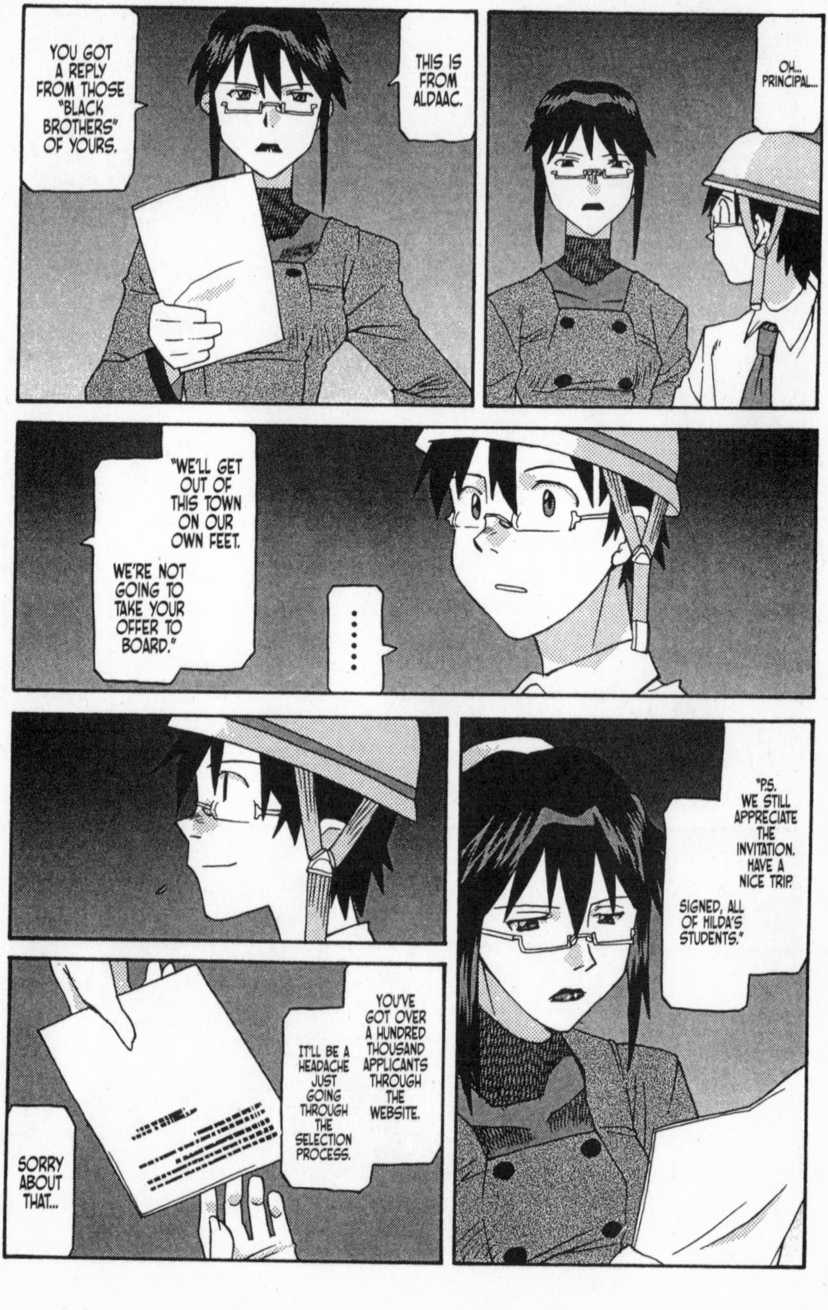
OH... PRINCIPAL...
THIS IS FROM ALDAAC.
YOU GOT A REPLY FROM THOSE "BLACK BROTHERS" OF YOURS.
"WE'LL GET OUT OF THIS TOWN ON OUR OWN FEET.
WE'RE NOT GOING TO TAKE YOUR OFFER TO BOARD."
......
"P.S. WE STILL APPRECIATE THE INVITATION. HAVE A NICE TRIP.
SIGNED, ALL OF HILDA'S STUDENTS."
YOU'VE GOT OVER A HUNDRED THOUSAND APPLICANTS THROUGH THE WEBSITE.
IT'LL BE A HEADACHE JUST GOING THROUGH THE SELECTION PROCESS.
SORRY ABOUT THAT...

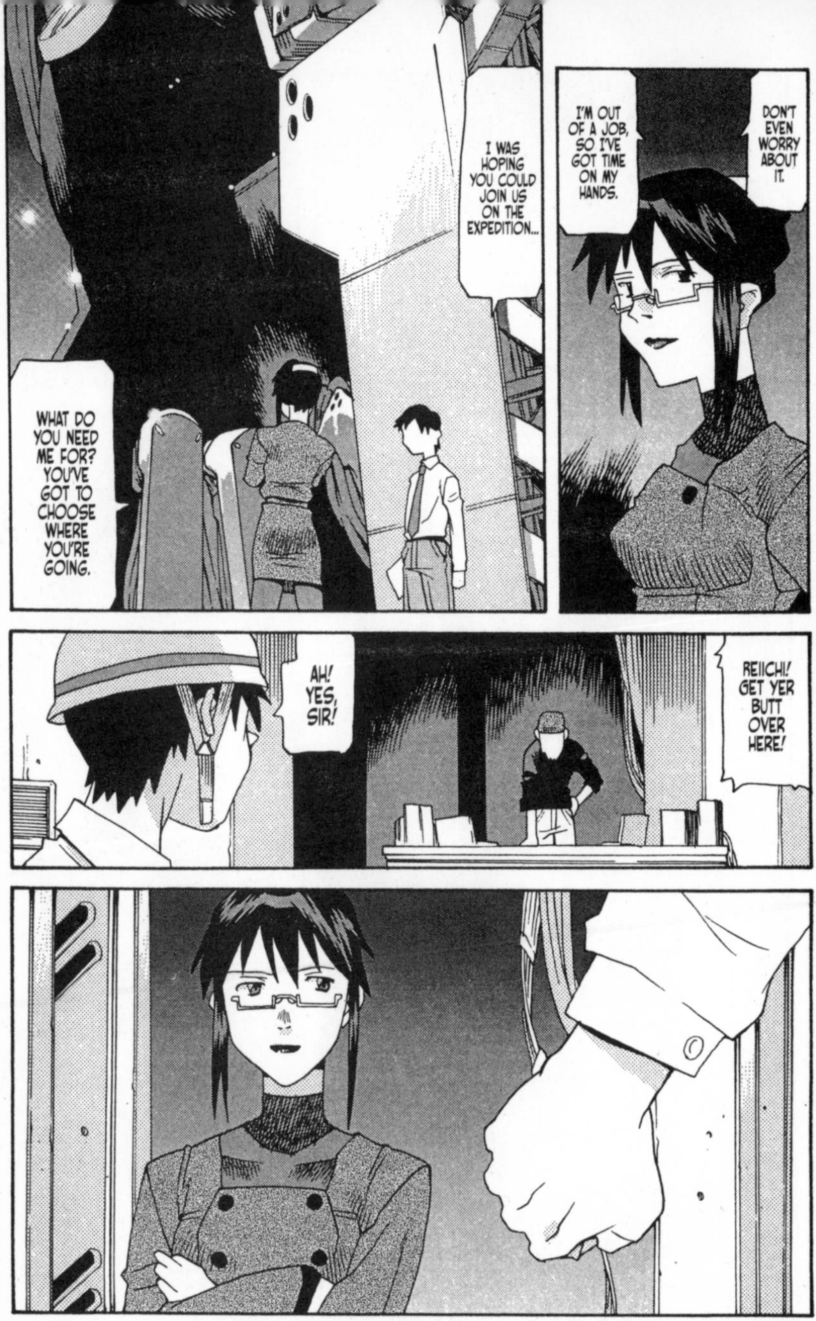
DON'T EVEN WORRY ABOUT IT.
I'M OUT OF A JOB, SO I'VE GOT TIME ON MY HANDS.
I WAS HOPING YOU COULD JOIN US ON THE EXPEDITION...
WHAT DO YOU NEED ME FOR? YOU'VE GOT TO CHOOSE WHERE YOU'RE GOING.
REIICHI! GET YER BUTT OVER HERE!
AH! YES, SIR!

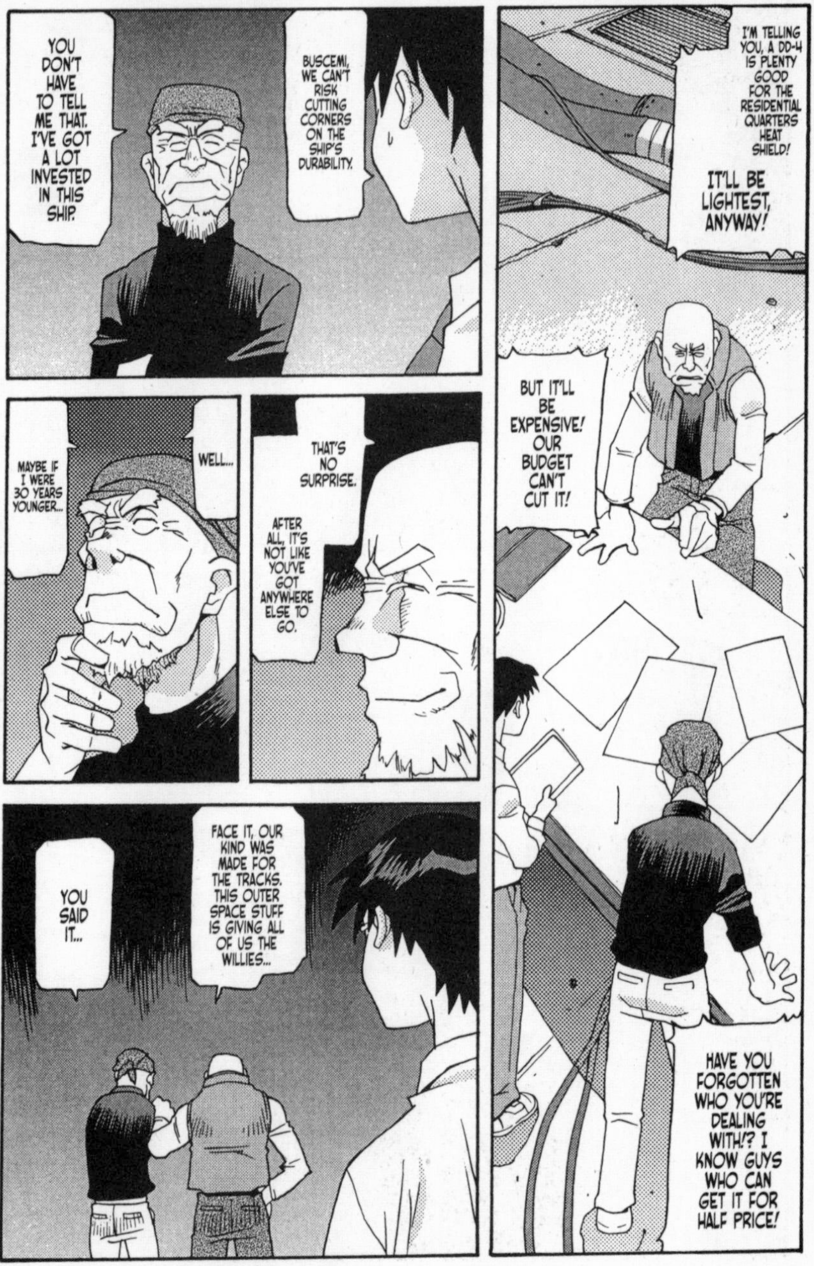
I'M TELLING YOU, A DD-4 IS PLENTY GOOD FOR THE RESIDENTIAL QUARTERS HEAT SHIELD!
IT'LL BE LIGHTEST, ANYWAY!
BUT IT'LL BE EXPENSIVE! OUR BUDGET CAN'T CUT IT!
HAVE YOU FORGOTTEN WHO YOU'RE DEALING WITH!? I KNOW GUYS WHO CAN GET IT FOR HALF PRICE!
BUSCEMI, WE CAN'T RISK CUTTING CORNERS ON THE SHIP'S DURABILITY.
YOU DON'T HAVE TO TELL ME THAT. I'VE GOT A LOT INVESTED IN THIS SHIP.
THAT'S NO SURPRISE.
AFTER ALL, IT'S NOT LIKE YOU'VE GOT ANYWHERE ELSE TO GO.
WELL...
MAYBE IF I WERE 30 YEARS YOUNGER...
FACE IT, OUR KIND WAS MADE FOR THE TRACKS. THIS OUTER SPACE STUFF IS GIVING ALL OF US THE WILLIES...
YOU SAID IT...

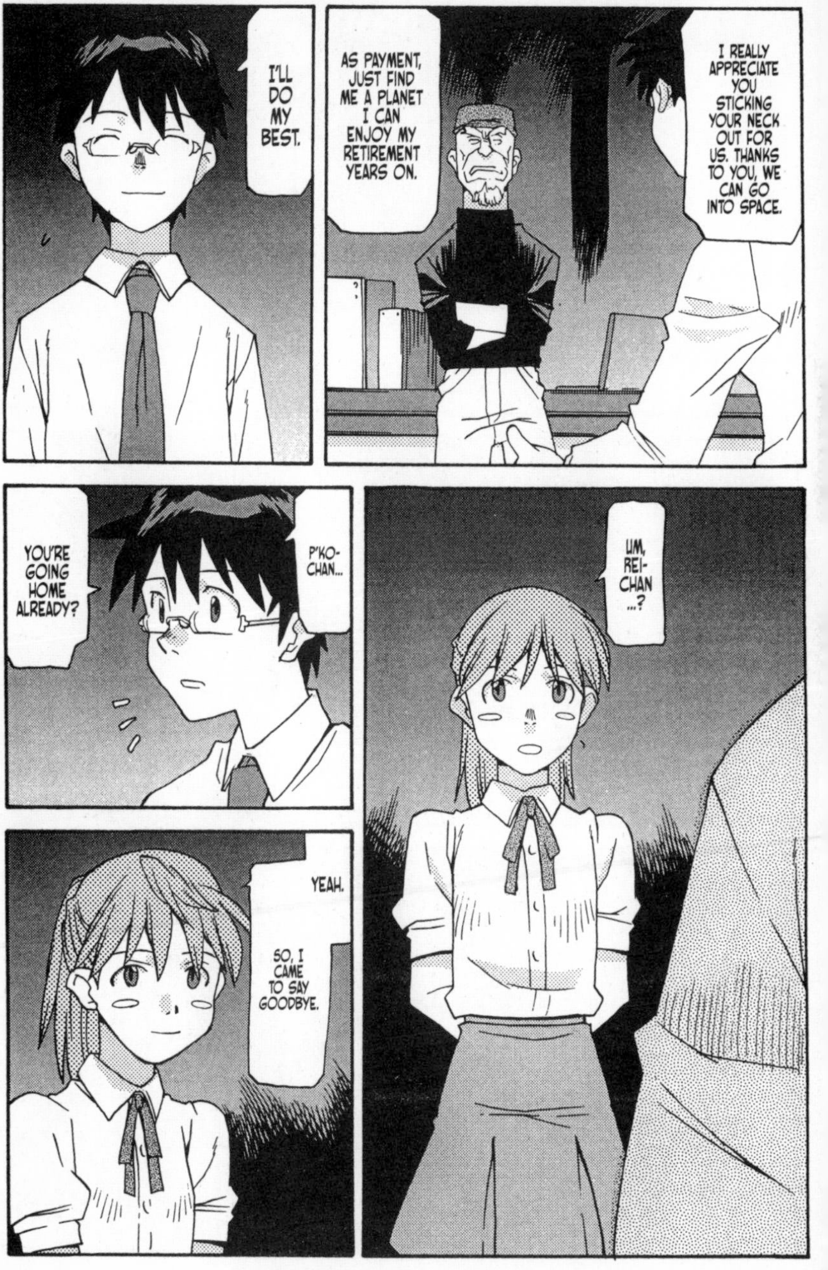
I REALLY APPRECIATE YOU STICKING YOUR NECK OUT FOR US. THANKS TO YOU, WE CAN GO INTO SPACE.
AS PAYMENT, JUST FIND ME A PLANET I CAN ENJOY MY RETIREMENT YEARS ON.
I'LL DO MY BEST.
UM, REI-CHAN ...?
P'KO-CHAN...
YOU'RE GOING HOME ALREADY?
YEAH.
SO, I CAME TO SAY GOODBYE.

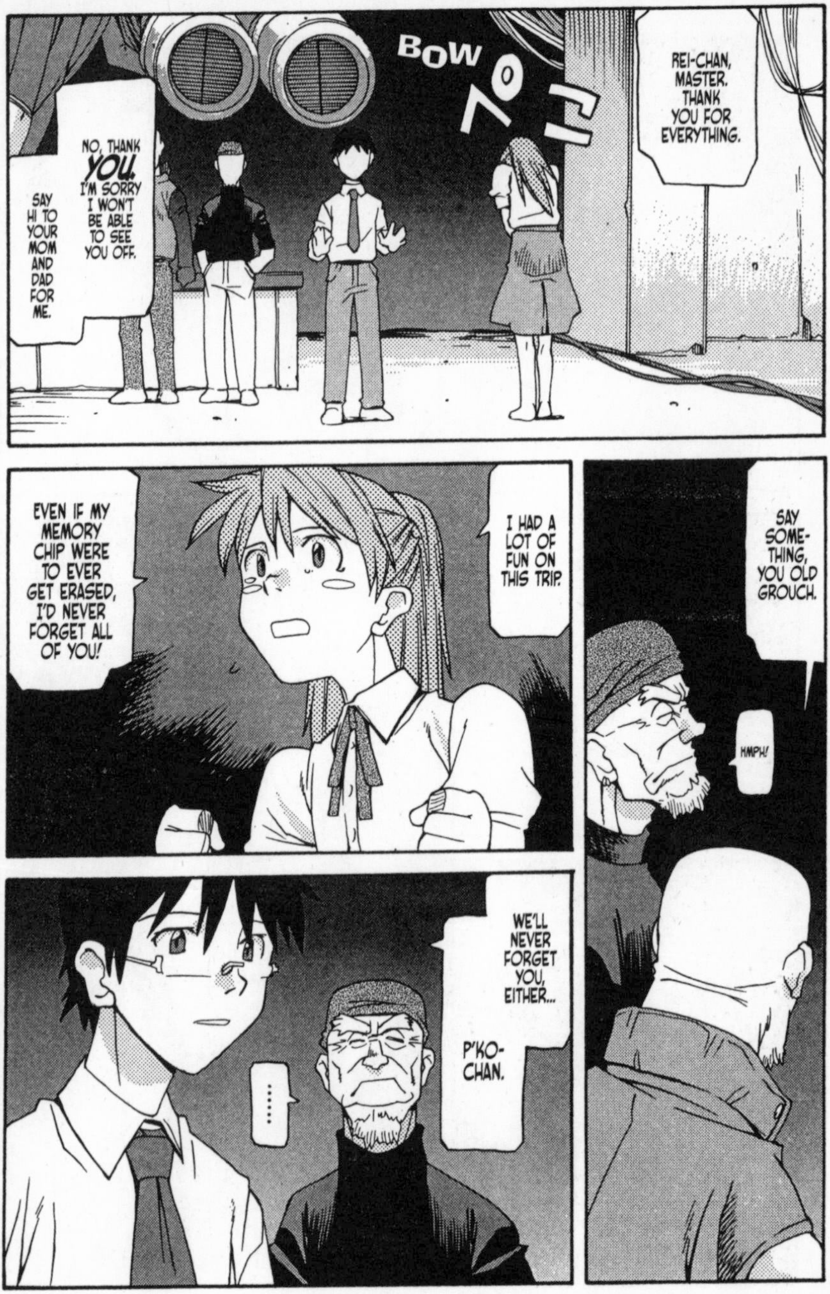
REI-CHAN, MASTER. THANK YOU FOR EVERYTHING.
BOW
NO, THANK YOU. I'M SORRY I WON'T BE ABLE TO SEE YOU OFF.
SAY HI TO YOUR MOM AND DAD FOR ME.
SAY SOME-THING, YOU OLD GROUCH.
HMPH!
I HAD A LOT OF FUN ON THIS TRIP.
EVEN IF MY MEMORY CHIP WERE TO EVER GET ERASED, I'D NEVER FORGET ALL OF YOU!
WE'LL NEVER FORGET YOU, EITHER...
P'KO-CHAN.
......

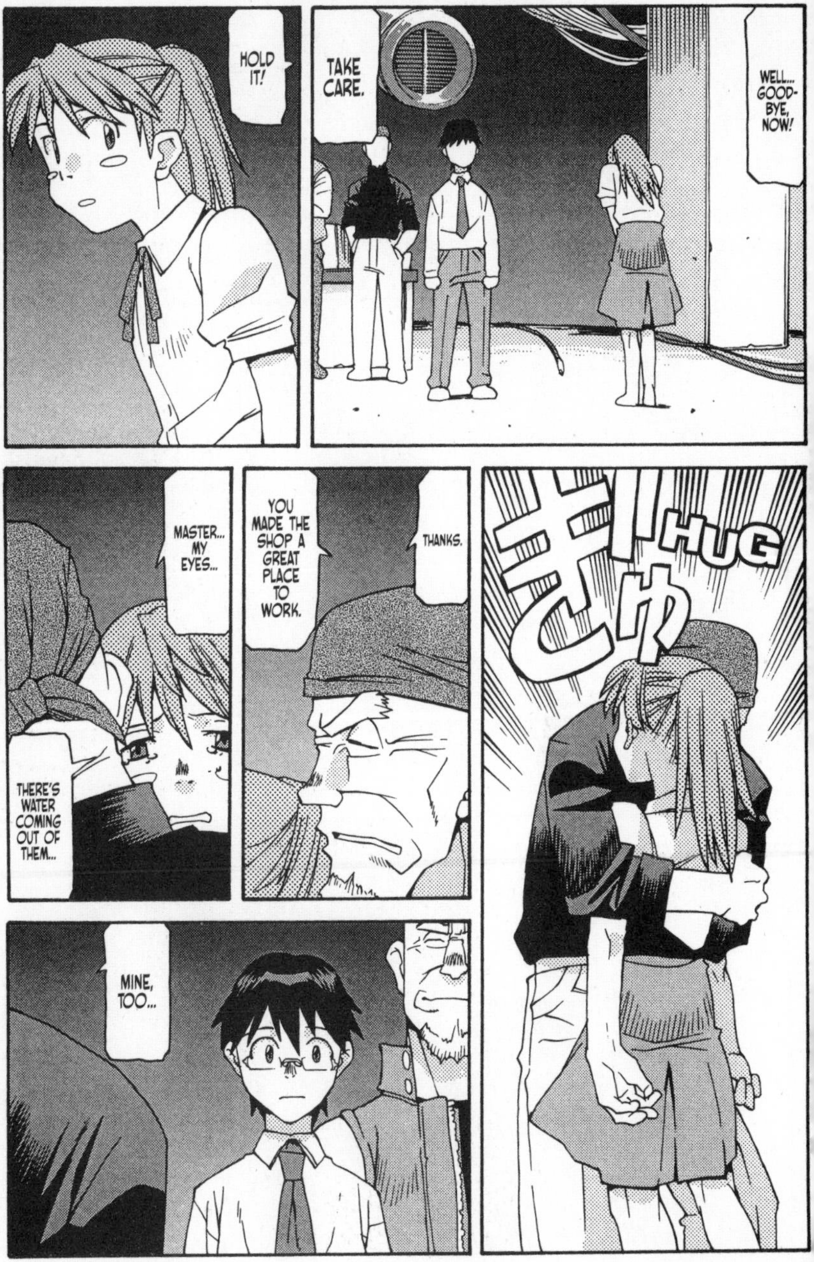
WELL... GOOD-BYE, NOW!
TAKE CARE.
HOLD IT!
ぎゅ
HUG
THANKS.
YOU MADE THE SHOP A GREAT PLACE TO WORK.
MASTER... MY EYES...
THERE'S WATER COMING OUT OF THEM...
MINE, TOO...

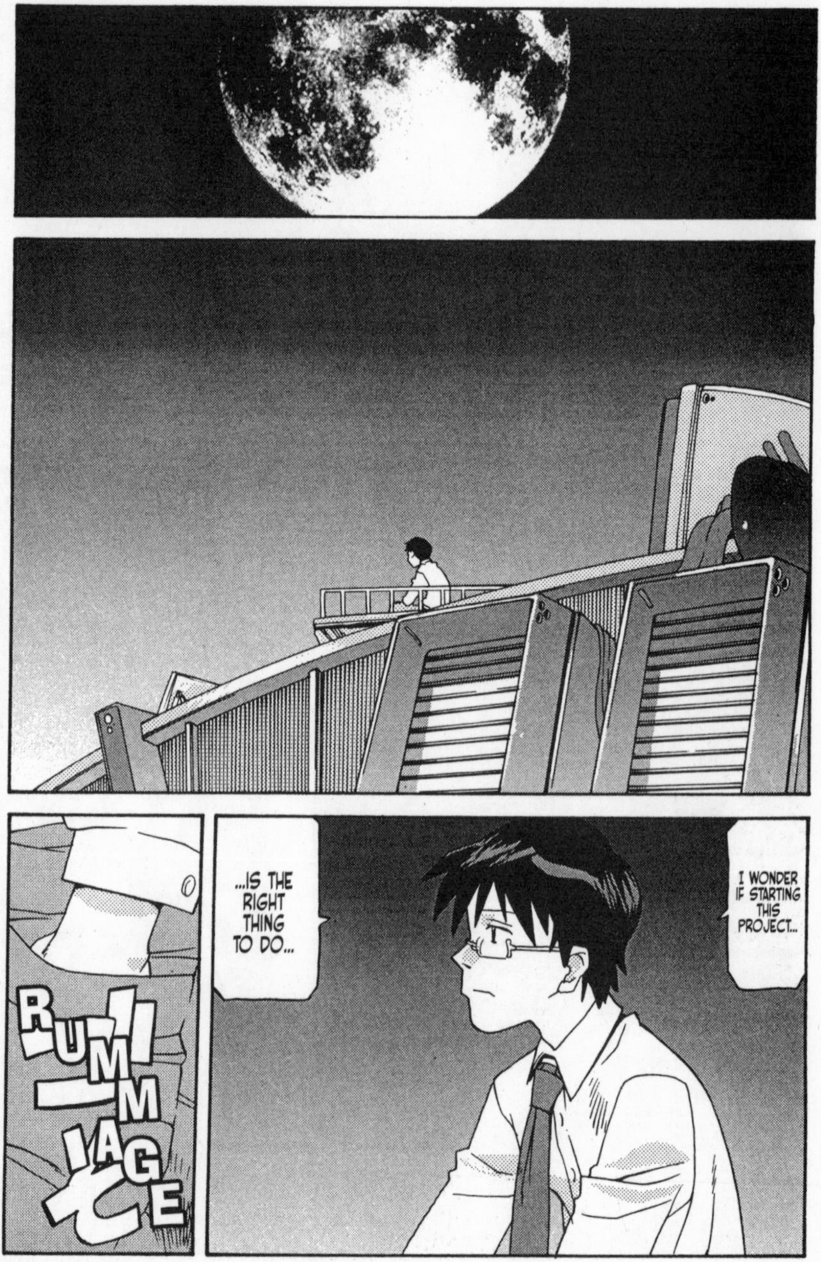
I WONDER IF STARTING THIS PROJECT...
...IS THE RIGHT THING TO DO...
RUMMAGE

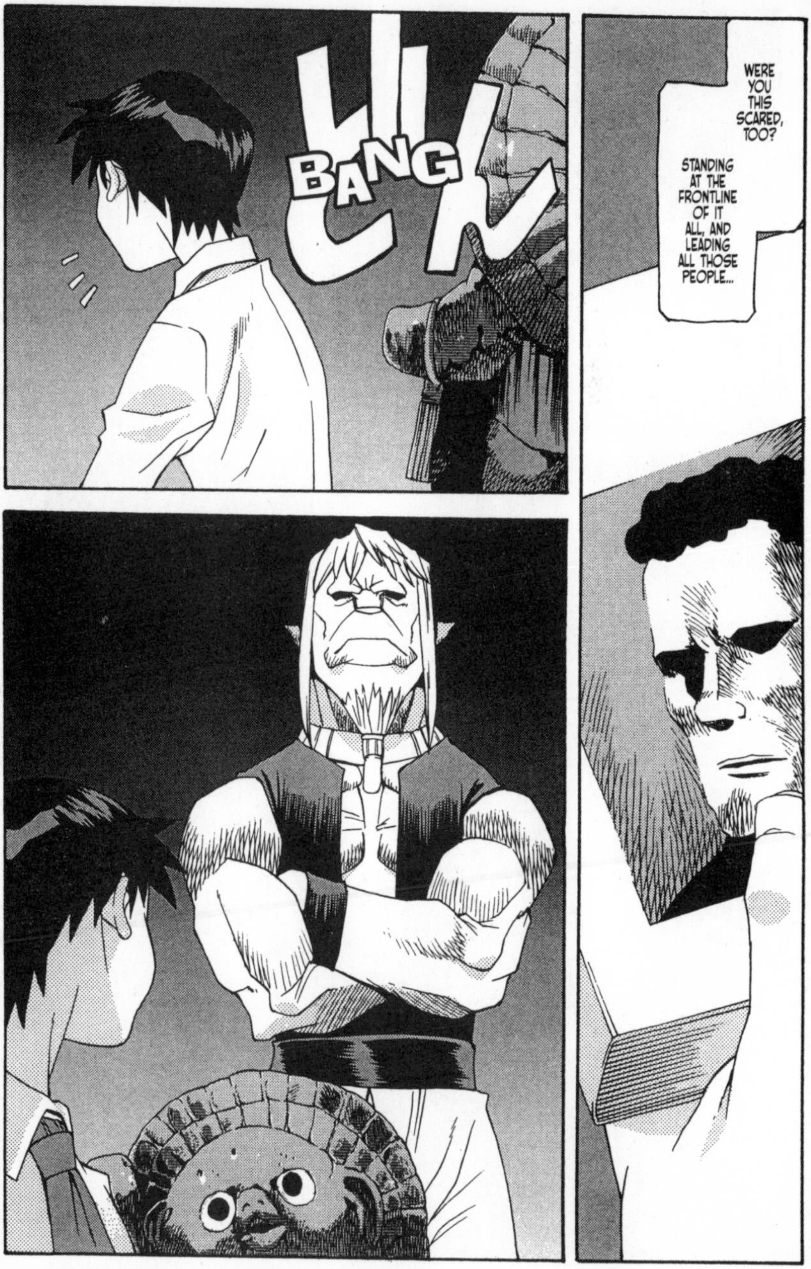
WERE YOU THIS SCARED, TOO?
STANDING AT THE FRONTLINE OF IT ALL, AND LEADING ALL THOSE PEOPLE...
BANG

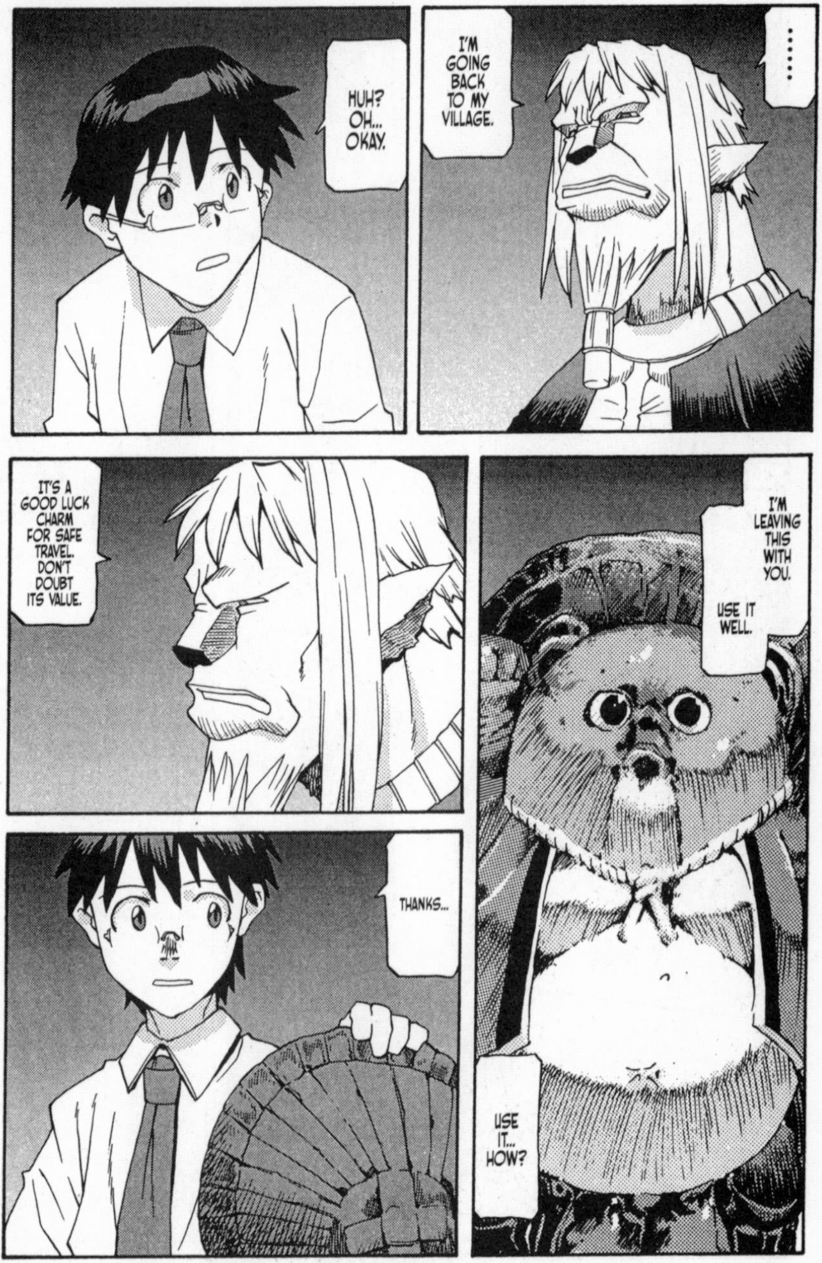
......
I'M GOING BACK TO MY VILLAGE.
HUH? OH... OKAY.
I'M LEAVING THIS WITH YOU.
USE IT WELL.
USE IT... HOW?
IT'S A GOOD LUCK CHARM FOR SAFE TRAVEL. DON'T DOUBT ITS VALUE.
THANKS...

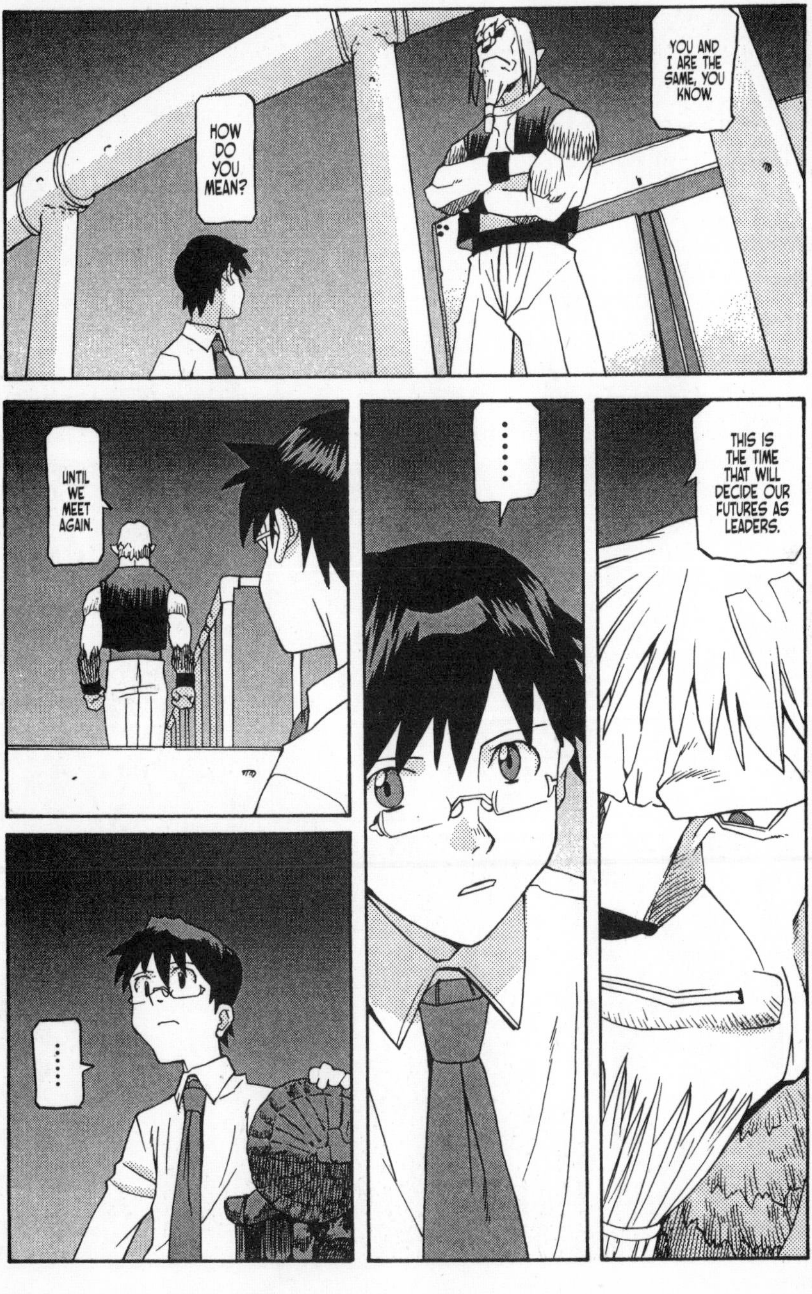
YOU AND I ARE THE SAME, YOU KNOW.
HOW DO YOU MEAN?
THIS IS THE TIME THAT WILL DECIDE OUR FUTURES AS LEADERS.
......
UNTIL WE MEET AGAIN.
......

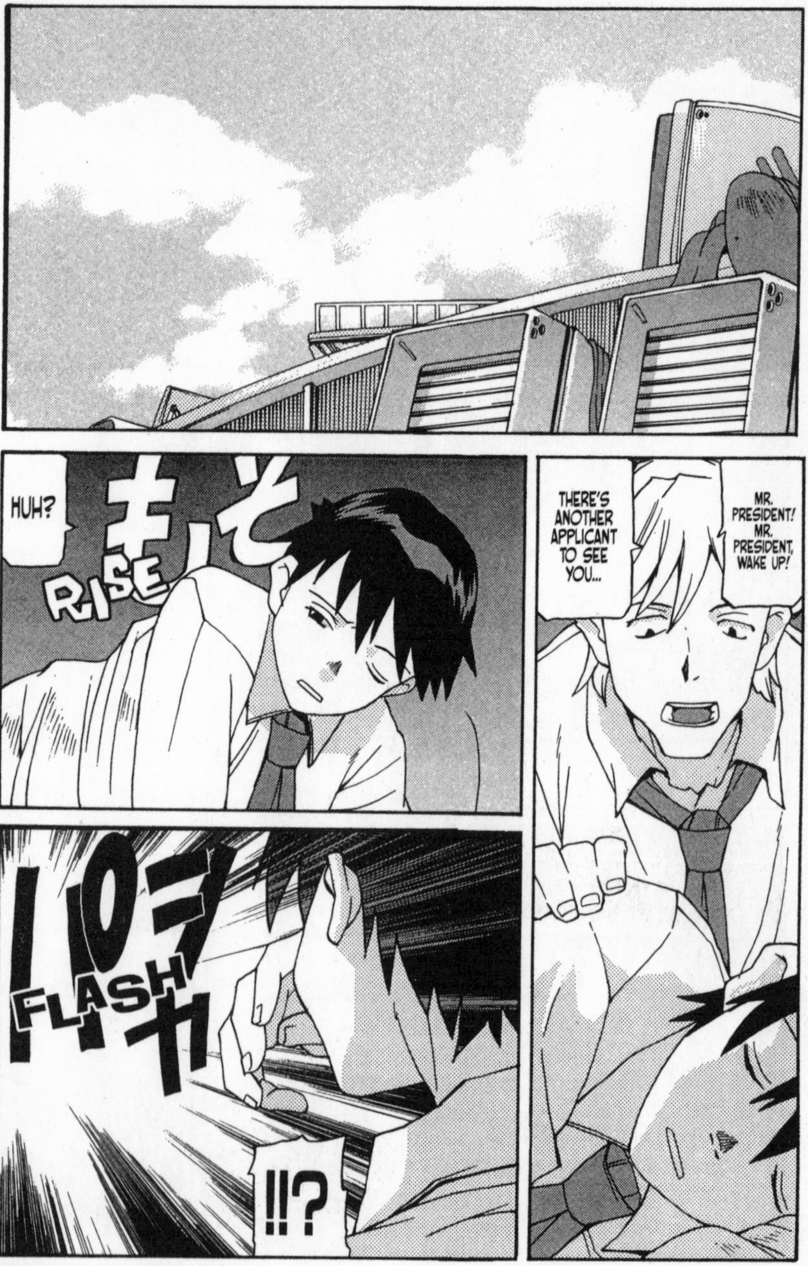
MR. PRESIDENT! MR. PRESIDENT, WAKE UP!
THERE'S ANOTHER APPLICANT TO SEE YOU...
HUH?
RISE
FLASH
!!?

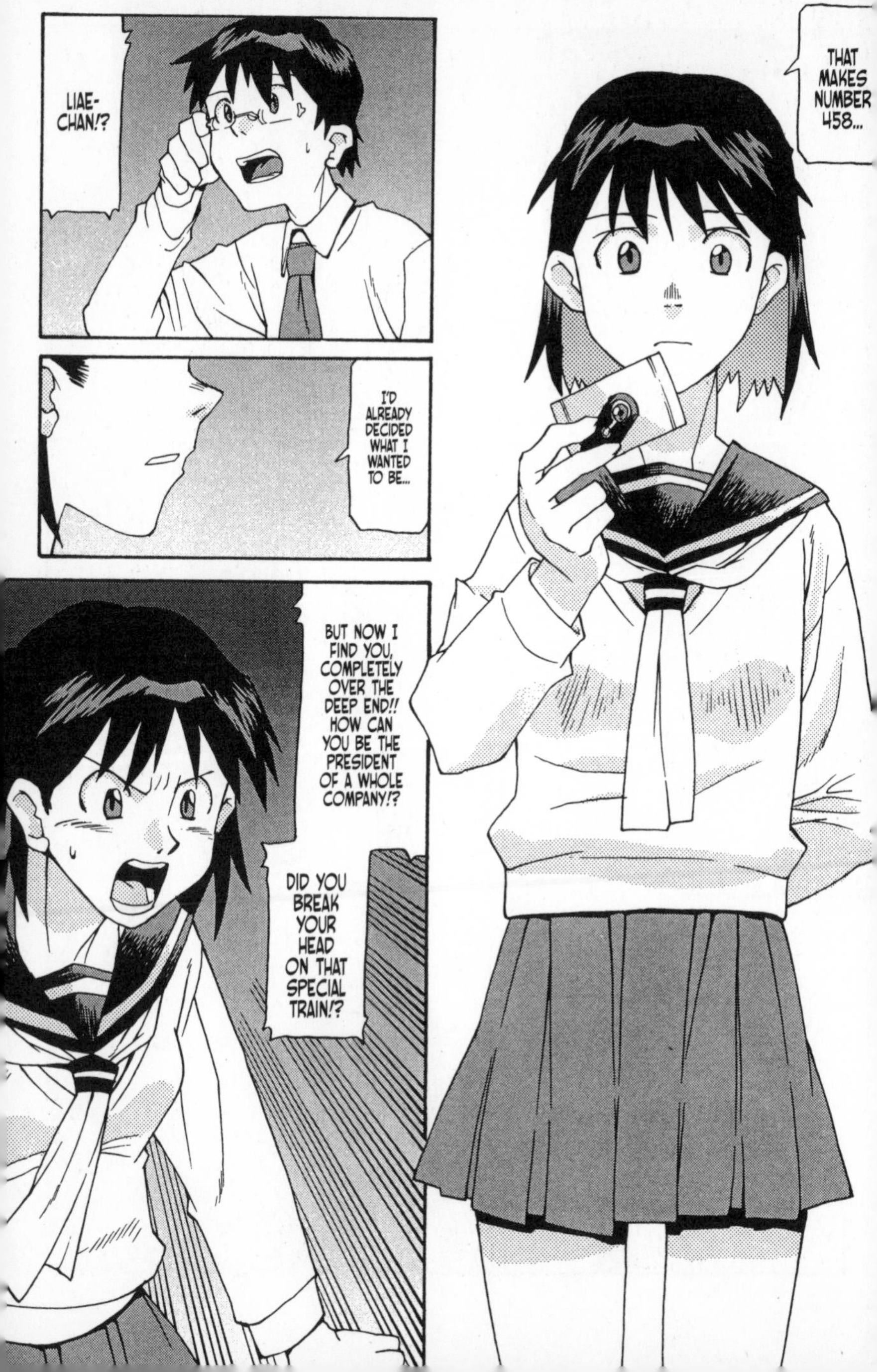
THAT MAKES NUMBER 458...
LIAE-CHAN!?
I'D ALREADY DECIDED WHAT I WANTED TO BE...
BUT NOW I FIND YOU, COMPLETELY OVER THE DEEP END!! HOW CAN YOU BE THE PRESIDENT OF A WHOLE COMPANY!?
DID YOU BREAK YOUR HEAD ON THAT SPECIAL TRAIN!?

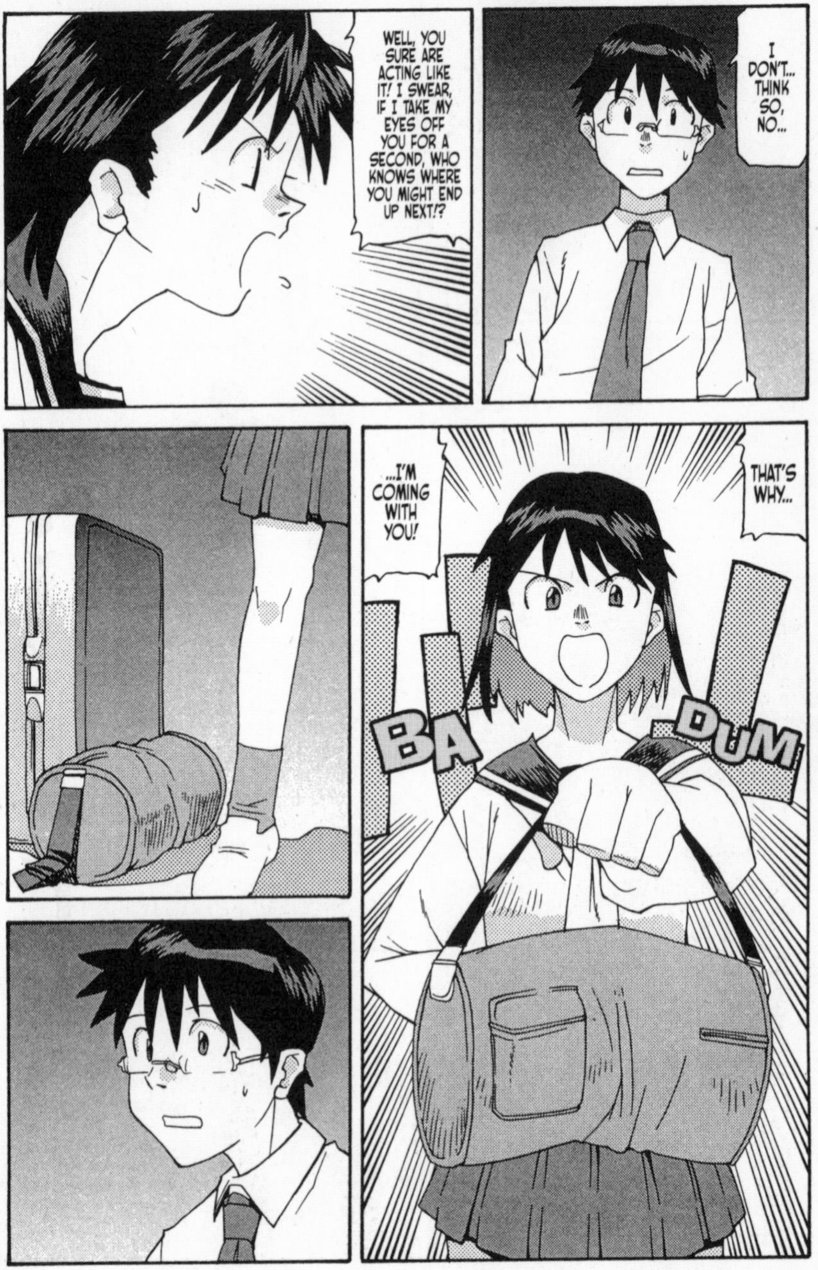
I DON'T... THINK SO, NO...
WELL, YOU SURE ARE ACTING LIKE IT! I SWEAR, IF I TAKE MY EYES OFF YOU FOR A SECOND, WHO KNOWS WHERE YOU MIGHT END UP NEXT!?
THAT'S WHY...
...I'M COMING WITH YOU!
BA DUM

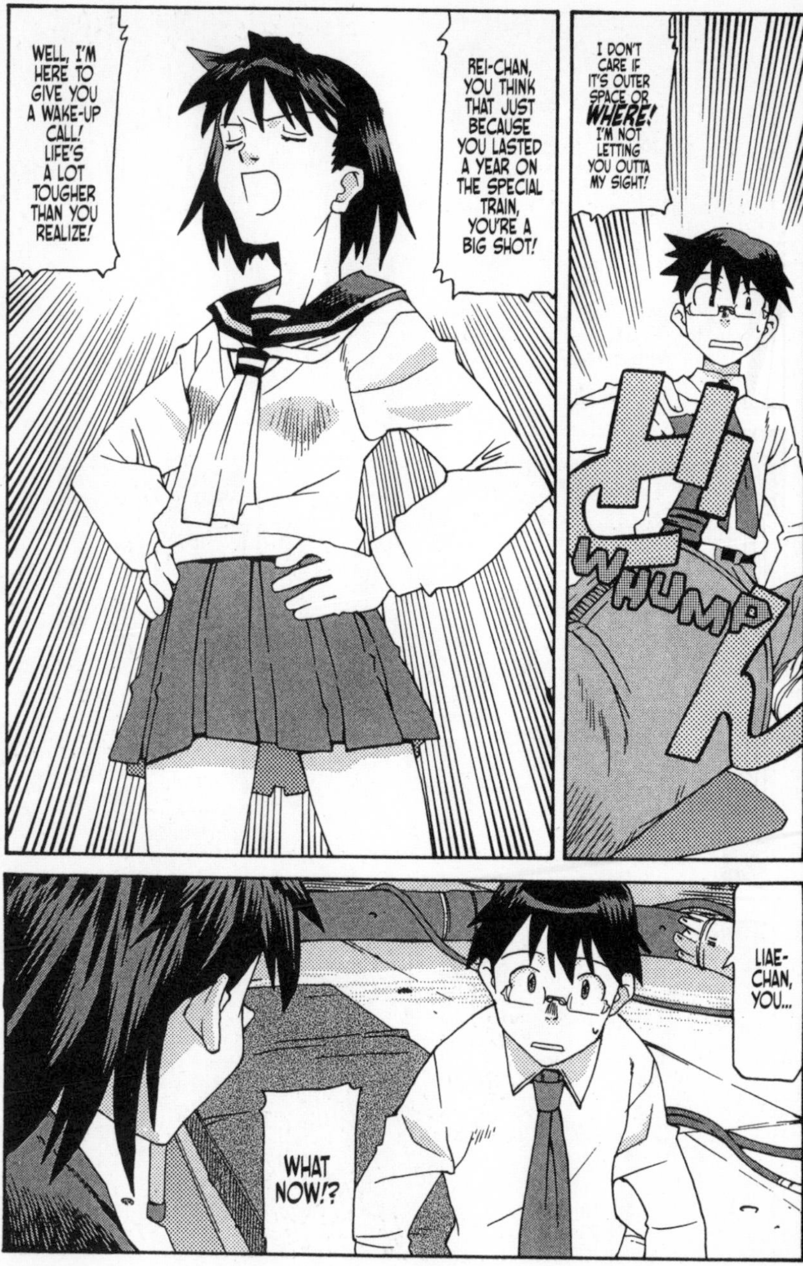

I DON'T CARE IF IT'S OUTER SPACE OR WHERE! I'M NOT LETTING YOU OUTTA MY SIGHT!
WHUMP
REI-CHAN, YOU THINK THAT JUST BECAUSE YOU LASTED A YEAR ON THE SPECIAL TRAIN, YOU'RE A BIG SHOT!
WELL, I'M HERE TO GIVE YOU A WAKE-UP CALL! LIFE'S A LOT TOUGHER THAN YOU REALIZE!
LIAE-CHAN, YOU...
WHAT NOW!?

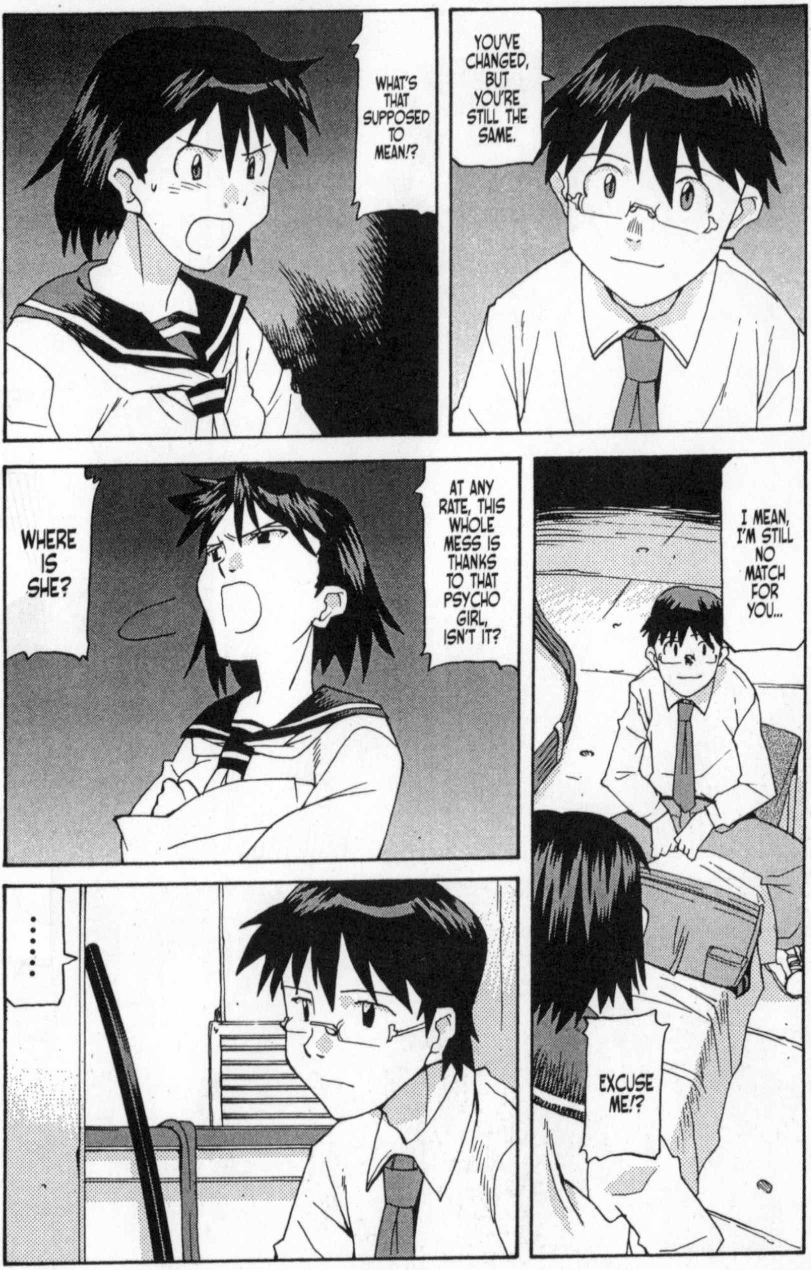
YOU'VE CHANGED, BUT YOU'RE STILL THE SAME.
WHAT'S THAT SUPPOSED TO MEAN!?
I MEAN, I'M STILL NO MATCH FOR YOU...
EXCUSE ME!?
AT ANY RATE, THIS WHOLE MESS IS THANKS TO THAT PSYCHO GIRL, ISN'T IT?
WHERE IS SHE?
......

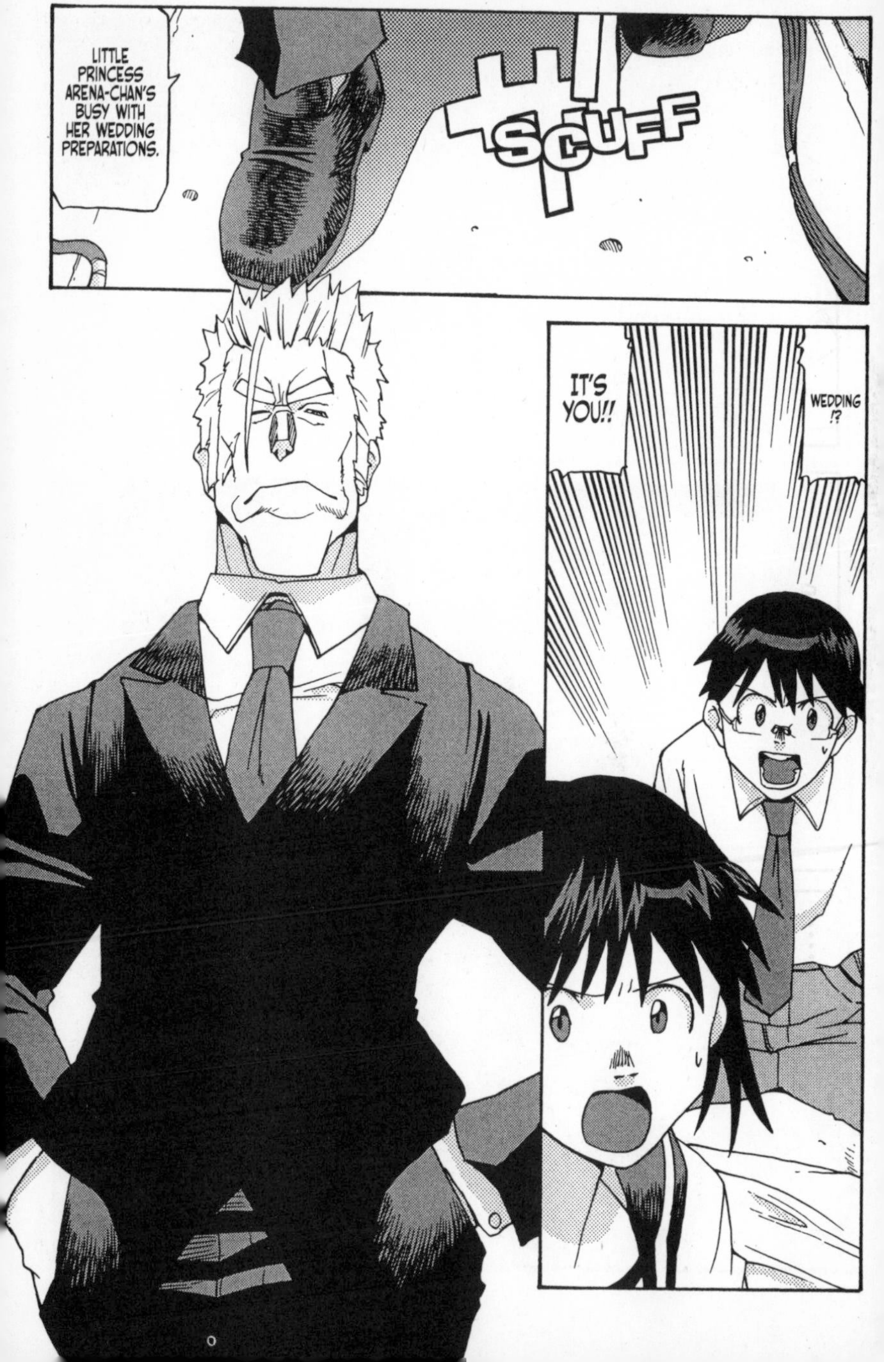
SCUFF
LITTLE PRINCESS ARENA-CHAN'S BUSY WITH HER WEDDING PREPARATIONS.
WEDDING!?
IT'S YOU!!

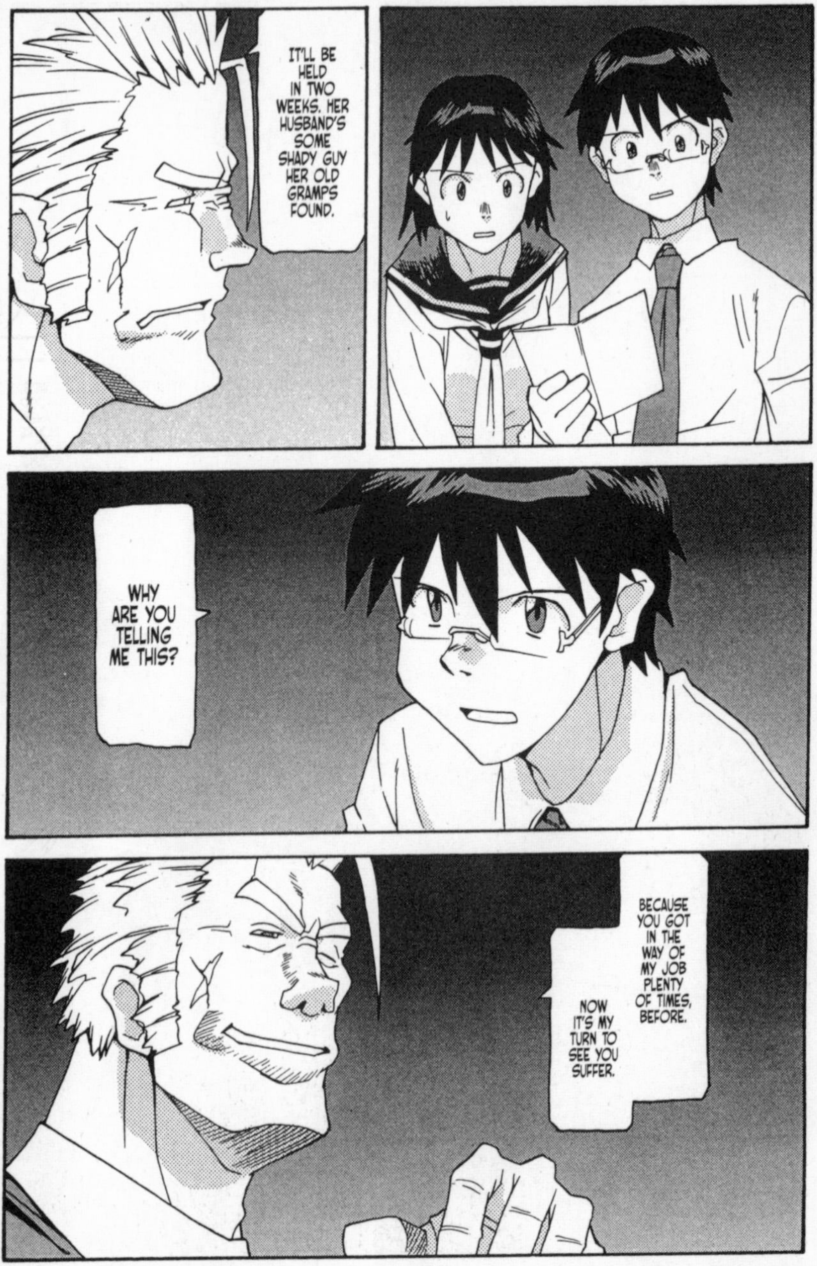
IT'LL BE HELD IN TWO WEEKS. HER HUSBAND'S SOME SHADY GUY HER OLD GRAMPS FOUND.
WHY ARE YOU TELLING ME THIS?
BECAUSE YOU GOT IN THE WAY OF MY JOB PLENTY OF TIMES, BEFORE.
NOW IT'S MY TURN TO SEE YOU SUFFER.

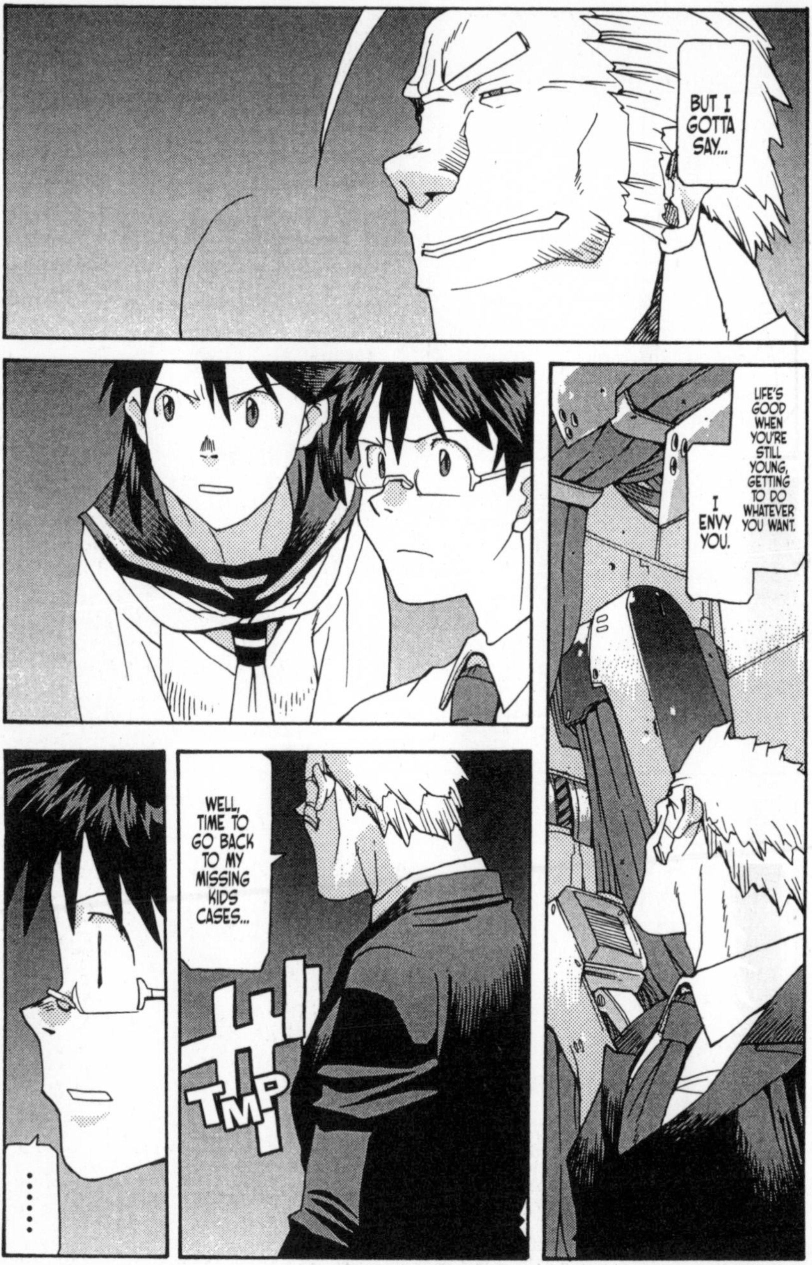

BUT I GOTTA SAY...
LIFE'S GOOD WHEN YOU'RE STILL YOUNG, GETTING TO DO WHATEVER YOU WANT.
I ENVY YOU.
WELL, TIME TO GO BACK TO MY MISSING KIDS CASES...
TMP
......

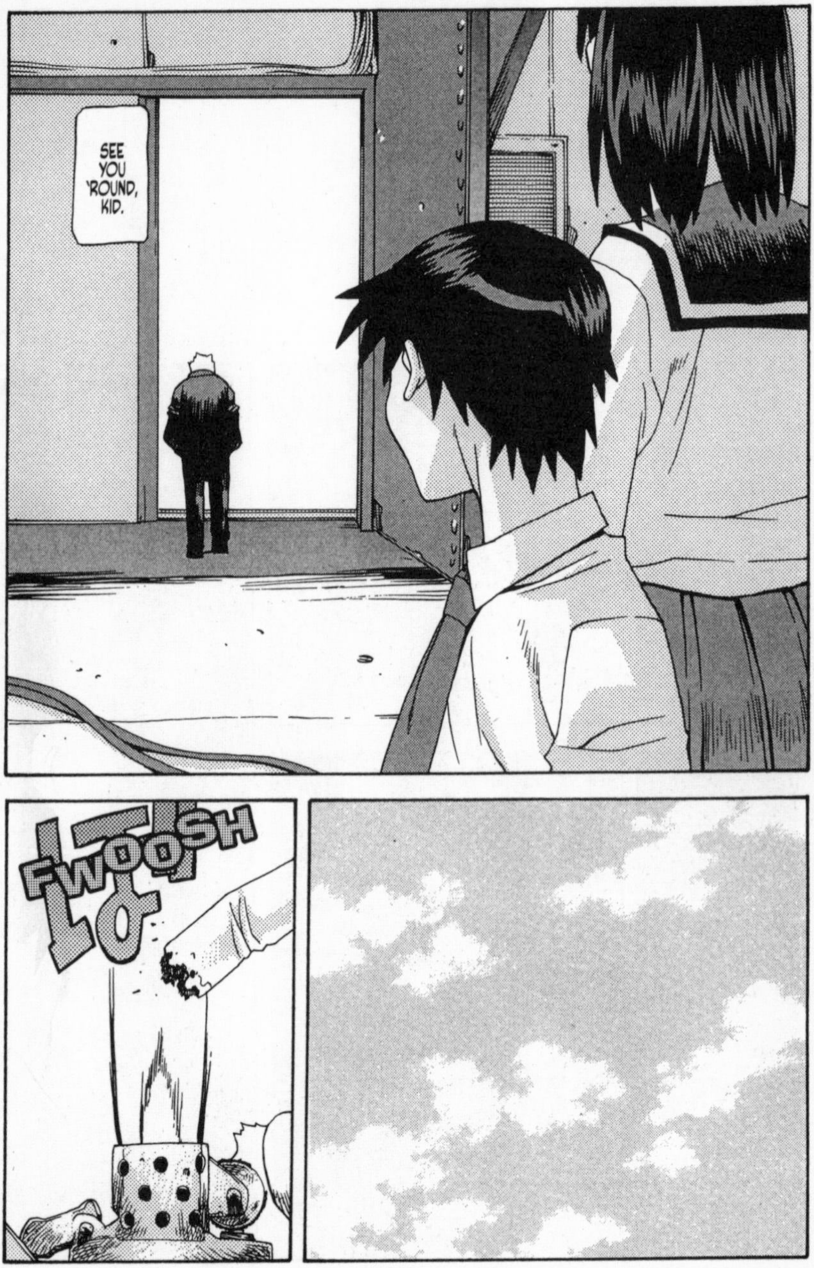
SEE YOU 'ROUND, KID.
FWOOSH

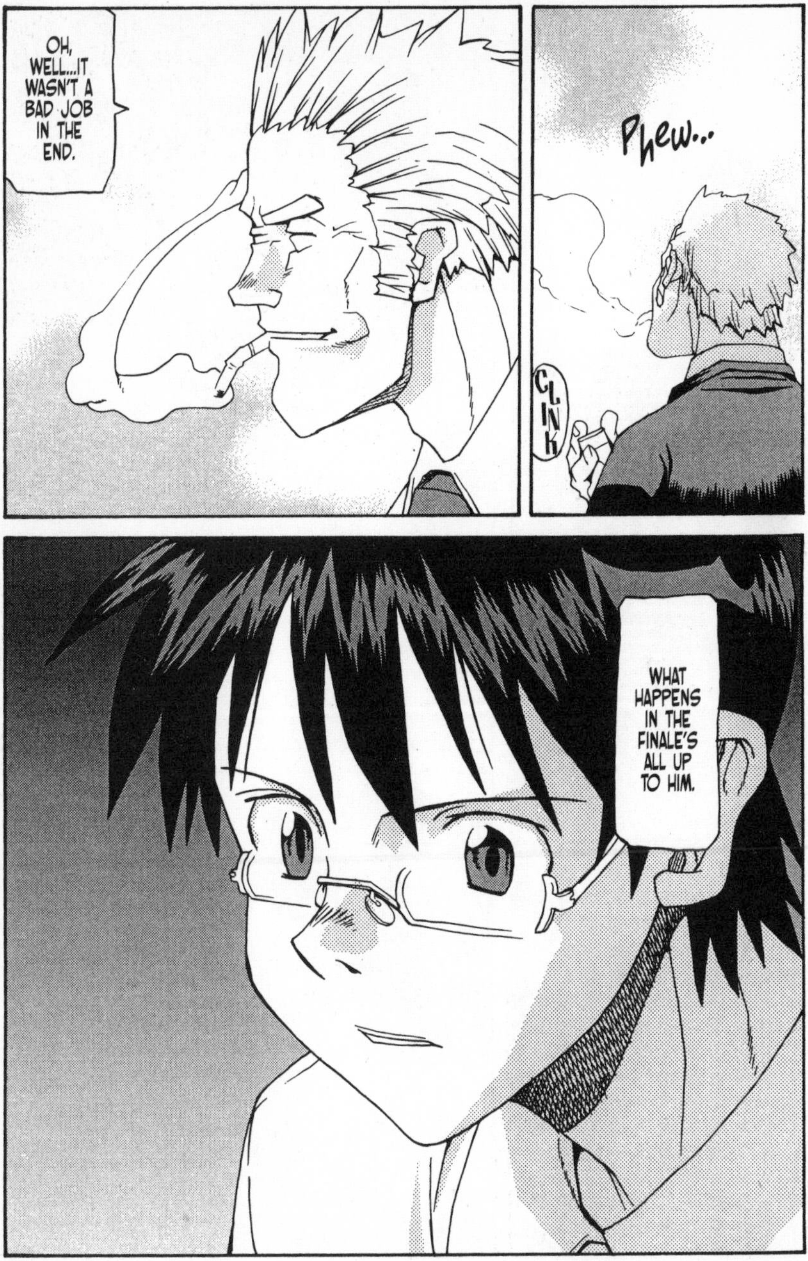
Phew...
CLINK
OH, WELL...IT WASN'T A BAD JOB IN THE END.
WHAT HAPPENS IN THE FINALE'S ALL UP TO HIM.

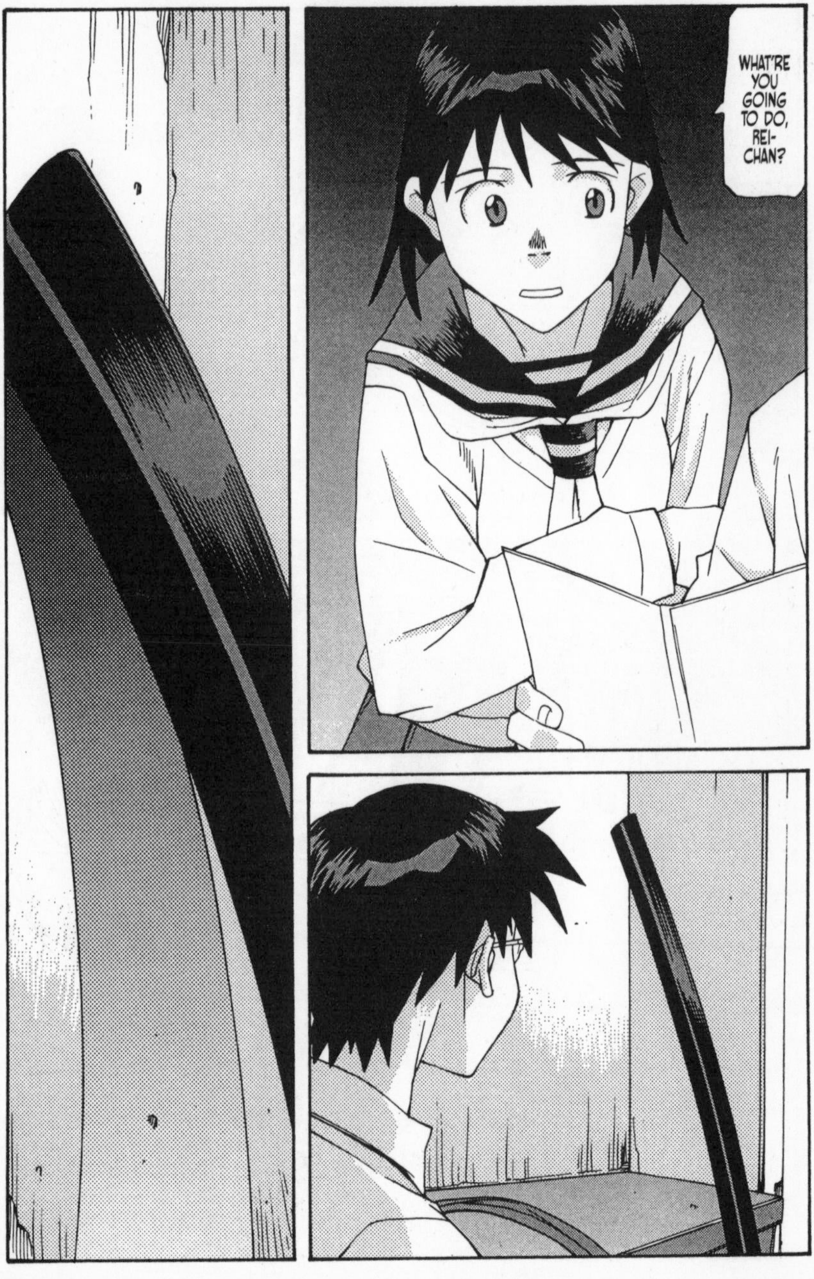
WHAT'RE YOU GOING TO DO, REI-CHAN?

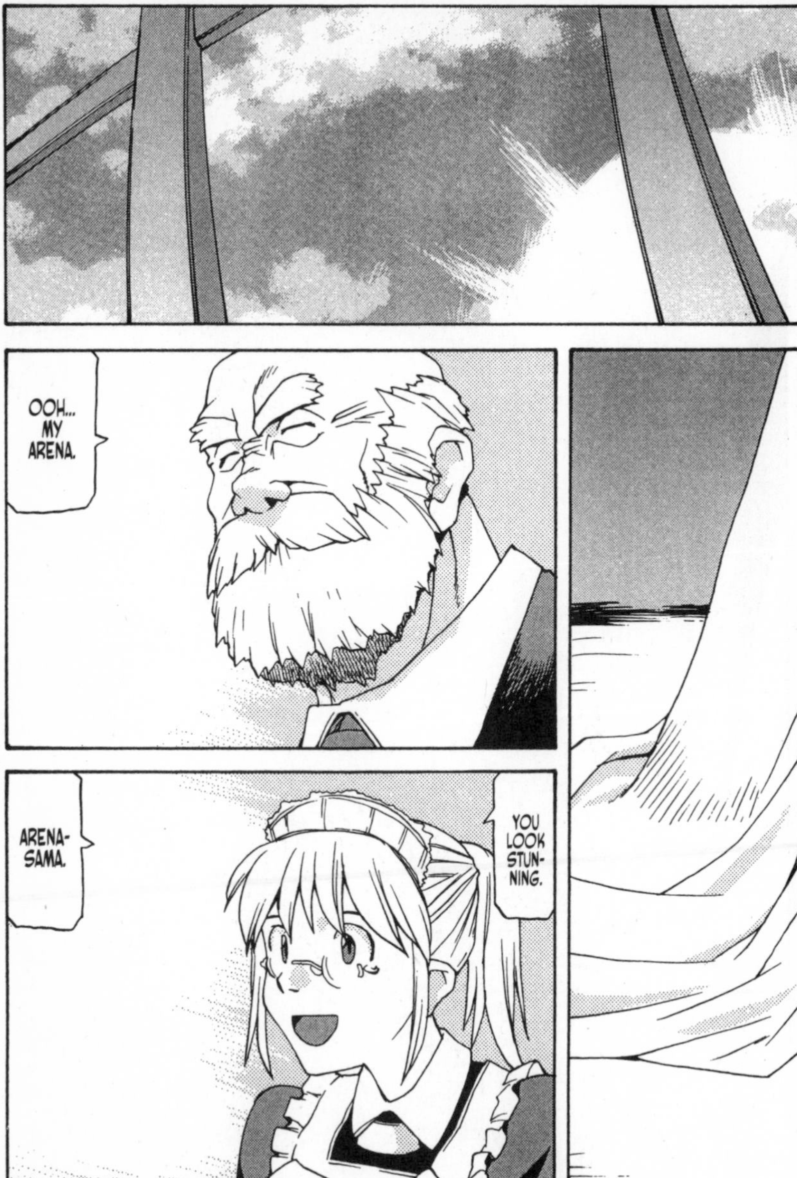
OOH... MY ARENA.
YOU LOOK STUN-NING.
ARENA-SAMA.

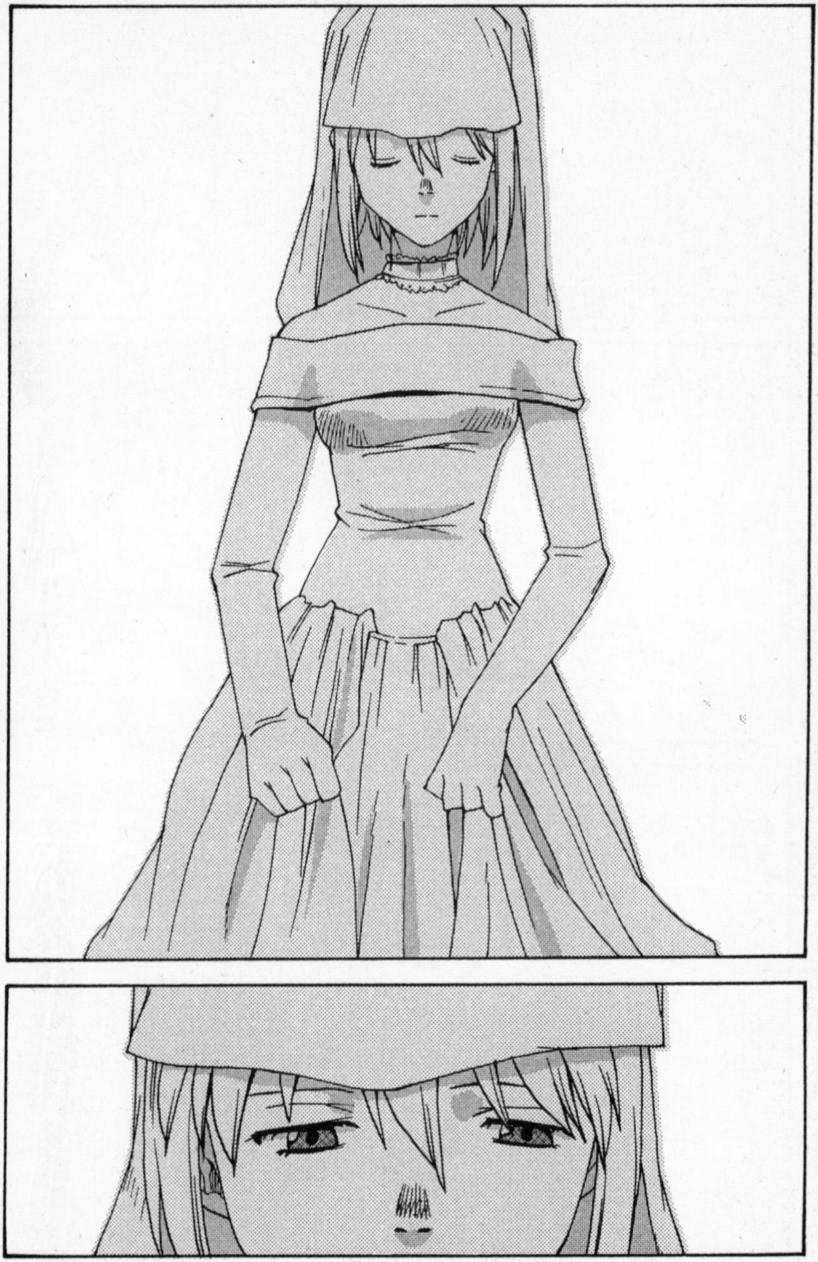

TRANSFER
ode.38
New Episode
INTO THE B ES
03.3.20
0038

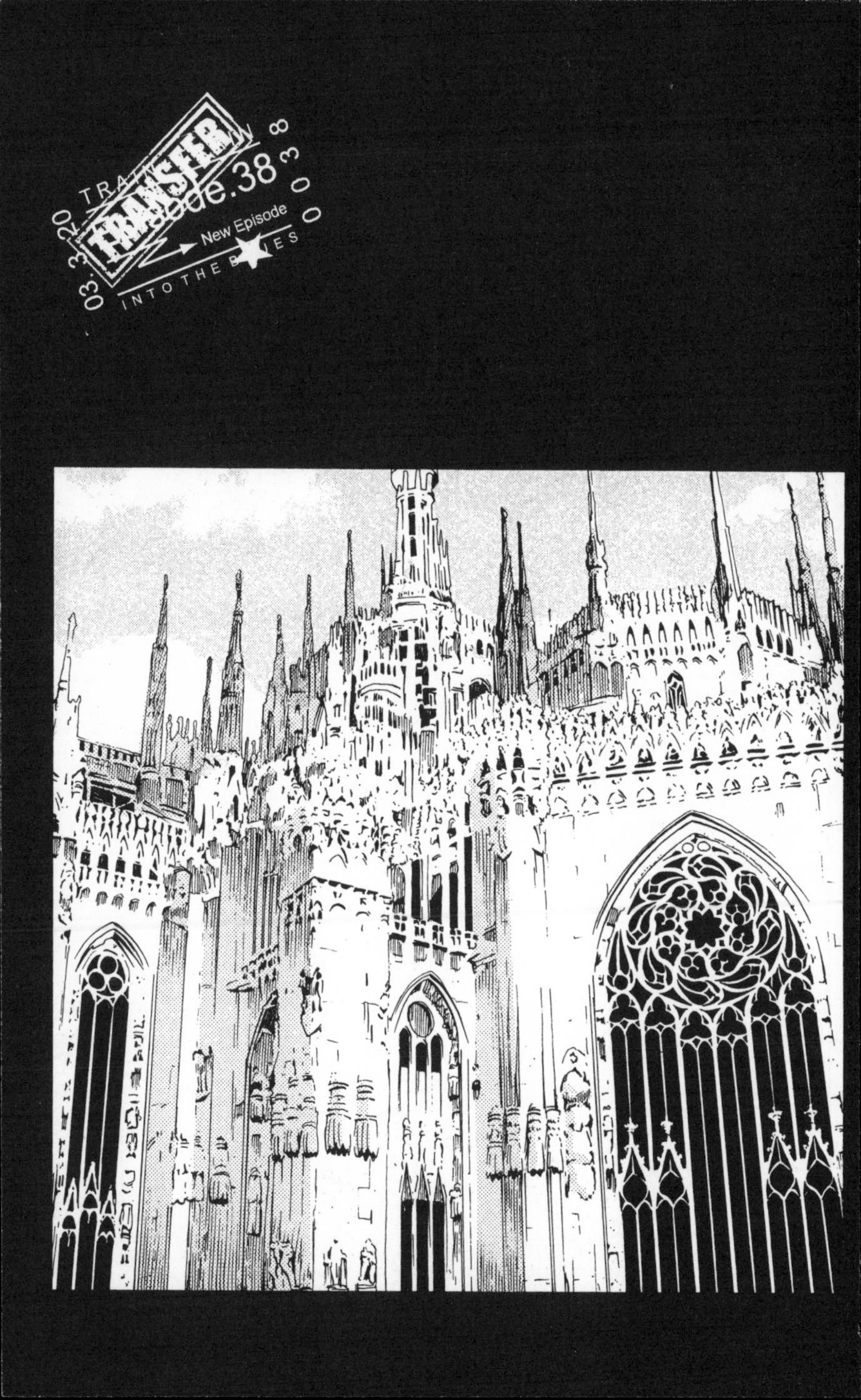

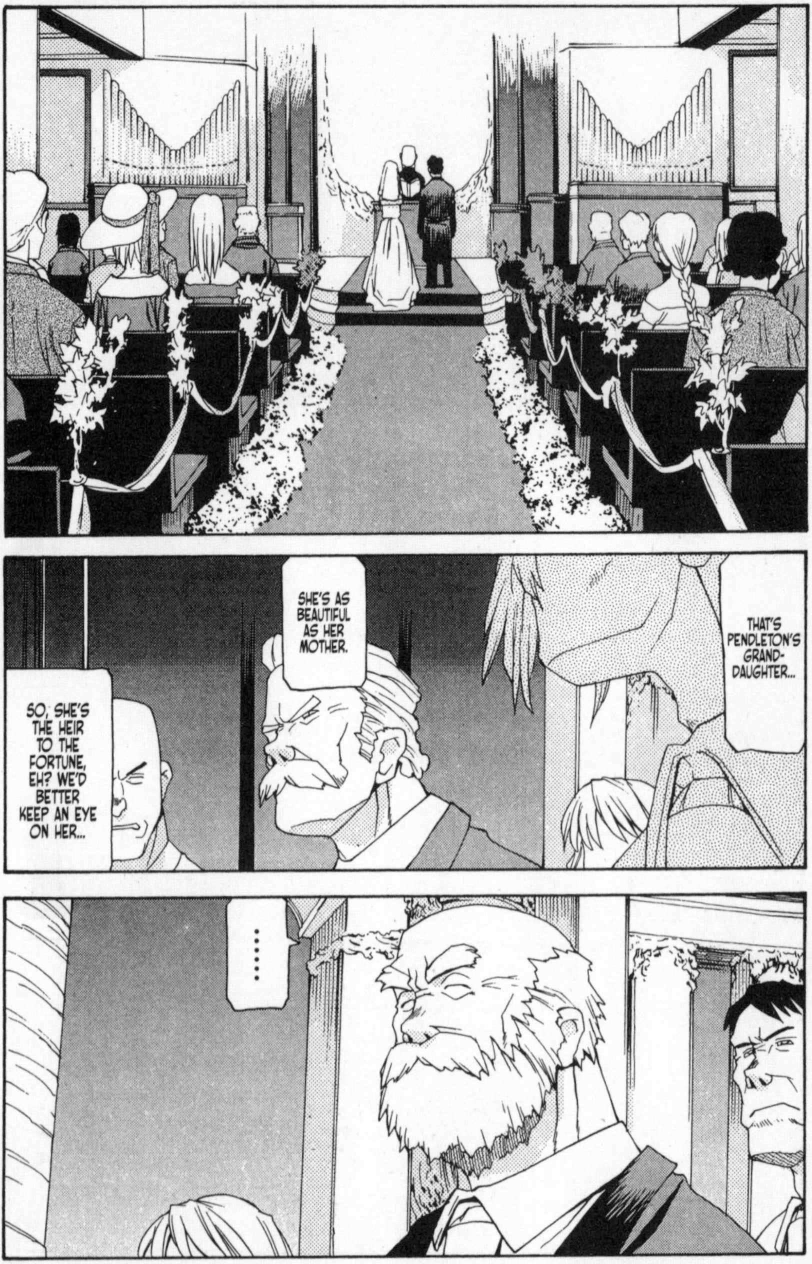
THAT'S PENDLETON'S GRAND-DAUGHTER...
SHE'S AS BEAUTIFUL AS HER MOTHER.
SO, SHE'S THE HEIR TO THE FORTUNE, EH? WE'D BETTER KEEP AN EYE ON HER...
......

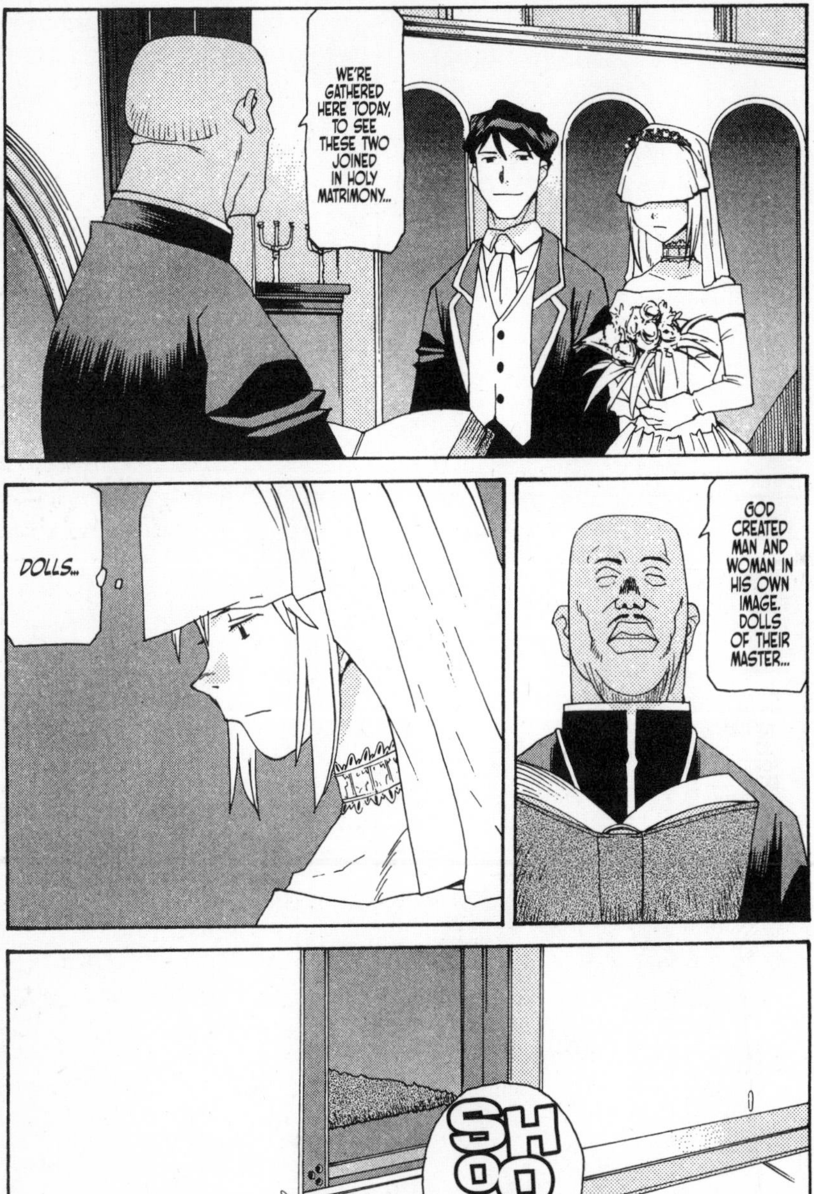
WE'RE GATHERED HERE TODAY, TO SEE THESE TWO JOINED IN HOLY MATRIMONY...
GOD CREATED MAN AND WOMAN IN HIS OWN IMAGE. DOLLS OF THEIR MASTER...
DOLLS...
SHOOP

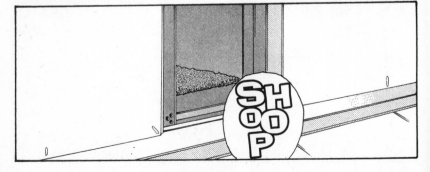

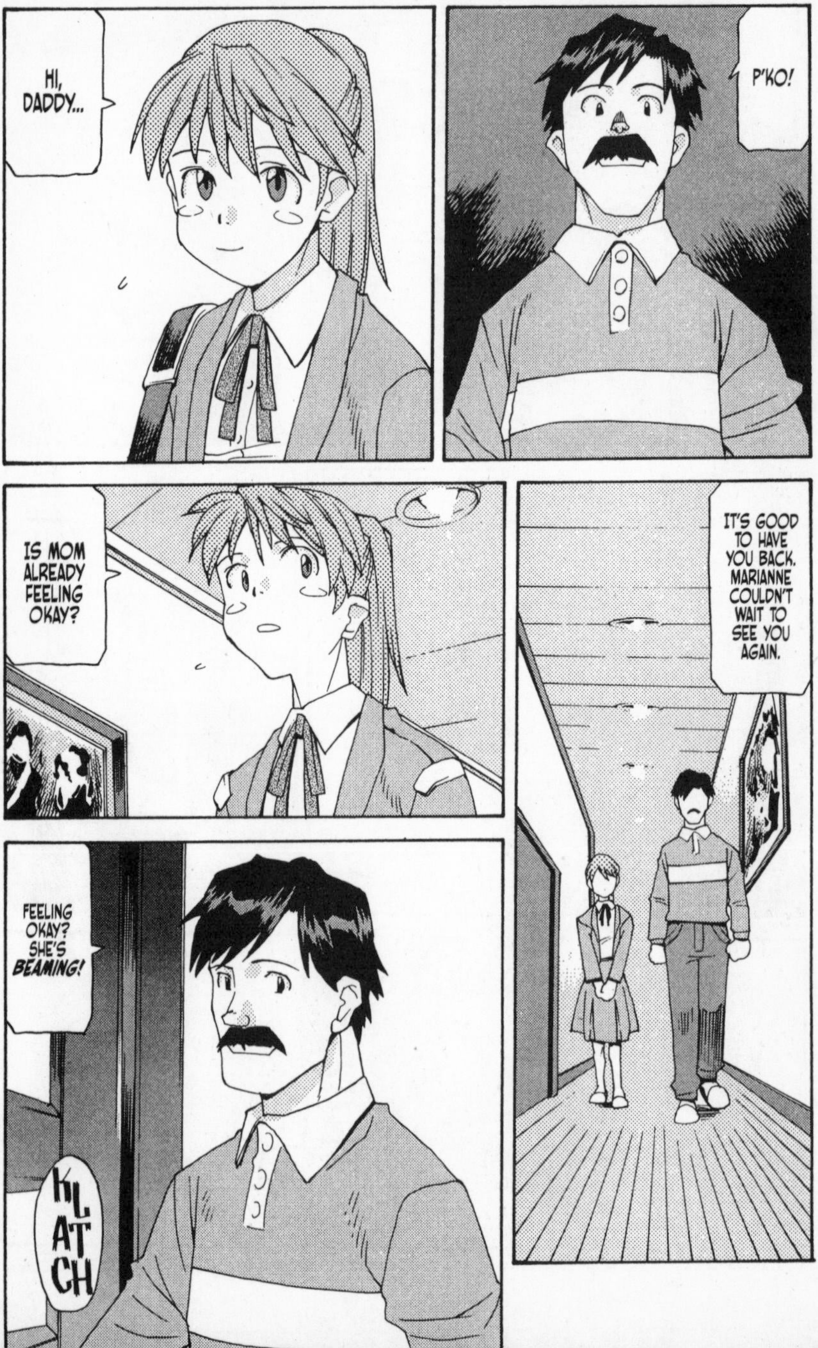
P'KO!
HI, DADDY...
IT'S GOOD TO HAVE YOU BACK. MARIANNE COULDN'T WAIT TO SEE YOU AGAIN.
IS MOM ALREADY FEELING OKAY?
FEELING OKAY? SHE'S *BEAMING!*
KLATCH

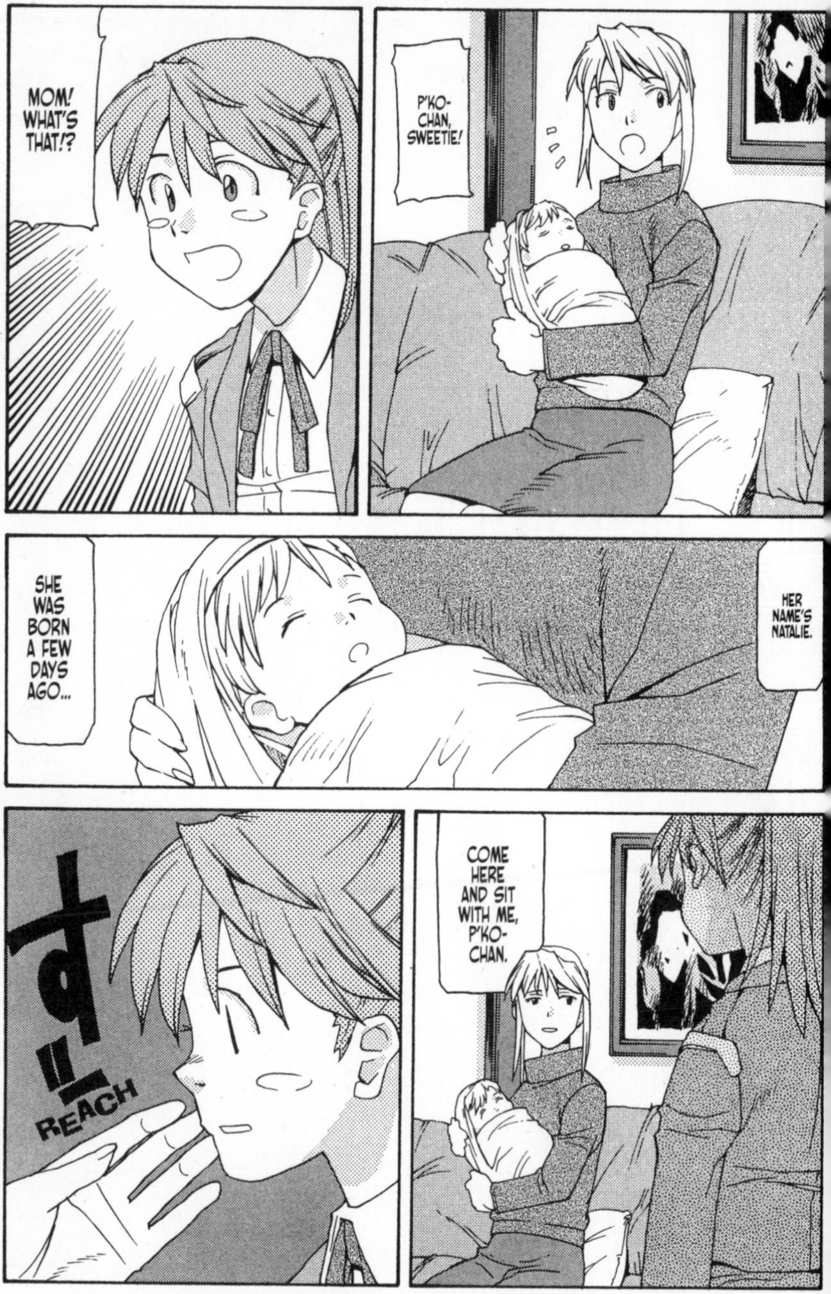
P'KO-CHAN, SWEETIE!
MOM! WHAT'S THAT!?
HER NAME'S NATALIE.
SHE WAS BORN A FEW DAYS AGO...
COME HERE AND SIT WITH ME, P'KO-CHAN.
REACH

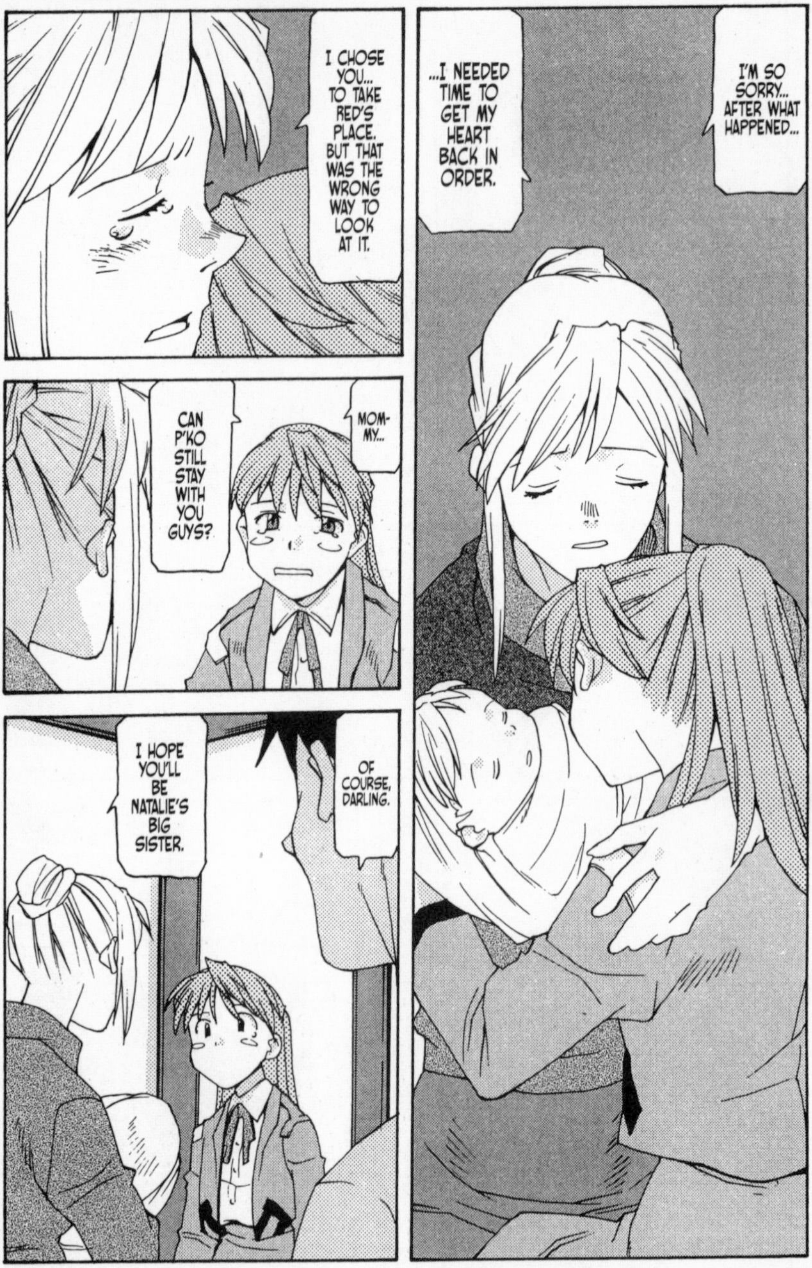
I'M SO SORRY... AFTER WHAT HAPPENED...
...I NEEDED TIME TO GET MY HEART BACK IN ORDER.
I CHOSE YOU... TO TAKE RED'S PLACE. BUT THAT WAS THE WRONG WAY TO LOOK AT IT.
MOM-MY...
CAN P'KO STILL STAY WITH YOU GUYS?
OF COURSE, DARLING.
I HOPE YOU'LL BE NATALIE'S BIG SISTER.

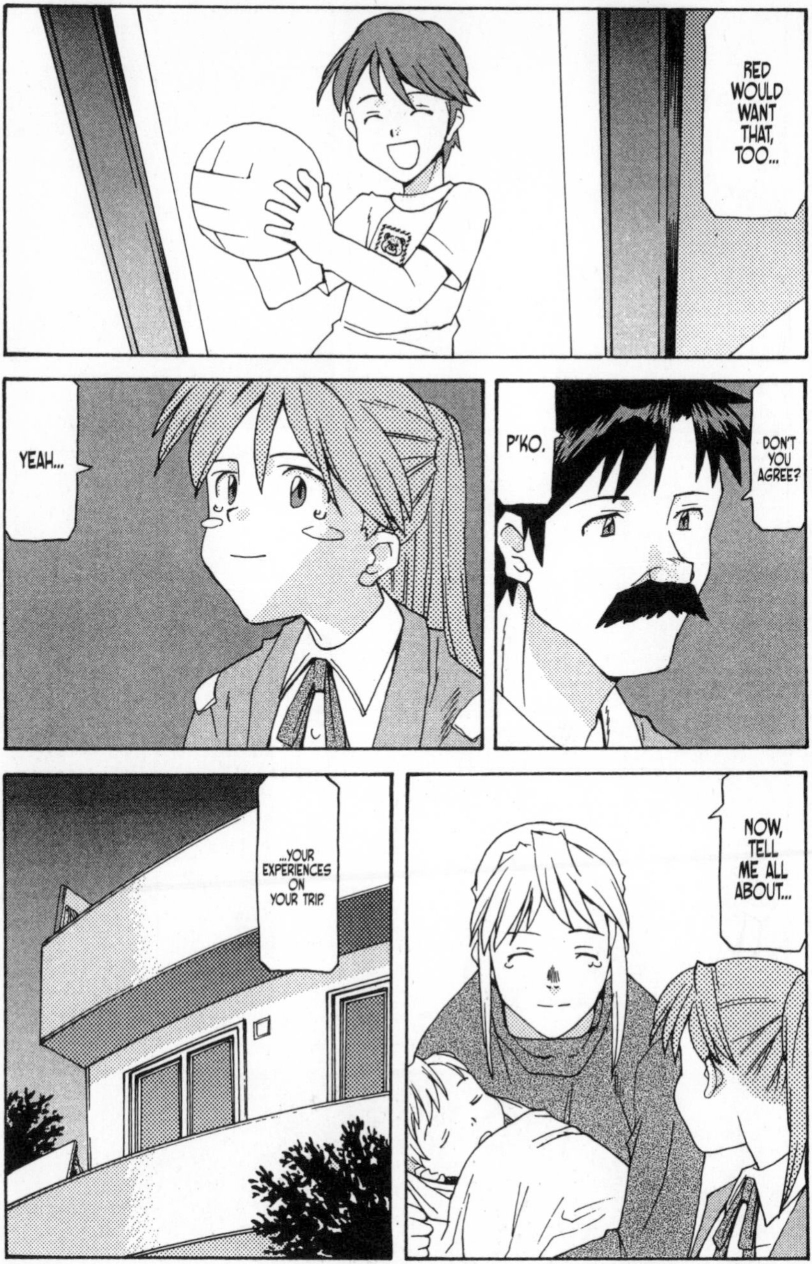
RED WOULD WANT THAT, TOO...
DON'T YOU AGREE?
P'KO.
YEAH...
NOW, TELL ME ALL ABOUT...
...YOUR EXPERIENCES ON YOUR TRIP.

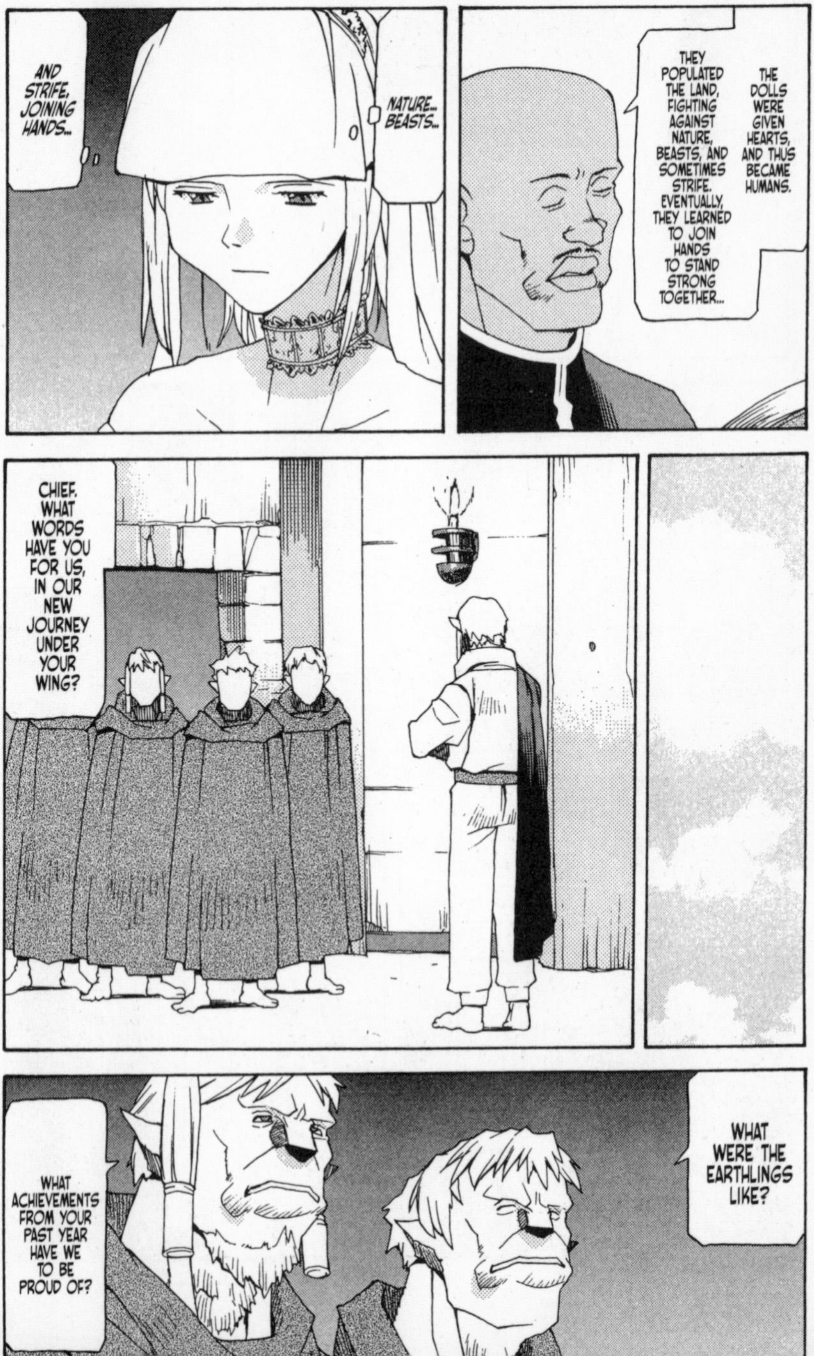
THE DOLLS WERE GIVEN HEARTS, AND THUS BECAME HUMANS.
THEY POPULATED THE LAND, FIGHTING AGAINST NATURE, BEASTS, AND SOMETIMES STRIFE. EVENTUALLY, THEY LEARNED TO JOIN HANDS TO STAND STRONG TOGETHER...
NATURE... BEASTS...
AND STRIFE, JOINING HANDS...
CHIEF. WHAT WORDS HAVE YOU FOR US, IN OUR NEW JOURNEY UNDER YOUR WING?
WHAT WERE THE EARTHLINGS LIKE?
WHAT ACHIEVEMENTS FROM YOUR PAST YEAR HAVE WE TO BE PROUD OF?

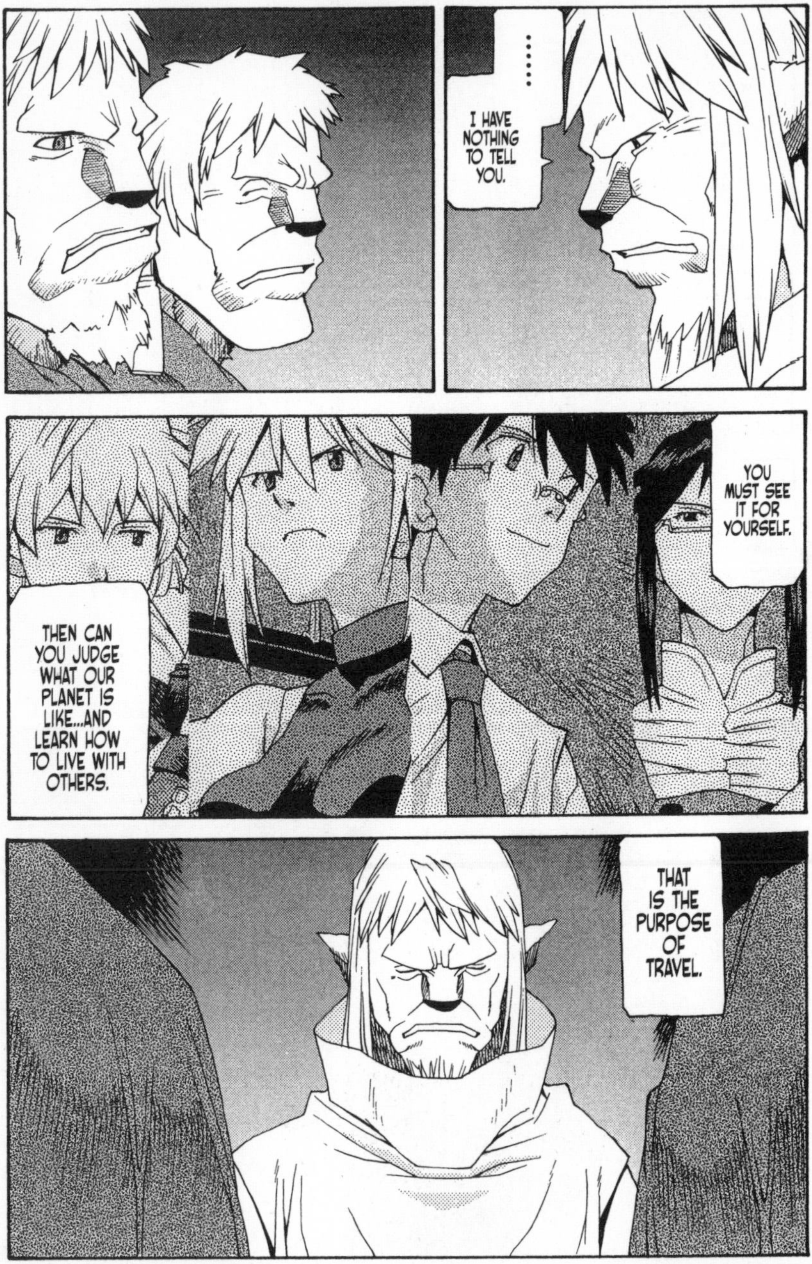
……
I HAVE NOTHING TO TELL YOU.
YOU MUST SEE IT FOR YOURSELF.
THEN CAN YOU JUDGE WHAT OUR PLANET IS LIKE...AND LEARN HOW TO LIVE WITH OTHERS.
THAT IS THE PURPOSE OF TRAVEL.

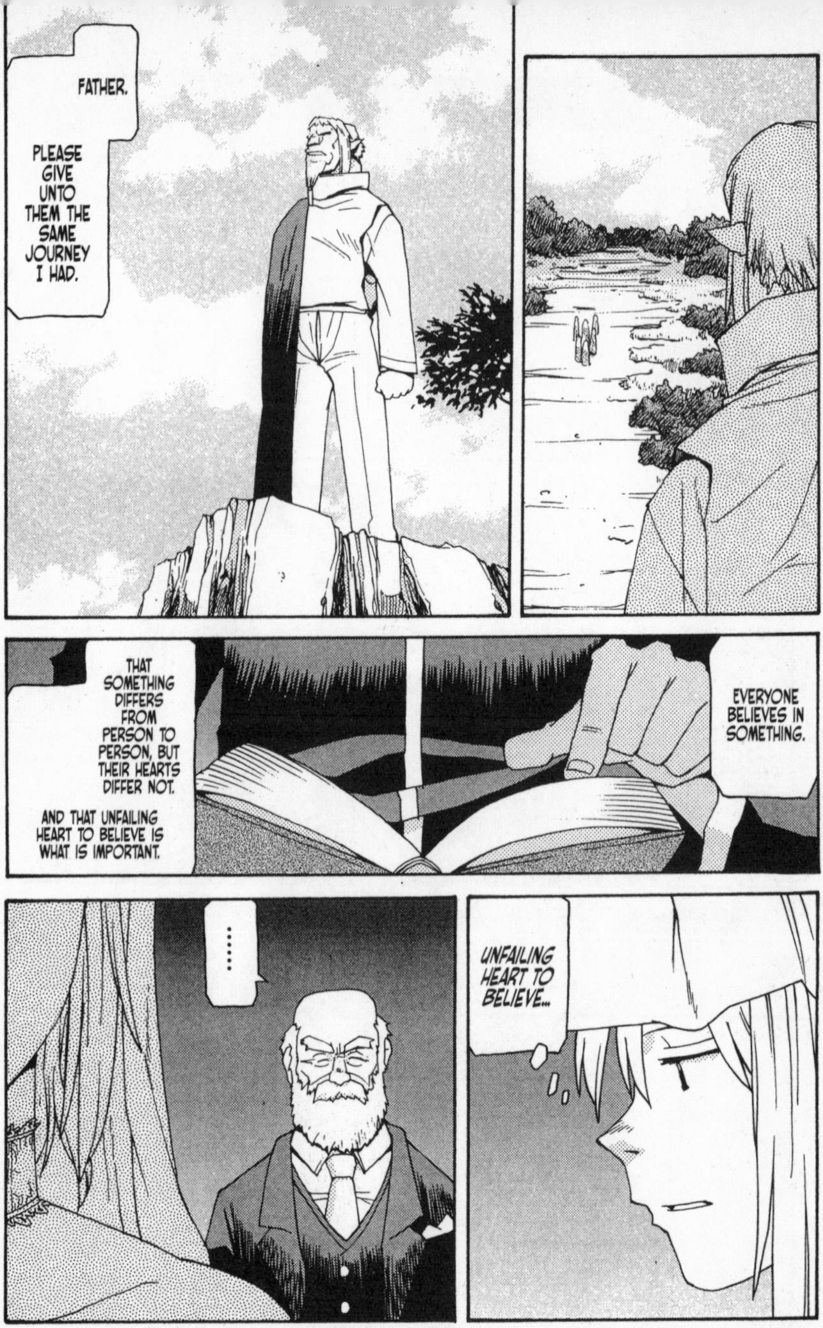
FATHER.
PLEASE GIVE UNTO THEM THE SAME JOURNEY I HAD.
EVERYONE BELIEVES IN SOMETHING.
THAT SOMETHING DIFFERS FROM PERSON TO PERSON, BUT THEIR HEARTS DIFFER NOT.
AND THAT UNFAILING HEART TO BELIEVE IS WHAT IS IMPORTANT.
UNFAILING HEART TO BELIEVE...
......

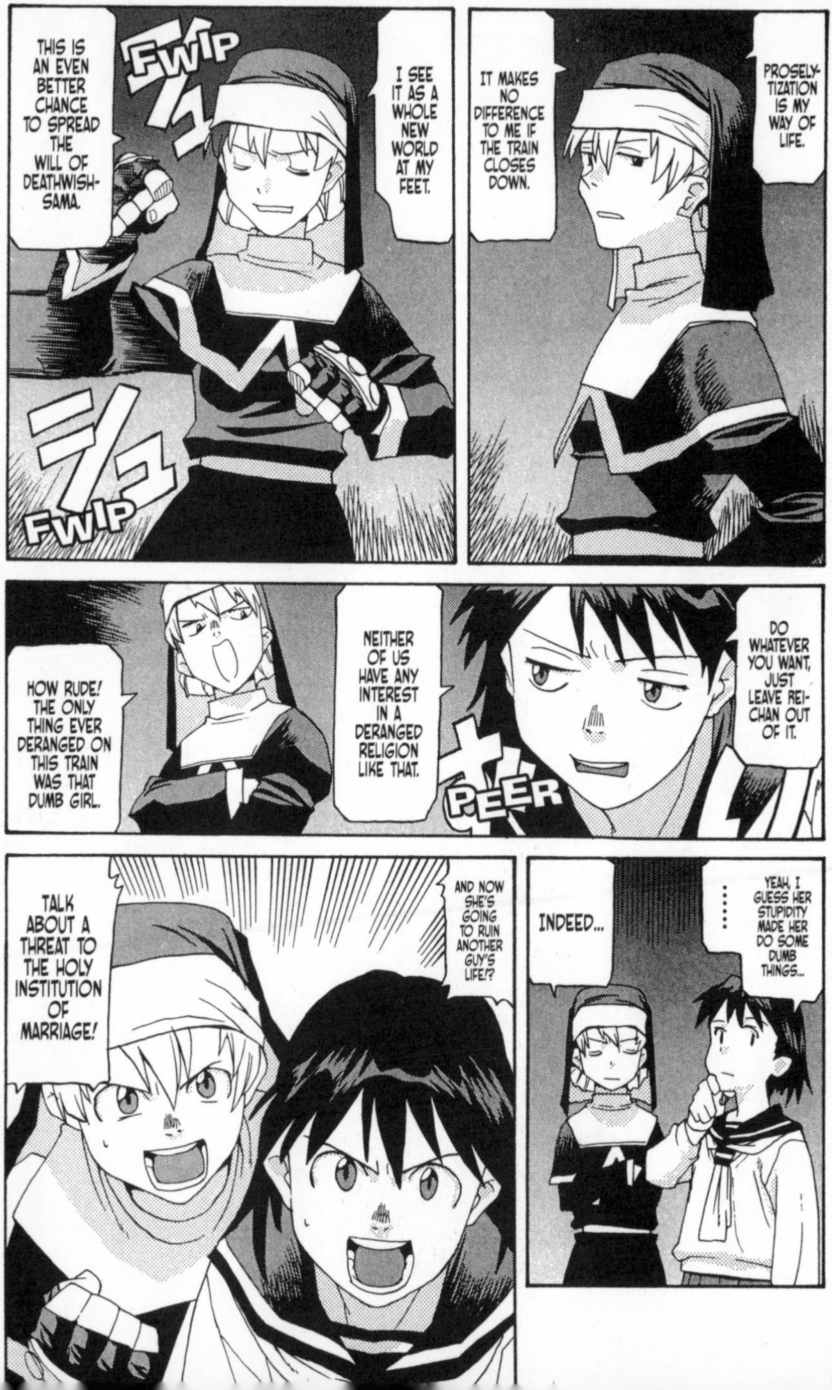
PROSELY-TIZATION IS MY WAY OF LIFE.
IT MAKES NO DIFFERENCE TO ME IF THE TRAIN CLOSES DOWN.
I SEE IT AS A WHOLE NEW WORLD AT MY FEET.
FWIP
THIS IS AN EVEN BETTER CHANCE TO SPREAD THE WILL OF DEATHWISH-SAMA.
FWIP
DO WHATEVER YOU WANT, JUST LEAVE REI-CHAN OUT OF IT.
PEER
NEITHER OF US HAVE ANY INTEREST IN A DERANGED RELIGION LIKE THAT.
HOW RUDE! THE ONLY THING EVER DERANGED ON THIS TRAIN WAS THAT DUMB GIRL.
YEAH, I GUESS HER STUPIDITY MADE HER DO SOME DUMB THINGS...
......
INDEED...
AND NOW SHE'S GOING TO RUIN ANOTHER GUY'S LIFE!?
TALK ABOUT A THREAT TO THE HOLY INSTITUTION OF MARRIAGE!

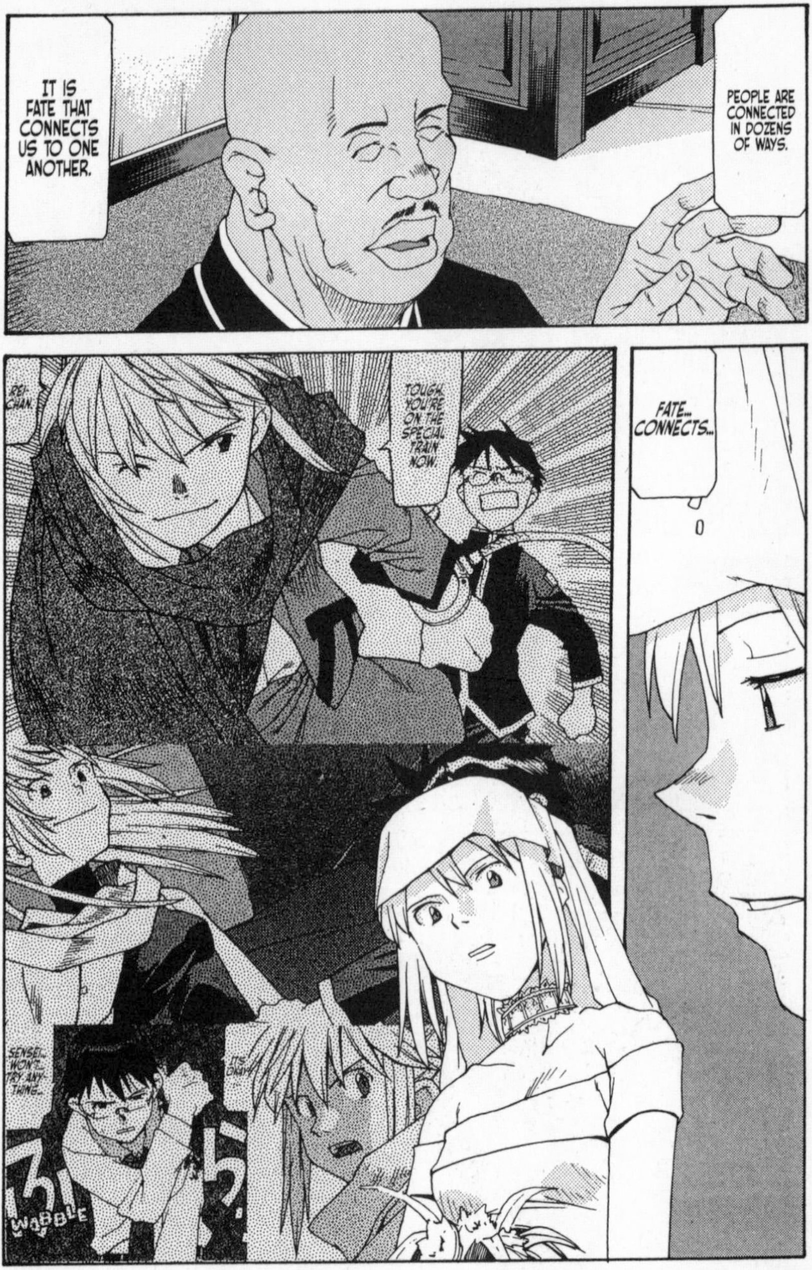
PEOPLE ARE CONNECTED IN DOZENS OF WAYS.
IT IS FATE THAT CONNECTS US TO ONE ANOTHER.
FATE... CONNECTS...
TOUGH. YOU'RE ON THE SPECIAL TRAIN NOW.
REI-CHAN.
IT'S OKAY!
SENSEI... WON'T... TRY ANY-THING...
WOBBLE

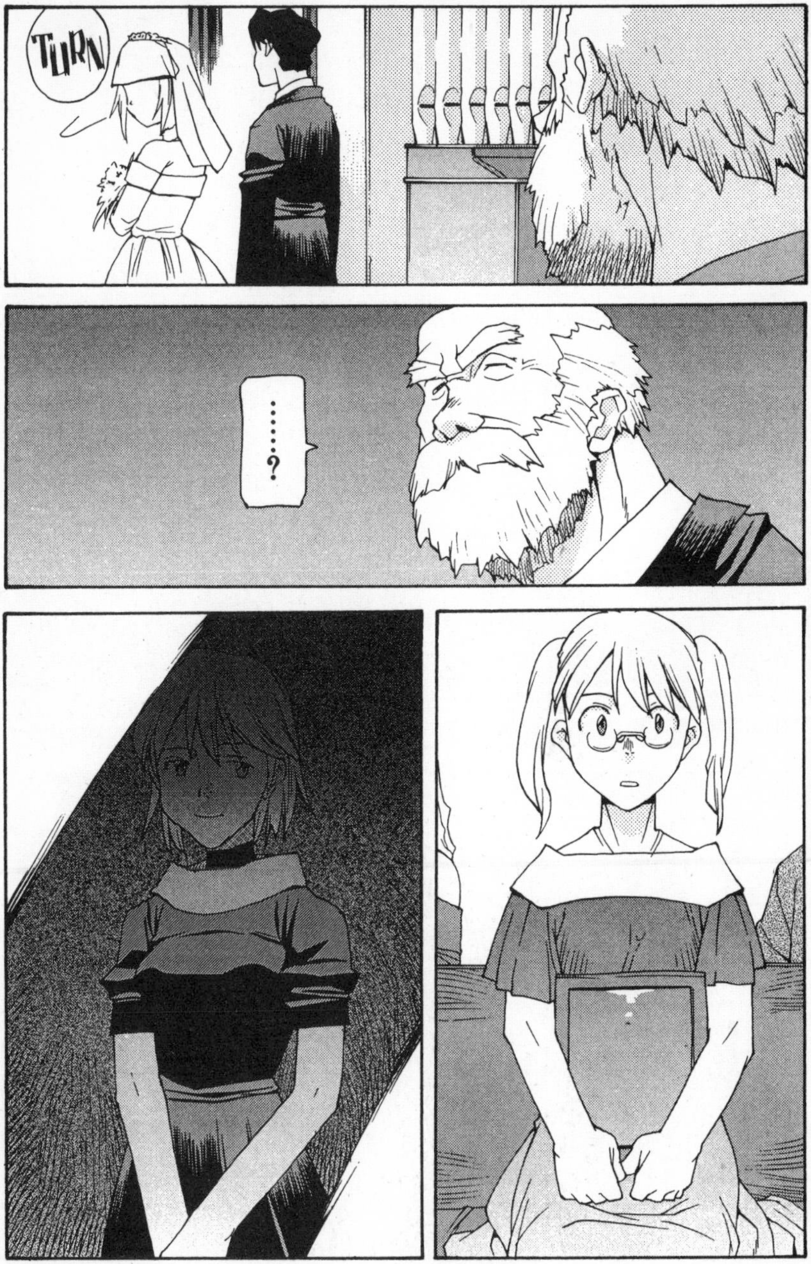
TURN
……?

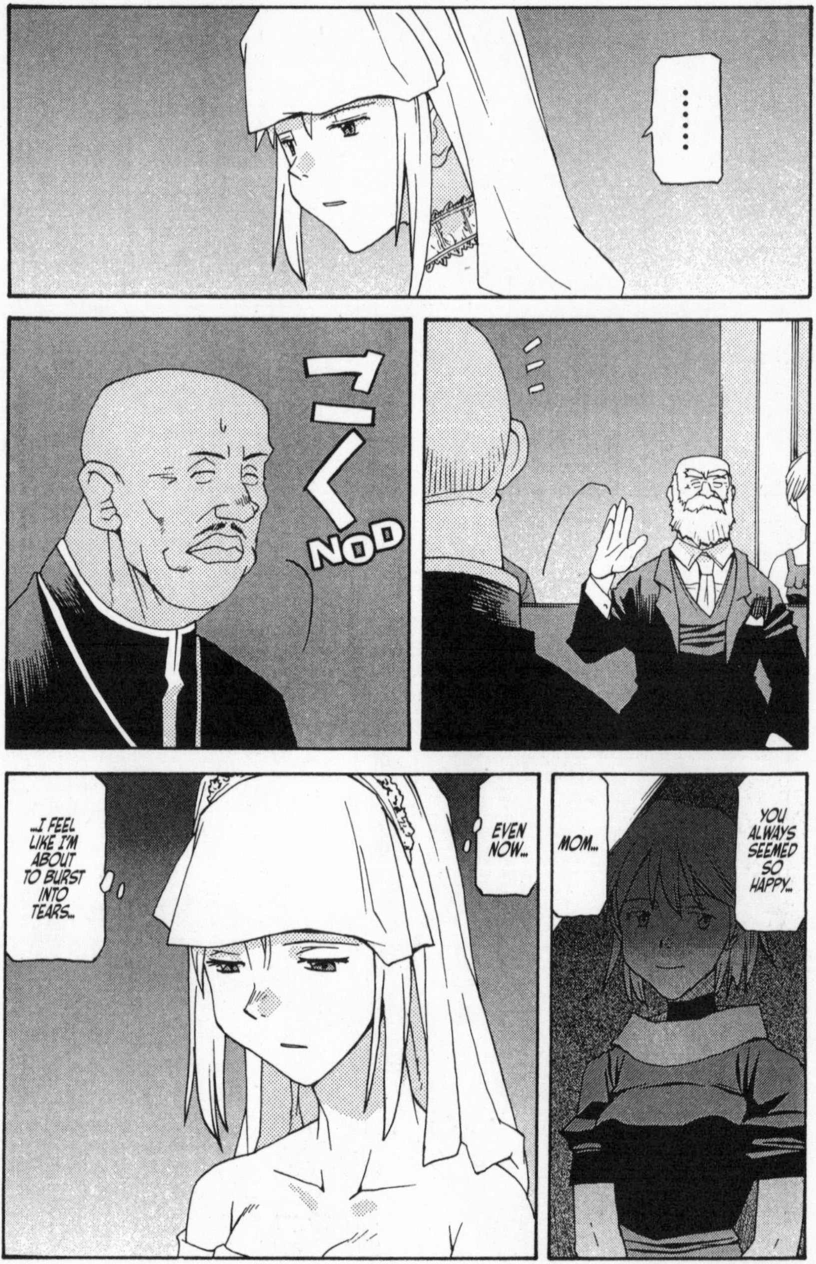
……
こく
NOD
YOU ALWAYS SEEMED SO HAPPY...
MOM...
EVEN NOW...
...I FEEL LIKE I'M ABOUT TO BURST INTO TEARS...

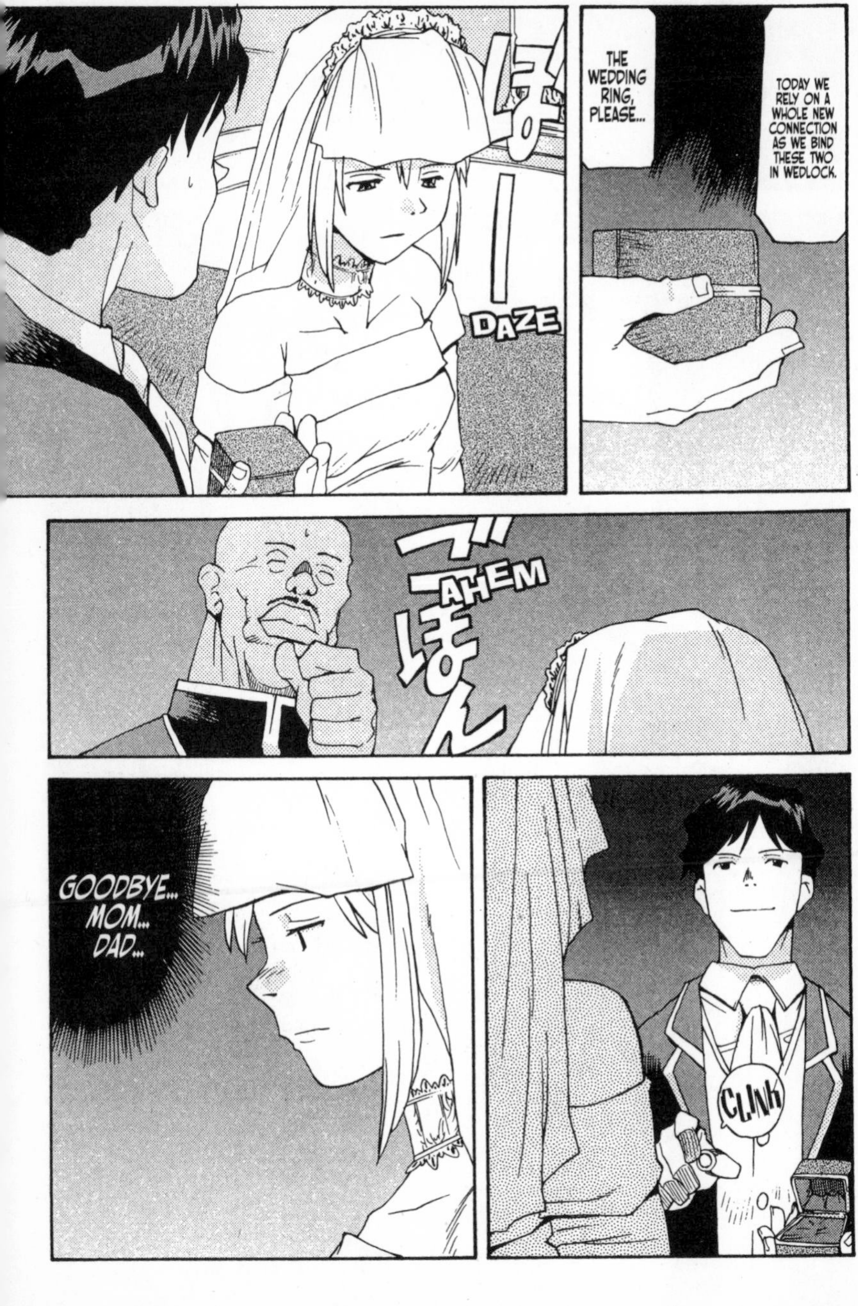
TODAY WE RELY ON A WHOLE NEW CONNECTION AS WE BIND THESE TWO IN WEDLOCK.
THE WEDDING RING, PLEASE...
ぼー
DAZE
ごほん
AHEM
CLINK
GOODBYE... MOM... DAD...

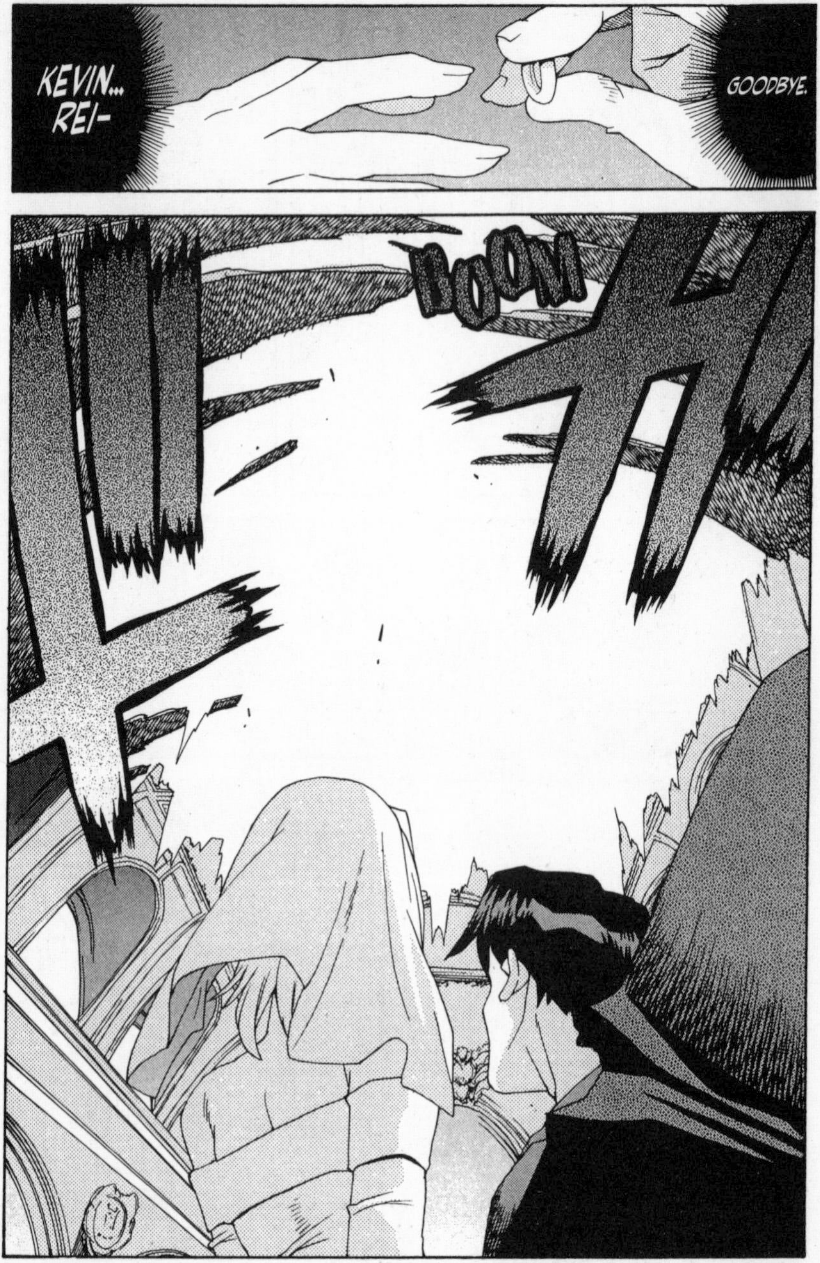
GOODBYE.
KEVIN... REI-
BOOM

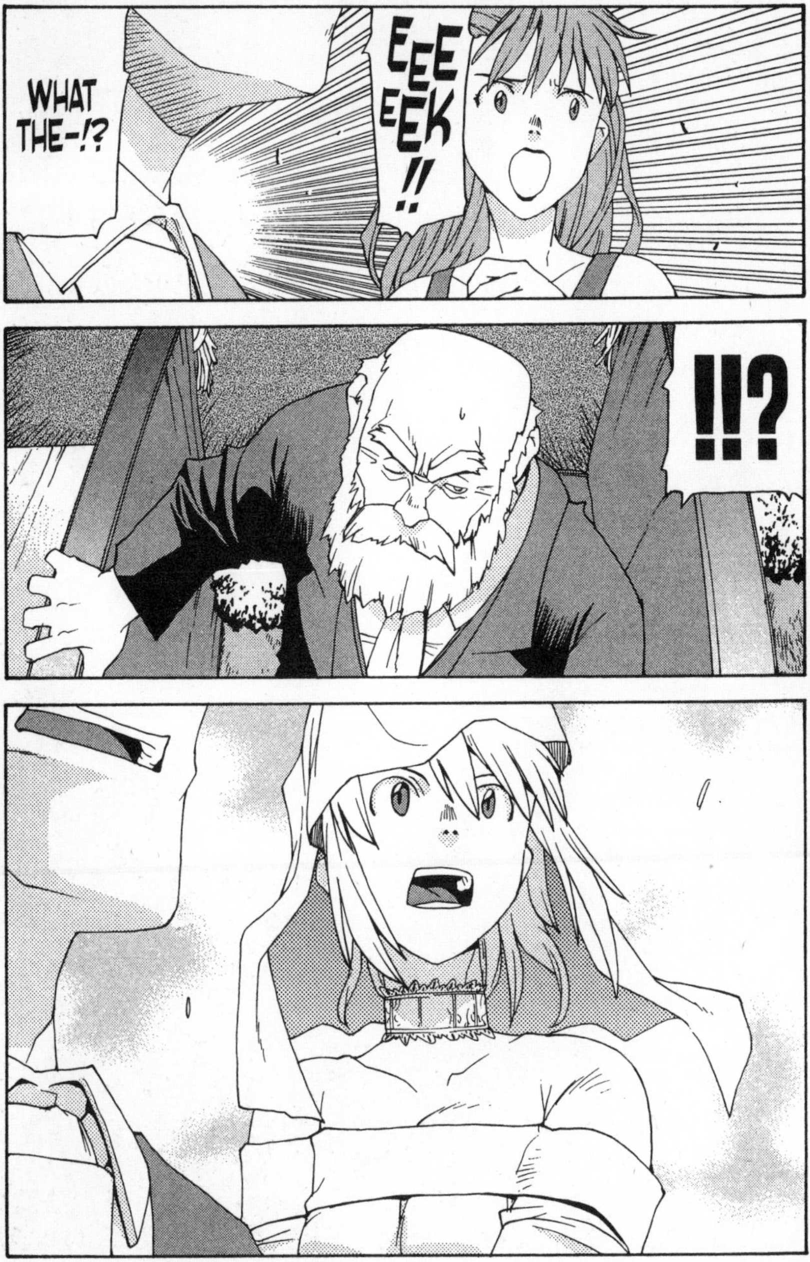
EEEEEK!!
WHAT THE-!?
!!?

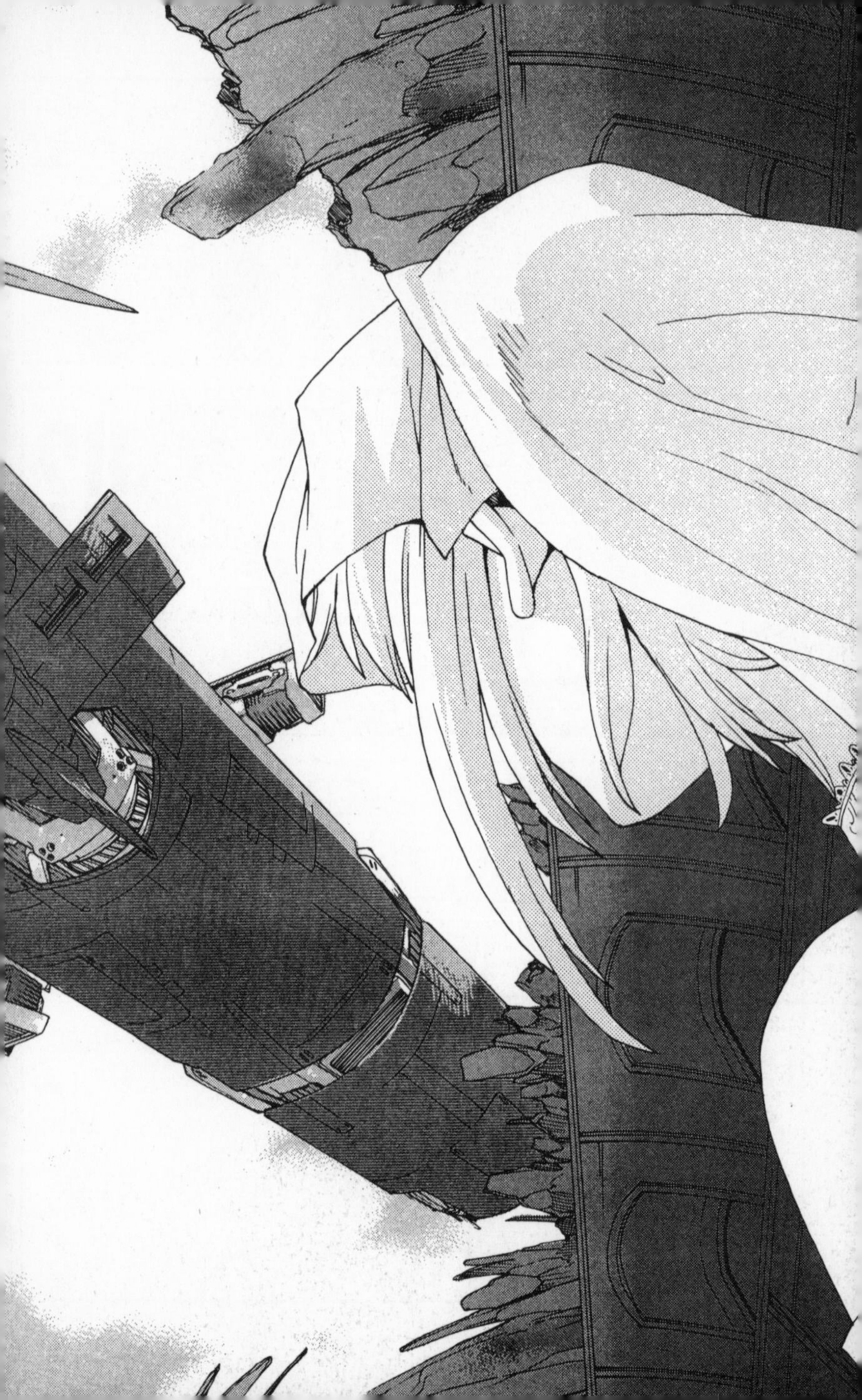

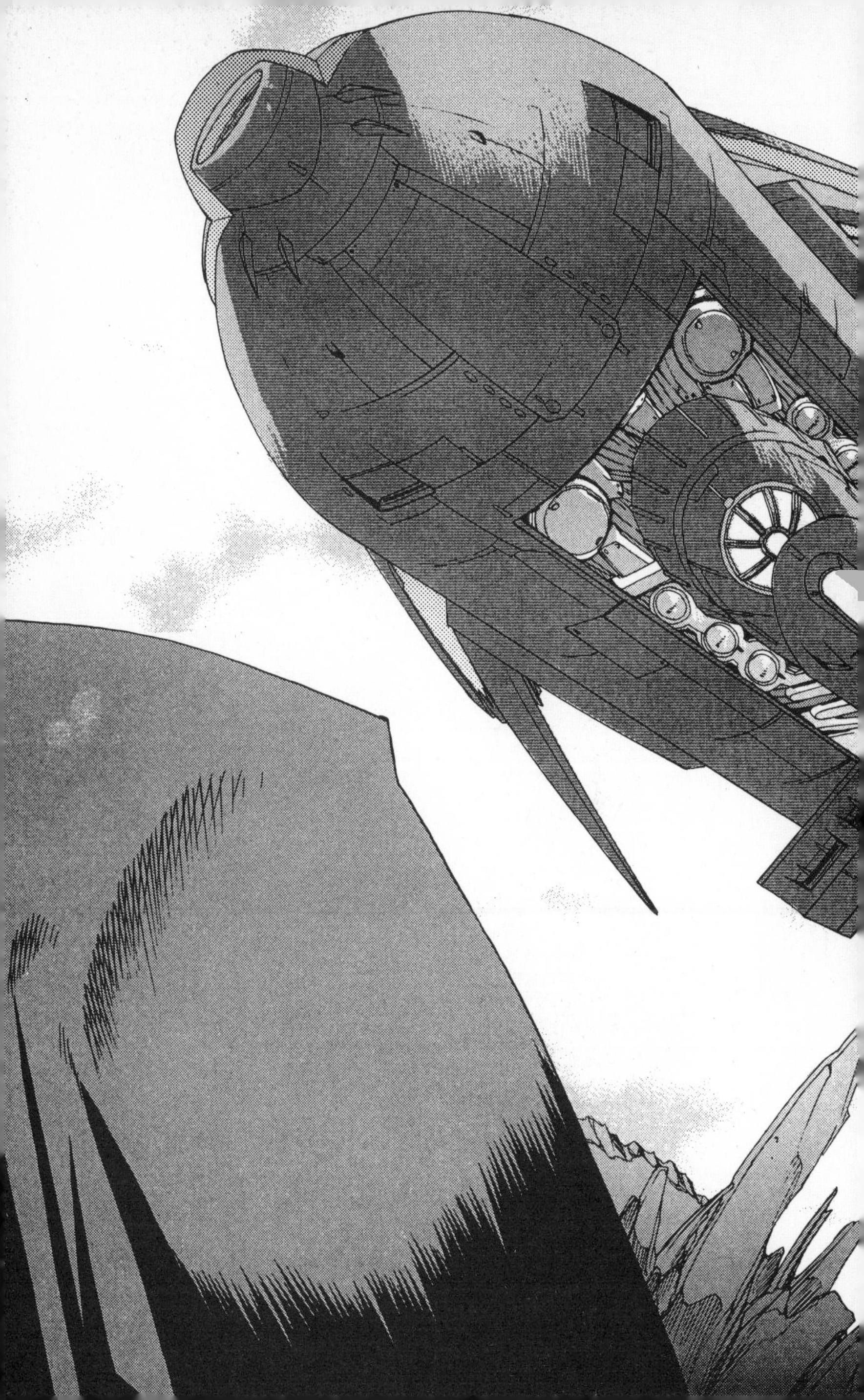

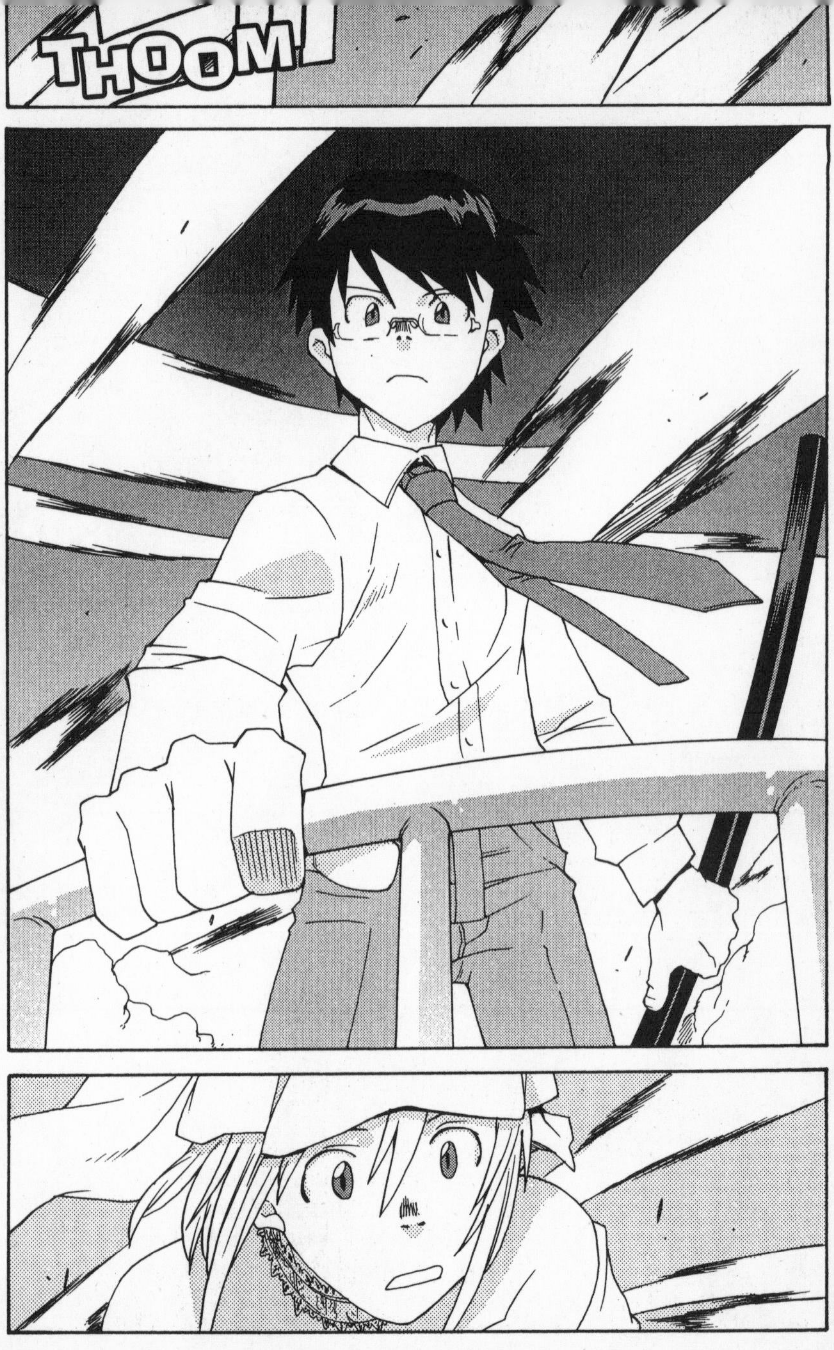
THOOM

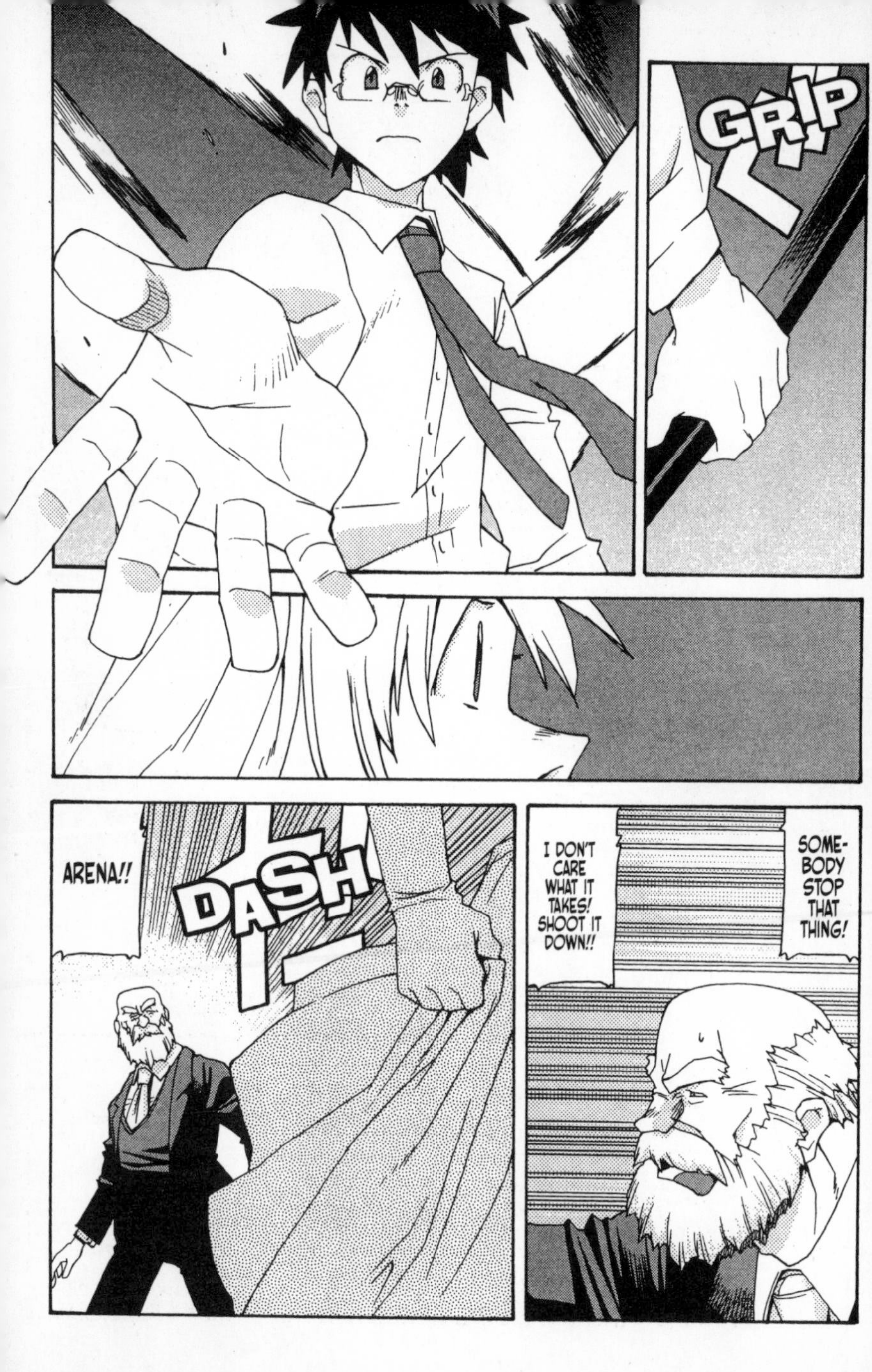
GRIP
SOME-BODY STOP THAT THING!
I DON'T CARE WHAT IT TAKES! SHOOT IT DOWN!!
DASH
ARENA!!

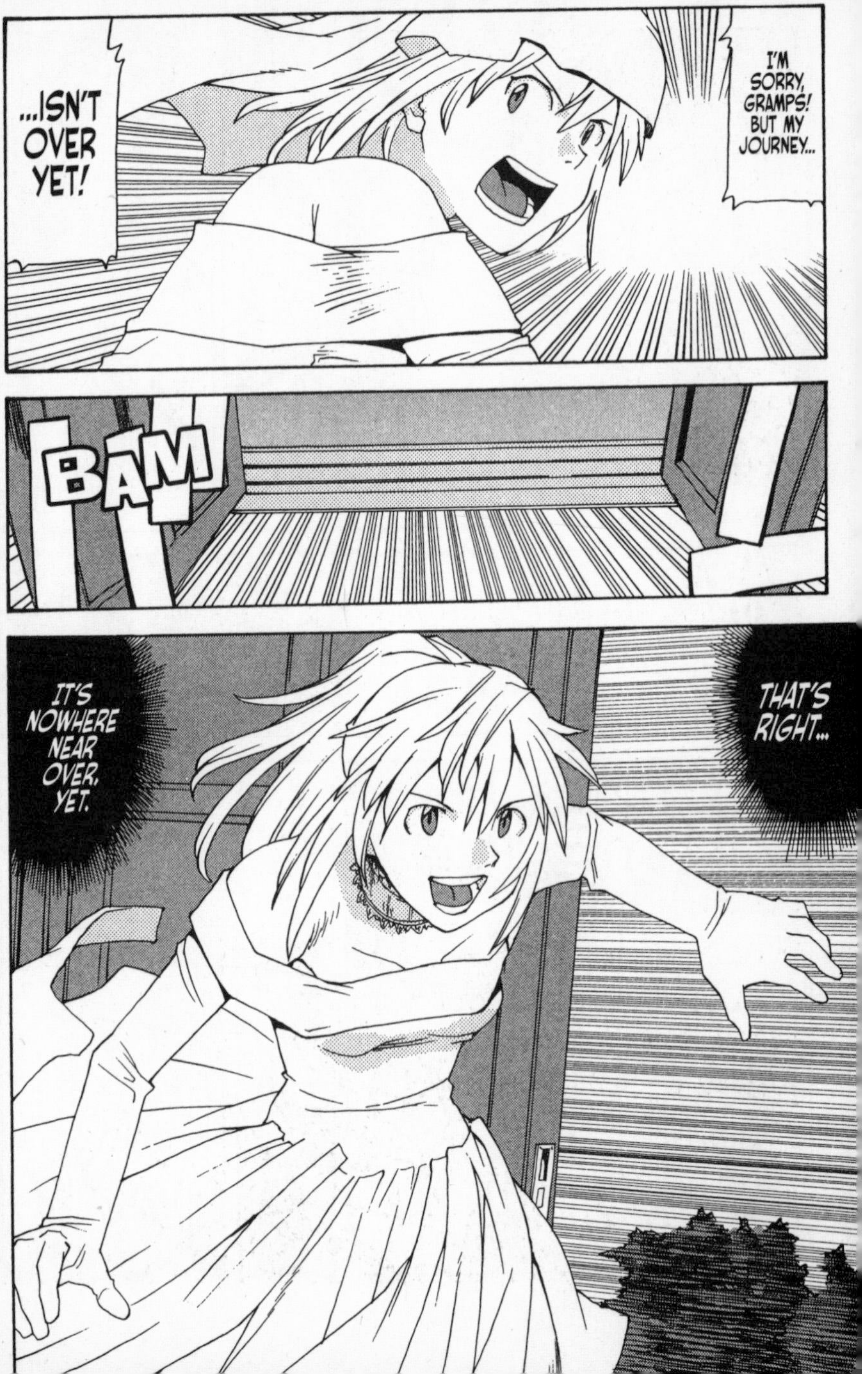
I'M SORRY, GRAMPS! BUT MY JOURNEY...
...ISN'T OVER YET!
BAM
THAT'S RIGHT...
IT'S NOWHERE NEAR OVER, YET.

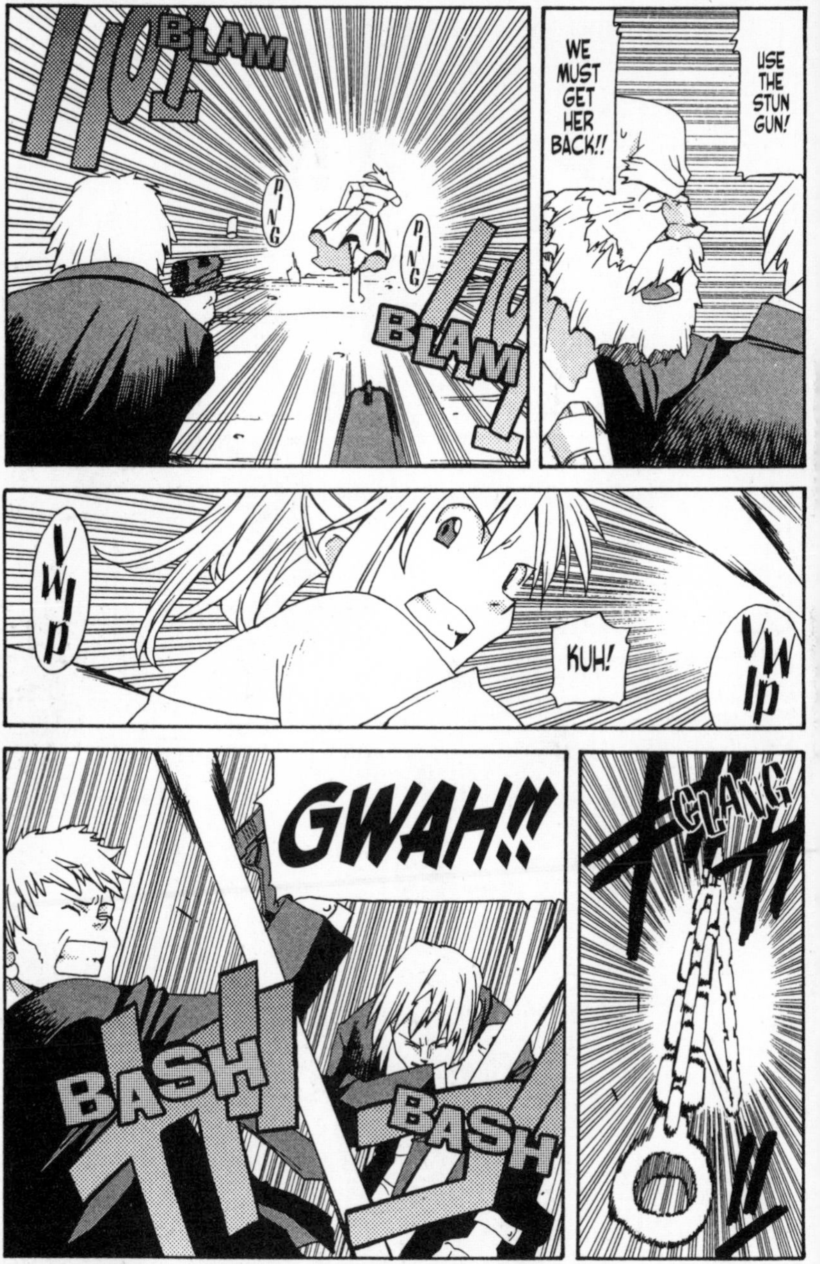
USE THE STUN GUN!
WE MUST GET HER BACK!!
BLAM
PING
PING
BLAM
VWIP
KUH!
VWIP
CLANG
GWAH!!
BASH
BASH

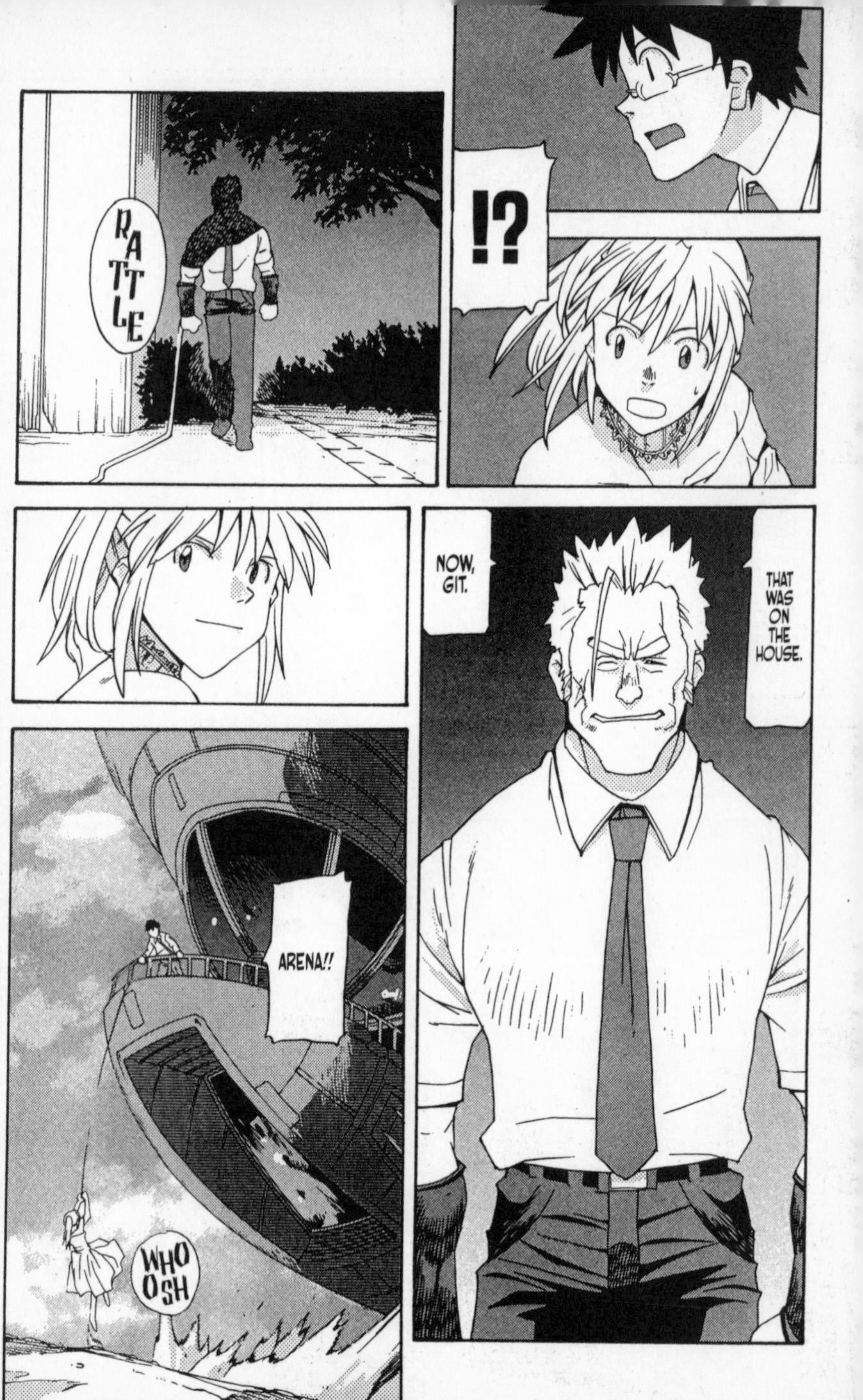
!?
RATTLE
THAT WAS ON THE HOUSE.
NOW, GIT.
ARENA!!
WHOOSH

PSSH

K-CLICK

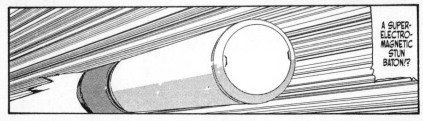

A SUPER-ELECTRO-MAGNETIC STUN BATON!?

SWOOSH

GRAB

SHNIKT

REIICHI! MY SWORD!!

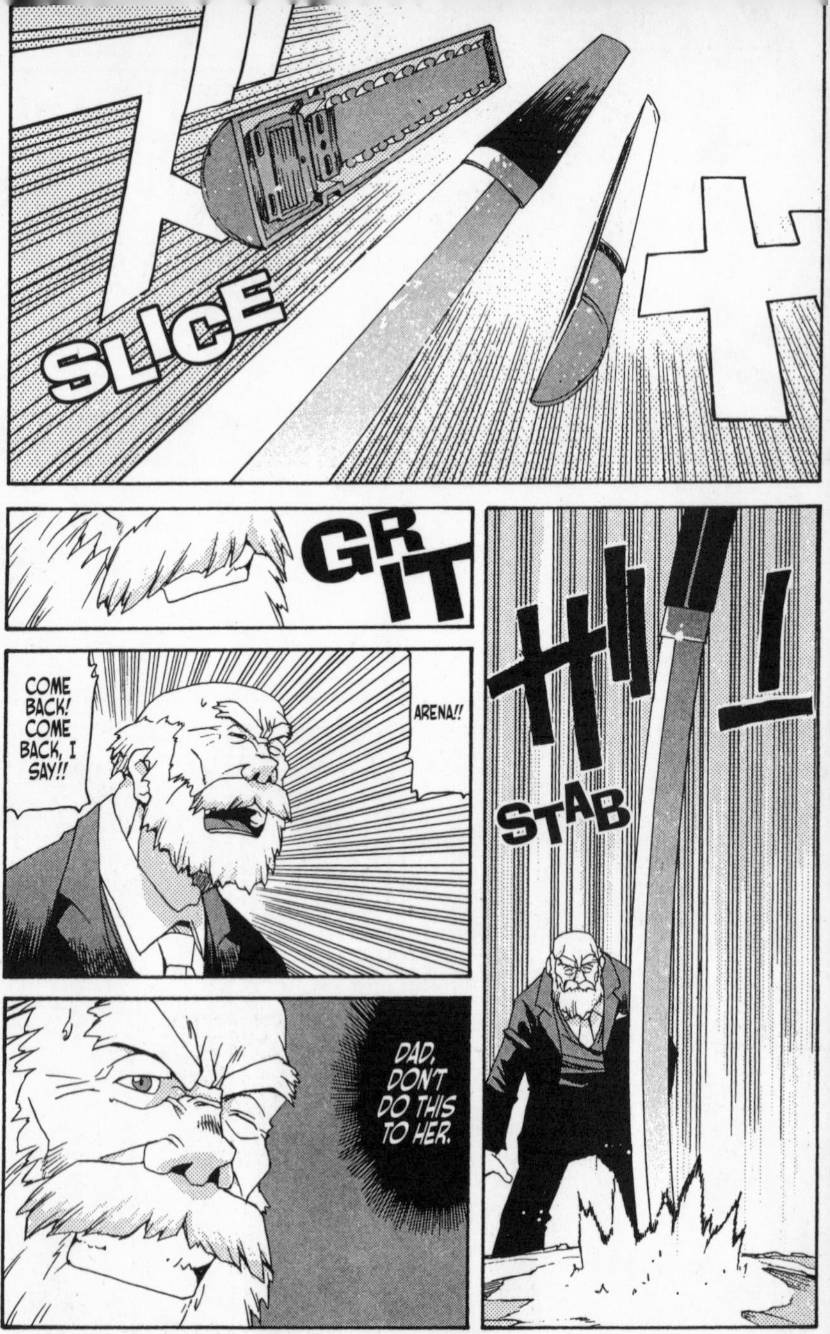
SLICE
STAB
GRIT
ARENA!!
COME BACK! COME BACK, I SAY!!
DAD, DON'T DO THIS TO HER.

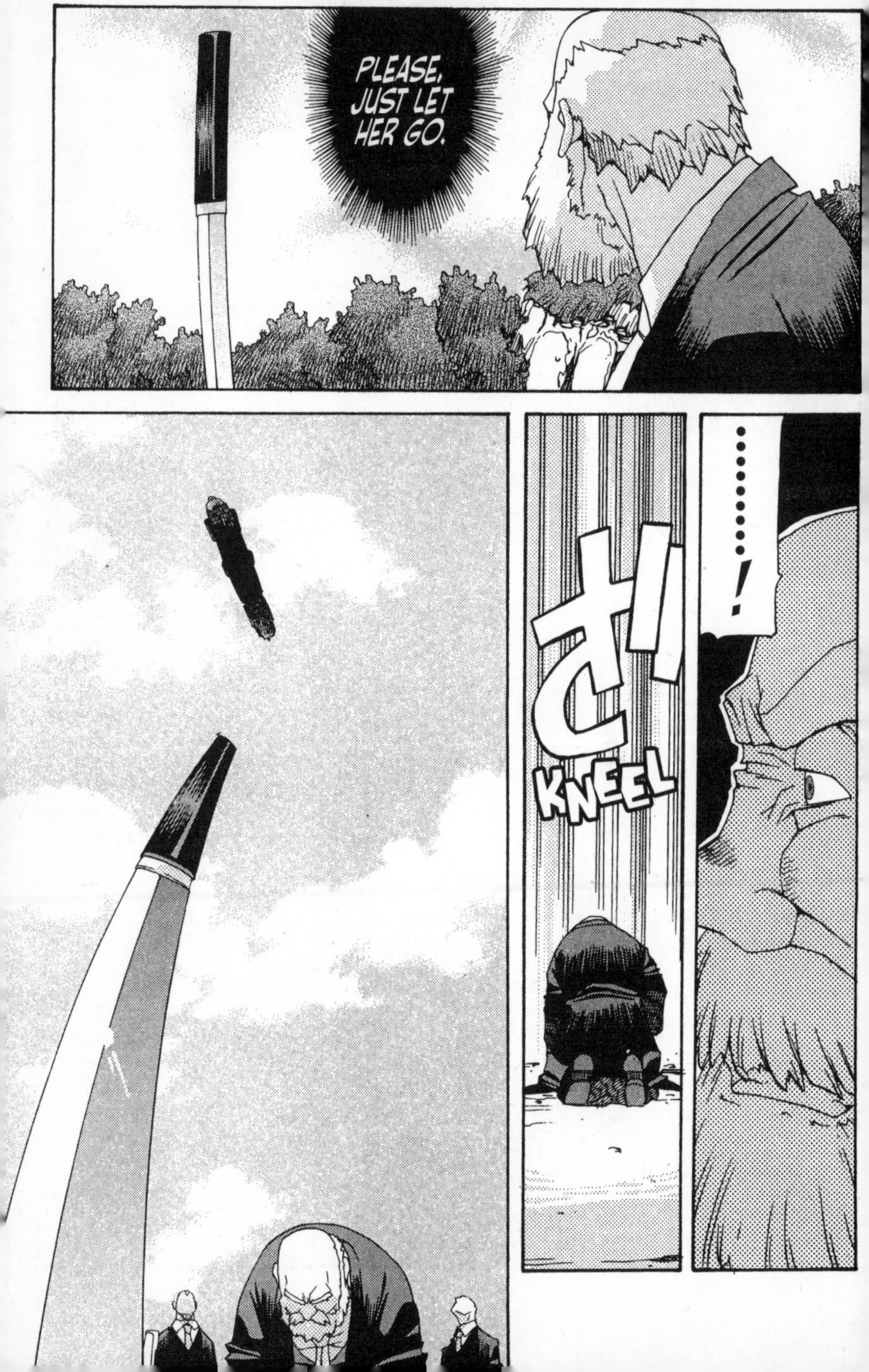
PLEASE, JUST LET HER GO.
......!
ざ
KNEEL

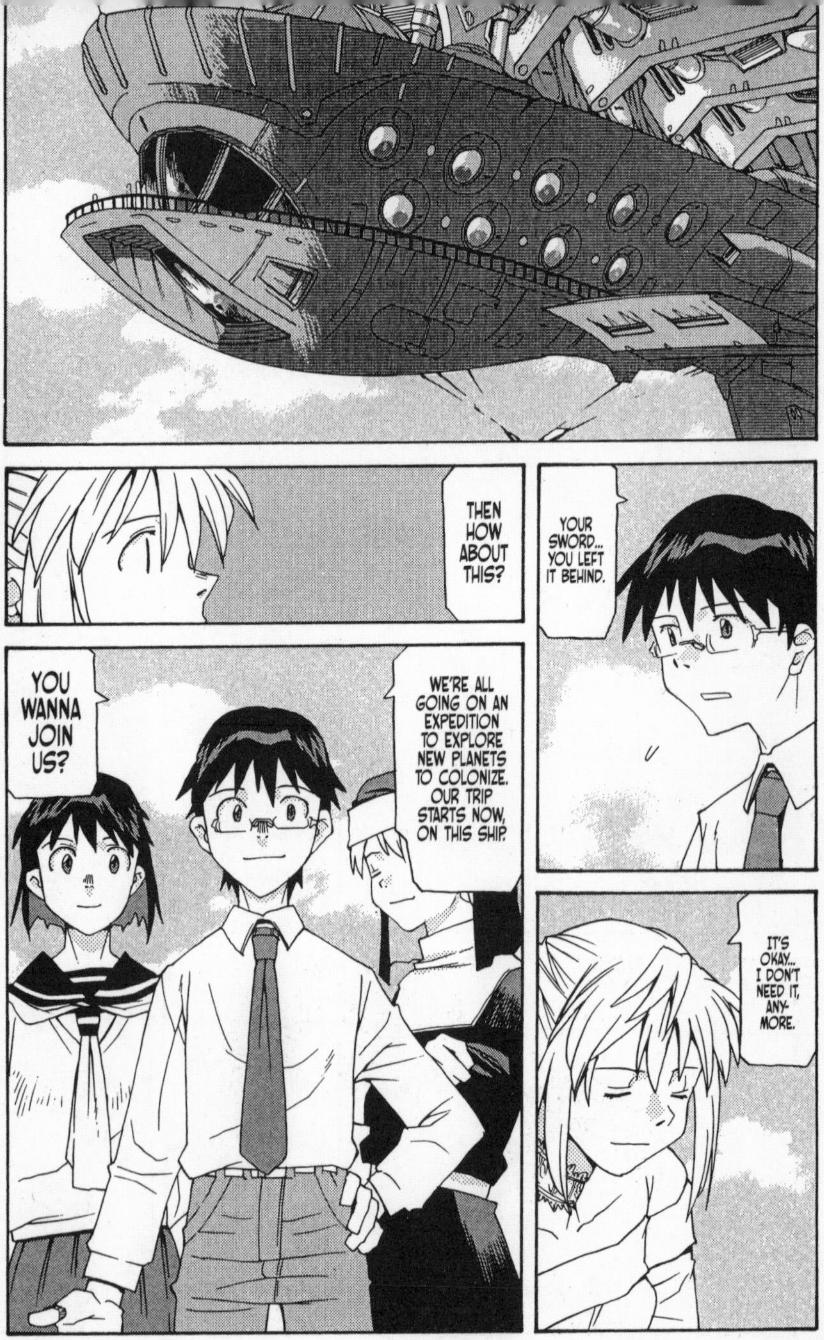
YOUR SWORD... YOU LEFT IT BEHIND.
IT'S OKAY... I DON'T NEED IT, ANY-MORE.
THEN HOW ABOUT THIS?
WE'RE ALL GOING ON AN EXPEDITION TO EXPLORE NEW PLANETS TO COLONIZE. OUR TRIP STARTS NOW, ON THIS SHIP.
YOU WANNA JOIN US?

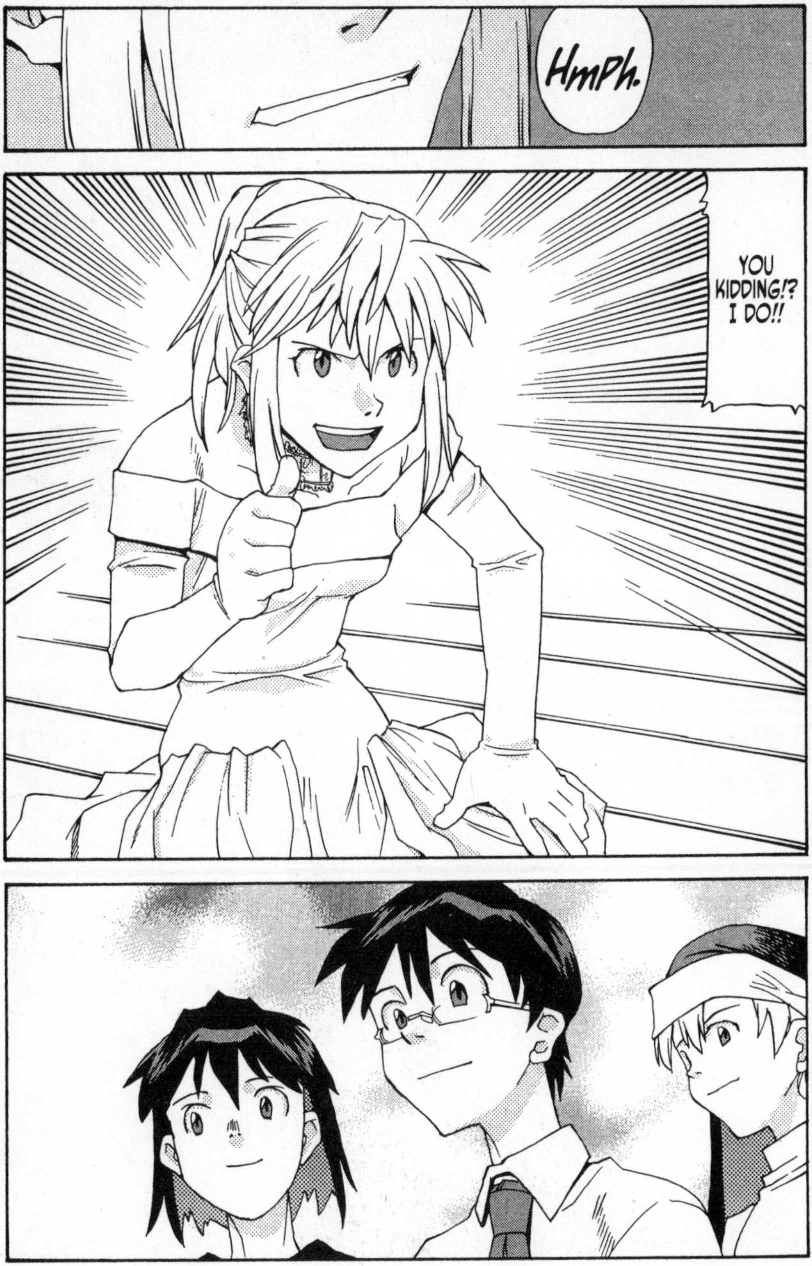
Hmph.
YOU KIDDING!? I DO!!

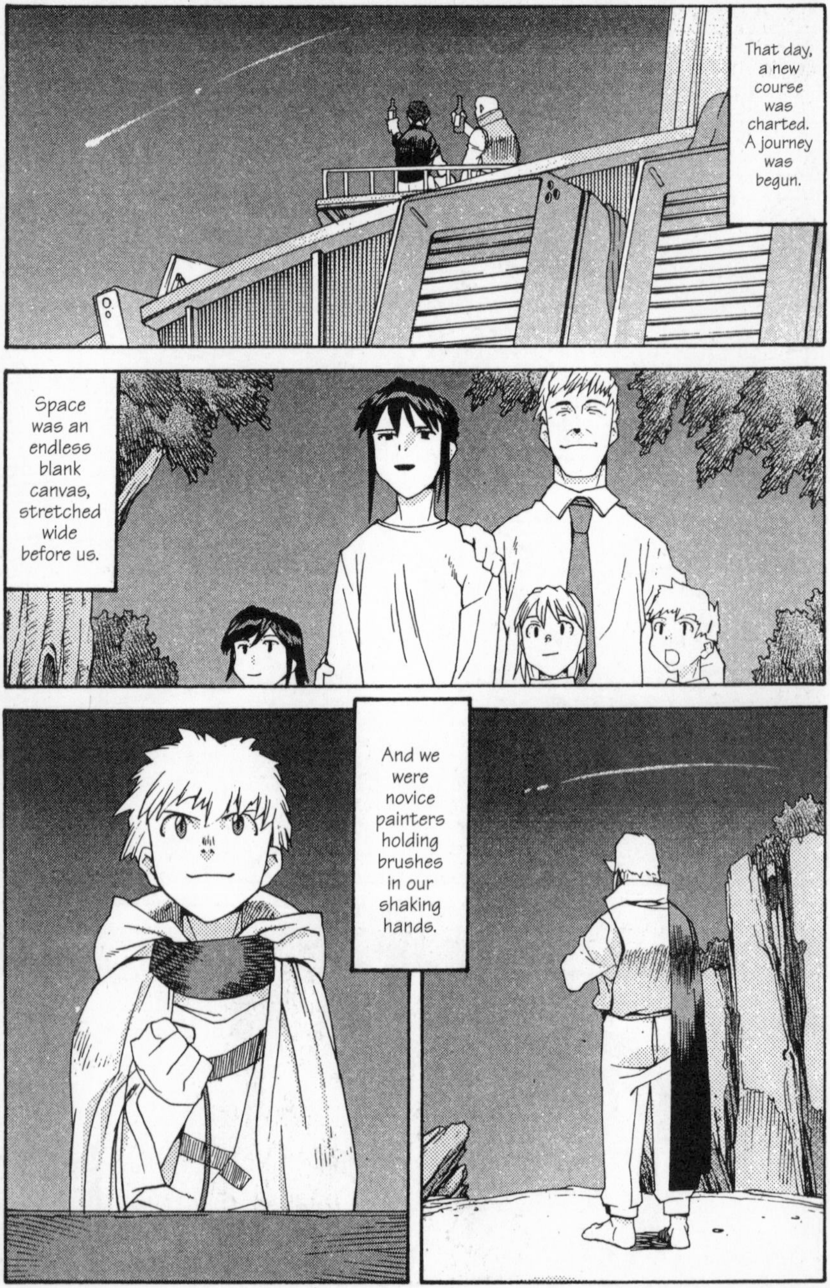
That day, a new course was charted. A journey was begun.
Space was an endless blank canvas, stretched wide before us.
And we were novice painters holding brushes in our shaking hands.

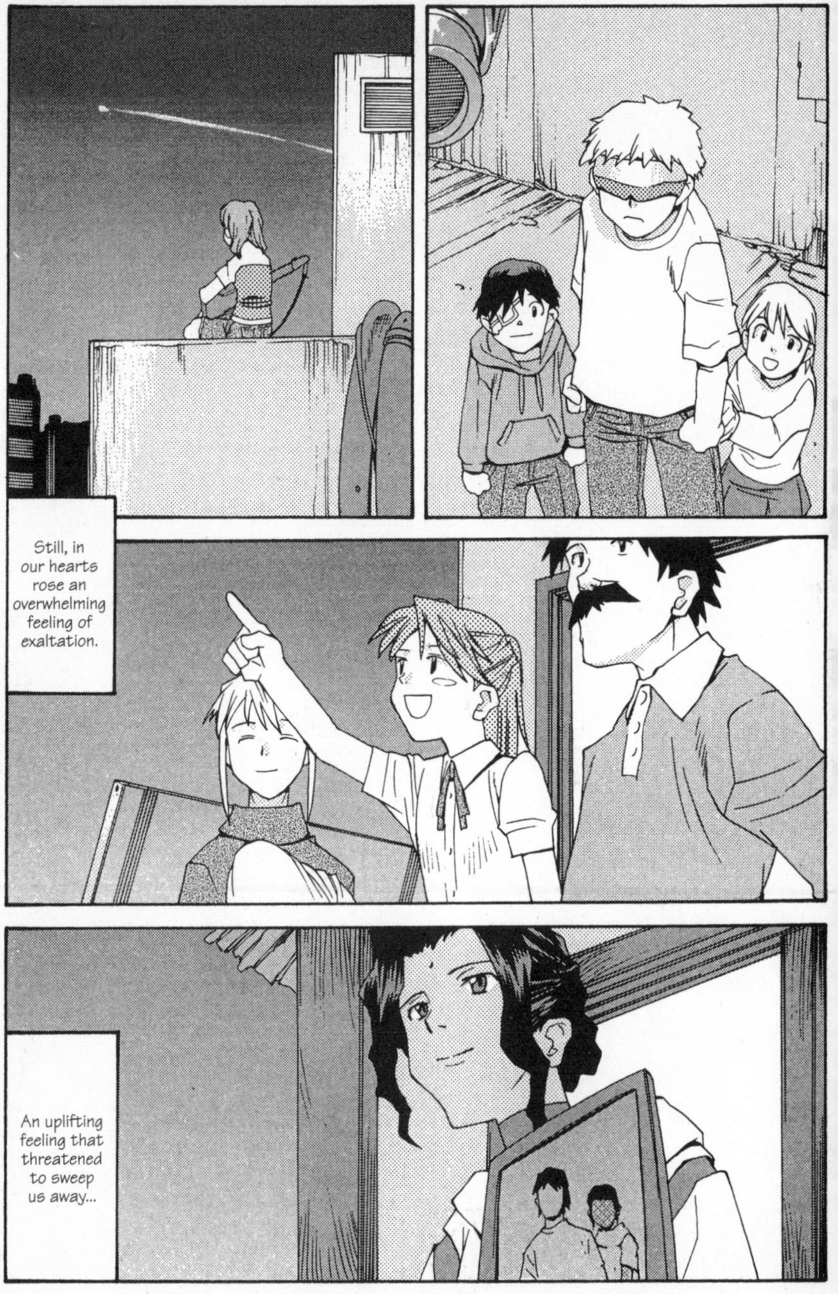
Still, in our hearts rose an overwhelming feeling of exaltation.
An uplifting feeling that threatened to sweep us away...

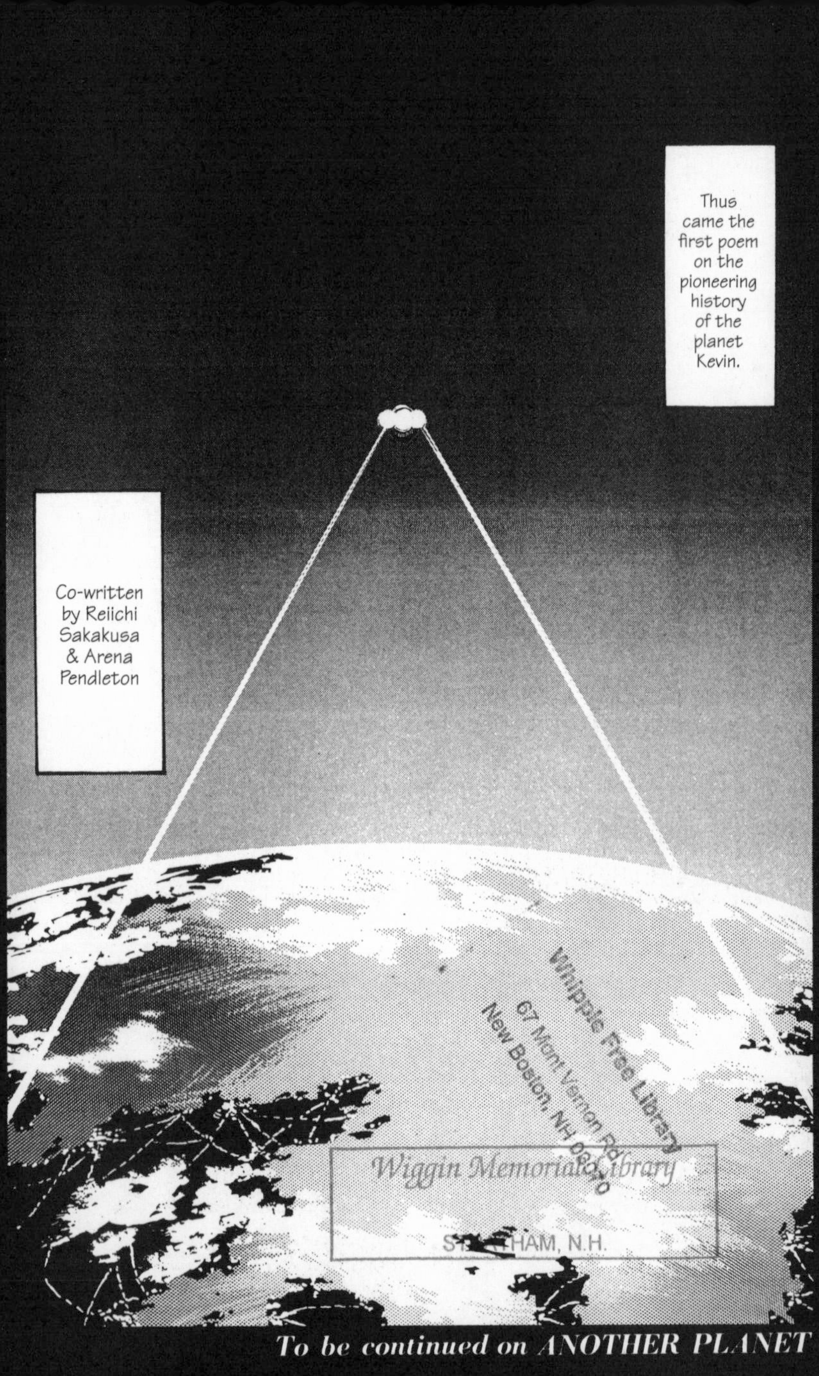
Thus came the first poem on the pioneering history of the planet Kevin.
Co-written by Reiichi Sakakusa & Arena Pendleton

To be continued on ANOTHER PLANET

Hideyuki Kurata
原作 倉田英之
Written by Hideyuki Kurata

"TRAIN + TRAIN" is what I consider my first real original work.
It made a heavy impression on me, giving me both good times and hard times. In this comic version of it, there was plenty I wasn't used to and I caused plenty of trouble for both Takuma-san and his studio staff. That's why I'd like to take this time to apologize for that.
At any rate, having finally reached the ending after this long, long serialization, I must say I feel a deep sense of satisfaction.
This story is about a girl and a boy unsure about the paths of their futures, and influencing one another to help them choose what it is they want to do. And so I wrote this story bringing to mind the simultaneous anxiety and excitement I'd experienced over choosing my own career, and the trouble I'd given my parents through the whole ordeal. Reiichi Sakakusa was alive inside me during that time and could very well be called the embodiment of all that anguish from those pubescent years of mine.
So in the end, neither Reiichi nor Arena reached the end of their journey. The future ahead of them seems to be more travel and that will last as long as they're alive.
Before I go, I'd like to thank you all for your reading and support of this story.

2003/3/19 倉田英之
March 19, 2003 Hideyuki Kurata

INTO THE BLUES!!

TRAIN + TRAIN

Tomomasa Takuma
作画 たくま朋正
Illustration by TOMOMASA TAKUMA

Arena and Reiichi finally reached their final station only to set them on the path to yet another station somewhere off in the future.
A station nobody knows the whereabouts of.
Still, I haven't a doubt that it'll bring about a journey filled with the kinds of ups and downs that suit them so well.
I hope to meet them again, somewhere along the way, but until then we'll have to end the tale of this journey here for now.

Thank you for your long-lasting support and encouragement.

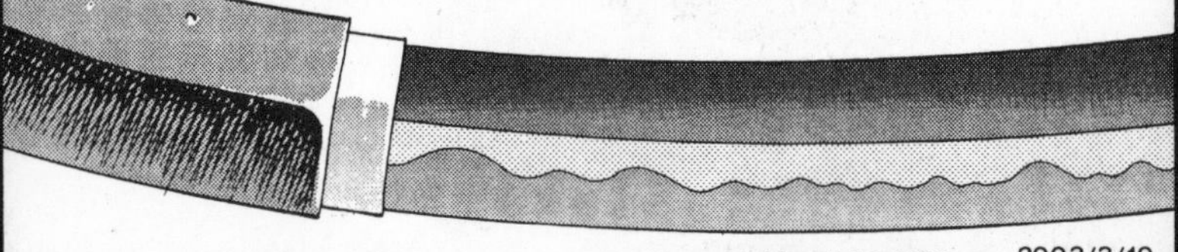

March 19, 2003
Tomomasa Takuma
2003/3/19
たくま朋正

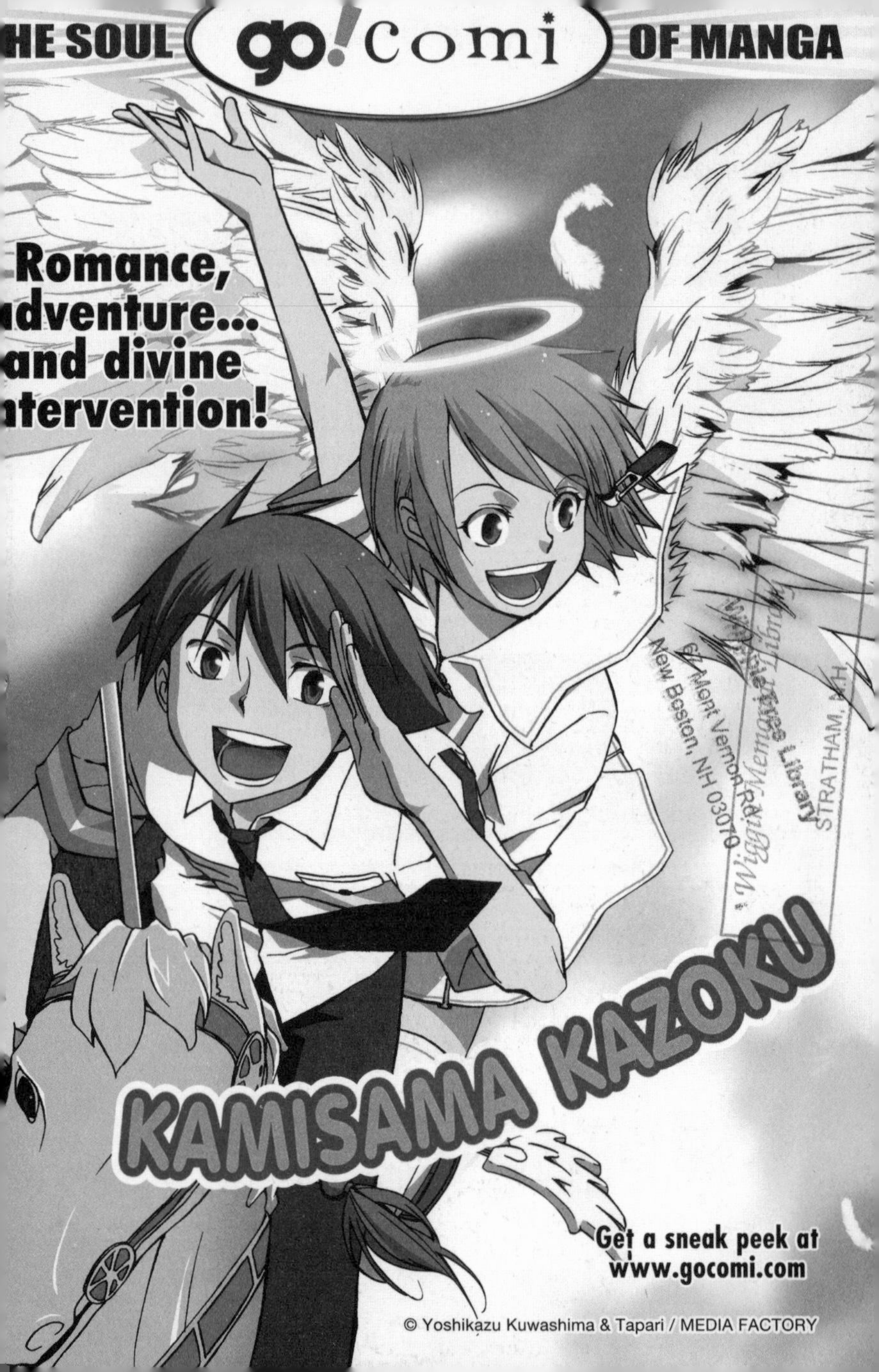
THE SOUL go!comi OF MANGA
Romance, adventure... and divine intervention!
KAMISAMA KAZOKU
Get a sneak peek at www.gocomi.com
© Yoshikazu Kuwashima & Tapari / MEDIA FACTORY

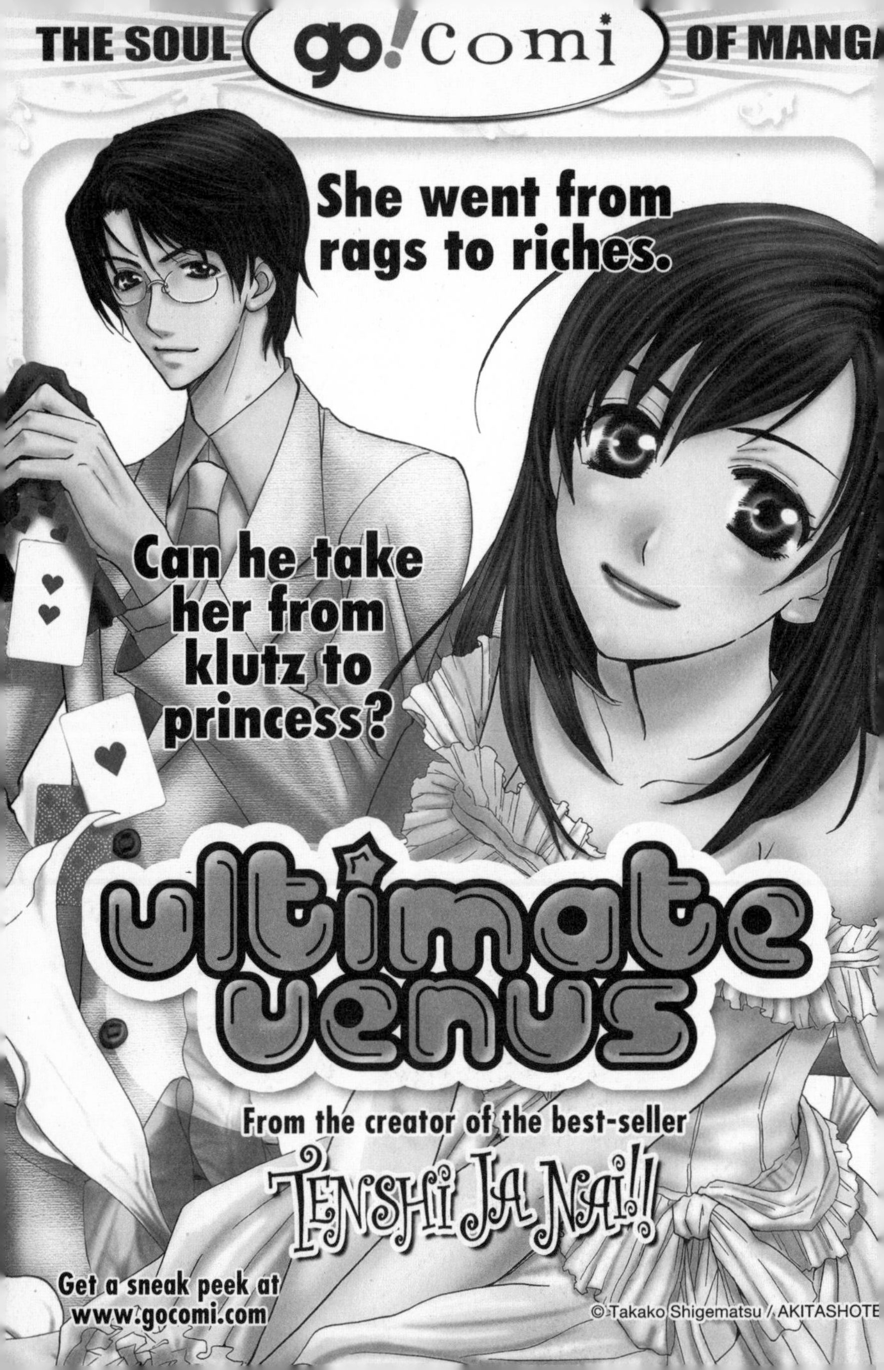
THE SOUL go!comi OF MANGA
She went from rags to riches.
Can he take her from klutz to princess?
ultimate venus
From the creator of the best-seller
TENSHI JA NAI!!
Get a sneak peek at www.gocomi.com
© Takako Shigematsu / AKITASHOTE

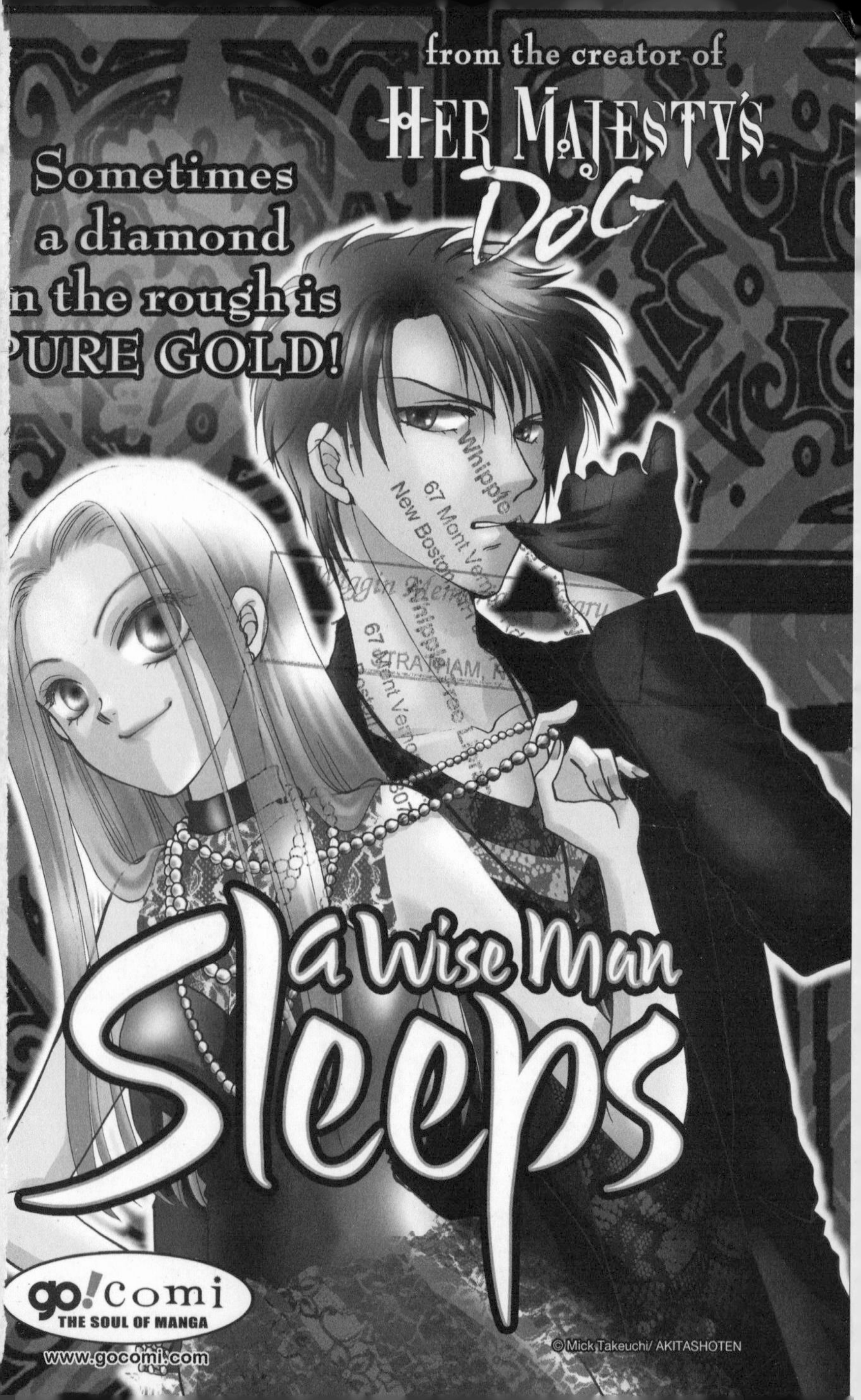
from the creator of
HER MAJESTY'S DOG
Sometimes
a diamond
n the rough is
PURE GOLD!
A Wise Man Sleeps
go!comi
THE SOUL OF MANGA
www.gocomi.com
© Mick Takeuchi/ AKITASHOTEN